Josef Albers   Albert Alcalay   Peter Alexander   Billy Apple   Carl Andre   Alexander Archi...   ...ard Artschwager   Richard Avedon   Milton Avery   Francis Bacon   Jennifer Bartlett   Georg Baseli...   ...rry Bell   Billy Al Bengston   Robert Benton   Joseph Beuys   Max Bill   Pierre Bonnard   Constanti...   ...er César   John Chamberlain   Chryssa   Chuck Close   George Condo   Joseph Cornell   Alan Davie   Stuart Davis   Giorgio de C...   ...em de Kooning   Robert Delaunay   Agnes Denes   André Derain   Philip-Lorca deCorcia   Guy Dill   Jim Dine   Jean Dubuffet   Sergei Eisenstein   Max Ernst   Fred Eversley   Rainer Werner Fassbinder   Lyonel Feininger   Walter Feldman   Federico Fellini   Alan Fenton   Barry Flanagan   Dan Flavin   Lucio Fontana   Sam Francis   Naum Gabo   Alberto Giacometti   Terry Gilliam   Fritz Glarner   Julio González   Adolph Gottlieb   Arshile Gorky   George Grosz   Philip Guston   Raymond Hains   Al Hansen   Barbara Hepworth   Eva Hesse   Alfred Hitchcock   David Hockney   Hans Hofmann   John Huston   Robert Indiana   Patrick Ireland   Robert Irwin   Alfred Jensen   Jasper Johns   Ben Johnson   Donald Judd   Wassily Kandinsky   Craig Kauffman   Ellsworth Kelly   Edward Keinholz   Paul Klee   Franz Kline   Lee Krasner   Nicholas Krushenick   Lawrence Kupferman   Akira Kurosawa   Henri Laurens   Fernand Léger   Sol LeWitt   Alexander Liberman   Roy Lichtenstein   Sven Lukin   David Lynch   René Magritte   Robert Mallary   Robert Mangold   Piero Manzoni   Conrad Marca-Relli   Brice Marden   Marisol   Agnes Martin   Henri Matisse   Allan McCollum   John McCracken   Barrie C. McDowell   Eleanor Mikus   Mirko   Joan Miró   Piet Mondrian   Claude Monet   Henry Moore   Malcolm Morley   Robert Morris   Ed Moses   Robert Motherwell   Elizabeth Murray   Eadweard Muybridge   Hans Namuth   Robert S. Neuman   Barnett Newman   Louise Nevelson   Robert S. Nueman   Barnett Newman   Georges Noël   Isamu Noguchi   Kenneth Noland   Isamu Noguchi   Jim Nutt   Claes Oldenburg   Tom Otterness   Blinky Palermo   Ed Paschke   Jules Pascin   Eduardo Paolozzi   Irving Penn   Ellen Phelan   Pablo Picasso   Michelangelo Pistoletto   Sigmar Polke   Jackson Pollock   Larry Poons   Kenneth Price   Robert Rauschenberg   Ad Reinhardt   Edda Renouf   Bridget Riley   Suellen Rocca   Aguste Rodin   James Rosenquist   Mark Rothko   Ed Ruscha   Robert Ryman   Lucas Samaras   Julian Schnabel   Kurt Schwitters   Martin Scorsese   George Segal   Richard Serra   Joel Shapiro   David Smith   Kiki Smith   Tony Smith   Richard Stankiewicz   Saul Steinberg   Frank Stella   Marjorie Strider   Clyfford Still   Antoni Tàpies   Paul Thek   Mark Tobey   Michael Todd   Jean Tinguely   Henri de Toulouse-Lautrec   Hugh Townley   Ernest Trova   Cy Twombly   Jack Tworkov   Dewain Valentine   Coosje van Bruggen   Victor Vasarely   David von Schlegell   Andy Warhol   Orson Welles   Tom Wesselman   Robert Whitman   Frank Lloyd Wright   Jack Youngerman   Fred Zinnemann   Joe Zucker   Josef Albers   Albert Alcalay   Peter Alexander   Billy Apple   Carl Andre   Alexander Archipenko   Chuck Arnoldi   Jean Arp   Richard Artschwager   Richard Avedon   Milton Avery   Francis Bacon   Jennifer Bartlett   Georg Baselitz   William Baziotes   Max Beckmann   Larry Bell   Billy Al Bengston   Robert Benton   Joseph Beuys   Max Bill   Pierre Bonnard   Constantin Brancusi   Roger Brown   Alexander Calder   César   John Chamberlain   Chryssa   Chuck Close   George Condo   Joseph Cornell   Alan Davie   Stuart Davis   Giorgio de Chirico   Willem de Kooning   Robert Delaunay   Agnes Denes   André Derain   Philip-Lorca deCorcia   Guy Dill   Jim Dine   Jean Dubuffet   Sergei Eisenstein   Max Ernst   Fred Eversley   Rainer Werner Fassbinder   Lyonel Feininger   Walter Feldman   Federico Fellini   Alan Fenton   Barry Flanagan   Dan Flavin   Lucio Fontana   Sam Francis   Naum Gabo   Alberto Giacometti   Terry Gilliam   Fritz Glarner   Julio González   Adolph Gottlieb   Arshile Gorky   George Grosz   Philip Guston   Raymond Hains   Al Hansen   Barbara Hepworth   Eva Hesse   Alfred Hitchcock   David Hockney   Hans Hofmann   John Huston   Robert Indiana   Patrick Ireland   Robert Irwin   Alfred Jensen   Jasper Johns   Ben Johnson   Donald Judd   Wassily Kandinsky   Craig Kauffman   Ellsworth Kelly   Edward Keinholz   Paul Klee   Franz Kline   Lee Krasner   Nicholas Krushenick   Lawrence Kupferman   Akira Kurosawa   Henri Laurens   Fernand Léger   Sol LeWitt   Alexander Liberman   Roy Lichtenstein   Sven Lukin   David Lynch   René Magritte   Robert Mallary   Robert Mangold   Piero Manzoni   Conrad Marca-Relli   Brice Marden   Marisol   Agnes Martin   Henri Matisse   Allan McCollum   John McCracken   Barrie C. McDowell   Eleanor Mikus   Mirko   Joan Miró   Piet Mondrian   Claude Monet   Henry Moore   Malcolm Morley   Robert Morris   Ed Moses   Robert Motherwell   Elizabeth Murray   Eadweard Muybridge   Hans Namuth   Robert S. Neuman   Barnett Newman   Louise Nevelson   Robert S. Nueman   Barnett Newman   Georges Noël   Isamu Noguchi   Kenneth Noland   Isamu Noguchi   Jim Nutt   Claes Oldenburg   Tom Otterness   Blinky Palermo   Ed Paschke   Jules Pascin   Eduardo Paolozzi   Irving Penn   Ellen Phelan   Pablo Picasso   Michelangelo Pistoletto   Sigmar Polke   Jackson Pollock   Larry Poons   Josef Albers   Albert Alcalay   Peter Alexander   Josef Albers   Albert Alcalay   Peter Alexander   Billy Apple   Carl Andre   Alexander Archipenko   Chuck Arnoldi   Jean Arp   Richard Artschwager   Richard Avedon   Milton Avery   Francis Bacon   Jennifer Bartlett   Georg Baselitz   William Baziotes   Max Beckmann   Larry Bell   Billy Al Bengston   Robert Benton   Joseph Beuys   Max Bill   Pierre Bonnard   Constantin Brancusi   Roger Brown   Alexander Calder   César   John Chamberlain   Chryssa   Chuck Close   George Condo   Joseph Cornell   Alan Davie   Stuart Davis   Giorgio de Chirico   Willem de Kooning   Robert Delaunay   Agnes Denes   André Derain   Philip-Lorca deCorcia   Guy Dill   Jim Dine   Jean Dubuffet   Sergei Eisenstein   Max Ernst   Fred Eversley   Rainer Werner Fassbinder   Lyonel Feininger   Walter Feldman   Federico Fellini   Alan Fenton   Barry Flanagan   Dan Flavin   Lucio Fontana   Sam Francis   Naum Gabo   Alberto Giacometti   Terry Gilliam   Fritz Glarner   Julio González   Adolph Gottlieb   Arshile Gorky   George Grosz   Philip Guston   Raymond Hains   Al Hansen   Barbara Hepworth   Eva Hesse   Alfred Hitchcock   David Hockney   Hans Hofmann   John Huston   Robert Indiana   Patrick Ireland   Robert Irwin   Alfred Jensen   Jasper Johns   Ben Johnson   Donald Judd   Wassily Kandinsky   Craig Kauffman   Ellsworth Kelly   Edward Keinholz   Paul Klee   Franz Kline   Lee Krasner   Nicholas Krushenick   Lawrence Kupferman   Akira Kurosawa   Henri Laurens   Fernand Léger   Sol LeWitt   Alexander Liberman

ADVENTURES IN ART

40 YEARS AT PACE

ADVENTURES IN ART

40 YEARS AT PACE

edited by
MILDRED GLIMCHER

with contextual recollections by
ARNE GLIMCHER

PaceWildenstein

LEONARDO INTERNATIONAL

CONTENTS

A LIFE IN ART

by Barbara Rose

When I was asked to write about the Pace Gallery, I knew that to some extent it would have to be a personal memoir. I had seen virtually every show since Pace opened in New York in 1963. Many of the artists I had championed showed with the gallery, and the story of Pace is very much that of the generation which came of age in the agitated but exciting decade of the sixties.

What defines a great art gallery? Certainly showing artists who make history. But great galleries also hold memorable exhibitions with unforgettable images, or organize shows whose visual juxtapositions open up new ways of seeing. The art dealers we remember are often identified with specific artists whose works they promoted over a long period of time and who form the core of the gallery. Among the artists Pace has represented, some for over three decades, are Agnes Martin, Robert Irwin, Lucas Samaras, Jim Dine, Chuck Close and the late Louise Nevelson and Jean Dubuffet.

Pace shows have the thoughtfulness and detail of museum exhibitions, and many have made history with their daring and innovation. I remember surprising and revelatory details of many exhibitions. However, the two that immediately come to mind as total revelations were the reconstruction of Mondrian's unrealized architectural project, *The Salon of Mme B*, and the extraordinary show of Picasso's unpublished and largely unknown sketchbooks, *Je suis le cahier*. Mondrian's elegance and formal order, based on the grid, were central to Arne Glimcher's taste from the outset. Harry Holtzman, the artist, had been instrumental in saving Mondrian from the blitz in London, where he lived as a refugee from Hitler. One of the founders of the American Abstract Artists, whose members included Ad Reinhardt and Lee Krasner—both of whom showed at Pace—Holtzman collected funds from young American admirers of Mondrian to bring the master to New York, where he became the group's unofficial leader.

When Mondrian died in 1944, he left Holtzman as the executor of his estate. One day Glimcher was looking through the Mondrian archives with Holtzman in the hopes of finding new material, when he came upon the plans for an architectural commission for a room. The drawings were black-and-white, but the colors of the planned panels that would turn the space into a three-dimensional Mondrian were indicated with capital letters.

Obsessed with realizing the project and aware that Mondrian had written that the ideal material for domestic interiors could have no texture or special characteristics, Arne decided formica most closely approximated the material described by Mondrian. Constructing Mondrian's room was a brilliant and daring scoop that permitted one to imagine what Mondrian himself might have been like as an architect as his work directly influenced architectural style.

Perhaps even more extraordinary was the coup of exhibiting a vast, historically crucial cache of unpublished drawings and notebooks, photos of which Arne found in the extensive archives of Claude Picasso. Going through this treasure trove of drawings, he was determined to curate a Picasso drawing show that would change the way Picasso was seen and understood. The result was the landmark exhibition *Je suis le cahier*, in which the sketchbooks that related to many of Picasso's most important paintings were shown for the first time. Based on the dates of the notebooks, however, Arne concluded that most of the drawings were done after the paintings as alternative versions or as later reflections. In the introduction to the catalogue, he proposed that sometimes the drawings rather than the paintings represented Picasso's final thoughts on a subject, thus revising the concept of drawing as preparation for painting; many of the paintings were preparations for drawings.

Arne's relationship with the Picasso family also allowed him to reveal two other major aspects of Picasso's oeuvre that had been largely overlooked: his greatness as a sculptor, especially in bronze, and the importance of his late paintings. At the time it was a risky thing to do, because museum curators and art historians disparaged the late works as inferior to the master's earlier achievements. Arne decided to show the late Avignon paintings, as they had been exhibited at the Palais des Papes in Avignon, before *Je suis le cahier*.

With a catalogue by James R. Mellow, *The Avignon Paintings* created a sensation. The show sold out.

Collectors and curators alike enthused about the works, and, after the Pace show, the Guggenheim Museum, the Tate Gallery, and the Ludwig Museum held exhibitions of Picasso's late works. "I'm interested in giving a new perspective to the span of an artist's work by extending the public's perception of an entire oeuvre. Artists are too easily identified by a signature style that becomes a trademark in the eyes of the public, especially the American public which tends to be myopic. Whenever possible, I want to encourage the awareness of other dimensions of an artist's career and provide a deeper insight and respect for a lifetime of work, rather than only for one period. The exhibition of Rothko's Surrealist period surprised many people who were only familiar with the sectional canvases. The exhibition not only revealed the breadth of Rothko's achievement, but the transformation of Surrealist influence into abstract language."

Arne began his career as an artist at the Massachusetts College of Art at the moment when Expressionist figurative painting ruled the art schools. Glimcher recalls his version of Action painting as a cross between Kokoschka and de Kooning, whose work he would eventually present in two major exhibitions. His ambition was to paint when he entered the MFA program at Boston University, where he met Brice Marden, whose dealer he would later become. He was already married to Milly Cooper, an art historian at Wellesley College. Ultimately, Arne didn't find his own work fulfilling, and he stopped painting. "I'd ask myself if the painting on which I was working was as good as Picasso. Then, like a Saul Steinberg cartoon, a huge 'No' resounded in the studio space." (Later he would befriend and represent the brilliant and witty Romanian-born artist, known to a broader public for his sophisticated *New Yorker* covers.)

Arne became a modest collector and low-rent art dealer, buying Käthe Kollwitz prints and selling some to friends for a modest profit that allowed him to keep others for himself. His biggest purchase in these years was Picasso's double-page etching, *The Dream and Lie of Franco*, which he bought for $125 a plate, paid for over time, and which still hangs in his home. Glimcher had been raised in comfortable circumstances. However, when he was twenty-one, his father died and his oldest brother informed him that he would have to get a job. "We were walking down Newbury Street in Boston, my mother, my older brother, Herb, and I," he recalls. "I

pointed out an empty shop and remarked that it would be a good place for a gallery. Herb said, 'Open a gallery.' So with $2,400 borrowed from my brother, the original Pace Gallery opened it's door."

Arne and Milly were still in school, so Arne's mother, who had run all kinds of businesses, baby-sat the gallery while they were in class. The first artists the Pace Gallery in Boston showed were those that were available—basically his professors at the Massachusetts College of Art, who were willing to show in an unknown gallery. He also began to buy Giacometti prints from Barbara Krakow's new Carriage House Art Gallery in her home. He paid $15 a print and sold them for $18 or $20. As often as possible, he and Milly would go to New York to keep up with the art scene.

On an earlier trip to New York in the mid-50s, Arne had an epiphany that would change his life. He saw Louise Nevelson's installation at The Museum of Modern Art. "It was not like any art I'd ever seen. It was more like theater and I responded—maybe because I was also an amateur actor." Glimcher's dedication to Louise Nevelson from that point on was total. Their friendship and collaboration was mutually sustaining, and he credits her with focusing him at an early stage on the importance of the installation of art, one of the signal strengths of the Pace Gallery. In 1963, he visited Nevelson in Los Angeles while she was on a Ford Foundation grant to produce prints at June Wayne's Tamarind Workshop. At the party of a film writer, he convinced her to officially join the Pace Gallery he was planning to open six months later in New York. Hollywood was an appropriate place to negotiate the contract since Nevelson would for many years be the gallery's star.

In 1972, Glimcher wrote a monograph on Nevelson for Abrams. Critical, historical, and biographical, it was a feat that few if any art dealers, who are not known for their writing skill, could have achieved. He traced Nevelson's development from Schwitters' *Merzbau*, Duchamp's ready-mades, and Mondrian's grids. Indeed, the number of artists in the gallery whose work was grid-based—Agnes Martin, Alfred Jensen, Ad Reinhardt, Chuck Close—reveals the extent to which a type of architectonic order is basic to Glimcher's taste. At the same time, he was attracted to theatrical extravagance, which explains, perhaps, why all the major artists associated with the Happenings—Claes Oldenburg, Lucas Samaras, Jim Dine, and Robert Whitman, as well as extravaganza specialist Julian Schnabel—all show at Pace.

Color theory had always been one of Glimcher's passions and Josef Albers was its reigning master. As a student Arne had pored over Michel Chevreul's *De la loi du contraste couleurs*, which had inspired Impressionists and Post-Impressionists. In 1962, when the gallery was still in Boston, Glimcher visited Albers at Yale, where he was teaching, to ask for an exhibition. Against the better judgment of Albers' wife, Anni, Albers gave him a show. Among those who saw the show was a dapper young man named Fred Mueller, who became Arne's business partner in the New York venture. Refined and elegant, Fred was a collector with an independent income, and eager to be in the art business.

Arne and Fred were friendly, articulate, and always on hand to talk and explain their artists' work to collectors. Because Arne and Milly by now had two babies, Fred Mueller did most of the gallery entertaining. I remember the elegant parties at Fred's, where artists, collectors, and critics mingled, and the friendship, food, and conversation were of the highest order. His apartment was filled with art from all periods and cultures. Indeed, his eclecticism, though typical in Europe, was rare at the time in the United States. Although Fred left the Pace Gallery in 1975 to open an antique shop, the two remained good friends until his death in the early nineties. "Fred was not only one of the classiest and intelligent people I ever met, but he was also one of the funniest and nicest."

Louise Nevelson's first show at the Pace Gallery in New York, an enormous success, put the gallery firmly on the map both in the United States and abroad. In his book on Nevelson, Arne describes visiting Louise in her new studio, at 29 Spring Street, filled with accumulations of objects from which she constructed her pieces. "In the early 1960s, a visit to Nevelson's studio was like a trip to a natural phenomenon, like seeing the Grand Canyon."

Throughout the history of the Pace Gallery, women—beginning with his mother and his wife, Milly—have had an important role. So Arne was surprised when he was picketed by the Guerrilla Girls, since he had shown Eleanor Mikus, Chryssa, and Marjorie Strider in the sixties, as well as Louise Nevelson, Lee Krasner, and Agnes Martin. Perhaps not coincidentally, none of the women who showed at Pace needed the feminist movement to be considered the equals of men. Today, the gallery roster also includes other women who avoid being ghettoized—Elizabeth Murray, Bridget Riley, Coosje van Bruggen, Barbara Hepworth, and Kiki Smith.

The Pace Gallery, with its immaculate white space, professional installations, and attention to detail, was immediately a noticeable addition to the major galleries that lined 57th Street from Madison to Sixth Avenues, among them Sidney Janis, Betty Parsons, Marlborough, Otto Gerson, and André Emmerich. It became a favored destination for the younger crowd, including this writer.

During the sixties and seventies, many of my friends exhibited at the Pace Gallery. In 1964, Sven Lukin, a young Latvian artist discovered by Betty Parsons, showed impressive three-dimensional shaped canvases. In 1966, Lucas Samaras, who had been my fellow student under Meyer Schapiro at Columbia, had his first show at Pace. Samaras is one of the most unpredictable artists imaginable, and Glimcher has been especially supportive of his forays into uncharted waters. He did not flinch even at the scandal of Samaras' large-scale Polaroid portraits of his friends, such as fellow artists George Segal and Jasper Johns, editor Betsy Baker, and art historians Diane Kelder and Kim Levin, all in the nude. I have to admit that both Arne and I were also among Lucas' somewhat reluctant subjects. Once you arrived at his apartment-studio, the instructions were to take off your clothes while he turned his back and to arrange yourself on a stage set that included a chair and a pile of the sleazy synthetic fabrics Lucas habitually collected. What Lucas did not say, however, was that once you were posed and he pushed the shutter, the shot was timed so that he could jump into the set with you, although he remained fully clothed. Thirty-five years later, the protean sculptor and installation artist, who fits no categories, is still with the gallery, still one of Arne's closest friends.

By the mid-sixties, the Pace Gallery was showing many of my favorite artists, including Craig Kauffman, Larry Bell, and Robert Irwin, the California light-and-space artists. For Glimcher, a turning point in his life was his 1966 meeting with Robert Irwin, the brilliant pioneer of art based on the viewer's perceptual responses. In Glimcher's estimation, Irwin's contribution is among the most crucial of the second half of the century. "Irwin is *still* the cutting edge. Meeting Bob was magic. I knew he represented the future, but, unfortunately it took the art world twenty-five years to recognize it." Irwin's mysterious, theatrically lit scrim installations that alter the viewer's perception of space and volume in subtle and changing perspectives have been among the most memorable Pace exhibitions.

In 1971, Arne's introduction of the Los Angeles-based group also included John McCracken, Fred Eversley, and Duane Valentine in a show called *A Decade of California Color*. At that point, Pace was the only New York gallery interested in their work, which was seen as a threat to the hegemony of the New York School. Since Arne's dedication to Mondrian was well known, the joke around town, based on the title of Mondrian's famous essay, was that the Pace Gallery was the home of Plastic and Pure Plastic art. But Arne remembers with pride, "Barney Newman championed my gallery when everyone said it was slick and plastic." Minimalist sculptor Donald Judd, who was writing criticism for *Arts Magazine*, was among those to support Glimcher's taste for an elegant, austere art. Today, the Pace Gallery represents the estate of Judd and also shows the fluorescent light installations of Dan Flavin. Pace has also represented the work of Robert Ryman since 1990, and more recently Sol LeWitt, another artist associated with Minimalism, exhibited the wall drawings for which he is best known at the gallery.

In retrospect, Arne's early, and consistent embrace of both Pop and Minimalism makes sense: he is the art dealer of his generation, which came of age in the sixties. He shared the taste and preoccupations of the artists he grew up with. "It was a decade of revelation when the secret of art as a perceptual tool became public," Arne says. "Suddenly beauty was not a pejorative term. It was all about a new aesthetic. Ravishing was complimentary."

Later, after Barnett Newman upheld Glimcher's enthusiasm for younger artists, Arne would show Newman and continue to exhibit Irwin and Bell. As the dealer for Judd's estate, he and Douglas Baxter, the gallery's president, would create extraordinary installations of Judd's works entirely in keeping with Judd's severe and refined aesthetic. But Minimalism was hardly the Pace Gallery's credo. Indeed, the Paul Thek installation of 1966 was probably the season's shocker, anticipating by decades the surrealistic installations of Louise Bourgeois and Robert Gober.

Another crucial moment in the history of the gallery was Arne's meeting with Jean Dubuffet (whose theater piece *Coucou Bazar* was a kind of Happening) in 1967 in Paris. "Annette Michelson introduced me to Dubuffet. She had returned from Europe, and I told her of my huge admiration for his work. We talked about the fact that Abstract Expressionism was the end of something, and Dubuffet was the beginning of something else. My dream was to show Dubuffet. Annette introduced me

to his dealer and made a strong recommendation on my behalf. But she warned me: 'Beware, Dubuffet has no servants, for he makes slaves of his friends.'"

I am grateful to Arne for an exceptional art experience. He sent me to Paris to spend a week with Dubuffet, one of the geniuses of this century, so that I could see the work that was going to be in the forthcoming *Théâtres de Mémoire* exhibition at Pace. Anyone who has known Dubuffet understands the seductiveness of the *monstre sacré*, and when he asked me to write his biography, I was tempted, but then remembered that he had driven three of my friends—Annette Michelson, Hubert Damisch, and Margit Rowell—to distraction over the project, and I politely declined. Somehow Arne managed to keep their relationship on an even keel for over seventeen years, until the artist's death.

Fascinated by the perceptual process in art, Arne went back to school at New York University during the seventies to study perceptual psychology. There he both taught and wrote a book with Dr. Paul Vitz on perception: *Modern Art and Modern Science: The Parallel Analysis of Vision*, which was adopted as a textbook by many universities. "During the modern period, both scientist and artist have been in a parallel investigation of perception, one cognitively, the other intuitively." As a result of his studies, he had become interested in the perceptual experiments that were contemporaneous with Mondrian's Plus and Minus series. In 1978, Arne assembled an exhibition on the theme of the grid, as he believed the grid to be the dominant organizing device in twentieth-century art. Rosalind Krauss was invited to write the catalogue that isolates this signal structural principle in modern art.

In the seventies, more formal art dominated the exhibitions held at Pace. However, the intellectual and conceptual content was very different from the purely optical Color Field painting being championed by Clement Greenberg. Interestingly, despite Glimcher's involvement with color theory, the Pace Gallery never represented the Greenberg School. For example, Jack Youngerman, although he painted intensely colored work, was never one of Greenberg's favorites. Nor was the mystical Alfred Jensen, who showed regularly at Pace from 1971 and whose estate continues to be represented by the gallery. The rigorously structured paintings of Georges Noël, who exhibited at the gallery in 1973 and 1977, had more in common with Tàpies and Minimalist art than with the hazy stained painting of the Greenberg School. And as for the two members of the first generation of the New York School that Pace started showing in the seventies—Lee Krasner and Ad Reinhardt—Greenberg openly detested them.

Both Reinhardt and Krasner were artists I was particularly close to, and I was grateful for Arne's help when I needed research material. Even though she was one of the greatest painters of her generation, Krasner was still virtually unknown when she left Marlborough for Pace in 1977. Arne was especially generous and far-sighted in financing the film I made on Lee, which brought attention to her work and won many prizes for documentary filmmaking. (I also secretly believed that being involved with the film inspired him to become a director—although of Hollywood features rather than documentaries.)

Installation is Arne Glimcher's absolute forte as well as one of his principle creative expressions. It is his way of realizing his dream of being the curator of his own museum. He redesigns and relights the gallery for every exhibition, one of the reasons that each show has a special coherence and flair. His interest in sculpture, which is particularly hard to install, punctuates the history of the gallery. He has done exceptional installations of the work of such masters as Archipenko, Julio González, Henry Moore, Joan Miró, Tony Smith, and Alexander Calder. The estate of the great Japanese-American sculptor Isamu Noguchi, who joined the gallery in 1975, is still represented by Pace, as are those of Donald Judd and Barbara Hepworth. Between 1987 and 1998, Richard Serra showed regularly with the gallery. Today, Joel Shapiro and John Chamberlain, two of the most internationally esteemed sculptors, exhibit their dramatic work at Pace.

In the eighties, Glimcher became more and more interested in historic work, in European art, and in comparisons between American and European art. Milly, meanwhile, had returned to school to earn a doctorate in art history at the Institute of Fine Arts. She wrote the catalogue of the de Kooning-Dubuffet exhibition that showed each of the two great artists exploring the theme of Women. Arne first presented the murals that Rothko painted for the Seagram building (which are now at the Kawamura Museum in Japan.) "They were like the blind arcades of Michelangelo's Laurentian Library, which [Rothko] visited on a trip to Italy."

When I asked Glimcher why he showed an artist, he reflected a moment and then answered, "Astonishment, I show art that astonishes me. For example, I wanted to do a Tàpies show from the moment I saw his work at Martha Jackson, in the sixties. They were the first paintings that I saw in which graffiti was transformed into art." Did his taste develop and change over the years? "Actually," he said, "the thrill for me is finding a new way of presenting the work so people see it as it's never been seen before. For example, I knew that Rothko was interested in Bonnard, and that inspired me to present the exhibition *Rothko/Bonnard: Color and Light*. Before the big MoMA retrospective showed his greatness, Bonnard was considered an Impressionist. I hope that our show provoked people to see Bonnard as a great and influential colorist. On the Saturday that *Rothko/Bonnard* closed, we had to stay open until 7:30 because there were lines down the block even though there was hardly any support from the press and few serious reviews." Like many of the ambitious historical shows put on by Pace, the news of this extraordinary *succès d'estime* traveled by word of mouth even beyond the art world grapevine.

The success of the Pace Gallery led Arne to open a second space on Greene Street in SoHo in 1990 for larger works. Many distinguished shows have been mounted at this site. In March 2000, Greene Street was filled with huge portraits by Chuck Close, whose daguerreotypes and holograms were being shown at Pace/MacGill on 57th Street. Glimcher's relationship with Close is one of the most important in his life. His continued support during the difficult times after the artist's disabling stroke, surely helped Close gain the confidence that permits him to innovate and produce on the most physically demanding and ambitious scale and redefine portraiture itself.

"I never wanted to be a 'gallerist,' people go to school now to become 'gallerists.' My ambition is for art, not business." At this moment in history, when so many gallerists are desperately turning to ephemeral sensation and trendy media, the consistency and quality of the works shown at PaceWildenstein are both exceptional and exemplary. This is, in other words, a gallery for grown-ups who value history, continuity, and aesthetics over shock, entertainment, and superficiality. At PaceWildenstein, taste—even if it is for difficult, reductive beauty, even if it is sometimes the most extravagant and convulsive beauty of a John Chamberlain or a Lucas Samaras—is not a bad word. The dedication of the gallery to educating the public, rather than catering to uninformed taste, is one reason that Pace/PaceWildenstein has made history for four decades, and continues to be a vital force in the art world.

1 9 6 0

BOSTON

Over the past four decades, Pace has been the locus through which many artists' work reached the public. We have also presented thematic exhibitions and exhibitions of lesser-known periods of the work of famous artists. Working in the art world and enjoying the privilege of "being there" when much of the art was created has been the fulfillment of living a life in art. This publication celebrates the artists and serves as a compendium or scrapbook of forty years of our enterprise. Originally, we planned to publish only photographs of exhibitions, believing that they would best capture the context of the art at each specific time. Researching the book, however, turned up an abundance of mementos, some humorous, some touching, and many long forgotten. Over five hundred exhibitions have been presented at Pace/PaceWildenstein, and we have published over three hundred catalogues with texts by many significant authors. Early on, the privilege of publishing distinguished authors became as integral a part of the gallery as the exhibition process itself.

In 1960, I was a senior at the Massachusetts College of Art, and my wife, Milly, was a junior art history major at Wellesley. That year we opened The Pace Gallery at 125 Newbury Street in Boston, where it remained until 1964. This book is the continuing story of that gallery.

THE PACE GALLERY

THE PACE GALLERY

125 Newbury Street   Boston, Massachusetts

Arnold Glimcher, Director   COngress 2-9383

MIRKO

ALBERT ALCALAY

DAVID BERGER

LAWRENCE KUPFERM

ROBERT S. NEUMAN

JASON BERGER

THE PACE GAL

125 Newbury

Boston, Massa

ARNOLD GLI

Director

The Pace Gallery has been formed to serve artists of established reputation and to develop younger artists of exceptional promise. The opening exhibition will present works by Mirko, Albert Alcalay, David Berger, Lawrence Kupferman, Robert S. Neuman, and Jason Berger. April 25 through May 16.

Gallery Hours: Monday through Saturday, 10:00 A.M. to 6:00 P.M.

FOUR SCULPTORS | ARP, CÉSAR, MALLARY, MIRKO
October 10 – 24, 1960

Four Sculptors — Arp — Cesar — Mallary — Mirko
October 10 to 24 — The Pace Gallery — 125 Newbury Street, Boston

Mirko
"Standing Figure"

The Italian sculptor Mirko was the director of the Carpenter Center at Harvard, located in the new Corbusier building—the architect's only American structure—and Mirko showed his own work at the prestigious World House Gallery (in the Carlyle Hotel) on Madison Avenue in New York. My gallery was in its first year, and World House didn't consider Pace significant enough to warrant an exhibition of Mirko's sculptures and refused my proposal for a one-man show. Desperately wanting to show this artist of international renown, I went directly to Mirko. With the help of mutual friends, and against the advice of his dealer, Mirko agreed to lend me a few sculptures for an exhibition, providing that I could place them in an agreeable context.

César was one of the most sought-after sculptors of the moment and was represented by the Saidenberg Gallery, which had yet to present an American exhibition of his work. Allan Stone, in his role as an extraordinary collector, had bought most of the great César sculptures from both Saidenberg and Claude Bernard in Paris. Neither Saidenberg nor Bernard had any idea that Allan was planning to open a gallery, and in a secret coup he opened his new gallery with César's first American exhibition. Scooping the Saidenbergs brought strong resentment from the art establishment. Stone, in the meantime, was very generous and supportive of my fledgling gallery, and we both showed the work of the Boston artist Robert Neuman. Allan lent me sculptures by César as well as by Robert Mallary for "Four Sculptors," and I borrowed Arps from the Hanover Gallery in London and from Denise René in Paris, with whom I had developed a relationship that would lead to three early exhibitions by Vasarely. The "Four Sculptors" exhibition would introduce me to Richard Solomon, who would eventually become my partner in Pace Editions.

As an art student I spent many weekends driving from Boston to New York to observe the scene. Each time I visited MoMA I was captivated by Nevelson's Sky Cathedral. Alfred Barr had brilliantly created an installation in a black alcove, producing an environment, a concept new to American art. I had never seen anything like it, and for years I assumed that this muscular, architectural sculpture was made by a man, having misread the label as Louis Nevelson.

In the early fifties Martha Jackson and Sidney Janis were the most powerful contemporary dealers in New York. The prominence of the Jackson Gallery and the audaciousness of its international exhibition program, was, in addition to Ms. Jackson's talents, the product of its perspicacious young director, Ivan Karp. Ivan would soon move to the Leo Castelli Gallery where he continued as a major influential figure in the avant-garde of the sixties, as the Castelli Gallery rose to preeminence.

Through Ms. Jackson's generosity and confidence, I was able to present an exhibition of Nevelon in my new Boston gallery. Nevelson's sculptures are large, but they broke down into units that I could load into a U-Haul truck myself and drive to Boston. It was to be Nevelson's first Boston exhibition and the first show of new work by a member of the New York avant-garde in a Boston gallery. The exhibition was to change the direction of The Pace Gallery, give it international recognition and allow me to attract other artists of stature.

I invited Mrs. Nevelson to Boston for the opening, offering accommodations at the Ritz Hotel and a round trip plane ticket for which I had no way of paying. It was only the success of the show that saved me. Already legendary for her eccentric costumes, I remember Nevelson arriving at the gallery on a warm May afternoon wearing enough layers of clothing to fill a closet, crowned by a huge fox hat. It was the beginning of a relationship that lasted twenty-nine years until Louise Nevelon's death in 1988.

ROBERT S. NEUMAN

3 BRITISH ARTISTS

PIETRO CONSAGRA

Robert S. Neuman, *No Pasar*, 1960
oil on canvas, 46⅞ × 44⅛"

ROBERT S. NEUMAN was born in Kellogg, Idaho, on the 9th of September, 1926. He studied at the California School of Fine Arts, San Francisco, at the California College of Arts & Crafts, at Mills College, with Max Beckmann, Oakland, California, and at the University of Idaho, Moscow, Idaho. Later he also studied with Willi Baumeister at the Staatliche Akademie der Bildenden Kunste in Stuttgart, Germany. In 1953 he was awarded a Fulbright Grant for Painting, and in 1956 he received a Guggenheim Fellowship for Painting and lived in Barcelona, Spain, during 1956 and 1957.

His paintings and drawings have been exhibited in Europe, the United States and Japan. Neuman's paintings are represented in the collections of the Carnegie Institute, Pittsburgh, the Institute of Contemporary Art, Boston, the San Francisco Museum of Art, and numerous private collections. In 1961 the grand prize of the Boston Arts Festival was awarded his painting "Cuadro Español"; other paintings have received awards from the San Francisco Museum of Art, the Institute of Contemporary Art, Boston, and the Providence, R.I., Arts Festival.

He is currently Visiting Assistant Professor of Art, Brown University, Providence, Rhode Island. He has lived in Boston since 1957.

ALAN DAVIE

EDUARDO PAOLOZZI

WILLIAM SCOTT

3 British Artists

THE PACE GALLERY   125 NEWBURY ST.   BOSTON

THE MONTH OF DECEMBER

PIETRO CONSAGRA

RICHARD STANKIEWICZ

PREVIEW: OCT. 22, 5 P.M. to 8 P.M.,

RICHARD STANKIE

RECENT SCULPTURE
OCT. 23 THRU NOV. 11

THE PACE GALLERY
125 NEWBURY STREET
BOSTON, MASSACHUSETTS

VICTOR VASARELY | PAINTINGS

March 12 – 31, 1962

This essay by Sam Hunter began our practice of commissioning texts by prominent writers and historians to introduce the exhibition on view.

Vasarely's ingenious geometric figures deceive the eye and delight the mind. Obeying a principle of optical reversal, his carefully engineered shapes double as spatial covers and openings, positive form and negative interval. Although these structures have an impersonal and mechanically processed look, they are surprisingly mobile and mysterious. Forms divide, subdivide, and multiply beneath our gaze, setting every inch of their surfaces in dynamic formal operation. Vasarely's restless activism of surface and wealth of formal mutation link his art with the best of contemporary abstraction, both of the "hard" variety and "soft." The artist's debt to the structural esthetics and schematic reductions of Mondrain, Moholy-Nagy and the classical constructivists is clear, and acknowledged; his use of ambiguity as an expressive device, however, places him solidly in our own time. The optical dipsy-doodle of his reliefs, in particular, subverts the closed geometric order of the old purist generation, and sets free a certain flexibility of spirit more in keeping with contemporary attitudes. One might describe these works as an effort to define the limitations of an art of intellectual control: at the least movement of the spectator's head the neatly regimented forms break ranks and scatter to unpredictable positions.

The ambiguities of Vasarely's paintings and relief constructions are both kinetic and optical. In the painted reliefs, patterns of composition and whole new formal constellations are created by the observer's own movements. Unlike Futurism, here, it is the spectator rather than the artist who provides the motor energy for change. The work of art unfolds itself sequentially, like the frames in a film, as he walks past. The eye, of course, would soon tire of such simple optical illusions and kaleidoscopic effects if they were not bound to a convincing pictorial space. We submit to the artist's visual sleight-of-hand, and even become active accomplices in his game because the shifting forms finally satisfy our deeper esthetic instincts.

Despite the chaste, diagrammatic simplicity of his work, and its limited sensuous appeal, Vasarely has no intention of establishing a new cult of the immaculate. Note how the bald contrasts of black and white are softened by subtle gradations of neutrals, and how often stripes of deep blue and purple enrich, and enliven, areas of black. Subtle modulations of color and tone, at the far end of the value scale, register the tremor of personal sensibility, and give an essentially human dimension to this otherwise coldly rational art, mitigating its formal rigors.

Even the stern father of the Rational Style, Piet Mondrian, in a rare moment of candor, seemed aware that it was not possible, nor even desirable, to suppress completely the accidents of individualistic expression. "The flat surface and the straight line provide the means for saying everything," he wrote in a little-known statement that deserves wider currency, "but it is the artist who does the saying." Vasarely took his cue from Mondrian, and from his followers, but he has managed to rehabilitate the stereotypes of non-objective expression by personalizing the idiom. If, as critics tell us, there is a new "realism" at work in the art of the neo-dadas, who turn to the brute materials and artifacts of contemporary life for inspiration, a comparable realistic, and individualistic, current may be found in "hard-edge" abstraction. A complex illusionism and visual play, suggesting multiple formal solutions, have replaced the innocent faith in a monolithic pictorial order of the great constructivist pioneers. In Europe today Vasarely bears a major share of the responsibility for reviving geometric abstraction and placing it in the service of contemporary moods.

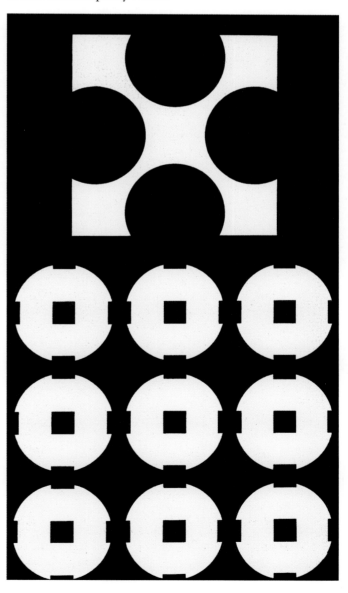

Exhibition announcement
© 2001 Artists Rights Society (ARS), New York / ADAGP, Paris

JOSEF ALBERS | **PAINTINGS**
November 5 – 24, 1962

THE PACE GALLERY TAKES PLEASURE IN ANNOUNCING AN EXHIBITION OF RECENT OILS BY JOSEF ALBERS, FROM NOVEMBER 5 THROUGH NOVEMBER 24, 125 NEWBURY STREET, BOSTON.

The greatest color theoretician since Helmholtz and Chevreul, Albers was the director of the Graduate School of Fine Arts at Yale. The protocol for a secondary dealer (one who does not represent the artist) is to ask the primary dealer for a show. My letters to Sidney Janis, Albers' representative, went unanswered. Frustrated, I sent Janis a packet of reviews of gallery shows and all of my announcements hoping to impress him. After weeks with no response, the package was returned stamped REFUSED! It lacked sufficient postage and the Janis Gallery would not accept delivery.

I called Albers directly at Yale and asked if I could visit him. I drove to New Haven and spent the day at his home. His wife, Annie, was inhospitable and clearly was against my having an exhibition of her husband's work. We talked about his work, color theory, and mutual artist friends. Against Annie's wishes I left New Haven with the promise of an exhibition. Albers interceded on my behalf with Janis. The Albers exhibition proved to have an even greater significance. In Boston, exhibitions opened on Sunday afternoons. Late Saturday evening, as I was struggling to complete the Albers installation, Fred Mueller came into the gallery. The heir to Mueller Brass (Detroit's manhole cover manufacturers), Fred was returning from six months in Europe after having financed and produced an Off-Broadway review entitled Another Evening With Harry Stoons. Despite its stellar cast, which introduced Dom DeLuise, Diana Sands, and Barbra Streisand, the Laugh-In-like review closed after one performance.

Fred was sophisticated, handsome, socially connected, knowledgeable in matters erudite as well as trivial; funny, genuinely nice, and obviously rich. He collected Asian antiquities and had a few modern paintings. That evening he bought the largest Albers out of the show. It was also the only one that I sold. He told me about his disappointment in the theater and his determination to get a job in a gallery, in preparation for opening his own.

ENJOY
Coca-Cola
TRADE-MARK ®

THE PACE GALLERY
125 NEWBURY ST.
BOSTON 16, MASS.

Stock up for

THE COCA-COLA COMPANY, LITHO. IN U.S.A.

MARISOL
OLDENBURG
DINE
ROSENQUIST
SEGAL
WARHOL
INDIANA
WESSELMANN

1960 - 69

the Holidays

Dec. 10 thru Jan. 2
Preview: Sunday
Dec. 9, 5-7 P.M.

"STOCK UP FOR THE HOLIDAYS"

A SURVEY OF POP ART

December 10 – 2 January, 1962

The exhibition of "The New Realists" at the Janis Gallery gave Pop art a credible endorsement, attracting the media that it parodied, and the notoriety expanded Pop's collector base. It was becoming chic to collect Pop art. A dealer synonymous with the great art movements of the twentieth century, Sidney Janis had audaciously rented a store-front space on West 57th Street and actualized the artists' intention of taking art back to the street. The exhibition was a sensation and inspired me to present my own version in Boston. I borrowed works from New York galleries and directly from the artists as well. Warhol, Indiana, and Marisol were Eleanor Ward's discoveries at the Stable Gallery. The Warhol paintings included Troy Donahue, Marilyn Monroe, Coke Bottles, Glass (Fragile), Campbell's Soup Can *and matchbook covers entitled* Close Cover Before Striking. *Marisol's* Equestrian Pope *was also in the show.*

From the Green Gallery, Dick Bellamy lent me George Segal's Man on a Bicycle, *Tom Wesselmann's* Great American Nude (Tondo), Still Life With Radio, *and Oldenburg's* Luncheon Pastries, Ice Cream Soda and Cookies, Box of Jockey Shorts, *and* Box of Shirts. *Martha Jackson lent Jim Dine's* Flesh Chisel. *The crucial artist missing was Roy Lichtenstein. Leo Castelli was unwilling to lend to the show as Roy's works were already in great demand.*

A few weeks prior to the opening, Milly and I were grocery shopping at Stop and Shop (Dick Solomon's family business) and noticed a poster in the window of an airbrushed Santa Claus knocking back a bottle of Coke. Under the image, in red Old English type were the words "Stock Up for the Holidays." It was just before Christmas. Dick Solomon secured

Window of Pace with *Man on a Bicycle* by George Segal

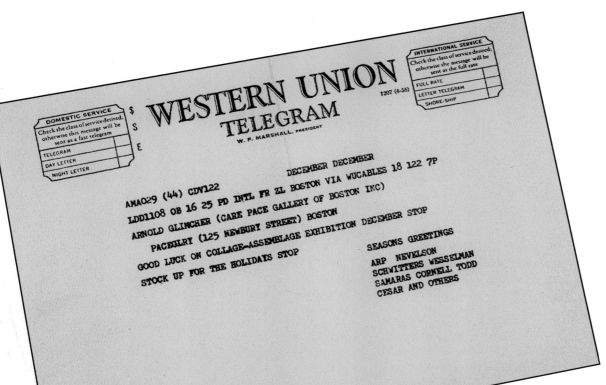

WESTERN UNION
TELEGRAM
1207 (4-55)
W. P. MARSHALL, PRESIDENT

DOMESTIC SERVICE
Check the class of service desired;
otherwise this message will be
sent as a fast telegram
TELEGRAM
DAY LETTER
NIGHT LETTER

INTERNATIONAL SERVICE
Check the class of service desired;
otherwise the message will be
sent at the full rate
FULL RATE
LETTER TELEGRAM
SHORE-SHIP

DECEMBER DECEMBER

AMA029 (44) CDV122
LDD1108 OB 16 25 PD INTL FR ZL BOSTON VIA WUCABLES 18 122 7P
ARNOLD GLIMCHER (CARE PACE GALLERY OF BOSTON INC)
PACEGLRY (125 NEWBURY STREET) BOSTON
GOOD LUCK ON COLLAGE-ASSEMBLAGE EXHIBITION DECEMBER STOP
STOCK UP FOR THE HOLIDAYS STOP

SEASONS GREETINGS
ARP NEVELSON
SCHWITTERS WESSELMAN
SAMARAS CORNELL TODD
CESAR AND OTHERS

JOHN CHAMBERLAIN

NOV. 16 — DEC. 7
PACE 125 NEWBURY ST., BOSTON

five hundred copies of the poster for me, and in the spirit of the artists' transformation of Pop culture into high art, I printed the artists' names in a border around the photo of Santa, inviting my collectors to "Stock Up for the Holidays."

Most of the artists, as well as Ivan Karp and Fred Mueller, came to Boston for the opening. As we couldn't afford to put them up in hotels, Tom and Claire Wesselmann stayed with Ann and Dick Solomon, Patty and Claes Oldenburg stayed with Milly and me. We arranged for Andy Warhol, Marisol, Indiana, and some of their friends to stay with other collectors. Though his work was not included in the exhibition, Larry Poons, along with his wife Thalia, came from New York by motorcycle to be a part of this collegial weekend. Claes Oldenburg brought a copy of his filmed happening Birthday Party *and we showed it at Ann Solomon's parents' home in Brookline. Sunday morning, Milly and I prepared brunch before they all returned to New York. Sam Hunter, then the director of the Rose Art Gallery at Brandeis University and an early champion of Pop art, came to our house with his friend, Virginia Wright, a young collector from Seattle.*

The exhibition was a great success both as a curiosity in conservative Boston and commercially. To my collector friends I made the baseless promises that I would buy the works back if they didn't like them. We sold several Warhols at $250 apiece, making a fine commission of $50 on each work. Dine's large Flesh Chisel *was sold for $800, Indiana's* Walt Whitman *also sold for $800 and three plaster Oldenburgs sold for between $150 and $200. Fred Mueller bought Tom Wesselmann's* Great American Nude (Tondo), *for $900.*

Top: Marisol, Dine, Indiana, Wesselmann, Wesselmann, Wesselmann
Bottom: Indiana, Oldenburg, Wesselmann, Warhol, Oldenburg, Rosenquist

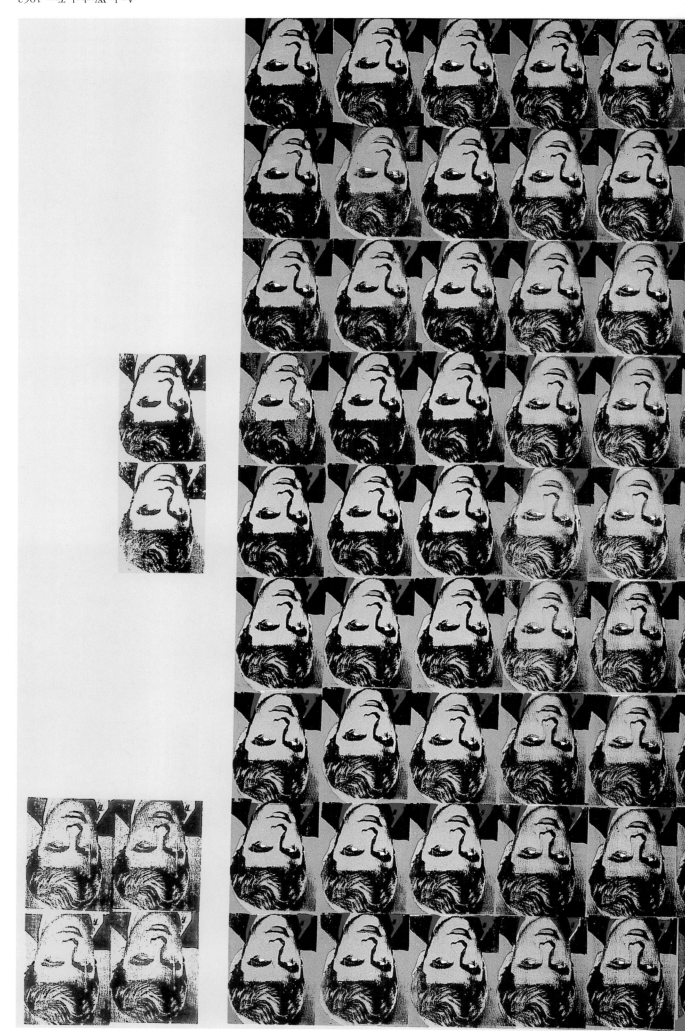

JOHN CHAMBERLAIN | SCULPTURE
November 16 – 7 December, 1964

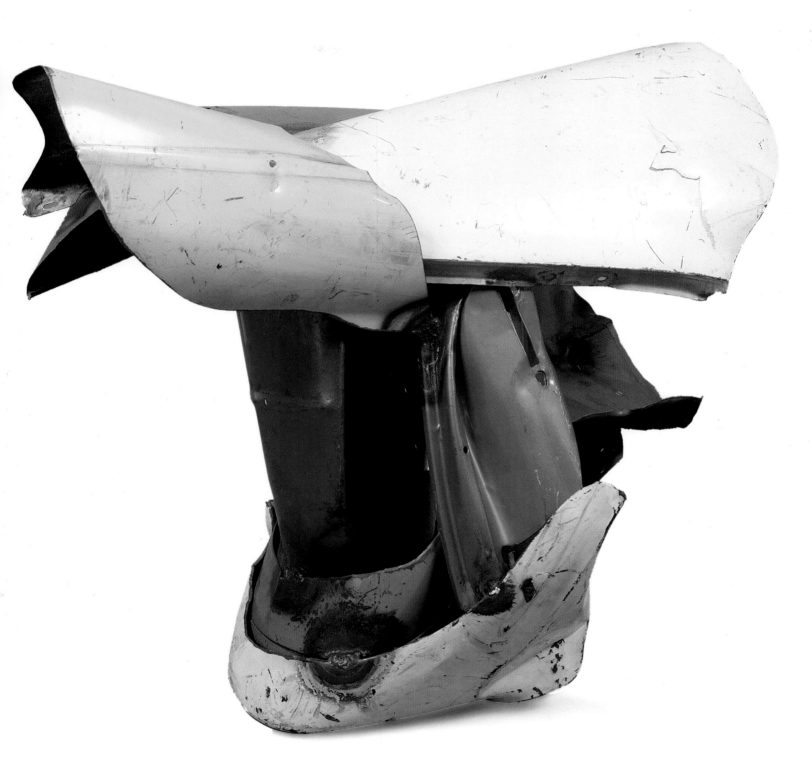

Untitled 1963, 1963
painted and chromium plated steel, 31¼ × 37½ × 27½"
Collection Whitney Museum of American Art
Purchase with funds from the
Howard and Jean Lipman Foundation, Inc. and gift
Photo Geoffrey Clements © 1998 Whitney Museum of American Art,
New York

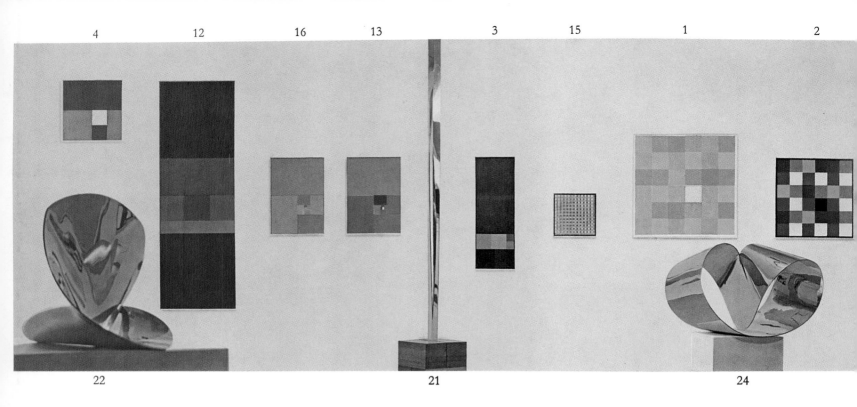

22   21   24

painting

1 field of eight color groups · 1955–62
   80:80 cm (31 1/2 : 31 1/2")

2 four complementary color groups · 1958
   62:62 cm (24 1/2 : 24 1/2")

3 group of four pairs of squares · 1958–61
   88:31 cm (34 1/2 : 12 1/4")

4 structure with three colors · 1959
   47:47 cm (13 1/2 : 13 1/2")

5 white square set in red · 1959
   88:88 cm (34 1/2 : 34 1/2") diagonal

6 yellow quarter · 1959
   66:66 cm (26:26") diagonal

7 eight equal sized planes · 1959–60
   47:47 cm (18 1/2 : 18 1/2") diagonal

8 red radiation · 1959–62
   43:43 cm (17:17") diagonal

9 condensation 4:3:2:1 · 1960
   113:113 cm (44 1/2 : 44 1/2") diagonal

10 light horizontal diagonal square · 1960
   141:141 cm (55 1/2 : 55 1/2") diagonal

11 red horizontal diagonal s
   57:57 cm (22 1/2 : 22

12 compr

max bill

born 12/22/08 · lives in zurich/switzerla

sculptures 1937–

18   23   19

14   four colors around white center · 1961
     141:141 cm (55 $^1/_2$:55 $^1/_2$″) diagonal

15   integration of four similar color pairs · 1961
     33:33 cm (13:13″)

16   six color pairs around pink · 1961–62
     60:42 cm (23 $^1/_2$:16 $^1/_2$″)

     sculpture

17   construction · 1937
     executed 1962 in granite · diameter 80 cm (31 $^1/_2$″)

18   construction with a cube and within a cube · 1944–45
     executed 1960 in gilded brass · 52:40:14 cm (20 $^1/_2$:15 $^3/_4$:5 $^1/_2$″)

19   construction from three circular planes · 1945–46
     executed 1961–62 in gilded brass · diameter 50 cm (19 $^3/_4$″)

20   endless loop from a circular ring II · 1947–49
     executed 1958 in gilded brass with white marble base
     53:14:38 cm (21:5 $^1/_2$:15 $^1/_2$″)
     collection mr and mrs alvin s. lane, new york

21   endless surface in form of a column · 1953
     executed 1958 in gilded brass · h = 250 cm (98 $^1/_2$″)

22   hexagonal surface in space with complete circumference · 1953
     executed 1960 in gilded brass · 35:50:40 cm (13 $^3/_4$:19 $^3/_4$:15 $^3/_4$″)
     collection mr edgar kaufmann jr., mill run, pa.

23   22 · 1953
     white marble on porphyry 50:50:60 cm (19 $^3/_4$:19 $^3/_4$:23 $^1/_2$″)

24   monoangulated surface in space · 1957
     executed 1959 in gilded brass · 38:70:46 cm (15:27 $^1/_2$:18 $^1/_8$″)

25   group of six cells · 1959
     white marble 37:57:52 cm (14 $^1/_2$:22 $^1/_2$:20 $^1/_2$″)

MAX BILL | SCULPTURES AND PAINTINGS
April 22 – 11 May, 1963

CLAES OLDENBURG

THE PACE GALLERY CORDIALLY INVITES YOU TO

PREVIEW AN EXHIBITION OF RECENT WORKS BY

CLAES OLDENBURG

SUNDAY MAY 10, 1964 8:00 TO 10:00 P.M.

THE EXHIBITION CONTINUES THROUGH JUNE 6

125 NEWBURY STREET   BOSTON

Oldenburg's first exhibition in Boston began a friendship that has continued to the present. Many objects in this exhibition were conceived for Oldenburg's Store, *which not only became a Pop icon, but represents one of the pivotal moments in installation and environmental art in America. In 1961, Claes rented a storefront space on East 2nd Street and, without warning to the neighborhood, installed his sculptures of food, clothing and pop cultural objects in the commercial context natural for the originals, thus eradicating the separation between life and art.*

Bringing elements from The Store *to Boston, and taking them out of their presentation context, was nevertheless counter to the artist's intention. But in the few years that had passed since the opening of* The Store, *the objects, by their own power, had been transformed into "fine art." They had acquired an audience and hence could be displayed comfortably in a gallery setting.*

Lingerie Counter, 1962
cloth soaked in glue and plaster and painted with enamel,
fluorescent light fixture, 53⅛ × 70⅞ × 8⅞"
Collection National Gallery of Hungary, Budapest
Gift of Peter Ludwig

Andy Warhol, *Arne, Eva and Fred,* 1980
silkscreen ink and diamond dust on synthetic polymer paint on canvas, 60 × 40"
© 2001 Andy Warhol Foundation for the Visual Arts, ARS, NY.

1 9 6 3

9 West 57th Street, New York City

I had been in discussion with Erica Brausen of London's Hanover Gallery about opening a gallery together in New York. Erica had already lent me a show of masterpieces by Bacon, Picasso, Matisse, Giacometti, Gonzalez, Richier, Magritte, and Arp, and in exchange I had arranged a Nevelson show at her gallery in London. Adding to the mix, I had developed relationships with Oldenburg, Warhol, Lichtenstein, Indiana, Marisol, Segal, and Wesselmann, as their works were beginning to find an audience of vanguard collectors. With my involvement in the contemporary American art scene and Erica's connections with modern masters, I thought that together we could create an important forum to which we could attract the new artists before they were all committed to other galleries. Erica's backers were cautious and by the time they agreed, all the Pop artists were affiliated with New York galleries. I explained the situation to Fred Mueller, who was not discouraged by the timing, and we formed a partnership and opened The Pace Gallery at 9 West 57th Street in New York. As the Pop artists were largely with Castelli and the Color Field artists were with Emmerich, Pace opened without an obvious focus, as a pluralistic gallery. A pejorative label at the time, over the next decade pluralsim would become our strength as artists preferred to be viewed as individuals rather than as part of a group.

ERNEST TROVA

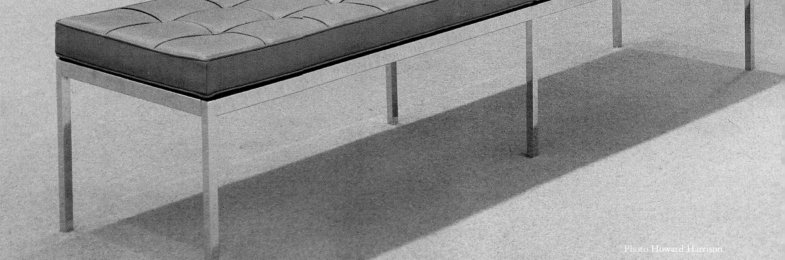

Exhibition opening
Top: Ernest Trova,
Richard Brown Baker
Bottom: Robert Indiana,
Ellsworth Kelly
Photos © Fred W. McDarrah

THE PACE GALLERY OF NEW YORK CORDIALLY
INVITES YOU TO PREVIEW ITS INAUGURAL
EXHIBITION OF PAINTINGS BY ERNEST TROVA
MONDAY, OCTOBER 28, 1963, 7 TO 10 P. M.
9 WEST 57 STREET

VASARELYVASARELYVASARELYVASARELY VASARELYVASARELYVASARE
ASARELYVASARELYVASARELYVASARELY VASARELYVASARELYVASAR
ASARELYVASARELYVASARELYVASARELY VASARELYVASARELYVASA
ASARELYVASARELYVASARELYVASARELY VASARELYVASARELYVASA
ASARELYVASARELYVASARELYVASARELY VASARELYVASARELYVASA
ASARELYVASARELYVASARELYVASARELY VASARELYVASARELYVAS
ASARELYVASARELYVASARELYVASARELY VASARELYVASARELYVAS
ASARELYVASARELYVASARELYVASARELY VASARELYVASARELYVAS

Announcements

VASARELY
MARCH 31—APRIL 18
PREVIEW
MONDAY, MARCH 30, 8:00 to 10:00 P.M.
PACE 9 W. 57 ST. NEW YORK

Catalogue

42

Photo Howard Harrison

VICTOR VASARELY | **PAINTINGS, SCULPTURE, PRINTS**
March 31 – 18 April, 1964

I had already shown Vasarely in Boston in 1962, through his Paris dealer, Denise René. Art as a perceptual tool has always been of primary interest to me. I had already shown Albers and Max Bill in Boston exhibitions, and prescient collectors began to acquire Op art. Our timing was excellent: Vasarely was accepted as the most important contemporary artist in the movement and the exhibition was a sell-out. The following year, the Museum of Modern Art would mount "The Responsive Eye," in which Vasarely was featured, and an avalanche of Op art infiltrated the media, influenced fabric, clothing, and houseware design and ultimately self-destructed.

LOUISE NEVELSON

RECENT WORK
November 17 – 2 December, 1964

THE NEW YORK TIMES   Saturday,   Nov. 21, 1964

Art: Sculptures by Louise Nevelson

Display at Pace Gallery Called Her Best Yet

By JOHN CANADAY

THINGS do move awfully fast. Only yesterday, Louise Nevelson was the star debutante of the art season, and now here she is, the grande dame of contemporary sculpture. Her new exhibition at the Pace Gallery, 9 West 57th Street, should establish her position for anyone who has had lingering doubts. It is her best show yet, and a beauty.

At 65 years of age, Mrs. Nevelson can recall a period of 30 years when she was unable to sell anything. After her first one-man show, at the pioneer Nierendorf Gallery in 1940, she carted the whole thing back to her loft studio and burned it. (A hard winter.) Then about 10 years ago we began hearing about her assemblages of fragments of old wood—balusters and other elements from destroyed houses—and in 1958 the Museum of Modern Art acquired its first Nevelson. She was in, and has ridden high ever since.

But as a creative artist she has never ridden so high as she does in her current show. Her work has had flair, spirit and the inexplicable quality called "presence," but it has never before been in addition so controlled, so disciplined. There has been a suspicion that much of the impact of her art has come from the force of its architectural dimensions. But now she has some small wall panels and some standing pieces only a foot high that are as powerful in presence as the big constructions that take whole rooms to themselves.

There are some easily de-

"Silent Music 2," 20-unit black curved wall with Plexiglass and bases, by Louise Nevelson, at the Pace Gallery.

finable changes, innovations for her—mirrored backgrounds, framed compositions and the smaller dimensions. But they do not account for the major delight, the sensation of absolute completeness that the new work creates.

Somebody tells me, at second hand, that at the opening of her new show last Tuesday Mrs. Nevelson was telling a story about Isadora Duncan's last performance, when everybody came to see what kind of dancing an old wo-

man could do. Isadora came out and just raised one arm in a certain way, and said, "Dears, that's what it's all about."

It would be both inaccurate and ungentlemanly to call Mrs. Nevelson an old woman (she is an unchronological kind of person, in the first place), and she must have many an exhibition left to go. But she can certainly point to this one and say, "Dears, that's what it's all about."

We did like it.

Nevelson's studio at 29 Spring Street, New York

By 1962 my relationship with Nevelson had become familial. She took a strong interest in our new baby and traveled with my mother. During the first years of the Boston gallery's existence, we had two successful exhibitions of her work. I visited her regularly in New York and even took my baby son, Paul, to her studio. During this period she left her dealer of long standing, Martha Jackson, for Sidney Janis. Nevelson was the sculptor whose work had the greatest affinity with the Abstract Expressionist painters. Pictorial in attitude and frontal in construction, like Rothko, she reached for the "sublime" and was interested in tragic themes. (Later, Nevelson would be the conduit to my relationship with Mark Rothko.) If David Smith's sculpture was about drawing in space (inspired by Picasso and Gonzalez), Nevelson's was about assemblage painting, a combination of Picasso's constructivist Guitars and Schwitters' Merzbau, dependent on physical objects and their attendant shadows to create form by illusion. She produced the first site-specific environment and installation works in America.

The Janis Gallery represented nearly all of the Abstract Expressionist painters. Nevelson, a strong feminist, wanted to desegregate this bastion of male power and be the first woman, and the first American sculptor, represented by Sidney Janis. She also wanted to be in a gallery with her peers, and they encouraged her. Nevelson was selected to represent America in the 1962 Venice Biennale. Before I learned of her affiliation with Janis, and hoping that she would join the gallery that I was planning to open in New York, I took out full page ads in all of the art magazines, with installation photographs captioned "Nevelson at Pace/Representing America in the XXXI Venice Biennale." To the Europeans, Pace appeared to be her representative. In Venice, Nevelson took me to all of the parties and introduced me to the international world of artists, collectors, and museum directors as her dealer. In Venice, through Erica Brausen of the Hanover Gallery, I met Giacometti. Erica and I, together with Nevelson watched him install his sculptures in the Italian pavilion. The space was large and white with high ceilings, and the dark patinated sculptures looked like little sticks timidly poking into the space of the rooms. Displeased with the effect, Giacometti painted the sculptures flesh color so that the already visually fragile figures appeared and disappeared like ephemeral specters, just out of perceptual grasp. It was a great triumph and Giacometti won the prize. Most of the sculptures had been lent by collectors and museums, some of whom were outraged that he had changed their sculptures. Later, I heard of owners having the paint removed and the sculptures restored to their original patina.

During the Biennale, it was announced that Nevelson was leaving Martha Jackson and Daniel Cordier for exclusive representation by Janis. Nevelson was sensitive to my disappointment, and one evening at a dinner given in her honor on the roof of the Danieli Hotel, she said: "Don't be so sad—eventually I'll be with you in New York, but for now this relationship with Janis will be good for you as well—I always go with the best." Nevelson finally achieved her objective of being with "the boys," but her move was ill-timed. Janis presented his Pop art

exhibition, and the Abstract Expressionists, threatened by the media support of Pop art and repelled by its embrace of pop culture, left Janis en masse for the new swank New York outpost of Frank Lloyd's Marlborough Gallery. Nevelson was left alone at the Janis Gallery.

Sporadic alcoholism haunted Nevelson all of her life. "I never drink a little," she would say, "when I drink it's a binge." Binges could last days or weeks and she could get so drunk that she'd collapse on the streets of Little Italy. The Don of Little Italy, where she lived in what was once a private sanitarium, was aware of her prominence as a cultural icon and protected her. He didn't necessarily understand her work, but respected it. Each morning Nevelson would find bits of old broken furniture leaning against her door. If she picked up something on the street—a bit of wood, a broken chair—invariably someone would rush over and help her carry it home.

The Janis Gallery was in a transition from which it would never fully recover. Marlborough was the new king of the art gallery world and Pace was about to open in New York. On New Year's Eve 1963, Nevelson's first show at Janis opened with a black tie vernissage. The economy having slumped, only one work was sold, and Nevelson was in debt to Janis for the advance of $20,000. She descended into the worst binge of her life contemplating suicide daily. She knew that she had made a mistake in going with Janis. She wanted to come to Pace, but she couldn't leave Janis without paying back the advance. Furthermore, all of her work was in Janis' warehouse.

I asked Leo what he thought of my opening a branch of Pace in New York and he said: "All New York needs is another gallery." Ivan was much more encouraging. It was June 1963 and every Monday Fred Mueller and Ivan Karp would pick me up at the airport in Ivan's car and we would visit artists' studios. "It's my party, and I'll cry if I want to . . ." played on his car radio. Ivan was genuinely in love with the new art, the new music, and pop culture. He knew that for the latest wave of the avant-garde to succeed, it had to be endorsed by more than just the Castelli Gallery. With his help we found our location, he introduced us to a young architect named Hanford Yang, and we assembled our first roster of young artists. We knew that if we could add Nevelson to the gallery, we'd be a gallery worthy of consideration. Ivan, who had been director of the Martha Jackson Gallery during Nevelson's tenure there, agreed. Fred and I had a total of sixty thousand dollars with which to reconstruct the space and open the gallery. We decided to give one third of it to Nevelson so that she could pay off Janis and get her work back. By now she was chronically alcoholic, and in the hopes of reestablishing her sense of security, we sent all of her sculptures back to her studio. With her work back and no demands made by us, she gradually came out of her alcoholism, let go of her anger and began to make new work. We wouldn't show her work until the following November. We borrowed additional money and gave Nevelson a small advance against future sales. At the end of our first year, we showed her new work to great acclaim and ended our first year in the black with cumulative sales of $90,000.

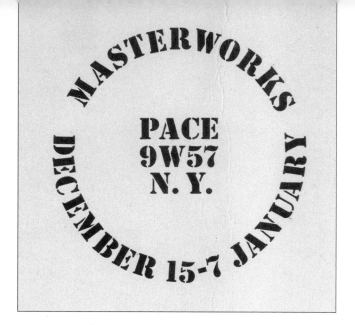

I met Erica Brausen at her Hanover Gallery in London in the summer of 1961, where she was presenting a sculpture exhibition entitled Modern European Masters. Among others, it contained Giacometti's Homme qui marche and Quatre figures sur socle, Matisse's Figure décorative, Picasso's Hand, Richier's Don Quixote, Magritte's Madame de Recamier, and sculptures by González, Arp, and Ernst as well. At that time, these now-iconic works were still difficult to sell. Throughout the summer-long run of the exhibition, despite the traditional visits of American collectors to Europe in search of art, none of the works sold. During my visit, I bought Francis Bacon's Man in Blue of 1954 for $15,000, and I asked Erica if it would be possible to have her sculpture show for my Boston gallery.

In an act of faith and kindness, Erica agreed to send me almost the entire exhibition on consignment. Although it met with great critical acclaim, ultimately, none of the sculptures sold. Irving Rabb, the only client to whom I had sold similar works, was on an extended vacation. He returned to Boston the last Saturday of the show, came into the gallery, and admired Giacometti's Four Figures on a Base. He said that he'd consider it, since it worked well with the other Giacomettis in his collection. I explained that the exhibition was being returned to London the following Monday. Sunday morning, Irving called me at home and asked what I would have to pay for the entire group of sculptures. The answer was $250,000. Irving advanced me the funds, we became equal partners in the profits, and he kept one of the Giacomettis.

Two years later, when we opened in New York, the still unsold Giacometti Homme qui marche and Matisse Figure décorative, graced our office, which had been decorated by my partner, Fred Mueller, with Ming Chinese furniture. In the course of the next two years, we sold the remaining works for a reasonable profit. The most satisfying transaction was placing Giacometti's Walking Man in the collection of The Art Institute of Chicago. Soon after, on a visit to Paris, Erica Brausen invited me to lunch with Giacometti at the Deux Magots. I was speechless at meeting this pale, plaster-dusted legend, and Erica, attempting to involve me in the conversation, said, "Alberto, Arne just sold your Homme qui marche to the Chicago Art Institute for a record price of $53,000." Giacometti smiled, then, pointing his spiny finger in my direction and raising on eyebrow, said, "You will be arrested!"

Alberto Giacometti
L'homme qui marche, 1960
bronze, 72 × 10 × 38"
©2001 Artists Rights Society (ARS
New York/ADAGP, Paris

Henri Matisse, *Figure décoratif*, 1908
bronze, 28⅜ × 19⅞ × 11⅞"

1ˢᵗ

INTERNATIONAL GIRLIE EXHIBIT

Your true Friend.

PACE 9 WEST 57

JAN. 7—JAN. 25
PARTY PREVIEW: JAN. 6, 8-10 P. M.

THE PACE GALLERY WISHES TO ACKNOWLEDGE THE COOPERATION OF LEO CASTELLI & IVAN KARP IN ASSEMBLING THE GIRLIES

Works by Marjorie Strider
and Tom Wesselmann

Opening of
*1st International
Girlie Exhibit*

Top left:
Ivan Karp

Top center:
Arne Glimcher,
Ray Johnson

Top right:
Andy Warhol

Photos ©
Fred W. McDarrah

At a time before feminist politics made the concept impossible, we presented a survey of the influence of the "pinup girl" on contemporary artists. Beginning with de Kooning's Women series of the fifties, this American icon had been transformed in a collision with Cubism. Unlike de Kooning, however, the Pop artists presented the image intact, and it was the post-de Kooning pinups that inspired our exhibition.

As a teenager, pinup art had always fascinated me, and I would spend hours copying the pinups of Frank Petty's new "Petty Girls," to the delight of my friends.* Wesselmann's Great American Nude was as much influenced by the American pinup as by Matisse. Lichtenstein's Girl with Beach Ball and Little Aloha, Marjorie Strider's pinups with three-dimensional breasts, Al Hansen's silhouettes of nudes made from Hershey wrappers, and Ben Johnson's ripe female forms were all included in the exhibition. With the help of Ivan Karp and the support of Leo Castelli, we mounted the show and most of the art world made the opening the event of the month.

*Frank Petty and Alberto Vargas were the kings of pinup art during the forties and fifties. They were so much a part of popular culture that Joan Caulfield and Robert Cummings starred in a movie on Petty's life called The Petty Girl.

Roy Lichtenstein, *Girl with Ball*, 1961
oil and synthetic polymer paint on canvas, 60¼ × 36¼"
Collection Museum of Modern Art, New York
Gift of Philip Johnson
©Estate of Roy Lichtenstein

ERNEST TROVA

Trova's first sculpture show was well received by the press and a frenzy of collectors. Before the opening it was sold out to major collectors, including Emily and Burton Tremaine, Vera List, Howard and Jean Lipman, Evelyn and Leonard Lauder, Richard Brown Baker, and Philip Johnson. Alfred Barr and Dorothy Miller bought three works for the Museum of Modern Art. The Whitney Museum made some acquisitions and scores of museums followed.

BEYOND REALISM

March 9 – 4 April, 1965

by Michael Kirby
Excerpt from Pace Catalogue

. . . Surrealism of that period was essentially intellectual-literary. Thought moves. It must have sequence. It makes, and is composed of, connections between things. Thus juxtaposition, the combination of disparate objects and images, became fundamental to Surrealism. The umbrella and the sewing machine meeting by chance on a dissecting table disrupted the usual combinations of associations and forced thought into new progressions. Just as the unconscious was indicated by the dreams and slips of the tongue that constituted the "psychopathology of everyday life," the artist trapped it with his own creations. The intellect, pressing upon materials it could not handle in the accustomed manner, was left with the significant imprint of irrationality. It was much like the mediums who make plaster casts of spirit hands: the unconscious was seen by the marks it left behind.

In addition to ideational sequence, the intellectual-literary aspects of Surrealism were also apparent in the inclination toward, and susceptibility to, interpretation. The symbols of the "hand-painted dream photograph" were traced back through the "dream work" to the "latent content." The visual language that was developed had a close relationship in both vocabulary and syntax to the young science of psycho-analysis, and "translation" was often an expected part of the experience.

It was not until the war drove Surrealist artists to the United States that one of the major professed ambitions of the group—a non-intellectual "pure psychic automatism"—could be realized. And it was achieved by the American Action Painters of the late 1940's and early 1950's. The spontaneous gesture, devoid of symbolic information or thought, presented new aspects of the unconscious.

More recently, a number of American artists have begun working with the unconscious in their own ways. Non-programatic, non-didactic, stressing individuality, their work does not comprise a "movement," but certain generalities may be made. The tendency is toward a sensory presence that creates the feeling of the unconscious rather than an intellectual stimulator that creates the *mental awareness* of the unconscious. The multiplicities, juxtapositions, and inventions of fantasy and Surrealism are abandoned. Symbols, interpretation, and representation—the processes of "standing for" something else—are forgotten. The works tend to be objects. They are things that we experience as directly as the things of everyday life. But their presence is not the everyday, rational one. It is the presence of the unconscious.

As in a dream, we are aware of irrational contradictions and incongruities: the small is of huge size, the light is actually heavy, the useful is useless, the rigid is flexible. And, as in a dream, these impossibilities are presented with a direct, dominating, incontrovertible reality. (In dreams, even the most bizarre and distorted images have the *feeling* of reality. The occasional simultaneous knowledge that "this is a dream" does not weaken the pervasive "realness.")

While the presence is direct, the feelings involved are complex, contradictory, and sometimes elusive. As is true in dreams, ambivalent effect—love/hate, attraction/repulsion—is felt, and, although the pathological and bizarre are not emphasized, a gross, visceral quality permeates much of the work. At a time when theories and ideas about the unconscious are commonly accepted, these works, in their nonintellectual character, make an important contribution to experience.

At its inception, the fascination with Pop art was largely based upon its reintroduction of recognizable imagery drawn from popular culture. After two decades of the Abstract Expressionist search for the sublime, to the sixties artists it seemed that Pollock, Rothko, Newman, and Reinhardt had fulfilled the history of reductionism and left no related space in which to work. Later we would learn that this was not true, as Minimalism, working off the beachhead of Pop seemed to once again carry reductionism to its logical conclusion.

Another fascinating aspect of the Pop period was the creation of surreal metaphors by altering states of the familiar. There is no more exquisite example than the work of Claes Oldenburg. The history of sculpture is the transformation of soft into hard. In the most perverse gesture, Oldenburg reverses the tradition by making hard objects soft. Permanence gives way to states of flux as Oldenburg's floppy objects are subject to constant gravitational changes. With Oldenburg as the linchpin we assembled sculptures by a group of artists whose subject was not so much the image as its physical and metaphoric transformation "Beyond Realism."

Richard Artschwager

Chryssa

Robert Morris

Claes Oldenburg

Michelangelo Pistoletto

James Rosenquist

Lucas Samaras

Majorie Strider

Paul Thek

Ernest Trova

Michael Todd

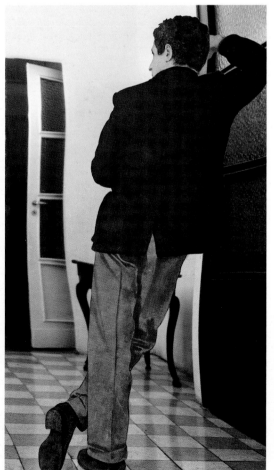

Michelangelo Pistoletto
Man with Yellow Pens, 1962–64
painted tissue paper on stainless steel, 78¾ × 39⅜"
The Museum of Modern Art, New York

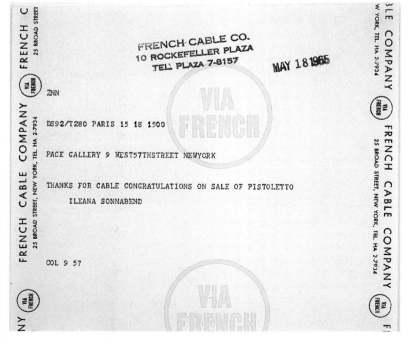

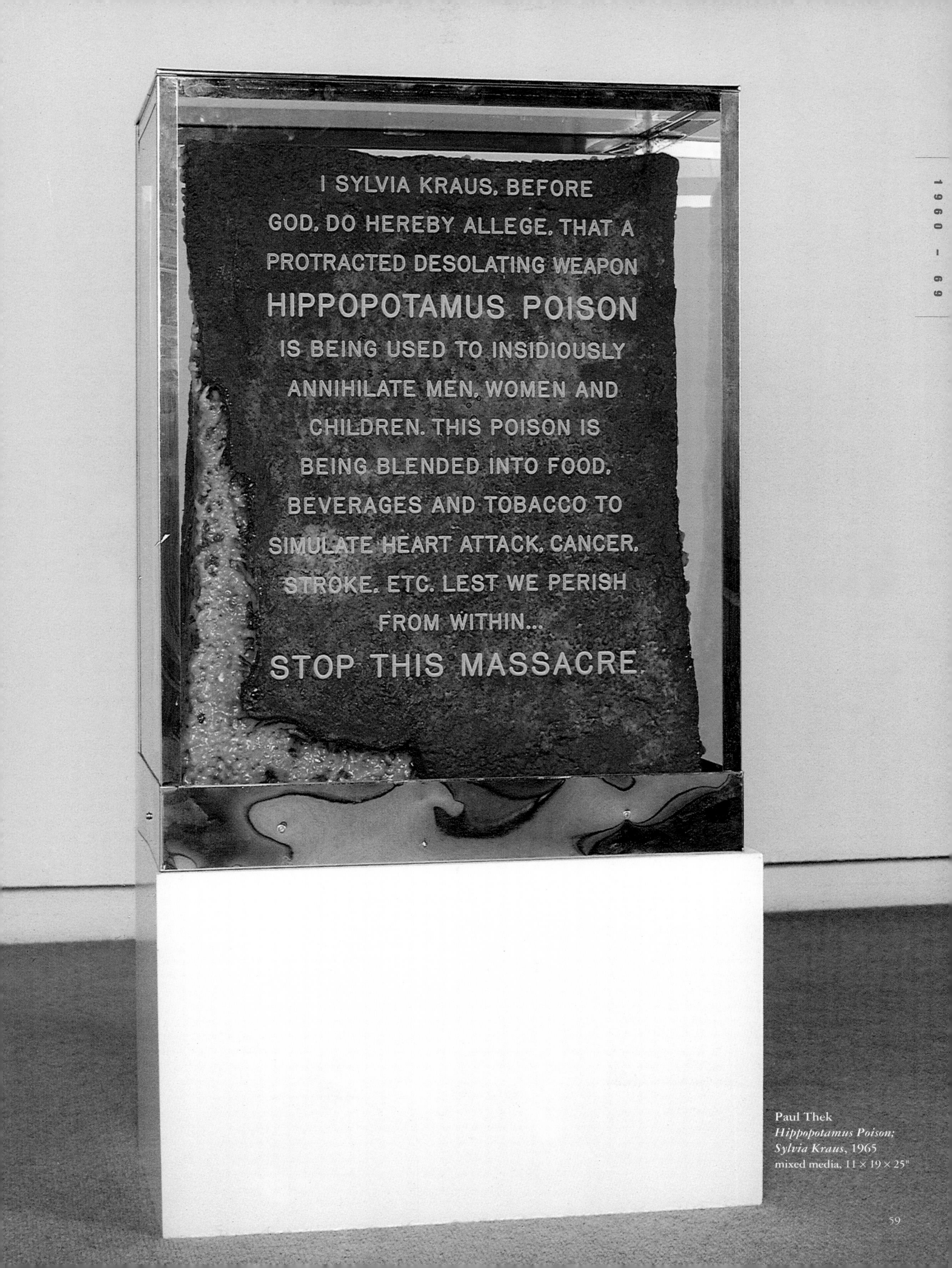

I SYLVIA KRAUS, BEFORE
GOD, DO HEREBY ALLEGE, THAT A
PROTRACTED DESOLATING WEAPON
HIPPOPOTAMUS POISON
IS BEING USED TO INSIDIOUSLY
ANNIHILATE MEN, WOMEN AND
CHILDREN. THIS POISON IS
BEING BLENDED INTO FOOD,
BEVERAGES AND TOBACCO TO
SIMULATE HEART ATTACK, CANCER,
STROKE, ETC. LEST WE PERISH
FROM WITHIN...
STOP THIS MASSACRE.

Paul Thek
Hippopotamus Poison;
Sylvia Kraus, 1965
mixed media, 11 × 19 × 25"

THE PACE GALLERY'S OPENING EXIBI-
TION MAY BE FOUND BY ERASING THE
SILVER DISCS WITH A MOIST TISSUE.
OCTOBER 9-NOVEMBER 3, 1965

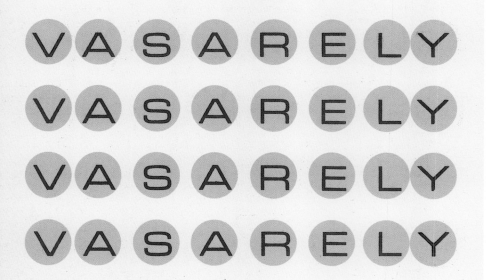

THE PACE GALLERY'S OPENING EXIBI-
TION MAY BE FOUND BY ERASING THE
SILVER DISCS WITH A MOIST TISSUE.
OCTOBER 9-NOVEMBER 3, 1965

The result of our 1964 Vasarely exhibition was the creation of demand for the works by collectors and institutions far exceeding the supply. It also ensured Vasarely a major place in the Museum of Modern Art's forthcoming blockbuster, "The Responsive Eye." Denise René, Vasarely's dealer in Paris, seemed pleased by our performance and grateful for the revenue from sales, which exceeded $250,000—the most successful Vasarely exhibition to date. What we didn't know was that Denise René was making a deal with Sidney Janis for Vasarely's next show. She had obtained from Janis a guarantee of $100,000 in purchases—which she told me was too large an amount to ask us for (though we could have guaranteed it based on our waiting list of clients for the work). Moreover, she wanted Vasarely in the context of Mondrian, Albers, and Herbin at the Janis Gallery. She also showed Albers and controlled the estate of Herbin. Fred and I were devastated, humiliated, and angry. Since the deal was final, I went to Paris and asked Denise to at least sell me some Vasarely paintings for the collectors on my waiting list. After all, I argued, I was responsible for some of the commercial acceptance of his work.

Out of guilt feelings and in violation of her contract with Janis, Denise sold me a group of extraordinary new color works, making me promise to be discreet in their disposition. We acquired other works in the market place, borrowed paintings from collections, and opened the season with "New Works by Vasarely." In an act of retribution, we published a catalogue preceded by an announcement that I designed for my amusement and Denise René's humiliation. I printed a card covered with water-soluble silver discs in four rows of eight across, instruction the recipient to discover the artist's name "by erasing the silver discs with a moist tissue." As they were mailed, I pictured the shock on Denise René's face as she, moist tissue in hand, revealed the name V-A-S-A-R-E-L-Y.

Fred Mueller and Arne Glimcher, ca. 1965

LARRY BELL

RECENT WORK
October 31 – 29 November, 1965

Above: Untitled, 1969
mineral coated glass with metal binding
14 × 14 × 14"

EDUARDO PAOLOZZI

SCULPTURES, DRAWINGS, PRINTS
January 8 – 2 February, 1966

Poem for the Trio MRT, 1964
welded aluminum, 85 × 86 × 44"

variations from Micky Mouse

E Paolozzi 1964.

Crash Table Mickey

variations in a theme of Micki

Akopotic Rose, 1965
welded aluminum, 109 × 73 × 50"

PAUL THEK

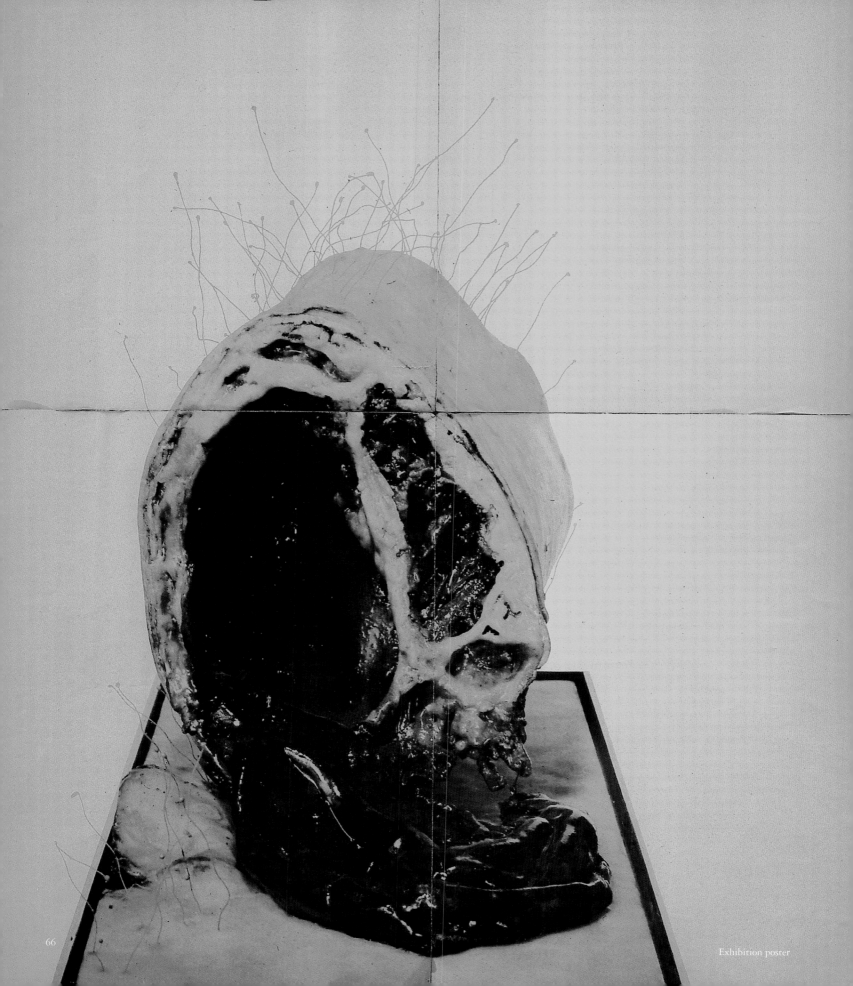

Exhibition poster

PAUL THEK | **RECENT WORK**
April 12 – 4 May, 1966

Fred Mueller and I heard about an artist making wax facsimiles of slabs of meat. It was too preposterous and disgusting to keep us away, and we arranged a meeting with Paul Thek at his studio. Part hippie (his last major work would be a tomb containing his effigy in wax, entitled The Dead Hippie*), part conjurer, and with the presence of a movie star, he showed us his work. At first we gagged, but we recognized his ability to turn revulsion into seduction, and after a couple of visits we succumbed to his sorcery. Paul wanted to encase the works in bilious yellow-green plastic cases, some with numbers and some engraved with texts. There was a woman named Sylvia Kraven who passed out manifestos in front of the Plaza Hotel warning of the government-sponsored toxins infiltrating the food supply in the form of hippopotamus poison. Thek engraved her text on a case enclosing a huge slab of wax meat glistening with mucus and veins and sprouting hairs on the patch of skin crowning the image. Other pieces of meat were encased in tall totemic columns with center sections opening to reveal reliquary fragments. Others had pipes piercing the plastic-like feeding tubes of science fiction movie specimens. The success of this little known and extremely powerful body of work lay in the experience of threat giving way to seduction and the repulsive transformed to the beautiful.*

We believed in Paul, presented an exhibition, and placed several works in museums and some, with more difficulty, in private collections. Ultimately searching for expanded consciousness, Thek let drugs overtake his life, and our relationship drifted apart before his untimely death. The experience of showing the work is still a source of pride.

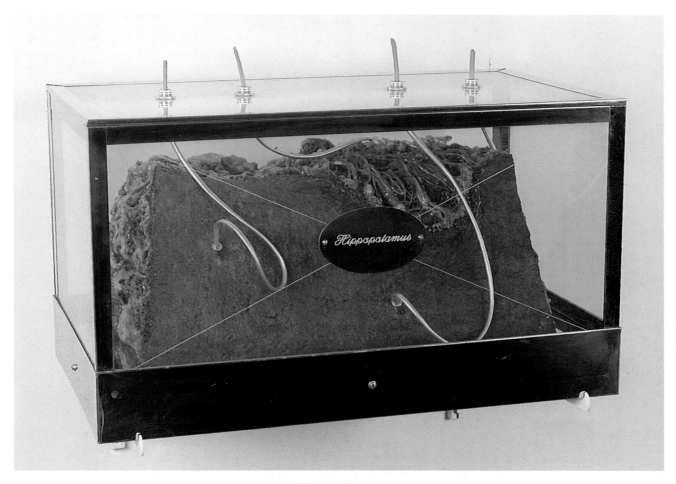

Hippopotamus, 1965
mixed media

1 9 6 6

When the Green Gallery closed in 1965, its director, Dick Bellamy, more a friend to artists than a dealer, secured a place for each of the Green artists in the gallery he considered most suitable. Dick proposed that we take on Lucas Samaras, as he knew of my interest in the work. Samaras had other ideas. If he couldn't join Castelli's gallery (and he couldn't), he wanted to join the Janis Gallery, where his friends, Oldenburg and Segal, were going. We also wanted Oldenburg and Judd, but fledgling Pace couldn't compete with either Janis or Castelli.

When Samaras visited the gallery, essentially to interview Fred and me, the meeting went well. At one point, Samaras proposed that we underwrite the building of a mirrored room. I immediately agreed. This level of commitment was greater than any of the galleries he was considering, and as a result, Samaras joined The Pace Gallery.

Samaras created a group of complex boxes and a series of drawings from X-rays of sculls, hands, and internal organs for his first exhibition at Pace. This was amongst the first work "about the body" whose influence can still be felt today. The mirrored room cost a formidable $5,000 to construct, which we took from our operating budget. We knew that if we didn't sell it quickly we'd be in serious debt, but during the first week of the exhibition, Seymour "Shorty" Knox, president of the Albright-Knox Art Gallery and visionary collector, bought the mirrored room for $17,000 and we divided the handsome profit of $12,000 with Lucas. The environment initiated our practice of underwriting artists' projects—which was rarely if ever done by galleries before us.

LOUISE NEVELSON

FOUR ENAMELED ALUMINUM SCULPTURES

January 9 – 3 February, 1971

Atmosphere and Environment I, 1966
black enameled aluminum, 78 × 144 × 48"

Louise Nevelson's first exhibition of outdoor sculpture was the beginning of her relationship with the Lippincott Foundry. They would provide the environment within which she would produce heroic scale sculptures and public commissions for the rest of her life.

Top right and left: Mirrored Room under construction
in the gallery space
Bottom left: Lucas Samaras, Helen and George Segal,
Judith Heidler, Fred Mueller, and Arne Glimcher
in front of *Mirrored Room* during the exhibition
Bottom right: installation view

Interior, *Mirrored Room,* 1966
mirrors on wooden frame, 8 × 10 × 8'
Collection Albright-Knox Art Gallery, Buffalo, New York
Gift of Seymour H. Knox

ROBERT IRWIN | DOT PAINTINGS
November 12 – 10 December, 1966

Excerpts from a conversation:
Bob Irwin and Milly Glimcher
June 23, 1999

M.G. How did you and Arne meet?

B.I. I actually think Larry Bell introduced me to everybody in New York; it was funny to have my student take me around. He was very gregarious. After having nothing happen (because I really had never courted anything), I got three offers simultaneously to show in New York. Suddenly, I had this incredible richness.

I got offers from Arne, and from Leo Castelli, and Sidney Janis. I had shown one painting in a group show at the Janis Gallery and the painting was sold to the Albright-Knox Gallery. I had previously been asked to have an exhibition of the *Dot Paintings* at the Green Gallery. I came [to New York], and I looked at the space, it was small, and for me, a little awkward. And at that time I was probably overly precious, but I felt that the paintings needed the right circumstances. I don't think they're nearly as *trés cher* now as I thought they were then. They work under a broader set of circumstances, but at that time. I was really cutting it fine. I decided that it was only possible to hang one painting there, which we [Irwin and Dick Bellamy] both felt was a little awkward, and so, the exhibition never happened.

Janis had peg-board walls, and I thought: God, he wasn't about to change peg-board walls for me, and obviously, I couldn't hang my paintings on those walls.

Arne was very different. He basically said: "We'll do whatever you want. We'll present them however you think they need to be hung." And basically, Arne never reneged on what he said. And, in retrospect, I think that Janis was not the right place for me, and as for Leo, with all the politics during the next ten or fifteen years, Pace was probably a much better place to be for me.

But, my decision was really very simple. It was based on what I could do and what Arne actually had offered. At that time, the gallery was not really a good gallery for me in the sense of the kind of traffic that went through. My work didn't really fit the profile of the gallery in the beginning.

M.G. The gallery didn't really have a profile at the beginning.

B.I. Let's not say "profile." It just didn't draw the kind of crowd that would be interested—the gallery was actually more sophisticated, in terms of the kind of people who showed there.

M.G. Arne likes to tell the story about your first show of the *Dot Paintings* at the gallery. As I understand it, when you finished the installation, there was a shadow cast by one of the ceiling bays so you painted the entire gallery the color of the shadow.

B.I. Well, what I did was like a reverse *trompe l'oeil.* No matter what color you paint the wall, there'd still be shadow there. So, what I did was to paint the walls a little darker, and then, I painted the area of the shadow a little lighter, and then it just matched right out, and the shadow appeared to be the same color as the wall. It disappeared. That kind of thing drove New Yorkers crazy, it was just too precious for them at that time.

M.G. Can we talk about the show of the "soft wall" and the show of the "hard wall" that you built down the center of the gallery?

B.I. Well, the "hard thing" came first, and the "soft" came second. I think the soft one was probably one of the better things I've done. The paintings were starting to become lost in the shadows, and I was not sure where it was going or what I was going to do. In the interim, I did a sort of bridge thing, which is what the columns were. I didn't know how to make non-object art, and for a moment, I thought that it was going to translate into the third dimension, that sculpture would be how I would break out of this thing. Then I realized that the same logic applied, the same thing that made a painting a painting made an object an object. For a while I really didn't know what to do, and that's why I wandered for a couple of years doing that peripatetic thing, just filling in the time trying to figure what was going on.

Although I didn't even have terms for them yet, I started with the idea of everything being rooted in the conditional, the reverse of the old aspiration of art being transcendent, timeless. There was nothing in time, but rather for me the real question was the contextual. That is, if you have a frame, a

Untitled, 1966
oil on canvas, 82½ × 82½"

context, then you have an axiom, which is just the mark you make on it. And if you have something beautifully put together, like a painting which is like a history of marks; when I put a mark on a canvas, everyone who is conversant with that history can compare that mark to all others which enables the most sophisticated kind of dialogue, incredibly layered. However, when you break the frame, you break this agreement and something major is lost: the whole contextual agreement of how we make all our critical decisions. You have to supply a new frame of reference, an extended frame of reference, if you want to have an extended view.

If you take the words "creative" and "freedom" and all the things that we talk about in terms of creative effort, can we hold the dialogue about what is art, to be the equal of making? And the answer, of course, is no. Is it about a state of mind and about a level of awareness, about a kind of attending, or is it about the objects? Obviously, it's not about the objects. We're educated to think of the object as the subject and what I was pointing out is that there is a *subject* from which all these objects have arisen. Each of those objects is art, but none of them is art *per se*. The real issue in every new generation of art is to re-examine the *subject* of art, and to modify that dialogue we've had over the centuries about how we can make an art that is specific to our time, and that has to do with addressing the subject. Most people are having a dialogue with the objects, which can be very interesting and sophisticated, and that's why it's easy to confuse the two. It's not because it's irrelevant. It's the opposite, and it is quite sophisticated.

Having broken the frame, I put myself in a position of having to look at things in a different way. Every one of those installations at the gallery was essentially starting with a set of givens, with just the space. And then, the issue becomes the nature of the space: how it feels being in the space, what kind of expectations you have, how do you enter. . . . Then, you try and do something that in some way engages you about that process and challenges you as a perceptual human being. The soft wall was very good in that basically you walked in and, by almost every clue you had, it was an empty space. But, if you stood there for a moment, you knew something was wrong.

We have all these innate structures which work very well for us, so that as you walk through the world, if you had to stop and examine everything you wouldn't be able to move. When you enter a room, very quickly, very subliminally, you make a read of the room to be sure everything's in the right place, nothing's going to fall on you, and you're not going to trip on anything. And then you just move into the room. The more sophisticated the situation gets, the less we actually look, especially in the art world, the less we engage firsthand. So, I tried to do things in which you were frozen for a moment allowing you to become a firsthand observer. Before you moved, you had go through the whole process of re-examining that structure. It was an obscure thing to do but for me, very fundamental. The soft wall was one of the best things I'd done because it had almost no other level of existence. It wasn't pretty or interesting or any of the other things that a lot of my works are, it was really bare bones.

M.G. The soft wall really made me understand what you were doing more than anything else except perhaps the show in Chicago at MOCA.

B.I. The *Black Line?* That was the other dynamite one, a real hummer. If, on occasion, you get one like the *Black Line*, you become an observer like everybody else, it's like, "Wow!"

The way it came about made it even more thrilling. The installation in the front room was more planned, and the back room was still filled with the last show that they weren't able to move out of the museum until literally two days before my opening. Suddenly, with two days to go, I had an empty room to deal with, but I'd been around the place long enough that I already had a pretty good feel for the space.

I went out and just bought black tape and put it down. I did a couple of other things, including making the light more intense in that space. It was twice, ten times better than the piece out in the front. It was not about what the piece was made of, but about a kind of observation.

And, in a sense, that really more than anything defines why I made the right choice in the first place when I came to New York because Arne said, "Whatever you want to do, we'll do." I might have presented something that obscure to someone else even in a more so-called experimental gallery like the Green Gallery and they might have been willing to do it, but for him to do it in his gallery tells you all you need to know. He never reneged on that relationship.

CRAIG KAUFFMAN

RECENT WORK
February 18 – 18 March, 1967

**Installation: Kauffman
The Pace Gallery
view 2**

**32 East 57th Street
New York, NY 10022
1967**

We arrived in New York too late to become the gallery of any specific art movement—they were all taken. Castelli was the Pop art gallery and Emmerich was the "Greenberg" gallery of Color Field painting. In addition, our sensibilities were pluralistic, but if there was to be one direction that the gallery would favor it was the perception-extending-sensibilities of Robert Irwin and Ad Reinhardt. We also soon began showing the new California artists. We were accused of being slick in our presentations, which, in the best sense of the word, we were. Fred was a man of extraordinary taste who lived in one of the most beautiful apartments in Manhattan. He had great style and instinctively knew the value of installation and how to juxtapose objects to enhance their properties. I had a strong minimalist sense of installation and began reconstructing the gallery space for each exhibition, so that it was proportionately suitable to the works being shown. In the gallery scene of the sixties, still influenced by the rough and tough Tenth Street aesthetic, installation seemed fussy and beneath concern. It took a decade before the style in which Pace presented art was not only accepted, but became the norm.

ROBERT WHITMAN

DARK
October 17 – 7 November, 1967

R. WHITMAN AT PACE 9W57 OPENING 4-7PM OCTOBER 17 –NOVEMBER 7

The exhibition consisted of three works in which laser beams—one wavy, one straight, one wide—each circumscribed its own specially constructed space within the gallery. Upon meeting its end, each laser began erasing itself and then retracing itself, the two cycles repeating continuouslly. The exhibition was eventually closed by the City Board of Health, which was concerned about ocular damage to gallery visitors.

LOUISE NEVELSON

The New York Times, January 28, 1968

A Triumph of Constructivism
by Hilton Kramer

The exhibition of sculpture by Louise Nevelson at the Pace Gallery, 9 West 57th Street, is, except for her retrospective at the Whitney last year, the best exhibition, of her work in some years. It is not a large exhibition, either in the size of the individual pieces or in number, but it marks a new development in her work—a development that is going to have an influence on other similar sculptors and that already displays a remarkable authority and realization.

It is interesting to look back on the changes than have overtaken Mrs. Nevelson's work in the past decade or so. A great deal of art history—both the way art is conceived and executed and the emotions it can be expected to embody—is reflected in them. Those exhibitions at the Grand Central Moderns Gallery in the 1950s that won Mrs. Nevelson her first eminence were quite different from the present occasion. They were like no other exhibitions at the time. They were extremely theatrical. They were intended to overwhelm—and they did.

For those exhibitions were not mounted as discreet displays of separate objects; they were designed as spectacular sculptural environments. (The word—and the idea—had not yet suffered its current devaluation.) Mrs. Nevelson had begun by using a flat pedestal as a base upon which abstract wooden forms were arranged to resemble still life and landscape motifs. These forms were painted a uniform mat black. Though each work embodied a distinct conception that was executed with great care, it lent itself to this sort of environmental-theatrical exhibition. And indeed, the method of exhibition, which made the whole more important than the parts (even where the parts consisted of splendid individual sculptures), led to a change in the sculptural conception. It led to the creation of those sculptural "walls" for which Mrs. Nevelson is now best known.

These walls absorbed the smaller pedestal sculptures into an infinitely expandable series of boxlike units that permitted a great variety of form within a fixed format. There was, at least at the start, a recapitulation and anthologizing of all the forms that had formerly existed as separate conceptions. The scale became architectural, but the imagery remained romantic, subjective, mysterious. The attention to detail was painstaking and finical. There was a geometer's precision in the way forms were fitted together. But the feeling remained that of a romantic dream.

Mrs. Nevelson has, over the years, subjected the sculptural wall to a great many variations, but within these variations there has been one clear tendency—a tendency toward greater clarity, simplification, order. A certain helter-skelter quality was gradually abandoned; there was less emphasis on labyrinthine detail and more on the rigorous architecture of the overall structure. Found objects gave way to precision-made parts. Improvisation gave way to stricter design. The deeply subjective and romantic ambience of the earlier constructions gave way to an atmosphere of dispassionate analysis. Where the first sculptural walls suggested a Surrealist-cum-Expressionist taste, the later walls have moved steadily in the direction of an unadorned Constructivism.

This, of course, is the direction taken by a great deal of painting and sculpture in the late sixties. David Smith, in the last years of his life, followed a similar course. Much of the most accomplished abstract painting of the sixties has done—and continues to do—likewise. The whole Minimal movement has been a celebration of this development. There are, no doubt, some interesting historical reasons for this, but there are also important aesthetic-syntactical reasons, and we see them with especial clarity in Mrs. Nevelson's work.

Canada Series III, 1968
clear lucite, 42½ × 27 × 7½"

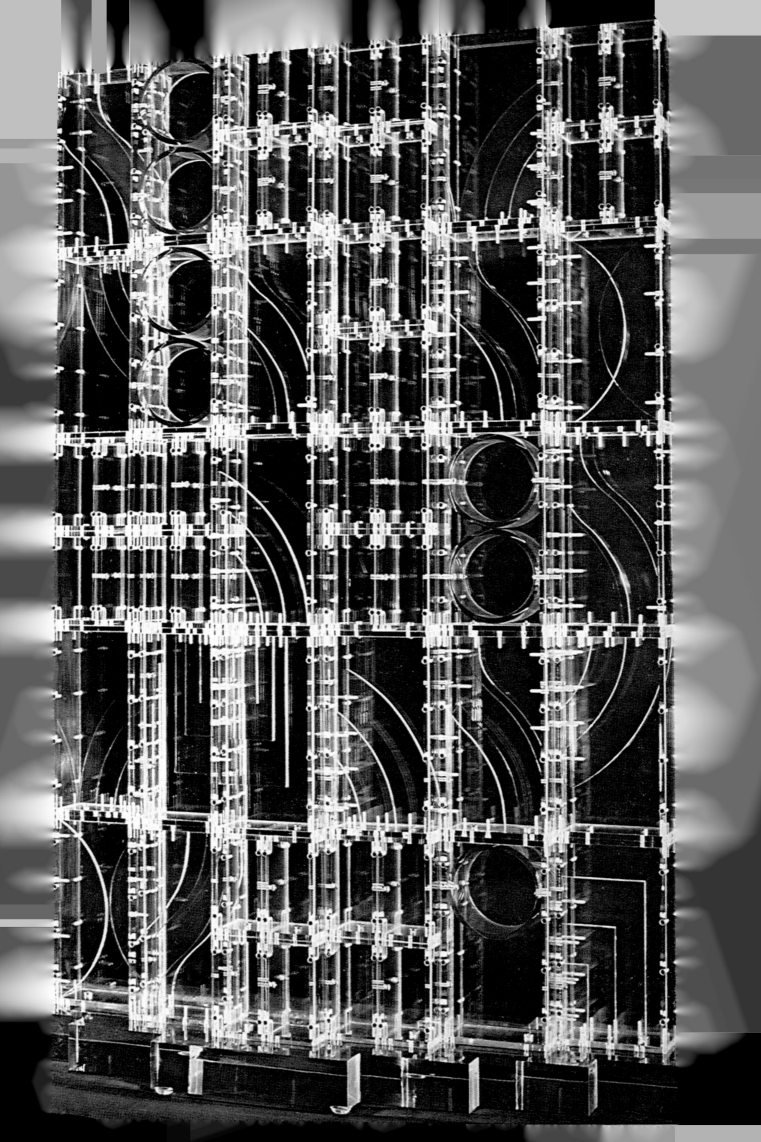

CHRYSSA

by Diane Waldman
Excerpt from Pace catalogue

Advances in technology have repeatedly been mistaken for advances in art. Just as oil paint did not occasion an art superior to that produced by egg tempera or succumb to the advances of acrylics, new technology cannot per se improve upon an art form. For an artist, however, it can offer exciting new possibilities toward the realization of an idea. Any artist, at any given time, must choose the appropriate vehicle for his needs; the use of either a traditional or contemporary method depends entirely upon the formal requirements of his idea, not vice versa. Conversely, as the use of technology increases, the definition of terms must also be expanded to accommodate it. The idea of the machine-made object as the illegitimate child of the handmade painting or sculpture places undue stress on the role of technology in the creative process. If we extend the definition of the hand to include the unique primary concept,

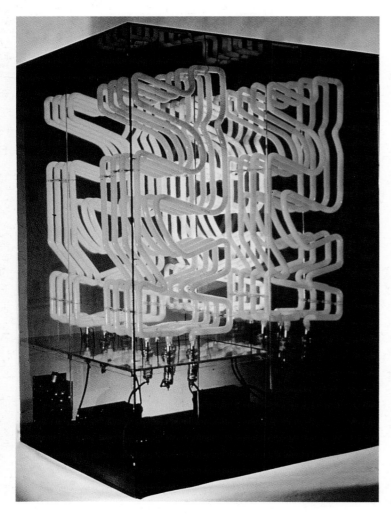

Study for the Gates #3, 1965
neon (yellow, orange, blue, green) and plexiglass
43 × 34¼ × 27½"

then it is possible to accept both the combination of sculptor/craftsman and the finished product. The machine-made object can bear the imprint of a personality as strongly as a handmade one. Ultimately, of course, the validity of the idea exists in its resolution, not in the means of its production. Chryssa has been one of the few to rise above the burden of recent technology. Most of the other light people have been content to illustrate other artists—reproducing a Noland target or a Lichtenstein cartoon in neon—rather than proceed to formal invention.

Although Moholy-Nagy and Thomas Wilfred were pioneers in the use of light, the first major event in its recent history occurred with Pop. The wholesale incorporation of the mass media into fine art was the logical culmination of the earlier interest in the found-object, particularly as it was expressed by Johns and Rauschenberg. The references to associations outside the context of a painting or sculpture that the found-object suggested were extended to include not only the object but its identifying label in a single work, or the label alone might stand for the object. The use of light remained peripheral to Pop, a part of the fascination for industrial graffiti. Chryssa's early use of light, in 1962, was an independent development. She has at best a tangential relationship to Pop, not in her use of light, but in her identification with the found-object. The transitory nature of her neon and metal fragments is rooted in its premises.

Chryssa shares with many of her contemporaries a love of letters. They are the most substantial part of her vocabulary to date, functioning both as a subject matter and form. The Tablets and Plaques (1956–59) and the Projections (1957–60) which preceded the neons were a fairly literal transcription from their common source—the commercial sign—to bronze, aluminum, and plaster. In the bronze plaques, the scrambling of word sequences blurs their identity and calls attention to the concept of "sign" rather than to a specific one. In the all-over pattern of other Plaques and the related series of paintings, the News-papers of 1961, Chryssa shares an affinity with Johns. The slight alteration of the signs themselves, whether a change of materiality or legibility, is an ironic play on the reality of the object. Pictorially, the bands of type are separated and contained by precise empty spaces which effectively remove the signs from the context of the present and lend them a remote hieratic authority that is somewhat related to ancient tablets.

A fondness for a relief surface and a frontal image, characteristic of the work of 1956–60, has persisted in the neons. The neons exist as a relief-in-depth by the repetition of a form until it occupies a cube, rather than as a free form in space. Chryssa's interest in relief first occurred with her earliest work, a series of small baked clay tablets, the Cycladic Books (1955–56). The only change in the surface of the books was a horizontal fold or crease that created a barely perceptible shift in plane. This becomes a more conscious formal device in the slightly raised surface of the later numerals. The creation of the secondary series of shapes by means of the shadows establishes a rippling pattern of light and dark, of positive and negative spaces, that is most exquisitely resolved in the neons. . . .

Chryssa first introduced the use of neon in an aluminum construction, *Times Square Sky,* of 1962. The assemblage of large metal letters forms the greater part of the work; the neon tubing spelling out the word "air" exchanges a specific context for an ambiguous one. In the combination of a concrete and an ephemeral form, the static sense of the massive metal letters is disturbed by the delicate thread of neon light. The fluctuation of the surface is even more apparent in later related works, in *Positive-Negative* and in her most ambitious piece to date, *The Gates to Times Square,* both of 1966. . . .

Chryssa's forms are dependent upon light for their full visual statement. Each neon is like a science-fiction plant awaiting electricity to bloom. Yet they are unique in that they have an independent sculptural existence when the light is turned off. The form takes shape as the fragmentation of a letter, enlarged and complicated beyond a reading. In her interest in the play between light and form, Chryssa establishes a concrete form which she then dissolves in light. To enhance the ephemerality of light, she has gradually moved closer to a more neutral form. One is confronted with several intriguing relationships: between the constant stable presence of the bent neon tubes and the changing nature of the light that they contain; between the intermittent glow of light and the long periods of darkness; between the fragmentation of a known form and the dynamic but unknown quality of the light. Both form and the absence of form, shadow and substance, are contained in the fragile glass tubes of her neons. . . .

As Chryssa moves toward a more abstract subject matter, it becomes possible for her to use color in a purely hedonistic way. Her color has way of bringing into question previous color experience, in that she is able to develop in her best pieces a pitched intensity that relates not to a general or descriptive color but, much like that of Morris Louis, that clarifies a specific color. One is much more aware of a yellow tube as yellow than of the concept "yellow." Simultaneously, the work makes reference to color illusionism. This is accomplished by the tight compression of the multiple tubes which eliminates a detailed reading and forces the eye to respond to a large slab of color. The same stacking principle allows the neon to bleed off at the edges, causing a halation as one color slides off into the next. . . .

In a literal sense, one could speak of her neons as being a reference to past and present, a dialogue between the traditional and the avant-garde, or more simply as the space between two thoughts. What began as an idea predicated on the use of existing forms, a sign or a numeral, has been turned inside out. We become involved with the inward workings, the skeletal structure of a form, and the concept that shapes them assumes a new totality.

Top: Christophe de Menil, Chryssa, Dorothy Miller
Bottom: Dorothy Miller, Arne Glimcher, Chryssa
during installation
Photos © Fred W. McDarrah

JEAN DUBUFFET | PAINTED SCULPTURES
April 13 – 18 May, 1968

Right: Dubuffet in his studio, 1967
Photos Luc Joubert
Courtesy Fondation Dubuffet, Paris

As an art student, I was shocked by Dubuffet's audacity and seduced by his alienation from everything I thought was fine art. In my Boston gallery, I bought and sold Dubuffet's lithographs, which became the center of the print activity on which the gallery was heavily dependent for revenue. In 1961, on my first trip to Europe to buy stock, with a $5,000 loan from the Brookline Trust Company, I met Daniel Cordier in Paris. His gallery, along with the Galerie Maeght and that of Claude Bernard, were at the center of the Paris art world. International in focus, Cordier showed in addition to Dubuffet and creepy French Surrealist artists, Nevelson and Rauschenberg. On my budget, I was unable to afford any of Dubuffet's paintings, but I bought a collage d'empreint *for $1,500. It was the gallery's first significant acquisition and would prove prophetic, although it was three years before it found a buyer.*

Dubuffet was represented by the Saidenberg Gallery, also Picasso's representative, something which irritated Dubuffet. The writer Annette Michelson was very supportive of my fledgling New York gallery and our mutual passion for Dubuffet created a bond between us. Her friend Sylvie Joubert, was a director of the Galerie Jeanne Bucher, Dubuffet's Paris gallery operating in association with Ernst Beyeler. Together Beyeler and Galerie Jean Bucher controlled the sale of Dubuffet's production and his exhibition program. Annette Michelson knew of Dubuffet's discontent with Saidenberg* and introduced me to Jean-François Jaeger who owned the Galerie Jeanne Bucher. After several trips to Paris, a meeting was arranged with Beyeler, and I was ultimately invited to meet with Dubuffet to see if he would consider changing representation in the States.

Prior to meeting Dubuffet for lunch in Paris at Le petit zinc, *Beyeler and Jaeger advised me on topics to avoid with the* monstre sacré. *He hated other artists, they said, and the reason my gallery was of interest to Dubuffet was that the artists were young and relatively unknown. The perversity of going with a gallery whose reputation did not deserve him was amusing. Above all, I was not to mention Louise Nevelson, as she was already too famous and they both had been in Cordier's gallery together. I was terrified!*

Beyeler and Jaeger carried the conversation and I remained silent, intimidated by Dubuffet's presence. Finally, Dubuffet said: "Tell me about the artists in your gallery." Backs straightened, knuckles whitened, and unable to go along with the charade, I told him about my artists and the current scene. He admired Claes Oldenburg,** did I know him? Yes, I had shown him in Boston. Then Dubuffet asked me to tell him all about Nevelson. "Une dame fabuleuse!—a great artist."

I realize now that Dubuffet, a cunning businessman (formerly a wine merchant) wanted to make the gallery's reputation, and so to speak, own my gratitude, which he always had. In 1967 he left Saidenberg and came with Pace. He reveled in the dismay of all of his friends and collectors. I remember being invited to dinner in Paris at Maurice Pinto's apartment. Pinto was voraciously collecting Dubuffet and had

put a significant part of his fortune into the collection. At dinner Pinto, obviously unhappy with Dubuffet's new association, wanted me to understand that he was accustomed to getting first choice of Dubuffet's work. I thought he owned too much of the work and generally disapproved of any collector being in control of such a large quantity of a single artist's work. My role was to extend the awareness of Dubuffet's achievement by placing work in American collections, especially those in which he was not already represented. At dinner Maurice Pinto turned to me and said: "What makes you worthy of representing Dubuffet?" "Someday I hope to be," I said.

*Ralph Colin was one of Dubuffet's biggest collectors and the president and founder of the Art Dealers Association. It was through Colin's intervention that Dubuffet found his way to the Saidenbergs after leaving Pierre Matisse. In the tradition of European dealers, Matisse hoarded Dubuffets. He bought all of Dubuffet's production, but sold only a small portion, holding back the best for investment. Matisse showed each new series, published catalogues, and brought Dubuffet's work to the awareness of museums and collectors. His investment paid off handsomely as the demand for Dubuffet's work increased and prices escalated. Dubuffet asked Matisse for an inventory of his work, and when he saw how little was sold in comparison to how much had been kept back, Dubuffet left the gallery.
**The admiration was mutual. Dubuffet's influence on Oldenburg's art can be seen indirectly in works such as The Street *(Museum Ludwig, Cologne) and directly in the early drawings, some of which Oldenburg actually signed "Dubuffet."*

1968

CHANGE OF ADDRESS

After five years at 9 West 57th Street, as we were just beginning to realize a profit, attract artists, and make our gallery a destination, the building was sold, and we were forced to move. I. M. Pei frequented the gallery and had become a good friend, supporting us as a collector and sending us his clients. I. M. looked at spaces with us, helped us decide on 32 East 57th Street, and agreed to design the interior, the cabinetry and even our partners' desk. The gallery only occupied the third floor of its present address—it would eventually expand to seven floors. I. M. designed a white box of beautiful proportion, entered on the right by a wedge-shaped funneling wall. The opposite wall was made of two-way mirror, behind which our office was located. This enabled us to see everyone who entered the gallery, creating in essence a "duck blind" that we hoped would prevent us from missing collectors, who at the time were a rare species. The two-way mirror soon became notorious—some people resented it—and we ultimately covered it over on the inside, allowing the gallery visitors their privacy and providing us with a much needed wall for what became our first private viewing space.

LUCAS SAMARAS | BOXES/TRANSFORMATIONS
October 12 – 12 November, 1968

by Lawrence Alloway
Excerpt from Pace catalogue

Peephole and Labyrinth

Peepholes involve the spectator in seeing bit by bit. There is neither the all-at-once impact of large-scale abstract painting nor the spatial unity of vanishing-point perspective in deep-space Renaissance pictures. Peepholes divulge the contents of a work of art in partial and successive glimpses. There are boxes of Samaras which actually have a peephole as the sole visual access to the interior, such as *Box 22*, 1964, where you open, and peer through, a nest of diminishing doors. Even where there is no actual peephole, however, Samaras organizes his objects on the basis of cells which we examine one at a time. The subdivisions of each work and the number of loose articles it carries forces us to draw close. Peering is how to see a Samaras. In many cases we open lids, doors, and drawers and brush aside crystals on glass to find a buried sexual image or a wound. Where we do not participate physically, we see Samaras' work in a similar way: the scrutiny of successive views and objects involves us in time as well as in space. Whereas abstract painting has reduced the temporal implications of art to an overwhelming hedonistic present moment of attention, both figurative art and objects explode the present moment of visual display. As in

15th century Flemish painting and illuminated manuscripts, close-up and distant view, eye-lashes and mountains, are adjacent in ways that stretch time into sequence beyond the simultaneity of a single view. In the case of Samaras time is present both in the sequence of movements by which we take in the work and in the objects themselves, laden with other times, like souvenirs and heirlooms.

If we take the peephole as a metaphor of the detailed way of looking that Samaras demands of the spectator, it must be stressed that there is not just one voyeur's post, as in a Dutch 17th century illusionistic cabinet. The focal points occur all over Samaras' complex structures which are, fundamentally, labyrinthine. A labyrinth is a structure of intercommunicating passages, some of them blocked, as at Crete. A labyrinth is the cavity of the inner ear, the turnings and windings of the intestines, the spirals of nautilus shells and nebulae, most of which figure in Samaras' iconography. Baroque calligraphy is labyrinthine and though his own non-referential calligraphy is not baroque, it is basically maze-like. The morphology of involution is the formal equivalent of the theme of the container which preoccupies Samaras. The historical background of the labyrinth, after Daedelus', includes the floor labyrinths of Gothic cathedrals, garden mazes in the eighteenth century, and topological knots; the anatomical and psychological background includes tattooing (outside the body), the organs and thought patterns within. The objects of affluence and cruelty, of secrecy and panoply, that Samaras constructs have persistent correspondences with the body. "Even now, taking a clock apart or tearing a newspaper sometimes gives me the shivers," he wrote. His objects and structures exist in a web of organic and inorganic substitution which melts classifications. "I guess spoken language always had great mumbo jumbo static noise for me whereas that other language that does not require speech but has to do with emotion or visual-mental perception was more available."

The theme of the labyrinth of formal complexity and of erotic transfers is persistent in both Samaras' art and writing. In one of his texts, *More Dickman*, there is a reversal of the indelible dinners, one of which was dedicated "For the Actor Bela Lugosi": "I came to

Transformation: Eyeglasses, 1966
mixed media
case size: 46½ × 24 × 15" in 2 parts
each 46½ × 24 × 15", two 15" bases

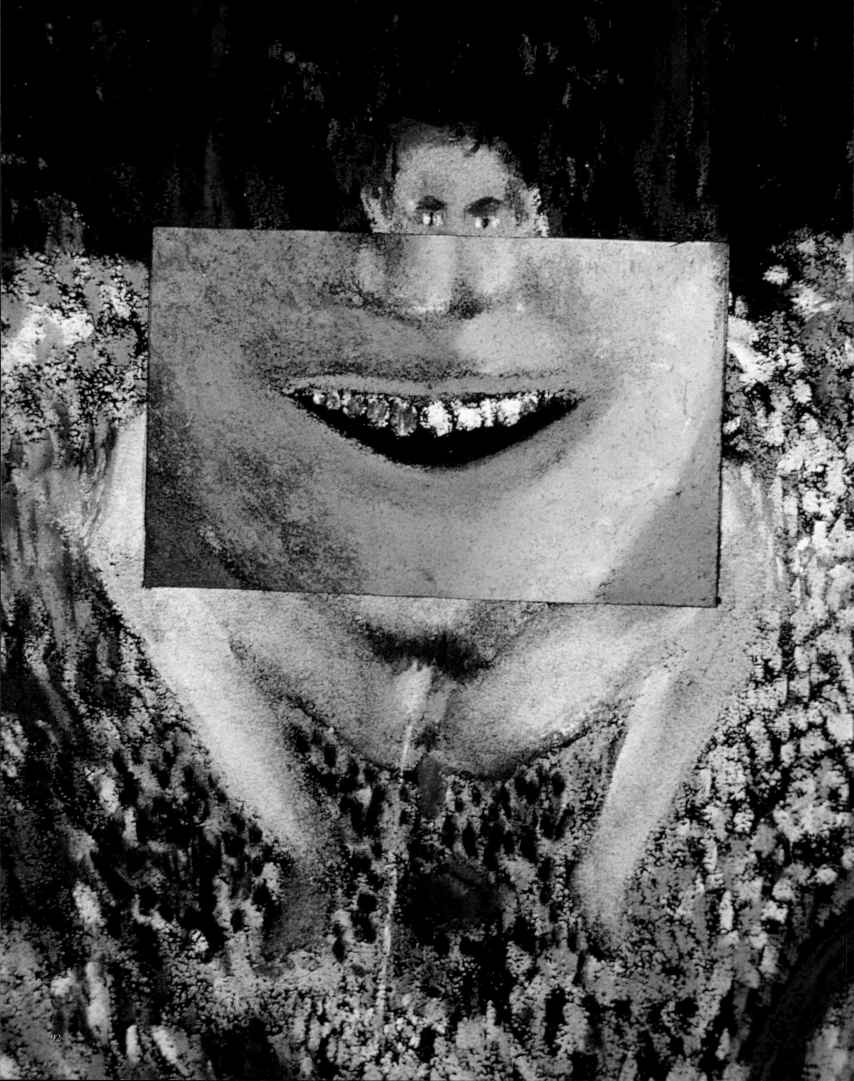

Times Square and the floor of Times Square became a gooeygoushey colored candy and people got gooeygoushey colored glued to the floor quickly turning into candy and the buildings also and the space was turning to a transparent Jello." This oral play is one element of Samaras' iconography and mirrors provide another. They first appear in a 1960 box which opens to reveal a mirror covered with tacks opposite a rag-face. In 1960–62 he played in many of Claes Oldenburg's Happenings and Oldenburg describes his part in *Fotodeath* as follows: "A man, Lucas, enters from left in a plain tight fastidious suit. He admires himself in many mirrors he takes from his pockets. He lies down with a tall mirror, posing himself in different ways, projecting himself upside down etc."[2] Mirrors occur frequently in the later boxes culminating in the project for a mirrored room, 1966. It seems a simple space compared to the crowded 1964 studio, but, in fact, it is more totally labyrinthine. The six sides of the rectangle will be mirror-covered, so that the room's inhabitants will always multiply to a Narcissistic mob. In a description of the home of Killman, one of the mythic figures in Samaras' texts, he writes: "next to the bedroom was the bathroom. It was a cube room that was completely mirrored, even the floor and ceiling. When he wanted to shit he shit on the mirror floor."

Additional information about Killman is relevant here: "He lived in a huge magnetized pin-covered building. Any living things passing flying crawling near the structure would be zook pinned to the walls. Birds, kites, cats, people, helicopters, embellished the skyscraper." Samaras' description of the exterior of the building cannot fail to bring his boxes to mind. As an environment, such as a room, is a big container, so a container, such as a small box, is a small environment.

Not only are different substances interchangeable to Samaras (metallic food and a gooey Times Square), but scale is flexible, too. The literal area of his objects is opened out by mirrors and glitter-surfaces or burrowed into by labyrinthine cells and divisions. Whether writing about a skyscraper or constructing a box, never large in scale though copiously detailed, there is a basic unifying reference. The body, like buildings, rooms, and boxes, is a container and Samaras' art stresses this connection. His objects are analogues and projections of himself, his body, and with the body go his memories, his appetite, his speculations. The works are so tenderly and intricately constructed because they are the repository of himself.

This is not meant to suggest that Samaras' art is like a journal; on the contrary, it is never occasional and discursive. It is the consistent and eloquent expression of an original view of life and art. It is not fetishistic because fetishes are details, viewed in isolation, whereas Samaras' view of the world is polymorphous and non-classifactory. Substance and scale differences are eaten up in his vision of the expanding body of the artist, secreted in the labyrinthine chalices and images he has deposited in the world.

2. Claes Oldenburg, quoted in *Happenings* by Michael Kirby (New York 1965).

Box #58, 1966
mixed media
18 × 16¼ × 8½", open
11¼ × 16¼ × 8½", closed

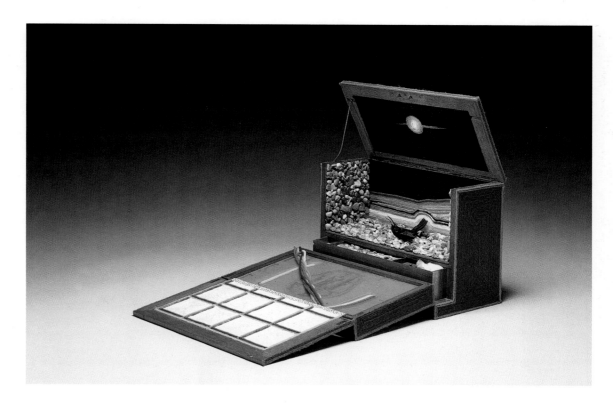

Untitled, 1962
pastel, 12 × 9"

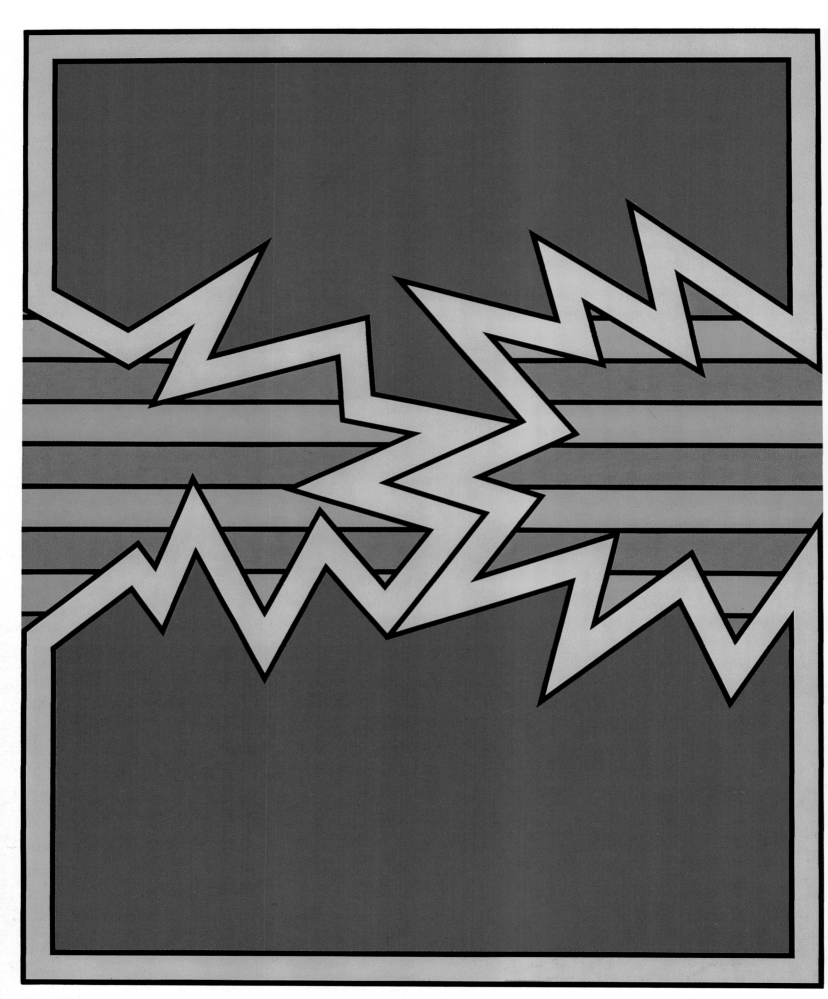

Electric Soup, 1969
liquitex on canvas, 90⅛ × 75"

NICHOLAS KRUSHENICK

PAINTINGS
April 26 – 21 May, 1969

Photos © Fred W. McDarrah

Krushenick with *Son of King Kong*, 1966

Photo Matthew Wysocki

ROBERT IRWIN | **ACRYLIC DISCS**
October 4 – 29, 1969

"The question for the discs was very simple. How do I paint a painting that doesn't begin and end at the edge? In other words, I no longer felt comfortable with that sense of confinement. . . I mean, we ordinarily start with the canvas as a fact, as more than a fact. We start with it as a truth so deeply hidden that we don't even question it. It's simply there. Obviously there's a good reason for that, or it wouldn't have lasted as long as it has. But for some reason my activities brought me up to question on what basis we assume that. Still, in the beginning it was a simple artistic challenge: How do I paint a painting that does not begin and end at an edge but rather starts to take in and become involved with the space or environment around it?. . ."

. . ."The reason for the circular disc as opposed to making them square, was that that eliminated the four corners, corners being really powerful focal points, whereas what I was after was an evenness of presence" . . ."The circle was simply the most neutral shape I could find. . ."

"Visually it was very ambiguous which was more real, the object or its shadow. They were basically equal. I mean, they occupied space very differently, but there was no separation in terms of your visual acuity in determining that one was more real than the other. And that was the real beauty of those things, that they achieved a balance between space occupied and unoccupied in which both became intensely occupied at the level of perceptual energy.". . .*

*Lawrence Weschler, *Seeing is Forgetting the Name of the Thing One Sees*, University of California Press 1982, pp. 99–104.

Untitled, 1968–69
acrylic lacquer on formed acrylic plastic, 54" diameter

YOUNG NEW YORK ART DEALERS

New York, 1969, Vogue Magazine

From left standing: Ivan Karp, Klaus Kertess, Fred Mueller
Seated: David Whitney, Paula Cooper, Arne Glimcher, Michael Findley and Dick Bellamy
Photograph Irving Penn
"Young New York Dealers, New York, 1969," copyright © 1970 by the Condé Nast Publications, Inc.

Paris, 15 septembre 1969

Mon cher Arnold,

Je m'apprête à composer une affiche pour votre exposition comme vous me l'avez demandé mais encore me faut-il d'abord donner pour cela un nom générique à ces constructions porteuses de graphies qui vont s'y trouver présentées, et le choix de ce nom m'a donné de l'embarras. Il serait souhaitable en effet qu'il oriente l'esprit vers que visent ces constructions, vers les positions mentales dont elles procèdent.

J'ai tout d'abord songé aux deux termes de *mont-joies* et de *cairns* qui l'un et l'autre désignent des monticules de pierres élevés en quelque lieu — une croisée de chemins — pour servir de repère aux voyageurs ou comme monuments commémoratifs. C'est là en effet un des aspects que peuvent présenter ces constructions et sous lequel il m'est arrivé de les regarder. Mais, outre que ces deux termes sont peu connus et risquent de demeurer à la plupart intelligibles, ils ne rendent pas compte du caractère figuratif (ou disons peut-être plutôt *allusif*) de ces dispositifs ou amoncellements, qui sont en effet étroitement liés à des évocations d'objets usuels, de meubles, de figures, sites ou paysages. Ces divers thèmes s'y trouvent délibérément traités dans la forme adoptée antérieurement pour toutes mes peintures de *L'Hourloupe*: celle d'une écriture méandreuse ininterrompue et résolument uniforme (ramenant tous plans au frontal, ne tenant nul compte du registre propre de l'objet décrit, de sa dimension, de son éloignement ou sa proximité) à la faveur de quoi s'abolissent toutes les particularisations, toutes les catégories (je veux dire tous les classements usuellement adoptés par notre pensée) et introduisent distinction entre une notion et une autre: entre la notion de chaise, par exemple, et celle d'arbre, celle de personnage, de nuage, de sol, de paysage, ou n'importe quelle que soit de manière que cette écriture bien constamment uniforme indifféremment appliquée à toutes les choses (et, il faut le souligner fortement pas seulement les choses qui s'offrent à nos yeux mais aussi bien celles qui, dénuées de tout fondement physique, sont seulement les productions de notre pensée, de notre imagination ou de notre caprice; les unes et les autres mêlées sans distinction) tend à tout réduire au même dénominateur et à nous restituer un univers continu, indifférencié: tend à opérer une espèce de liquéfaction des catégories dont notre pensée fait habituellement usage dans le déchiffrement (mieux voudrait dire le chiffrement) des faits et spectacles du monde. A la faveur de quoi la circulation de l'esprit d'un objet à un autre, d'une catégorie à une autre, soit libérée, et grandement accure sa mobilité.

C'est cette écriture uniforme, départicularisante, appliquée indifféremment à tous les objets, et étendue même, sans aucune rupture, aux phénomènes mentaux aussi bien qu'aux physiques, que j'ai associée à l'idée d'un nouveau logos. C'est d'où procèdent les titres que j'ai maintes fois attribués à des ouvrages appartenant au cycle de *L'Hourloupe*, comme ceux de "Borne au logos", "Epanchement du Logos", "Elément de Logos", "Site logologique", etc. Peut-être objectera-t-on que le terme de logos est employé ici à l'inverse de son sens puisqu'il désigne communément l'opération de l'esprit qui nomme et classifie, alors que ma propre opération est plutôt au contraire d'effacer les catégories et régresser vers un continuum indifférencié. Mais la visée de ces ouvrages est, en détériorant le logos institué, d'en proposer un autre, ou, pour dire mieux, d'en suggérer un autre, de manifester le caractère arbitraire et spécieux du logos qui nous est familier, et la possibilté qui demeure offerte de rechiffrer le monde et fonder la pensée sur des logos tout autres.

En considération de ce qui précède j'ai envisagé de donner aux ouvrages présentés dans votre exposition le nom de *Logogriphes* qui est formé du mot logos associé au mot grec désignant un filet ou, par extension, une énigme. Mais ce terme pourrait s'appliquer indifféremment à toutes les figures de *L'Hourloupe* — à celles du jeu de cartes notamment — et il ne rend pas assez compte des particularités que présentent les sujets qui sont cette fois montrés: celle d'être exécutés non sur une toile plane mais sur des solides tridimensionnels; celle aussi de ne comporter que de simples tracés noirs sur des fonds blancs; celle d'être constitués de pièces amoncelées les unes sur les autres; celle, surtout, d'être dotés d'un statut équivoque, dont résulte une indécision entre la fonction d'objets matériels et celle d'immatérielles figurations d'objets. Je veux m'expliquer sur ce point important dont je crains qu'il apparaisse d'abord obscur. Quand un peintre figure une chaise, interprétant et dénaturant l'aspect de celle-ci à son caprice, aucune confusion n'en résulte pour le regardeur du tableau entre la figuration proposée et la chaise réelle à partir de laquelle a opéré le peintre. Si maintenant cette figuration n'est plus seulement peinte sur une toile, mais érigée en un objet tridimensionnel, l'esprit du regardeur est alors enclin à ne plus y voir un ouvrage mental — l'interprétation mentale d'une chaise — mais bel et bien un objet physique: une nouvelle chaise qui lui est offerte pour s'y asseoir. Dans le cas des ouvrages qui donnent lieu à notre exposition il s'agit, bien sûr, d'évocations strictement mentales. La matérialité dont ils sont dotés est spécieuse; elle ne saurait être un instant prise à la lettre. Ils sont des érections matérialisées de productions mentales. Leur objectivation est fallacieuse. Ils sont des matérialisations d'opérations mentales tout à fait étrangères au monde des corps, au même titre — et plus encore sans doute — que l'est, au regard du spirite, l'ectoplasme. C'est par là qu'ils n'appartiennent pas, me semble-t-il, au registre de la statuaire, mais plutôt à celui de la peinture: peinture à laquelle a été cette fois insolitement donné *corps*, peinture corporalisée, objectivée. C'est pour marquer cet aspect particulier — très particulier — de ces travaux que j'ai pensé un moment à leur donner le nom de *Figures-corps*, ou celui de "Semblances-substances", ou encore, pour expliciter la mise en oeuvre qui y est faite de seuls graphismes noirs à l'exclusion d'aucun coloriage, celui de *Graphies-corps-prenant*. J'avais aussi retenu le nom — évidemment trop long — de *Dérives mentales dotées de corps physique*.

Ces diverses appellations m'ont ensuite paru quelque peu lourdes et malvenues. Je leur ai, pour finir, préféré le nom, assurément plus imprécis, prêtant aussi probablement davantage à des malentendus pour des personnes d'esprit futile (mais n'importe, ces ouvrages ne s'adressant de toute façon pas à des personnes futiles) de *Simulacres*, par lequel le côté de fantasme qu'ils comportent me paraît suffisamment (et pas trop) explicité. Le sens de *simulacre*, après tout, selon le dictionnaire, est celui d'une apparence sensible qui se donne pour une réalité. On appelle ainsi les fantômes.

A vous amicalement.

Jean Dubuffet

JEAN DUBUFFET

SIMULACRES
November 8 – 1 January, 1970

A DECADE OF CALIFORNIA COLOR 1960–70

November 7 – 25, 1970

PETER ALEXANDER
CHARLES ARNOLDI
LARRY BELL
BILLY AL BENGSTON
FRED EVERSLEY
PATRICK HOGAN
ROBERT IRWIN
CRAIG KAUFFMAN
JOHN MC CRACKEN
ED MOSES
KENNETH PRICE
ED RUSCHA
DEWAIN VALENTINE

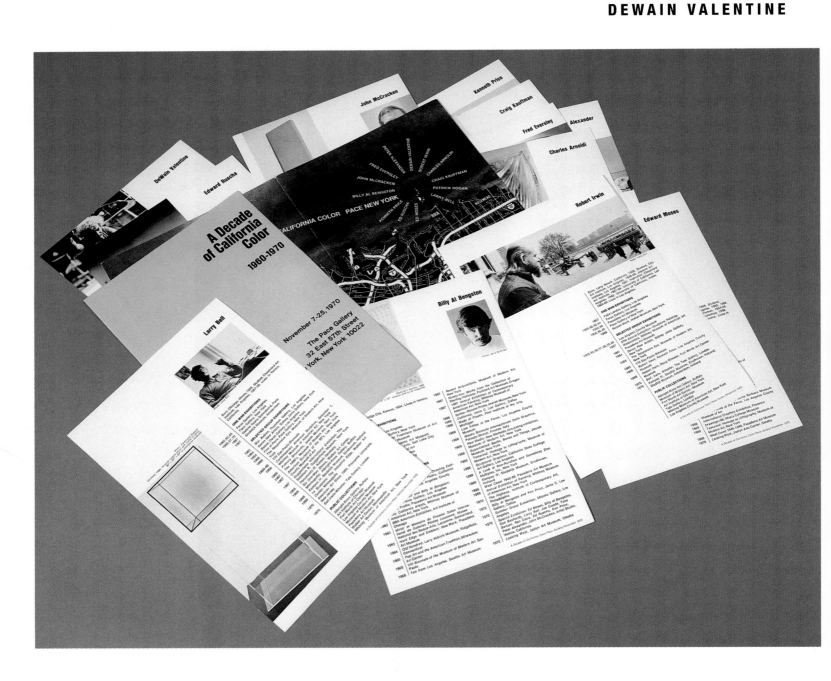

CRAIG KAUFFMAN

RECENT WORK

March 21 – 8 April, 1970

Untitled, 1969
sprayed acrylic laquer on heat rolled plexiglass
108 × 49 × 9"

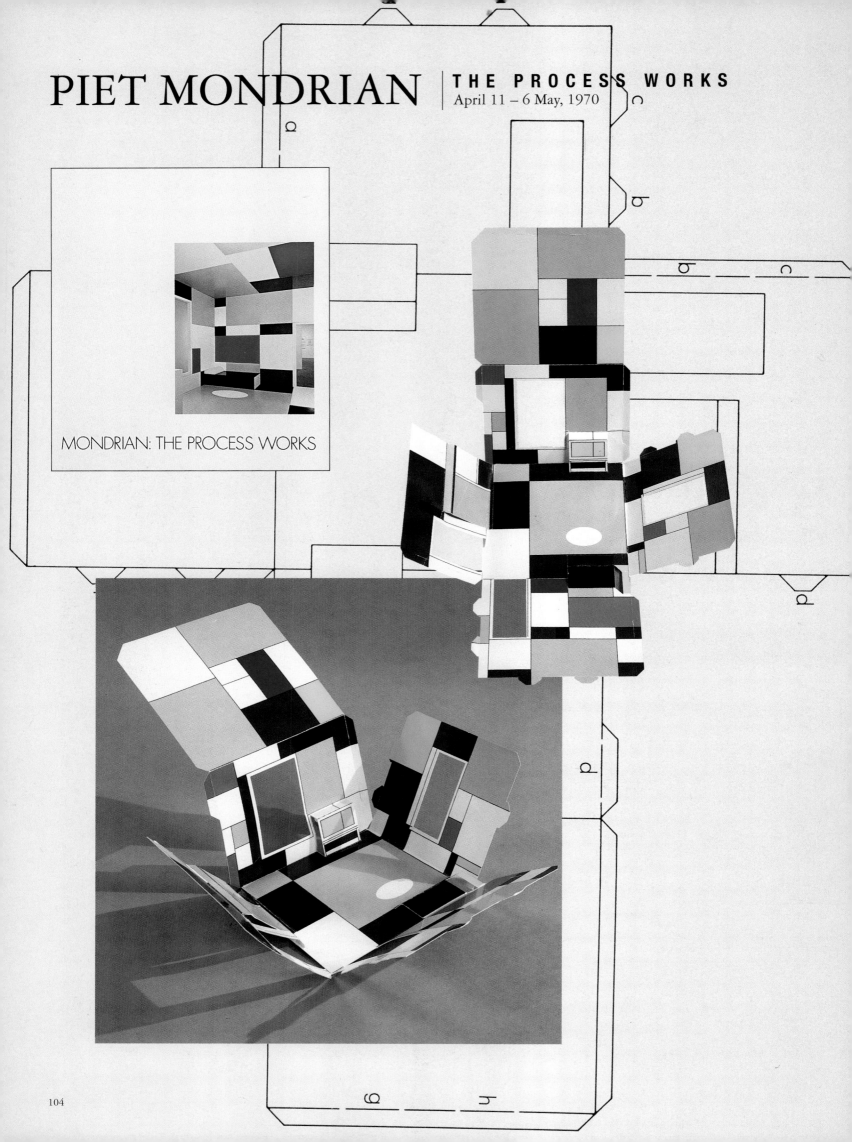

PIET MONDRIAN

THE PROCESS WORKS
April 11 – 6 May, 1970

MONDRIAN: THE PROCESS WORKS

Piet Mondrian's Environment Part 2
by Harry Holtzman
Excerpt from Pace catalogue

Piet Mondrian's studios are justly famous and historic; especially the first well-known one in Paris, 26 Rue du Départ, Montparnasse, and the last one in New York City, 15 East 59th Street, Manhattan. Both were seminal and inspiring to the generations of artists and architects who saw them. Mondrian's studios were his only opportunity to partially realize his radical conception of total environment, consistent with his aesthetic toward the inseparability of art and life.

The Paris studio was occupied by Mondrian before World War I, to which he returned immediately after the war ended. He resided there until 1938—ironically ousted by "urban renewal." He occupied the New York studio for only four months before he died, 1 February 1944.

There are no available photos of the later studio in Paris briefly occupied before he moved to London after the Munich Pact in 1938; nor of the London studio in Hempstead where he was "blitzed," which he left in 1940 for New York. His view toward these places was something like his attitude toward his first New York apartment, in which he worked contentedly until October, 1943. They were all too small, too full of his paintings to lend themselves to extreme development, although the stimulating touches of color were inevitably there. . . .

In October 1943, much revitalized by his productive and happy life in New York, Mondrian moved from the small apartment at 353 East 56th Street, to the final, vastly more satisfactory studio space on 59th Street. Although he lived there only four months before his fatal pneumonia, the stimulation and excitement of his last painting, *Victory Boogie-Woogie*, on which he continued to work, immediately reflected itself in this new environment which he developed with amazing energy and speed.

For Mondrian, the "bourgeois" approach to "furniture" and "comfort," among other things, belonged to a mode of life and values that failed essentially to meet the real human potential of environmental needs and satisfactions. He once commented humorously upon a visitor's complaint that there were no "comfortable" chairs in his studio. He had a canvas folding deck-chair, a metal stool (with round red top and white legs), another white rectangular stool which could also open up to form a short ladder (I had lent him that because he admired it). He said, "If it is *too* comfortable, people will stay too long! When I want to *rest*, I lie down on my bed."

So it was by deliberate choice that Mondrian selected his *objets trouvés*: the wooden packing-crates for his paintings, the canvas-stretchers for paintings; the rectangular wooden orange-crates and apple-boxes that he found at the fruit-store usually thrown out after use. From these he made the most essential of his new "furnishings," but he chose them because they were ready-made for his purposes. The only conventional objects were his couch; a standard drafting table which could be height-adjusted, with a tilting-top on which he could place his paintings when applying paint in the horizontal position; his white easel was also a commercial folding variety with a single vertical post, so that the painting appeared suspended in space, only the lower support visible.

Especially the walls of the studio itself and of the bedroom-study were well developed and interrelated; and each room had a structure of two orange-crates interconnected by horizontal wood strips and rectangular cards of primary colors. One cluster of orange-crates in the studio was used for storing paints and brushes and for the white glass palettes. In the bedroom-study another cluster for books and writing, and a unique writing table entirely constructed by Mondrian, quite reminiscent of his paintings. He also made another table for the kitchen, a room which remained otherwise undeveloped—he didn't live long enough. Both the tables were entirely new expressions in his work, incidental but important. . . .

Rita Reinhardt introduced me to Harry Holtzman, an artist of some renown, Mondrian's closest friend, and the legatee of his estate. Holtzman had already sold most of the Mondrian estate to Sidney Janis, retaining a group of drawings and sketchbooks, pages, and notations on the backs of cigarette packs. There were also some larger drawings and unfinished paintings, and the intriguing architectural plan for the Salon de Mme. B., a work commissioned in the twenties but never realized. Although the material first appeared to be the dregs of the estate, further examination revealed that it contained important information for understanding Mondrian's working process. I conceived the idea of building the Salon de Mme. B. from Mondrian's plan, and with Harry Holtzman's permission it was realized. In Mondrian's text, "Home, Street, City," he writes about a material for the interior that is descriptive of all the properties of Formica. Harry Holtzman still retained Mondrian's paint tubes and palette. Although the paint was mostly dry, we took them to the chemists at American Cyanimid, and from the pigment they matched colors and produced the panels out of which we constructed the Salon de Mme. B. For the exhibition announcement, I designed a three-dimensional folding model of the room.

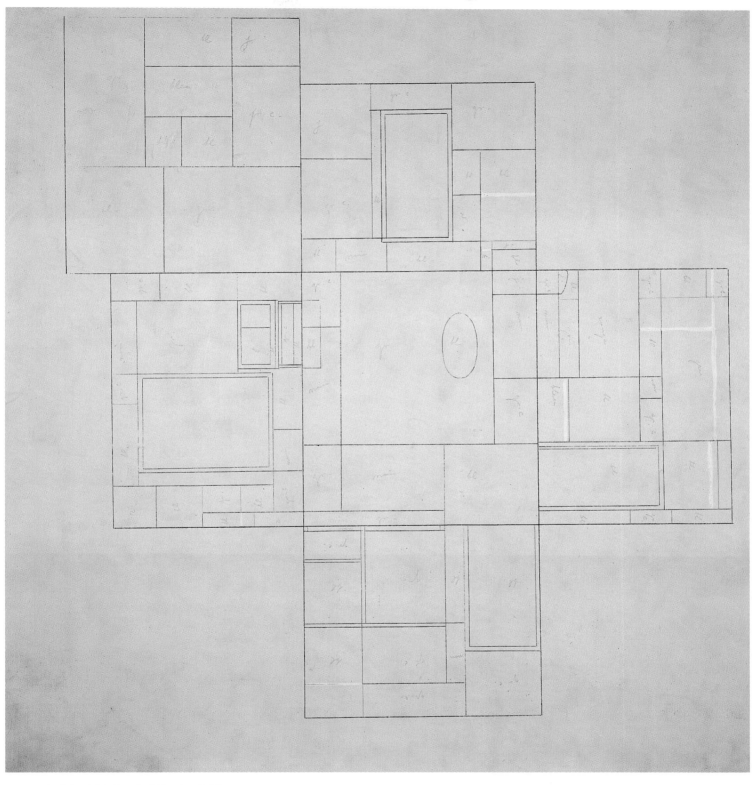

Drawing for *Salon de Madame B. à Dresden,* 1926
ink, pencil with gouache corrections on paper, 30 × 29¾"
©2001 Mondrian/Holtzman

The only other "architectural" effort of this kind, more properly called *environmental*, in my view, was a hypothetical room interior designed by Mondrian in 1926. It appeared in *Vouloir*, no. 25, 1927, in the context of his essay *Home-Street-City (Le Home-La Rue-La Cité)*[1] with the title *Salon de Madame B . . . a Dresden*. It was then presented as an exploded elevation in black and white values. The drawing Mondrian kept, exhibited here, indicated the colors only with words. It is most probable that Mondrian must have built a small cardboard model in order to work out the amazingly complex relationships. I feel certain of this because I saw another model of a stage set, far less complex, in his studio in Paris, in 1934.

The enterprising directors of the Pace Gallery of New York, with my consultation, have constructed this room for the first time (within six to eight inches short of full scale). The cooperation of the Formica Corporation made possible Mondrian's vision of this ideal material by producing colors according to my specifications. *"Roughness, rustic appearance . . . must be removed. . . .* Surfaces will be smooth and bright, which will also relieve the heaviness of the materials," he wrote in *Home-Street-City*.

Mondrian must have worked intensely over many months to achieve the integral unity of the composition; the varied continuity of interactions, so constantly different—but always completely unified—from every point or angle of vision—in all directions—within the room. The most surprising effect to so many is particularly in the felt reaction of the satisfying equilibrium, excitement and tranquility in an environment completely free of "objects" or "decoration." Only the slightly rounded yellow pillow of the couch, the oval white rug[2] on the gray floor may come as a surprise, as apparently random elements deliberately separated but related through the color—contradictions only to the stereotype of Mondrian's attitude. . . .

Human culture has been gently touched—but permanently and powerfully opened—by the contributions to perception of a great artist whose work is inseparable from the historical image of the XXth Century.

1. Also published in Dutch, in *i 10*, 1927, vol. 1, no. 1; and in English, in *trans/formation: arts, communication, environment*, 1, 1950.
2. Because the floor of the room will have much traffic during its travels, it was decided to inlay the oval with Formica instead of using some cloth; similarly for the couch.

Fabricated *Salon* based on Mondrian drawing, in the gallery

11, 1969, pencil on paper, 13″ X 8½″
er 12, 1969, pencil on paper, 13″ X 8½″
nber 12, 1969, pencil on paper, 13″ X 8½″
ember 12, 1969, pencil on paper, 13″ X 8½″
er 13, 1969, pencil on paper, 13″ X 8½″
mber 13, 1969, pencil on paper, 13″ X 8½″
cember 13, 1969, pencil on paper, 13″ X 8½″
ember 13, 1969, pencil on paper, 13″ X 8½″
cember 14, 1969, pencil on paper, 13″ X 8½″
December 14, 1969, pencil on paper, 13″ X 8½″
h, December 14, 1969, pencil on paper, 13″ X 8½″
on, 1969-70, no. 16 (detail of C shown opposite),
0″ X 15″ X 28″
ober 29, 1969, pencil on paper, 8½″ X 13″
October 30, 1969, pencil on paper, 8½″ X 13″
vember 1, 1969, pencil on paper, 8½″ X 13″
n, November 2, 1969, pencil on paper, 8½″ X 13″
October 13, 1969, pencil on paper, 8½″ X 13″
ch, October 15, 1969, pencil on paper, 8½″ X 13″
 formation, 1969-70, no. 17 (detail of D shown opposite)
, 34″ X 19″ X 16″
ood, 34″ X 19″ X 16″
sformation, 1969-70, no. 18, burned wood and acrylic,
X 40″
ch, October 23, 1969, pencil on paper, 8½″ X 13″
Sketch, October 31, 1969, pencil on paper, 8½″ X 13″
detail), October 30, 1969, pencil on paper, 8½″ X 13″
ransformation, 1969-70, no. 19 wool, wood, jewels,
acrylic on wood, 42″ X 16″ X 18″
Transformation, 1969-70, no. 20 (in progress), Corten steel,
18″ X 19″
r Transformation, 1969-70, no. 21 wool on wood,
r Transformation, 1969-70, no. 22 (detail of E shown opposite),
8½″ paper, 19″ X 50″ X 40″
1969-70, no. paper, 19″ X 50″ X 40″
25″ X 25″

A

B

63

C

D

Youngerman, ca. 1974
Photo J. Salb

JACK YOUNGERMAN
RECENT PAINTINGS AND SCULPTURE
February 13 – 10 March, 1971

ERNEST TROVA

NEW SCULPTURE

January 9 – 3 February, 1971

Trova, ca. 1970

LOUISE NEVELSON

SEVENTH DECADE GARDEN
May 8 – 19 June, 1971

Nevelson at Lippincott Foundry, ca. 1971

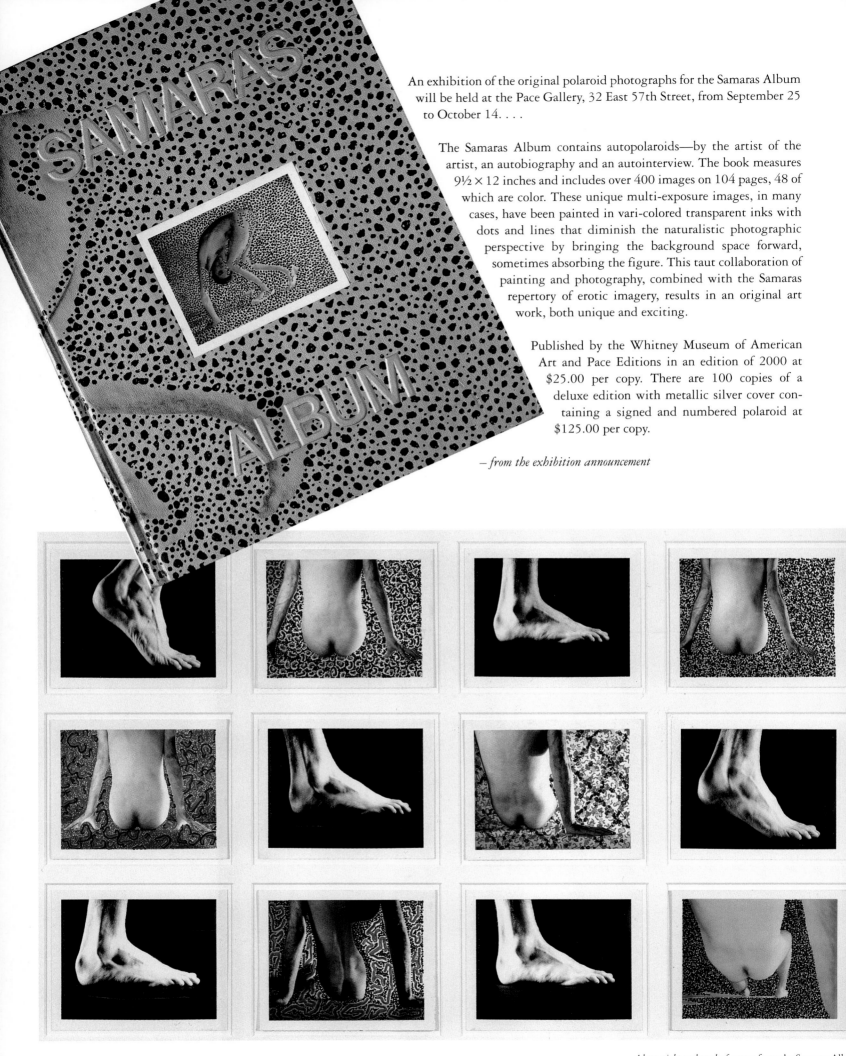

An exhibition of the original polaroid photographs for the Samaras Album will be held at the Pace Gallery, 32 East 57th Street, from September 25 to October 14. . . .

The Samaras Album contains autopolaroids—by the artist of the artist, an autobiography and an autointerview. The book measures 9½ × 12 inches and includes over 400 images on 104 pages, 48 of which are color. These unique multi-exposure images, in many cases, have been painted in vari-colored transparent inks with dots and lines that diminish the naturalistic photographic perspective by bringing the background space forward, sometimes absorbing the figure. This taut collaboration of painting and photography, combined with the Samaras repertory of erotic imagery, results in an original art work, both unique and exciting.

Published by the Whitney Museum of American Art and Pace Editions in an edition of 2000 at $25.00 per copy. There are 100 copies of a deluxe edition with metallic silver cover containing a signed and numbered polaroid at $125.00 per copy.

— from the exhibition announcement

Above, right and overleaf: pages from the Samaras Alb

116

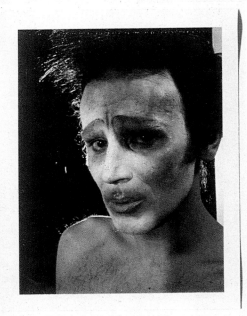

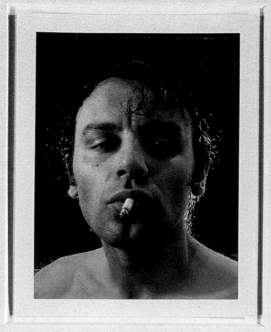

Tuesday, December 14th, 1971
from 8 to 11 p.m.
32 East 57th, New York City

Arne, Fred and Dick
invite you to join us in celebrating
the opening of the new second floor
Pace Gallery and Pace Editions
exhibition space
R. S. V. P. 421-3292

1971

Second Floor Gallery Opens

Several weeks after opening the Boston gallery, while we were wondering, waiting, hoping, and despairing that we would ever sell anything, Richard Solomon came in and ended our anxiety. Milly and I were both still at school, she an undergraduate in art history at Wellesley, and I a student in the Graduate School of Fine Arts at Boston University, where Brice Marden and I took classes together. While Milly and I were both at school, my mother "baby-sat" the gallery, and it would become on-the-job training for her own gallery. A year after we moved to New York, we would close the Boston gallery and she would open her own gallery in Columbus, Ohio, which she ran successfully for the rest of her life.

Richard Solomon reserved the most valuable work in the gallery, a Mirko sculpture, $1,500. He asked to take it home on approval and my mother agreed. By the time I got back to the gallery she was both filled with doubt and overjoyed that something might sell. She confessed that she had given the Mirko to a butcher at the local supermarket chain of Stop and Shop. Now she wondered if indeed, we would ever see it again or if he could afford it. Dick bought the sculpture and we subsequently learned that his family owned the grocery chain and our wives had grown up together, even been at summer camp together.

Milly and I moved to New York and coincidentally, so did Ann and Dick. He was working at Clairol and collecting art when the print renaissance occurred in the early sixties. We had become close friends and, mindful of his Harvard Business School training, I urged him to leave Clairol so that we could start a print-publishing business together. He agreed to produce some projects. And after issuing portfolios of prints by several of the gallery artists, we realized a project that still remains one of our best—BOOK by Lucas Samaras. An elaborate die-cut multimedia object, it contains silkscreens in ninety-eight colors with fold-out paper objects, and tiny books, concealed in pockets, that hold some of Samaras' short stories. Silkscreens on velvet and fold-out surprises dazzled the print world for sheer virtuosity, but few books were sold.

With inventory piling up, no exhibition space in which to show it, and Dick Solomon dissatisfied with his career in the cosmetics industry, we rented additional space on the second floor at 32 East 57th Street to open Pace Editions. Subsequently, our involvement with prints would extend back from modernism to the Renaissance, specializing in works by Dürer and Rembrandt.

1. ARP, JEAN
   Feuille de Crystal, 1954
   marble, 25" x 12" x 12"

17. KLEE, PAUL
    Adrasteapolis, 1925
    watercolor, 18½" x 12"

*34. MONET, CLAUDE
    Iris, 1923
    oil on canvas, 78¾" x 59"

35. NEVELSON, LOUISE
    Seventh Decade Garden III, 1971
    direct-welded, painted aluminum, 86" x 36" x 2

36. NICHOLSON, BEN
    Greek Island, 1965
    38¼" x 75¾"

*37. PICASSO, PABLO
    Bouteille, Verre, Fourchette, 1912
    oil on canvas, 28¾" x 21¼"

38. PICASSO, PABLO
    Combat de Faune et de Centaure, 1946
    ink, 19⅝" x 25⅛"

39. PICASSO, PABLO
    Etude pour les Demoiselles d'Avignon, 1907
    oil on canvas, 29½" x 13"

*40. PICASSO, PABLO
    Femme au Fauteuil Jaune, 1932
    oil on canvas, 51¼" x 38¼"

41. PICASSO, PABLO
    Femme nue couchée, 12/1/1954
    Chinese ink, 13½" x 17¼"

42. PICASSO, PABLO
    Jeune Peintre au Travail, 1964
    oil on canvas, 16" x 13"

43. PICASSO, PABLO
    Nu Allonge, June, 1920
    pencil and pastel, 8" x 10½"

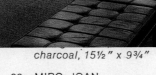

1933

44. PICASSO, PABLO
    Personnages, 19
    pencil, 2

charcoal, 15½" x 9¾"

11. DUBUFFET, JEAN
    Papa Flumette, 1967
    oil on canvas, 39¼" x 32"

12. GIACOMETTI, ALBERTO
    Femme Debout I, 1960
    bronze, 105¼" high

13. GIACOMETTI, ALBERTO
    Grande Tete, 1960
    bronze, 37½" high

14. GIACOMETTI, ALBERTO
    Portrait d'Annette, 1958
    oil on canvas, 36¼" x 28½"

15. GIACOMETTI, ALBERTO
    Tete d'Homme
    ball point pen, 6¼" x 6½"

*16. GIACOMETTI, ALBERTO
    Tete de Diego, c. 1956-58
    bronze, 16½" high

28. MIRO, JOAN
    Blue Painting, 1926
    oil on canvas, 23½" x 28¾"

29. MIRO, JOAN
    Personnage et Oiseau dans la Nui
    watercolor and collage, 43

30. MONDRIAN,
    Class

BEYELER AT PACE
PAINTINGS, SCULPTURE AND DRAWINGS
November 6 – 31 December, 1971

Pablo Picasso, *Femme au fauteuil jaune,* 1931
oil on canvas, 51¼ × 38¼"
©2001 Estate of Pablo Picasso/Artists Rights Society (ARS), New York

FERNAND LÉGER

LÉGÉR
THE LATE WORKS AT
PACE 32E57 NY10022

THE LATE WORKS
February 5 – 15 March, 1972

La partie de campagne, 1954
Collection Museum Ludwig, Cologne
Courtesy Rheinisches Bildarchiv, Cologne
© 2001 Artists Rights Society (ARS), New York / ADAGIP, Paris

Exhibition announcement

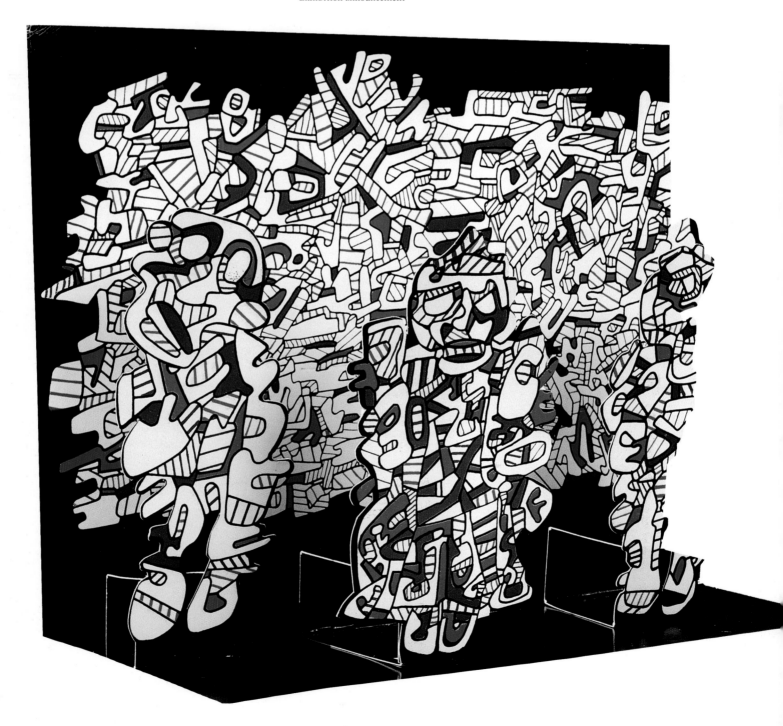

JEAN DUBUFFET
PRATICABLES
March 25 – 30 April, 1972

The exhibition consisted of 'klegecell' (a kind of epoxy or resin) panels painted with the Hourloupe *red, white and blue tracery, which determined the irregular outline of each panel. The panels were studies for pieces which would later be part of* Coucou Bazar, *the performance work Dubuffet would present at the Guggenheim Museum, during his retrospective, the following year. At selected times the exhibition also included dancers wearing costumes which were also used in* Coucou Bazar, *(le bal de l'hourloupe).*

127

ART FOR MCGOVERN

Andy Warhol, *Vote McGovern,* 1972
screenprint on Arches paper, 42 × 42"
© 2001 Andy Warhol Foundation for the Visual Arts / ARS, New York

Top: Gorden Parks, Alan King
Middle: Conrad and Sidney Janis
Bottom: Eunice Kennedy Shriver, Louise Nevelson
Photos © Fred W. McDarrah

130

LARRY BELL

KANDINSKY | WORKS ON PAPER
March 10 – 4 April, 1973

Catalogue cover
© 2001 Artists Rights Society (ARS), New York / ADAGP, Paris

Nina Kandinsky still lived in the same apartment in Neuilly, a suburb of Paris, that she had shared with her husband, Wassily Kandinsky, since their arrival in Paris in 1933. She invited Milly and me to visit her, and together we chose the drawings that would comprise our exhibition.

Entwurf zu "Kreise im Kreis," 1923
India ink and watercolor on paper 18¼ × 16¾"
© 2001 Artists Rights Society (ARS), New York / ADAGP, Paris

JEAN DUBUFFET

Jean Dubuffet and Arne Glimcher at
Vincennes studio, Paris, Spring 1972
Photo Richard Solomon

Milly Glimcher, Margit Rowell, wearing robes designed by Dubuffet, and Arne Glimcher at Vernissage of Dubuffet's retrospective at the Guggenheim Museum, 1973

For over two years, Dubuffet worked on a theater piece entitled Coucou Bazar, *which he planned to present at the Guggenheim Museum along with with his retrospective exhibition of 1973. The ballet theater piece was conceived as a three-dimensional kinetic painting created from the vocabulary of the* Hourloupe Cycle, *with which he had been preoccupied for a decade. It would be its finale. Dubuffet conceived a piece devoid of hierarchy, in which figure and ground—actors and sets, foreground and background—would exchange traditional roles. Some of the figures were flat, motionless cutouts while others were extravagant, three-dimensional gigantic costumes propelled by dancers. The weight and awkwardness of the costumes prescribed the movements. At times, the sets would move, while the figures froze, motionless. At other times, the action would be generated by the dancers, all unfolding to electronic music by Ilhan Mimaroglu, a musician of Algerian descent. It was extraordinary and was later presented at the Grand Palais in Paris; Gianni Agnelli sponsored another performance in Turin for which Dubuffet wrote his own electronic score.*

In preparation, Dubuffet created studies in the form of sculptures from which the costumes were made, and collages from which the set pieces were constructed. On May 5, 1973, we opened "Studies for a Spectacle," an exhibition of objects that had functioned as Dubuffet's sketchbooks for Coucou Bazar. *For the presentation at the Guggenheim, I designed a spiral-bound program printed on brown wrapping paper with die-cut collaged elements and "tipped-in" texts in an edition of 525. The edition included twenty-five artist's proofs, and a special edition of ten, each one containing an original drawing by Dubuffet. These were sold for the benefit of the museum to recover some of the production costs.*

Milord la chamarre, 1973
enamel paint on aluminum, 24'6" high
Seagram Plaza, New York, December 1974
© 2001 Artists Rights Society (ARS), New York/ADAGP, Paris

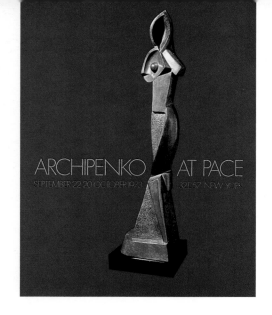

ARCHIPENKO AT PACE | September 22 – 20 October, 1973

ALFRED JENSEN | **RECENT PAINTINGS**
October 27 – 24 November, 1973

About My Work

"My work is done by a method of inductance (charge) thinking. It is done by conceptions being placed side by side in patterns, of magic things that influence one another and not by acts of mechanical causations. The patterns coalesce when they resonate. When my patterns are in relation, they are what they are according to numbers. The idea of correspondence has great significance and replaces the idea of causality, for things are connected rather than caused. Thus lovely things summon others among the class of repulsive things. This arises from the complementary way in which a thing of the same class responds. This idea that things belonging to the same class resonate with or energize each other has guided me in producing my 1973 paintings."

– A.J.

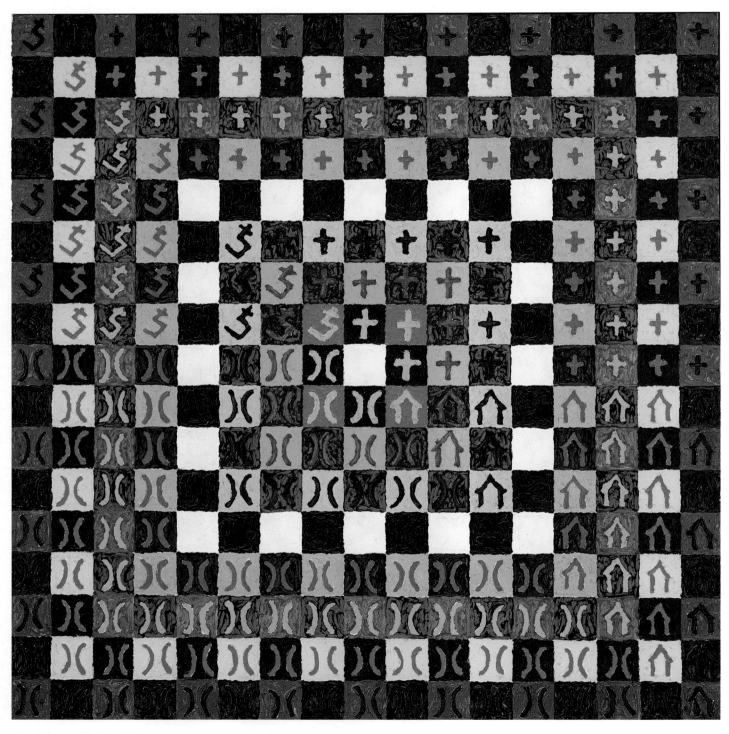

River Diagram, Lo Shu, 1971
oil on canvas, 60 × 60"

ROBERT IRWIN | **HARD WALL**
December 1 – 28, 1973

Untitled (Wall), 1973
wood and sheetrock
69" × 53' × 4½"

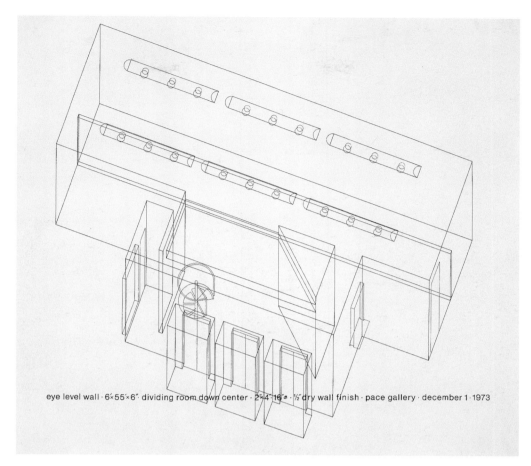

eye level wall · 6˝×55´×6˝ dividing room down center · 2×4˝ 16˝° · ½ dry wall finish · pace gallery · december 1 · 1973

Drawing for *Eye Level Wall,* 1973

Untitled (Wall), 1973
wood and sheetrock
69" × 53' × 4½"

Photo Larry Bell

Photo-Transformation, 1974
SX-70 Polaroid, 3 × 3"

LUCAS SAMARAS

by Arne Glimcher
Excerpt from Pace catalogue

The kitchen is tiny and cluttered with the visual dazzle of dishes and silver stacked to dry and accumulations of postcards, passports, plugs, icons, fruit, binoculars, cameras, tinfoil, mylar, paper towels, honey, sponges, a meat grinder, garbage bags, and spices. On a table stacked with pencils, brushes, film, photographs, books, and flowers, illuminated by a small lamp and surfaced in the random pattern of newsprint, Samaras reveals the versatility of his essential self in a series of tableaux he calls photo-transformations.

The stage on which these tableaux are enacted is directly opposite his only available audience, the television set that shares his kitchen. His camera records the collective drama positioned next to the television that stimulates his fantasies while playing in a constant technicolor dialogue. "I can do anything better than you can." In a gesture of reciprocity and seduction he returns frames of images inspired by the television's repertory as well as subjective reactions to incidents in his life.

The result of this theater is the production of a series of demonic, comic, and seductive hallucinatory transformations of himself. Previously in boxes, pastels, sculptures, drawings, acrylic paintings and autopolaroids, self-images were cannibalized and spoons, forks and knives were isolated for anthropomorphic focus.

His new work is still obsessed with the formation of imagery on associative parallels, i.e. himself as boxes, dinners, chairs, rooms, mandrills, monsters, wizards, etc. and the development of these objects' and images' roles within those contexts by implied function.

To realize these feats Samaras required a medium of immediate expression, and the lag between concept and output of expression has been significantly diminished by the use of the Polaroid SX-70 camera. In previous works he dealt with this need by employing assemblage techniques, which facilitated the selection or recognition of existing images, without having to sculpt them into existence. Selection itself became a sculptural act as it now becomes a painterly act in the photo-transformations. This desire for immediacy is not unique to Samaras, it is rather a major tendency in twentieth century art that has led to other solutions for other artists. The desire to produce a work as immediate and fresh as its preconscious model, motivated certain Surrealists to produce automatic works as it did de Kooning to produce action paintings. Process itself becomes the tool for the recognition of visual concepts within the pigments by finding external matches for internal schemas. Thus these transformations exist as a king of improvisational theater of painterly expressionism.

The photo-transformations are divided into two types: images in which the figure is transformed by actual physical contortion and extravagantly illuminated or painted with colored lights; and others in which the posed and lighted image is later distorted by altering the process of the film's development. As the image begins to appear, Samaras tests the limits of his fantasies' credibility by manually blending or mixing the photo-emulsion pigments using the surface itself as a palette in a kind of expressionistic finger-painting. The presumptive forms and gestures are thus altered by the puppeteer who exaggerates attitudes by linear embellishments and fields of patterns. Even in instances of the most monstrous distortion, photo naturalistic clues to the object's original identity remain.

The pin boxes of the early sixties have been extended into the image of a figure lifting the flayed sheet of skin from his torso to reveal the contents of steaming, spiky red flesh. His mouth is transformed into an incinerator consuming the fingers being fed from the edges of his lips. A parallel sequence occurs in his 1969 film "Self", in which the camera focuses on a mouth devouring family photographs. The performer from the Happenings of the early sixties now appears as a sphinx with none of the elegance of antiquity but rather the naked clumsiness of a new genus created by the arrangement of its own familiar elements.

Like a gigantic facial mask that confuses proportion, steely grey buttocks become the central expressionless hippo face out of which spring the arms and legs of a man. In these works Samaras continues his scrutiny of combinations and possibilities for the transformation of his environment as an extension of himself.

AFRICAN ACCUMULATIVE
SCULPTURE

September 21 – 19 October, 1974

Pace Editions had been functioning for three or four years, exclusively devoted to publications. Then Dick's affinity for tribal art extended the business to include African and South Seas sculpture. Andre Emmerich suggested that we see a young dealer in African art from Los Angeles' Franklin Gallery who wanted to relocate to New York. We hired Brice Holcombe to direct the African Art Gallery. To publicly inaugurate the enterprise, Holcombe curated an exhibition entitled "African Accumulative Sculptures." The exhibition and catalogue, with a scholarly text by Professor Arnold Rubin, examined the process of additive sculpture-making by accumulation of artifacts. As process can become subject in twentieth century art, and time a prime ingredient, the exhibition was particularly compatible with the focus of the gallery. As director of "Pace Primitive," Brice Holcombe presented memorable exhibitions, including "African Spirit Images" and "Art of the Cameroon Grasslands." He continued as director until his untimely death in 1984.

African Accumulative Sculpture
Power and Display
by Arnold Rubin
Excerpt from Pace catalogue

Substance

. . . As something of a corollary to earlier statements regarding the interweaving of African art and African life, anything resembling a concept of "art for art's sake" appears to be rare to the point of non-existence. Also as anticipated earlier, this finding should in no way be taken to mean that aesthetic decisions are not made, but rather that they find their place within a much wider set of values. In general, African peoples manifest an exquisite sensitivity to objects and experiences, structures and relationships, but primarily as means to ends rather than as ends in themselves. For most African communities, the overriding objective of all beliefs and practices is the survival, orderly and effective functioning, and prosperity of the community and of the individuals who make it up. In such a context, "usefulness" tends to be of extremely broad definition; moreover, each community typically relates to its natural, supernatural, and cultural environments with rigorous pragmatism and a notable lack of sentimentality. Rarely is there any compunction, for example, over melting down and recasting bronze ornaments or other configurations which have gone out of fashion, or are otherwise no longer relevant to any particular functional context. Nor does any serious distress accompany acknowledgement of the fact that, despite reasonable care, most masks and figures will eventually have to be replaced due to fire, insect damage, weathering, or breakage. Many types of objects are made for one period of use—often quite brief—and then discarded. Far from representing a tragedy, the fairly high rate of attrition of monuments in most African communities has the effect of providing work for comparatively large numbers of artists in each generation, for whom the products of only the preceding two or three generations are usually available as models and standards. In a broader sense, the entire body of inherited cultural patterns representing the accumulated experiences, accomplishments, and wisdom of the past, is typically re-evaluated in each generation and re-interpreted or adjusted where deemed desirable in the light of available options and altered circumstances.

Such a pattern of perceived and implemented distinctions between ends and means, and of continuous cultural stock-taking and re-adjustment, may help to clarify the difficulty which many Africans living in traditional contexts have in understanding the Western collector's motivation and rationale. Whatever else the objects in question may be and do, they are first of all perceived as making statements about the self-identification of the makers and users. Conceptions of what we call style, form, iconography, use and function—the total configurations of houses, pots, weapons, thrones, and images of ancestors, for example—represent entities intimately bound up with particular cultural continua. Peremptory removal of an object whose presence sanctions crucial political, religious, or social functions may render the exercise of those functions difficult if not impossible, representing a grave threat to the orderly life of the community; only an enemy would seek to remove such an object. On the other hand, if a new structural component in the areas of juridical authority or enculturation of the young, for example, has supplanted an earlier one, objects associated with the supplanted system may be cast out. More often, however, prudence will dictate that the earlier complex receive at least token maintenance for a period of time, by virtue of its earlier importance to the community (and the power it will have accumulated thereby), or as a reserve or "backup" system in case the new system proves unsatisfactory. While the owners or custodians of such formerly important objects may agree to part with them, they often express puzzlement at what possible use members of another group could have for relics at the same time useless and intimately bound up with the identity and cumulative experience of an alien people. Deprived of their functional roots, the formal appeal as well as the effective power of the objects wither away. As an even more important consideration, such objects will also be regarded as almost certainly hazardous to an outsider who is by definition ignorant of their proper use. . . .

In Africa, qualities are exploited through the organization and concentration of available "capability" in POWER contexts. An analysis of POWER materials such as horns, beaks, shells, etc., reveals that they are what may be called signature elements for the creature from which they have been taken, representing the distinctive capacity and equipment for survival which characterizes each: for birds, their beaks or feathers; for the various types of antelopes, their horns; for snails, their shells; and so on. Imitations in carved wood or other materials may, it seems, also serve. By virtue of the magnificently articulated survival-system he represents, the leopard is typically accorded special significance in such transfers or borrowings; claws, fangs, and pelt may be utilized, or pelt-markings emulated through spotting with paint. (We may note in passing that leopardskin is recognized as one of the most widely distributed attributes of high political or religious office in Africa. It seems very likely that transfer of "capability" of the sort being discussed is involved in this pattern of association, rather than

merely metaphoric allusion.) Incantations, blood sacrifices, and libations of "spiritous" liquors may be used to introduce additional essences. . . .

Accumulation in African Sculpture

William Fagg has argued that the principle of "increase" serves to organize life and art in African and other "tribal" societies (e.g., Fagg 1960: 471–2; Fagg & Plass 1964: 148–58). He proposes that a special sensitivity to life-forms characterizes such societies, by virtue of their closeness to nature in connection with subsistence pursuits. This sensitivity, according to Fagg, is reflected in the frequency with which the exponential or "growth" curve appears in their arts—the helical spiral described by many types of germinating seeds, for example, or the tendrils of vines, or certain horns and shells.

There is certainly nothing to dispute in the proposition that enhanced security, reflected in multiplication of children, food supplies, animals, or other types of wealth, represents a pervasive goal for members of the societies in question (and very likely a universal human goal as well). It seems to me, however, that the concepts of transfer and accumulation as outlined above may provide a more valid framework than "increase" for considering both the design characteristics Fagg has noted and possibly other distinctive features of African (and other "tribal") societies. . . .

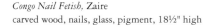

Congo Nail Fetish, Zaire
carved wood, nails, glass, pigment, 18½" high

149

ROBERT IRWIN | SOFT WALL
December 7 – 4 January, 1974

Robert Irwin at Pace
by Larry Rosing

Art in America
March/April, 1975

Robert Irwin's newest piece at Pace was almost invisible. A scrim (actually curtain material) was stretched parallel to the longest wall of the gallery and about two feet in front of it. The cloth, like the walls of the gallery, was white. The edges were inconspicuously stapled to the walls, floor and ceiling; no marks or wrinkles interrupted its perfectly flat surface. White paper on the rug behind the scrim helped to further conceal the measure, even the existence of that narrow space. The front of the scrim was lighted from the ceiling by a row of floodlights pointed straight down, and the light striking the fabric surface made the already dense material even more wall-like. The lights were shaded so as not to light the gallery space, which instead received alternate pools of warm and cool light from a second row of ceiling lights.

Irwin's concerns have gradually led him away from painting and object-making, and toward pieces like this scrim which try to define and give form to particular spaces. In the late fifties, he was an Abstract-Expressionist painter. In the early sixties he gave up the personal surface of Abstract Expressionism for close-valued Color-Field painting. His last objects, made at the end of the sixties, were a group of near-white aluminum discs and a series of banded, semi transparent plastic discs, both dependent on lighting and installation. For the last four years he has worked in increasingly environmental

ways, including thirty-seven "land pieces" in the deserts of the western U.S.

Irwin considers his recent work to be pure research rather than art-making. He sees it as a parallel with the work of certain theoretical scientists and mathematicians. The research area that has engaged him is in the limits of visual perception.

The aluminum discs of the late sixties demonstrate this: each is slightly convex and (from the proper viewpoint) is invisibly supported about two feet from the wall. Four lights, symmetrically arranged, make ambiguous the disc's position in space and especially its relation with the wall. Each disc appears to be white, but as you look at one a color rainbow appears at the edge and grows slowly inward towards the center. The discs, as this color is gradually perceived, elicit a feeling of spiritual revelation.

Although Irwin considers his work to be pure research, it is often quite moving. This was the most recent in a series of scrim pieces. Each of the earlier installations transformed its space and gave it a marvelous presence, mystery and purity.

A year ago Irwin transformed this same gallery space into a magical environment by building a solid wall, its top just above eye level, which bisected the gallery and left the far side fascinatingly inaccessible. Like the discs and the scrim pieces, it was carefully lighted; like them, it induced a quiet meditativeness.

Irwin's "soft-wall" exhibition marked the quietest month with the least attendance in the gallery's history. It wasn't so much that no one came—it was that nearly no one stayed. Elevator after elevator would open, people would peer in, and then deciding that there was no exhibition, leave. However, awaiting the brave souls that ventured into the exhibition was an extraordinary perception-extending experience. With the investment of a little time, the viewer sensed that something was wrong, out of kilter, with the space. Eighteen inches in front of the back wall of the gallery a theatrical scrim was stretched, causing the wall to blur or seem out of focus, while the three other walls were sharp. The space itself became palpable. It remains one of Irwin's best works.

ROBERT IRWIN
by John Russell

Robert Irwin (Pace Gallery, 32 East 57th Street): For some years now Robert Irwin has patrolled the frontiers of invisibility, never quite crossing them, but never quite turning his back on them either. His new piece at the Pace is there through January 4, and to many visitors it suggests that Mr. Irwin has crossed those frontiers once and for all.

What he has done is to partition off one side of the gallery with a wall simulated in muslin. The proportions of the space are altered, therefore, and that part of the gallery that lies behind the simulated wall is present merely as a soundless echo (or as a tall thin stripe at either end, where the convergence of side wall and end wall makes itself felt as a shadow). Some delicate masking of the gallery's lighting has also a part to play.

I won't say that the experience compares with one's first entry into Chartres Cathedral, but the job is done with Mr. Irwin's habitual discretion and finesse. Downstairs there are some very fine drawings by Picasso, Dubuffet, and others that come across all the more strongly after the exquisite evasions of Mr. Irwin.

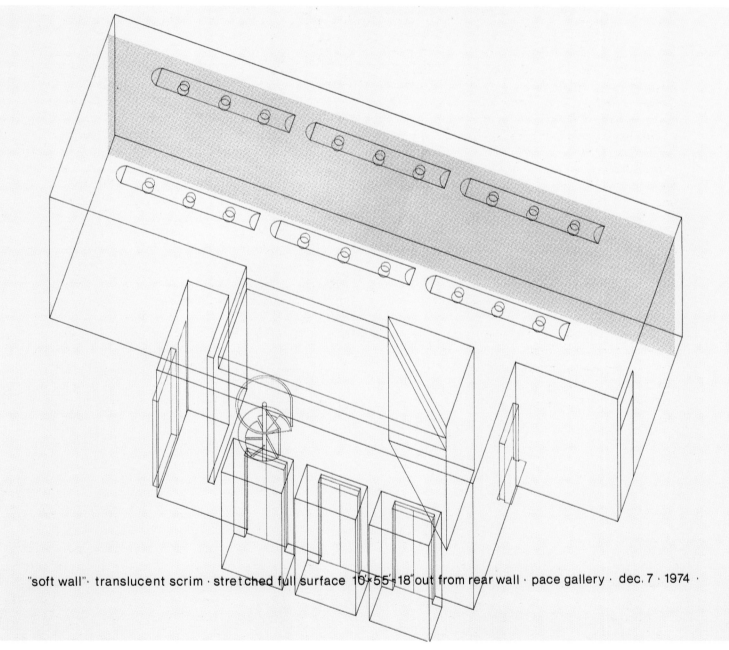

"soft wall"· translucent scrim · stretched full surface 10ʹ×55ʹ×18ʺ out from rear wall · pace gallery · dec. 7 · 1974 ·

Drawing for *Soft Wall*, 1974

Arne Glimcher and Agnes Martin, New Mexico, ca. 1974

By the mid-sixties, the gallery had established itself, at least to the handful of collectors that mattered, as a Saturday stop on the Rialto. We broadened our stable and during the week had periodic visits from most of the artists in the community. Barnett Newman was a regular. He was the only one of the Abstract Expressionists who embraced the new art, and didn't feel threatened by its high visibility. Barney was especially supportive of the work of Bob Irwin, Larry Bell, and Don Judd. Newman was a major influence on them, and he recognized and appreciated their respect for his work. When the pristine aesthetic of the gallery was challenged as slick and chic, Newman understood it and defended us. He was also very close to Agnes Martin, and she became a regular visitor to the gallery. Fred Mueller owned one of her paintings and, occasionally, we would visit her studio on Coenties Slip, stopping into the studios of Ellsworth Kelly and Robert Indiana as well.

AGNES MARTIN

NEW PAINTINGS
March 1 – 1 April, 1975

Untitled #20, 1974
acrylic, pencil and gesso on canvas, 6 × 6'

Agnes was generally considered to be among the most radical artists by her peers, though she regarded herself as an Abstract Expressionist. Her work was beginning to be collected by museums and a few significant private collectors. By the mid-sixties Agnes, Kelly, Youngerman, and Lenore Tawny had lost their leases at Coenties Slip and Agnes, for personal considerations as well, gave up painting and left New York. Agnes always insisted that her work was separate from her life and in no way referential to the physical world. The accolades that her work was beginning to win, were intrusive, and she was not inspired to create new work.

She bought an air-stream trailer and headed back to New Mexico, where she had previously lived and taught art, settling on a mesa in Cuba, New Mexico. After an absence from painting of six or seven years, she built a studio, planted vegetables, and began painting again. One day in early 1975, Agnes appeared at the gallery, said she was painting again, and asked if we'd show her new work. A visit to New Mexico revealed the first red and blue paintings of 1974.

LOUISE NEVELSON

DAWN'S PRESENCE – TWO/MOON GARDEN + TWO
February 14 – 13 March, 1976

DAWN'S PRESENCE – TWO
MOON GARDEN + TWO
1969 - 1975

NEVELSON

THE PACE GALLERY
32 EAST 57/NEW YORK
FEBRUARY 14-MARCH 13, 1976

Louise Nevelson and Betty Ford at the dedication of
Bicentennial Dawn, 1976
Photo Edward Byrn

Moon Gardenscape II

154

General Service Administration, er its mandate to spend one per on art in all new federal build construction, commissioned Louise elson to create a massive sculptur environment for the new James Byrne Federal Courthouse in ladelphia. Nevelson was moved to the work "Bicentennial Dawn" he patriotic fervor engendered by bicentennial celebration in 1976.

Bicentennial Dawn, 1976
multi-unit sculptural environment in
white painted wood, installed
at the James A. Byrne U.S.
Courthouse in Philadelphia, Pa.

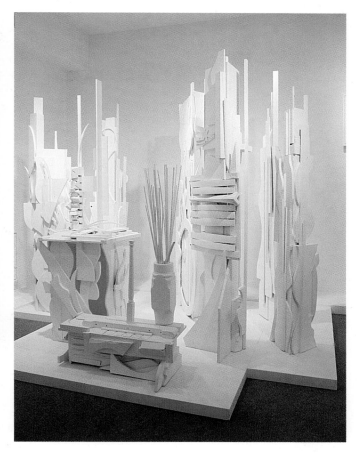

Installation at Pace: *Dawn's Presence - Two,* 1969–75
white painted wood, 102 × 135 × 105"

JULIO GONZALEZ

100TH ANNIVERSARY EXHIBITION
March 27 – 24 April, 1976

Homme cactus #2, 1939–40
iron, 30¾' high

AGNES MARTIN

Untitled #2, 1975
acrylic, pencil and gesso, 6 × 6'

AD REINHARDT
PAINTINGS
October 2 – 30, 1976

As students, in the late fifties, Milly and I came to New York to see the de Kooning landscape show at Janis. De Kooning was by far the most influential artist of his time, as evidenced by the work being produced in art schools—my own included. The Betty Parsons Gallery was across the elevator lobby from Janis, at 15 West 57 Street, separated by a glass wall. After spending the whole morning at the de Kooning show, while waiting for the elevator we peered through the glass wall into the Parsons Gallery. Betty, a formidable character, sat at her desk just behind the glass, forcing an encounter with each entering visitor. The gallery was devoid of people and there were what appeared from the doorway to be a series of same-size blank, vertical black panels around the gallery. We weren't certain that they were paintings, and thought that perhaps they were panels on which paintings were to be hung. Too uncertain and insecure to allow ourselves to appear stupid, and fearful of the forbidding Miss Parsons, we left without seeing what we ultimately realized was Ad Reinhardt's exhibition of vertical black paintings.

Years later, Ad visited Pace regularly and was very forthcoming in his admiration of the gallery's aesthetic. We became friends and I spent a lot of time in his studio. Like Newman, he encouraged our exhibitions of West Coast artists, and was also a great friend and admirer of Louise Nevelson, who introduced us. I was doing extensive research in perceptual psychology at New York University, which would result in the publication of a book entitled Modern Art and Modern Science: The Parallel Analysis of Vision, co-authored with Paul Vitz.

Abstract Painting, 1960
oil on canvas, 60" × 60"

Reinhardt, who operated at the threshold of perception, was of great interest to me, as was the work of Robert Irwin. Their art and philosophies continue to influence me to this day, and they were crucial to the development of the perceptual theories in my book.

Reinhardt and Rothko were at the top of our wish list, for their work was most relevant to the artists we represented, and if we could get them to join the gallery they would create a context for the younger artists already there and, we hoped, entice others to come. Ad had been with Betty Parsons for many years, and he accepted and found humor in the fact that she couldn't sell his paintings. He even developed a sense of pride about it. Fred and I each bought one of Ad's paintings from Betty, but not without having to sit through a private view of her own constructions first. After a couple of years of discussion, in 1967, Ad agreed to join the gallery but wanted an unofficial association for several months before a public announcement was made that he had changed galleries. During the period of transition, he agreed to give us works to sell. In 1967, Ad sent me the humorous postcard reproduced above, confirming the plans for a show.

On August 31, 1967, Ad died suddenly and the Reinhardt estate went to the Marlborough Gallery. Among other considerations, Marlborough offered to buy a significant amount of work from the estate, ensuring financial security for Ad's widow and daughter. Reinhardt was lost to us for a decade, and when the Rothko Estate became associated with Pace, Rita Reinhardt returned Ad's paintings to Pace for representation. Finally, we were able to present the exhibition described by Ad in the postcard (minus the Eurasian odalisques and soft music), and the postcard itself served as the exhibition announcement.

LUCAS SAMARAS

Samaras

The crawling things
are feasting

it might as well

to other times
we'll meet again
and until then
weave me another
multicolored sweater

Photo-Transformation, 1973–74
SX 70 Polaroid, 3 × 3"

the crawling
the feasting
and the mothering
forget
forget.
I'm traveling
on an almost empty plane
back from teaching in Tampa
time to temper
a lover
spooning down
some tepid food
looking out
over the haunting
blue ash tender
engulfing shroud
hovering below
the deep darkening
sunset
melding
into my once
delicious ancestress
who loved
uncultivated colors
and would have beamed
to own
such gaudy gowns.
Go away mother
journey with
the splendid sun
in a recurring bloom
now at last
if chance allows
I can embrace
my love past due.
Smile as you remove
your aromatic garment
from my throat
hasten your glow
to other lands
your scent

the ancient awesome
portions of my brain.
I'll continue
to implicate nature
with my future
and sleep among flowers
of dazzling stifling hues.
I must awake.
Erect in a sweat
after biting my lip
no one to hit
but myself.
Well it's better
than spitting the wall
hit splitting my head
or getting the bed wet.
Hungry angry.
But what is this urge
to hurt my lips
and force my feet
to talk to each other
whenever I seek
to sleep.
The mansion fell
upon itself
in a huge
Medieval centrifuge.
My skin uneasy
with rashes and bumps
my soul is patched with cotton puffs
and lemon rind
the burning confined
to the section
on loss and decline.
Others gave away
their clothes
or gambled
their unlucky lives
with pills and knives
I gave away my privacies
clean wrapped
and decorated

I kissed them hard
and slipped them
under doors, in books
telephones or britches

came back
mangled derided
hardly recognized
and shelved themselves
among the spices.
I went to the park
to get some nature
manmade or not
it eased the pressure
in the mind department
and aired the moldy darks
of my abode.
Fear smear.
Some hurts are smart.
from another angle.
A patchy rat
busy as a bat
crossed by path.
Sporting sandals
I walked fast
almost on toes
after that.
A dog walking woman
cautiously regarded
a felled double bent
boy athlete
with a leg cramp.
Deciding not to turn
I approached
kneeled and told him
soothing things
my fingers plied
his lumpy kinks.
Rising relieved
as his friends came by

a sweetness in my body.
Upset it
forget it.
The faded bench
by the statue
of the hero
on the rearing
horse ferocious
was bedroom
and bathroom
to the woman
with packed bags
minimal delights
stockings blotchings
open wounds
lipstick mistake
and no undies
thighs folding unfolding
dry fish journey
to a mess
with consequences.
Cute fat and ugly
fugly cugly
I steered clear
from her stares
and her smells
and her style.
They never last
beyond a season
more reason
to go catch
their saintly act
less abstract
than the silent
speed magician
holding court
between the sitting
bronze scribes
Walter Scott
and Robert Burns.
Better yet
to come upon

Photo-Transformation, 1973–74
SX 70 Polaroid, 3 × 3"

he told them the particulars
and from a distance
I heard him call
hey, thanks a lot mister

the tribe of men
who sun themselves
like swampy snakes
all stakes cast

en a quick swish
of their warm pink parts
privacy displayed
on gaming charts
or walk along
the majorettes
all thighs
out of steel
and out of step
roasting
in their shells
looted futures
passing wind
in the beauty parlor
grind
attending
to everyone's behind
and all around
this open living room
this grounded sea
this unsafe space
my father's ark
is nowhere to be found.
But if it were
could I go in
without a partner
or would I change
my living pattern
to pluck a fiery
pot luck spouse
Geometric mounts
with windows
and smokestacks
I don't mind that.
Daedalus bound in Babel
and Peenemunde.
There are enough
sparks spires
to reconstruct
and stroke
my fancy fires.
Cities built
to scale
in shallow
pools of water.
I know
how lovely
young flesh
seduces me
to touch itself
how sadly
self sufficient
Its mind
reduces me
to clutch myself.
Poetic profound
pathetic potatoes.
No vacations
without lovers
no confessions
without observers
nothing doing
without dreams
or hard desires.
Time to generate
new relatives
the old ones
magnify my faults.
Nothing to ache about
nothing to fake.
By the pea green lake
tea stain dragon flies
delicately linked
in hovering delight.
Shades of choppers and birds
and shouting men in boats
did not distract
their sweet biology.
If I were younger
I would squash them.

Close your eyes
you fool
and kiss me
and you'll be kissing
all the forms
you've ever kissed.
Open your eyes
you fool
and find
that my face
can be your
hiding place.
Use it refuse it
abuse it excuse it.
I'm so much better
than my body
I'm so much better
than my talk
I'm so much better
than my work
and so much worse.
Cycling jogging
walking or strolling
my mind is still
my arms and legs
move in place
space flows
in an unending barrel
only one creature
in the treadmill
me.
I sat on a hill
idyllic construction
of unkept grass
sun tickled trees
mangy brooklet.
He came by
addicted and tall
I had no money
he stalled
for something
of mine
unwilling
to lose face
with his near by friend
so I gave him
my half eaten chicken
chicken that I was.
Ten years later
he was small
gimme your money
quite unstable
gimme your money
almost in tears
gimme your money
that he was going to cut me up
if I didn't give him
everything I had
and swished his big
dull knife
in quick dull strokes
a stuttering
Hispanic
body artist
expressionist
ready to carve
well at least
he wasn't English
clutching
a cultured pen.
I gave him some cash
and curiously
gave him some more
glad I wasn't bitten
by a young beserk
with human rabies
and that blood
was kept in place.
Honor dishonor
I got to be a donor.

All this was not —
without erotic horror.
Let other people's misery
enter my thoughts
through a refinery.
Worse things
are apparent
elsewhere.
Elderly sibylic
sensualist Dutch
so sensitive
so saurian
so stabbed.
Let's all share
in the indignity
of lost controls.
Further down
on the edge
of the lake
a half submerged fire
hubcapped a more
compact ecology
bright green marble
August algae.
Near by
a dark raw chicken head
gory transplanted
island story.
Automatic
skotomatic.
Mutual ritual
Everything is fine
stomach devine.
Get new keys
torsos of trees
graffiti targets
in hardened poses
talked whenever
my back was turned
tussled their leaves
grandmas with frills

their cluttered lives
they flash
their tortured smiles
and burst with hives.
Half bare lovers
in a golden daze
fondled and fooled
my busy instruments
without intent.
I asked to be
their lubricant.
Let me watch you do
whatever you will
but do not tell.
Hostility
senility.
My legs stood stiff
on the left center steps
to bad breath Bethesda
sharing it's water
illegal baptisma
a sunstroked mass
of black injected
island goo
blood infected
island stew
melodious flesh
ears agape
sizzling rape
convulsing skin
smell of vulturine
volcanic extract
organic abstract
I go so ecstatic
I could blow my brains
and follow the echoes
on trains
a well trained
scientist.
Eyes sparking
batteries full

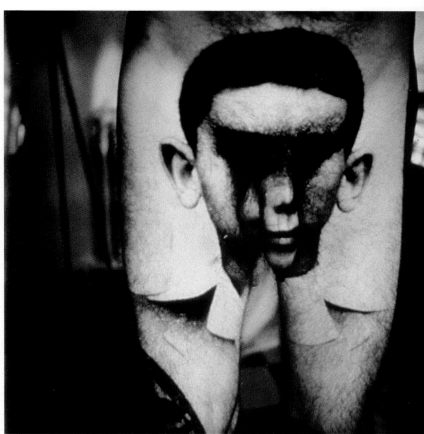

Photo-Transformation, 5/13/76
SX 70 Polaroid, 3 × 3"

Come and meet
my other side
aint he nice
aint she nice.
My presence
disturbs

back at my room
in a yellow collapse
relax relax
a bed dismattrassed
with springs and bones
unhook the phone
my spine all notched

163

jects—items of clothing, and tools from the hardware store—to his paintings, which, except for these objects, were executed in the established second-generation Abstract Expressionist manner. I once characterized this Neo-Dada style as "Expressionism with objects, or de Kooning plus Duchamp," and I still think it an apt description.

The claim was sometimes made in those days that Neo-Dada, because of its use of "real" objects and "real" space, was somehow closer to "life" than painting that confined itself to a flat surface. It was all a fiction, of course, but a lot of people believed it at the time. Now the use of such objects, which created certain problems for museum conservators but otherwise left real "life" undisturbed, looks like just another aesthetic convention, which it always was. . . .

[The] new paintings . . . are, in my opinion, quite the best paintings he has yet produced, perhaps the first truly serious paintings he has ever produced. About Mr. Dine's gifts as a draftsman and graphic artist, there has never been any ground for doubt, though there has sometimes been ample reason to question what he chose to do with those gifts. But as a painter—that, as they say, was another story. It was mostly a story of evading the essential problems of pictorial art by employing objects that diverted our attention from a surface the artist was unable or unwilling to face on its own terms.

* * *

The new paintings are large, grand and ambitious—actually an amalgam of painting and drawing that shows the artist grappling with the problem of transmuting the perceptions of the draftsman into the visual weights and measures of pictorial art. Only in the motif that is repeated in every picture . . . the motif of the "Robe" that is familiar to us from the clothes that used to hang, limp and wrinkled and disconsolate, from Mr. Dine's Neo-Dada constructions—are we reminded of the earlier work. But the handling of this motif is so different here, and the emotion it is made to yield so distant from the facetiousness of the old days, that we feel we are in the presence of something new—new, at least, for Mr. Dine.

Indeed, the artist I am most reminded of in these paintings is someone I would never have expected to compare to Mr. Dine in any respect—the late Mark Rothko. Never mind what Rothko would have thought of a nine-foot painting of a man's robe—Never mind either, that Rothko did not "model" his forms the way Mr. Dine does, with a kind of bravura drawing and a very traditional eye for light and shadow and contour. The comparison remains persuasive, all the same, for there is a similar feeling for large masses of somber, close-valued color projected on a monumental scale. Mr. Dine is less of a purist, and he lacks Rothko's sense of tragic detachment and absolute control, and he still relies on drawing to keep his image and his surface alive, not quite trusting the power of color alone, but he nonetheless comes remarkably close to Rothko's universe—and comes to it from a very different direction, too. In the slate grays and cloudy reds and other melancholy hues of the "Robe" paintings, even in the more intense reds of "The Cardinal," Mr. Dine has struck a deeper and more meditative note in his work.

He still works in a tonal tradition, eschewing the radical transitions and simplifications of the pure color abstractionists that derive from Rothko, yet he has learned something from their handling of color and space. What may be the most interesting thing about Mr. Dine's new paintings is, indeed, the way we see two quite separate traditions converging in them. Ten years ago, the aesthetics of color abstraction and the imagery and ideology of Neo-Dada painting seemed to inhabit two very separate worlds, and they seemed destined to remain separate and irreconcilable. But in Mr. Dine's new paintings we see something like a synthesis of these separate artistic worlds, and they add up to a very affecting as well as an unexpected artistic experience.

The New York Times, Sunday, January 9, 1977

"The Best Paintings Jim Dine Has Yet Produced"
by Hilton Kramer

Jim Dine belongs to the generation of American artists that came to fame—and thus to their first museum retrospective—early. (Has anyone calculated by how many years the Pop Art movement changed the age at which artists were to be considered "ripe" for such retrospectives? My own impression is that Pop, combined with the general accent of youth in the 1960s, altered the very notion of what a museum retrospective ought to be, effectively separating it from the concept of artistic maturity.) When the Whitney Museum of American Art organized Mr. Dine's retrospective in 1970, he was 35—an age at which Willem de Kooning, for example, had not yet had his first one-man show in a gallery. By 1970, the museum retrospective had become a showcase for young art, and Mr. Dine was one of the many artists to benefit from the new dispensation.

It should not be a source of surprise, then, to find that Mr. Dine's art has undergone some changes since that time. He remains, to be sure, recognizably the same artist, attached to the same motifs, indulgent of some of the same affectations and reveling in some of the same gifts that he has made a virtual signature of his work. Yet in his new show at the Pace Gallery, 32 East 57th Street, opening Saturday and continuing through Feb. 12, he has moved in a direction that would have surprised his admirers a decade ago and will surely disappoint anyone still yearning for the kind of "fun" we were offered up in the 60's. He has become a more sober and a more somber artist, and in some ways—dare one say it?—a more "traditional" artist. I think he is also a better artist now than he was at the time of the Whitney show, but not everyone is going to think so. An artist who recognizes in himself a loyalty to the kind of art he seemed to spurn in his youth is not always forgiven.

* * *

It will be recalled that Mr. Dine made his name as one of the young avatars of the Neo-Dada movement. He was associated with the first "Happenings," and he attached real ob-

JIM DINE

PAINTINGS, DRAWINGS, ETCHINGS — 1976

January 15 – 12 February, 1977

Afternoon Robe, 1976
oil on canvas, 72 × 66"
Collection Whitney Museum
of American Art, New York
Gift of Anne and Joel Ehrenkranz

LEE KRASNER

Several years had passed since Lee Krasner had been productive as an artist. Always overshadowed by Pollock, after his death she devoted her energy to the placement of his works in major institutions and the recognition of his achievement as central to the ongoing history of art. Barbara Rose was always a champion of Lee's work and one of her closest friends. Barbara suggested that we meet with Lee and select a small retrospective exhibition that would encourage a reassessment of her work, free from Pollock's shadow.

At the time, Lee had begun work on new paintings collaged from 1930s charcoal Cubist figure drawings. The new work was compelling in its ability to integrate the images into allover patterns that allowed the arcs of charcoal to interact as brushstrokes reminiscent of the allover patterns in her paintings of the 1950s. The collaged drawings were arranged on the canvas in grids, occasionally interrupted by blocks of pure color. The works looked very fresh and we encouraged Lee to continue with the series. Instead of presenting a historical overview of her art, her first show of new work in many years was presented at Pace. A series of historical exhibitions followed, reestablishing her reputation and generating a significant demand for her work both from museums and private collectors.

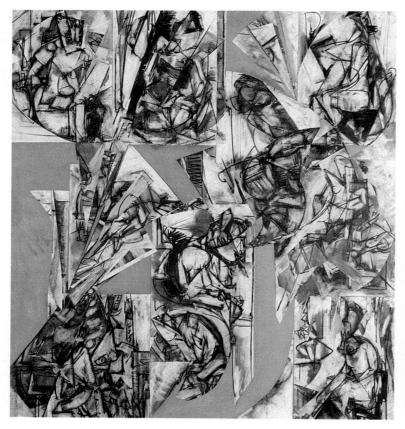

Imperfect Indicative, 1976
collage on canvas, 78 × 72"
©2001 Pollock-Krasner Foundation/Artists
Rights Society (ARS), New York

Lee Krasner during her exhibition
Photo © Fred W. McDarrah

Catalogue cover

LEE KRASNER
eleven ways to use the words to see

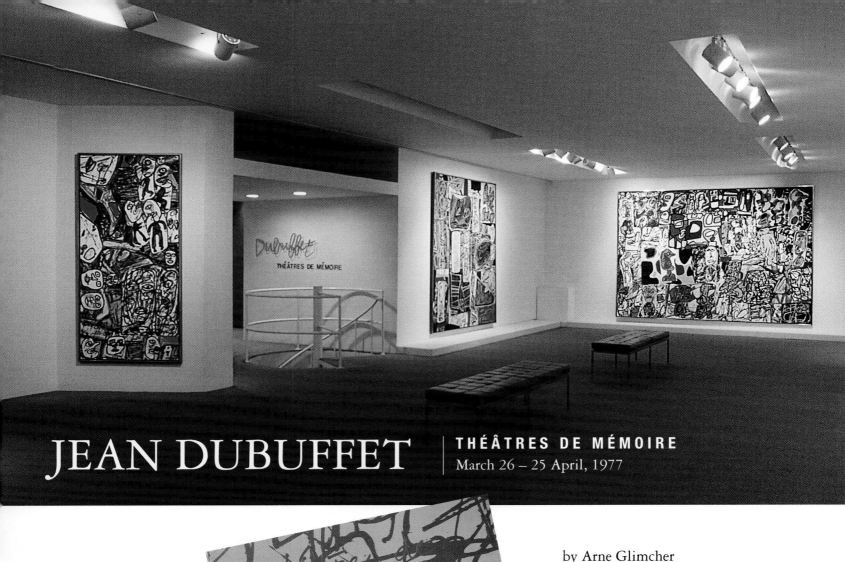

JEAN DUBUFFET | **THÉÂTRES DE MÉMOIRE**
March 26 – 25 April, 1977

Jean Dubuffet in his studio
Photo Kurt Wyss
Courtesy Foundation Dubuffet, Paris

by Arne Glimcher
Excerpt from Pace catalogue

During the early sixties, Dubuffet revealed the scaffolding upon which the fabric of the *Paris Circus* was hung. The opulent, luminous multi-layered surfaces were reduced to the flat, dry brush notes *(Rue de L'Entourloupe,* 1963) of which the *Circus* gouaches were nearly always constructed. The stenographic quality in the gouaches served as structural cartography for the canvases, as the paintings were exceptionally 'finished' in the context of Dubuffet's oeuvre. As the works became looser, the cellular structures, employed particularly in the portrayal of creatures within the *Paris Circus* paintings, were isolated, defined and separated from their environment by coursing black outlines. In turn, Dubuffet filled their interior chambers with red, white and blue stripes. These seed colonies, floating in their amniotic fluid *(Scène de Chasse,* 1962) proliferated into all-over linear networks. With the progression of the *Hourloupe* cycle, Dubuffet denounced the seductiveness of oil pigment for the immediacy of acrylic paints, allowing himself the spontaneity of single application picture making. Unlike the *Macadams, Portraits, Corps de Dames, Matériologies,* etc., in which the medium heightened the expressiveness of the formal arrangement; in the *Hourloupe,* and the works that follow, the pigment's role is to facilitate immediate notations and capture the path of the idea directly.

The artist's hand also grew increasingly less evident in favor of the instant perception of the signs in his new visual alphabet. It was with this language that Dubuffet constructed his most complete private universe, an option to consensus reality, in which he fulfilled his potential as sculptor (*Four Trees*), architect *(Villa Falbala)* and theatrical puppeteer *(Coucou Bazar)*. Within this cycle, paintings also left the confines of the easel to intrude upon and indeed to rival the space of the "real" world. In the *Praticables* and *Découpes*, the paintings were no longer rectilinear, but free form agitated panels that claimed space in the manner of objects, projecting from the wall.

Although the *Hourloupe* cycle is suggested within the Paris Circus, it is not necessarily the continuing legacy of the Paris Circus, but a tangent that might logically not have been taken. In 1974, after completing the lexicon of possibilities with the *Hourloupe*, it is as though Dubuffet returned to the fluid in which the *Hourloupe* cells originally floated and seized the other options not taken at that time. The decrystallization of the interlocking spatial structures of the *Hourloupe*, which reached their conclusion in the austere series, *Paysages Castillans, Sites Tricolores* of 1974, began with the illustration of Jacques Bern's book *"Le Flux Meme. . ."* In these images, the outline of the puzzle shapes that characterize *Hourloupe* are in evidence, but the obsessive interior patchwork has been replaced by random scribbles that neither express or define the forms, but rather deliberately act in chaotic opposition to them. A series of collage drawings entitled *Récits* followed and became the catalysts for the *Parachiffre* paintings of 1974 and 1975. The drawings are constructed of collaged shapes in the same manner as the collages of the *Hourloupe*, however, the process of making the paintings is quite different, indeed reversed. The page was first covered with layers of modulated color over which lines were scribbled or written, often applied directly from the tube, resulting in an overall pattern. Finally, the compound form was isolated (outlined) by painting-in the background field on which the image floats. The scrofulous ridges of the underpainting form crackling linear patterns in the background. . . .

The compulsive flood of paintings produced between 1974 and 1975 led Dubuffet out of eleven years of occupation by the *Hourloupe* and placed him at the juncture in 1962 when he opted for the *Hourloupe* rather than the *Théâtres de mémoire*. Reclaiming his territorial rights, Dubuffet is now continuing an evolution which circumvents and encapsulates the *Hourloupe* cycle, like an island, from the flow of his work.

The *Théâtres de mémoire* are an avalanche of experimentation. The formal structure of these enormous works is premonitory in the 1975 series of collage drawings, entitled *Conjectures*. The primary images are elements cut from the paintings of 1974 and 1975 and assembled into blizzards of discordant energy. Like the tapestry of memory, "The Theaters" are woven from multiple elements, sharing no relative size or stylistic consideration. Some are familiar, some the hybrids of compound associative images and yet others make their debut in Dubuffet's world. Elements cut from the *Parachiffres*, *Mondanités*, and *Lieu abrégés* were synthesized with additional pieces created

especially for the new works in progress. Typical of the process of his assemblages, Dubuffet works directly from the previously prepared materials making decisions with scissors and glue rather than from drawings. The works are composed on the studio floor, adding and subtracting successive layers until the nearly completed work is transferred to the wall. . . .

Resonating with the volatility of memory, the *Théâtres de mémoire* harbor figures both in and out of focus, sharply delineated, richly realized, and sketchy to the point of appearing unfinished. Recognizable symbols and amorphic images just out of reach of recognition exist tangential to one another. There is no central focus or fluid organization of the page and pictorial space abruptly changes from section to section. Changes in scale further confuse the spatial organization. All of the parts instigate activity or imply the potential for activity. None is passive. Figures are often cut out with borders surrounding their outline, encapsulating them in the deluge of activity. This device not only represents the integrity of the figure, but also of the element on which it has been glued. No interaction or figure/ground relationship is allowed to develop. Unlike the *Circus* whose chaos was unified by a recognizable geographical logic, the *Théâtres de mémoire* are a cornucopia of discordent images, sites and spores of new creations. Cars do not ride on streets, people do not exist within landscapes, but window shades float in space, staircases lead to nowhere. A camel (or is it a locomotive) floats in the sky and clouds displaced from the heavens are inserted in patches of earth. Dubuffet described the *tableaux d'assemblages* of 1956 as ". . . a kind of continuous universal soup with an intense flavor of life," and although the "theaters of memory" are formally very different, that description is applicable. . . .

The *Théâtres de mémoire* are gravid with ideas. The scatalogical juxtaposition of elements of incompatible size question the scale of memory stored images. Are the kernels of memory all miniaturized and filed in scale directly related to importance of surrounding events? Although the changes in scale appear random, they serve to designate centers of activity. Giants overlay landscapes populated by Lilliputians reminiscent of audiences miniaturized by the immense size of faces filling a cinema screen—audiences that unquestionably accept these colossi. But, an implication of scale based on hierarchy of importance would be in direct opposition to Dubuffet's philosophy in which he resuscitates discarded values to coexist equally with that which was previously reverential. . . . The question of scale is best approached like a natural phenomena. It is organized like the forces of nature organize and reorganize geology. Reminiscent of the diagrams in Natural Science museums describing the layers of the earth, the *Théâtres de mémoire* are a time line eroded through fossils trapped in successive layers of shale and shifted by earthquakes and volcanic eruptions until Paleolithic fossils are juxtaposed with current organic decomposition. They recall the past only to reveal the future and the revelations unearthed by each new excavation do not provide answers but rather raise questions.

Overleaf: Mêle moments, 1976
acrylic on paper mounted on canvas, 98 × 142"

169

CHUCK CLOSE | **RECENT WORK**
April 30 – 4 June, 1977

Chuck Close in his studio
Photos Heidi Faith Katz

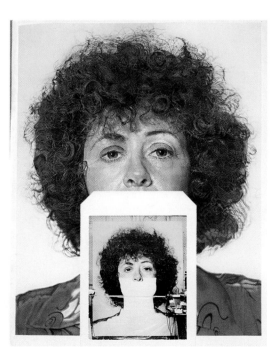

Catalogue cover

Linda, 1975–76
acrylic on linen, 9 × 7'

Still Life: Two Ceramic Oranges in New York, 1977
oil on canvas, two panels, 78 × 54" each

JIM DINE | NEW PAINTINGS
April 29 – 9 June, 1978

The Night Forces Painterliness to Show Itself in a Clearer Way, 1978
oil on canvas, 96 × 96"

The Still Life Painted on the Same Things and Then Varied and Then Married, 1977
oil on canvas, 3 × 12'

A Still Life with a Red Pepper as October Changes Our Valley, 1977
oil on canvas, 72 × 84"

Excerpt from Pace catalogue

"These are Annunciations—it's just an announcement. A frame of reference is usually something that's in my imagination. The painting becomes a completely different thing. . . .

I like the idea of subject matter in painting; I was really bored with painting as referring only to itself. The subject matter, my interpretation of the subject matter, made certain things happen; made it easier for me to make certain decisions. But in the end, I just want it to look like a good painting, without having any of these things attached to it. . . .

You paint a panel and it usually means something has to happen to the panel next to it, you have to make changes to that panel. See, you're always going back and forth. You're trying to figure out, to make a color brighter, bring the value up, take it down. On these, there are variations, but they are more within a constant framework. I'll put layer on layer of yellow, but in the process of working toward the yellow that

I want, the yellow also gets much more intense. You're building up the surface every time you build on the layer. It makes it more dense, because of the nature of the wax and the way the surface looks finally. See the difference between this one and that one. The surface loses a kind of crispness and it goes softer and waxier, the more paint you have. Richer. . . .

In the earlier painting, it's much looser, it's kind of overall field type of painting. Every mark eliminates another mark. But on these, it's drawn in a completely different manner, so you have these lines, but they tend not to be seen, it's not at all that evident. Very vertical free-hand drawing. I think it makes the space and the surface tension tighter. And that's what I'm after, either a real tension or a kind of— where the space opens up and it's soft, and then you go into it and it bounces back. Lately, I've been trying to get tension. And that has been the whole reason for the color getting more intense. . . ."

— B.M.

Conturbatio (Disquiet), 1978
oil paint and wax on canvas, 84 × 96"

MARK ROTHKO | **THE 1958–1959 MURALS**
October 23 – 3 December, 1978

Living across the street from Mark Rothko's studio on 69th Street, I visited him routinely. Louise Nevelson had introduced us and in time a friendship developed; Rothko allowed me to observe the development of his work over the period of our relationship. We often discussed the new art scene, which he held in great disdain. He loathed the celebrity that surrounded Pop art and disapproved of art as entertainment, a notion that was infiltrating the art world. For Mark, art was a serious endeavor, an expression of high tragic themes, transcendent, and ultimately sublime.

Rothko was clearly the greatest colorist of his generation, employing color itself to embody meaning. I asked him if Matisse had been his greatest influence, since he had titled one of his 1954 paintings Homage to Matisse. *He admired Matisse but told me that to see great color one must look at Bonnard. This response surprised me because Bonnard seemed out of sync with the time, too beautiful when toughness was the aesthetic currency. Rothko admonished me to forget about toughness and just look at Bonnard. I came to love Bonnard, the memory persisted and decades later I conceived the exhibition "Rothko and Bonnard: Color and Light," as a homage to Mark.*

On one of my studio visits to Mark, in the fall of 1969, he said that he wanted to sell a group of paintings for $500,000 and that if I could raise the money he wanted me to have them. Rothko was represented by the Marlborough Gallery but said that he was planning to sever that relationship and also withdraw from exhibiting his work in America. I believe it was a protest against the commercialization of the New York art scene but he agreed to a European exhibition at a suitable gallery. I called Ernst Beyeler in Basel and offered him half of the deal. Unfamiliar with the work or exactly who Rothko was, Beyeler agreed to come to New York and visit the studio. He was charming, Rothko liked him, and we agreed to Mark's average price of about $32,000 a painting. We were eager to select the works, but Rothko was tired and asked us to return the next day to make our selection. The next day, Mark answered the door, his eyes filled with tears, and he said it was out of his control, he wasn't free to sell the paintings. With no other explanation he closed the door. I never saw Mark Rothko again.

gram Building murals was presented to him. It absolutely supplied him with a whole new dimension. Now, I have a feeling we haven't talked nearly as much about that as we might; however, there was another area of concern that made this terribly important to him. For many years, he had the concept that his work must or should hang together in some manner that would create a permanent environment, fixed only by the work itself.

A.G. John Fischer's article refers to Rothko's reverence for the Laurentian Library as an environment, and William Scharf remembers that Rothko was fascinated that the Laurentian Library was dedicated to monastic scholarship.

D.R. I read that article, and he refers to an enclosed space where all the doors and windows are bricked up. I read that to mean exactly the same as many statements that Rothko made to me about his desire to control the environment and by controlling that environment he would give each of those pictures an added importance so that a symbiotic relationship developed between the pictures themselves, to the point that the entire environment in its particularity of each picture and its entirety of the many pictures together formed one experience.

A.G. This would allow Rothko to alter the perception of his paintings in general.

D.R. Yes, right, total to a part and the parts to a total, and the end achievement obviously was his great dream. Rothko would be able to place a person in an environment that he totally controlled and therefore this person could not help at least see the message. And by this, he would finally communicate. And this is why I wanted to go back and talk a little bit about his early involvement with mythology, which I believe continued throughout his entire life.

A.G. He always claimed a relationship to tragic themes.

D.R. Yes. He wanted to reach the deeper level in each human being, very much like Jung's writings—oddly enough, I never spoke directly to Mark about it, but you know he was a very widely read man and I'm sure that he knew Jung's writings quite accurately.

A.G. Fischer also recalled their visit to Naples after Pompeii, where Mark told Fischer that he felt a deep affinity between his own work and the murals in the House of Mystery. Fischer goes on to relate a story about his daughters in conversation with some Italian boys, telling them that Rothko was an artist. One of the girls said to Mark: "I told them you are an artist and they asked whether you came here to paint the Greek temples." "Tell them," he said, "that I have been painting Greek temples all of my life without knowing it. . . ." That's another example of his affinity with mythology.

D.R. Yes. And of course being a man very much of his time, he was enriched, or at least enlarged, by Jung and Freud. Now it will always be questioned in my mind as it is open to question in almost any painter's work, how much subject matter there is to be reached in the course of painting and how much of the subject matter is adjusted to fit the painting after the fact. It seems pretty clear or obvious to say that it's a little of both. Mark was always such a verbal man about his concerns, and he certainly offered verbal road maps of his way. I'm not sure about his identifying these particular paintings in a particular building like the Laurentian Library, I'm just not quite sure. Some of that association may have come later.

A.G. Fischer was not a part of the art world. He was a magazine editor and as such, there was no way he could have been aware of these associations without Mark having told him.

D.R. Oh, I'm sure Rothko did tell him. What I guess I'm trying to say is simply that I don't believe that these paintings are the result of Rothko's thinking only of that particular situation.

Coming home from work some months later, I noticed police cars and a crowd around Rothko's studio. I asked a cop what was going on, and he told me that the artist had committed suicide. Subsequently, I witnessed the contents of his studio being emptied into waiting trucks and I thought that an extraordinary chapter of my life—my relationship with Mark and his work—had ended.

Mark's daughter, Kate, on behalf of herself and her brother, filed a lawsuit against the Marlborough Gallery and the executors of the Rothko estate to reclaim her father's paintings, be reimbursed for the true value of the work, and for damages incurred. The executors, one of whom was a vice president at Marlborough, had sold the entire collection of Rothko's work to Marlborough for an average of $12,000 a painting with a long, interest-free payout. Reports of the trial appeared daily on the front page of The New York Times. *Other galleries were implicated and it was an embarrassing moment in the history of art dealing.*

The trial was going poorly for the Rothko children as Marlborough justified the low price per painting by claiming that no other gallery had been prepared to buy in quantity. They defended their price as a bulk discount. Gus Harrow, the assistant attorney general who was canvassing the galleries, came in and asked me if I had done any business with an artist named Mark Rothko. After relating the whole incident with Beyeler, he asked me to testify to refute Marlborough's claim that no one else would have purchased in bulk. I agreed to testify.

My decision to testify was met with hostility in the art world. Ralph Colin, a major collector, the president and founder of the Art Dealers Association of America, and a close friend of the Saidenbergs, whose gallery was implicated in the law suit—called and asked me not to testify. He argued that art dealers shouldn't testify against one another. But I felt that I had to testify in an effort to restore confidence in the industry.

Although I had been assured that my testimony would take no longer than two hours, I was subjected to two days of hostility from the defense lawyers, the scope of which I had never encountered. The first attack was designed to discredit me by accusing me of lying—they tried to prove that I had never been in Rothko's studio, which was preposterous. I was also accused of testifying in order to get the Rothko estate. One line of questioning asked me the value of Rothko's work in the early 1950s, mid-1950s, 1960s etc. After answering all the questions, the defense lawyer asked me my age at the dates in question. When I responded, he said, "Do you expect us to believe that you knew the value of

Rothko's work when you were in your teens and early twenties?" I countered with: "Don't you know legal precedents that were set long before you were born?" His attack had been so vicious that the spectators broke into applause and the judge threatened to clear the courtroom.

Ernst Beyeler came to corroborate my testimony. In his testimony, it was revealed that on the same trip during which we visited Rothko together, he had made a deal with Marlborough to buy some Rothko paintings, apparently covering all bases in the event that I did not consummate the deal with Rothko. He testified in a closed courtroom, so I learned about it in The New York Times.

Marlborough lost the trial, and Kate and her brother, Christopher, retrieved the paintings that Marlborough hadn't sold in what appeared to be bulk transactions to European collectors. Months passed and I received a call from Kate's lawyer, who was surprised that I hadn't contacted Kate about representing the Rothko estate. Kate was living in Baltimore and he said that every dealer in New York except me had been there making a pitch for the estate. I felt that in good conscience, my testimony excluded me from the competition, but he assured me that Kate wanted to see me. I had never met Kate before. She and her husband, Ilya, met me at the train, and we spent the afternoon together, developing an immediate rapport. After receiving approval from the surrogate court, The Pace Gallery be

Dan Rice Interviewed by Arne Glimcher
Excerpt from Pace catalogue

A.G. Was this the first time that you remember Rothko being involved with murals?

D.R. Yes, indeed, this project itself—that of murals contained in a particular space, in a public building—was very interesting to Rothko. He seized on the project with enthusiasm as though it were a release. The major difference that appeared in these paintings immediately and changed their character was that he simply turned the paintings on their side. This instantly made the separations between large areas much more positive, creating a much more positive role to the imagery. They became columns rather than a space separated horizontally.

A.G. Do you mean that they became less susceptible to landscape associations?

D.R. Yes. It refers back into the Surrealist period and to the complexity of his endeavors and concerns that were behind all of that labor, with its mythological associations. The one constancy throughout his painting life was the attempt to humanize painting. On the surface, it seems such an oddity that the work became more and more abstracted, off the course to the man on the street—less and less discernible.

A.G. No longer specific in its associations.

D.R. Exactly, yes, and leaving the figurative work and subsequently the Surrealist period meant for Rothko a reaching into a deeper level of communication. I believe he actually felt that he had gone as far as he could in painting until the proposal for the Sea-

A.G. Rothko's first set of paintings did not please him. He then made the set that we're showing, which gave him his concept for the last works. These are the intermediate paintings. I am not suggesting that these are a set of murals, because the last group was created as the final set of murals. But if you study the group and the relationship from painting to painting, they clearly deal with similar issues and create a dialogue.

D.R. There's no doubt about that at all. Rothko spent a good deal of time in experimentation with exact dimensions and combinations. While working on the exact mural series themselves he was very reflective, gathering all the paintings together again and jumbling them up. It would be very difficult to say that one was intended as a part of the murals and one was not. There were, even given the exact dimensions, three separate sets of murals, two of which were rejected, plus a lot of individual paintings that were done almost in exact terms. There was a lot of play about the end wall which gave him a lot of problems. You remember the situation, one end, the narrow end, was of glass. There was to be one long full wall with three large separate paintings. The further small end and then the long wall that involved the doors would have the three paintings going across the top. And it was the small end wall that gave him the most problems in the end and in which he did most of his real experimentation. He toyed with the idea of putting real color in the end wall because he thought quite definitely of these paintings—as he put it, no-color paintings— not dealing with color. He wanted to feel a spatial relationship that not only held the paintings together, but that was the declamatory statement. But not of color. This was an extreme break from his previous work, where color was the impact, and the nuance of paint application came later after the first impact with wonderful spatial play of positive, negative. . . .

D.R. He accepted the mural project because he realized the challenge that it offered him to build an environment. And this idea was further enhanced by the use that the room would be put to. He was terribly attracted to the original idea that the room could be seen as virtually a proscenium, or at least one long wall could be seen through the open doors from the cafeteria where the workers of the building ate. That to him was extremely important. This man was very engaged with sociological ideas. He used to tell me he went to jail a couple of times in political demonstrations, back in the 1930's.

Now that involvement was still very, very much in his thinking, even though not as literally apparent in his painting. It was still there as a part of his world and I dwell on it only because it became apparent when he was delighted that his paintings were going to be seen by these people, by the plebeians, as it were, and not just the board members or the executives, but by the workers. In this way, it would be raised as though on a proscenium. He was dismayed when the architectural changes came about and it was impossible for him to go through with the project. His refusal to let them have the murals hinged on this. One day, Mark told me that he was going to take Mell to dinner there and look the place over. I had arrived early in the studio the morning after and he came through the door like a bull, as only Rothko could, in an absolute rage. He said quite explosively—no good mornings or anything . . . slamming his hat down on the table and pounding, "Anybody who will eat that kind of food for those kind of prices will never look at a painting of mine." And that was it. Now at just what point of time after that he got around to telling them they couldn't have the murals, I really don't know, but his mind was clearly made up that night. . . .

Dan Rice was Rothko's assistant and they remained friends throughout Rothko's life.

Grids, You Say

by Rosalind Krauss

Excerpt from Pace catalogue

Grids?—you say—What is there to write or to read about grids? Hasn't everything been said already? Isn't it true that nowadays one must, in order to add anything at all, move into those equally arid spaces: the very academic or the very technical?—By which you point to the way that grids do not appear to be the suitable subject for discussion, seeming to be beyond—or is it above, or below?—discourse. Grids, we think, are inimical to the space of the page on which writing or reading takes place, because that page is one we can imaginatively inhabit. In their position as emblems of all that is quintessentially modern in art, grids are like that other symptom of modernity, the large city. As with the teeming metropolis, the grid is fine to visit—to look at (quickly)—but one wouldn't want to live there—in the sense that habitation, like reading, takes time.

Yet whether this gives us pleasure or pain, grids *are* the emblems of modernity, and so we must find a way of discussing them, of making their space and that of the page more available to one another. Here is one attempt.

When I was a teenager I saw a play called *Inherit the Wind*, a play that was intended, in theatrical parlance, as an actor's vehicle, for it staged the gladiatorial combat between two great figures, William Jennings Bryan and Clarence Darrow, as they clashed in a spectacle of oratory in the arena of the Scopes trial. From my place, sitting in the audience, I found the actors, going through their paces of declamatory vehemence or implacable determination, admirable; but I found the ostensible matter of the play completely bizarre. For between Darwin's theory of evolution and the biblical scene of Creation, as an explanation of how man arrived on this planet, there did not seem to be a serious choice. It was obvious to me that whatever role the story of Genesis had to play, in my or anyone else's spiritual life, it had to be highly symbolical. And from my adolescent perspective, this forced march of the spiritual into the realm of the purely fictitious did not strike me as much of a problem. So when the William Jennings Bryan character, exercised over the man-from-monkey issue to the point of heart-attack, thundered from his stretcher that we would "inherit the wind," I found it rather comic. There is, of course, a way to find it *seriously* comic—although I was too young to know that at the time. Nietzsche spoke of it this way when he wrote, "We wished to awaken the feeling of man's sovereignty by showing his divine birth: this path is now forbidden, since a monkey stands at the entrance."

But if the split between spirit and matter that was presided over by 19th Century science is what became the legitimate heritage of 20th Century schoolchildren, it is no less the heritage of 20th Century art. And the grid is its emblematic form.

There are two ways in which the grid functions to declare the modernity of modern art. One is spatial; the other is temporal. In the spatial sense, the grid states the absolute autonomy of the realm of art. Flattened, geometricized, ordered, it is anti-natural, anti-mimetic, anti-real. It is what art looks like when it turns its back on nature. In the flatness that results from its coordinates, the grid is the means of crowding out the dimensions of the real and replacing them with the lateral spread of a single surface. In the over-all regularity of its organization, it is the result not of imitation, but of aesthetic decree. Insofar as its order is that of pure relationship, the grid is a way of abrogating the claims of natural objects to have an order particular to themselves; the relationships in the aesthetic field are shown by the grid to be *sui generis* and, with respect to natural objects, to be both prior and final. The grid declares the space of art to be at once autonomous and autotelic.

In the temporal dimension, the grid is an emblem of modernity by being just that: the form that is ubiquitous in the art of *our* century, while appearing nowhere, nowhere at all, in the art of the last one. In that great set of chain reactions by which modernism was born out of the efforts of the 19th Century, one final shift resulted in breaking the chain. By "discovering" the grid, Cubism, De Stijl, Mondrian, Malevich . . . landed in a place that was out of reach of everything that went before. Which is to say, they landed in the present, and everything else was declared to be the past.

One has to travel a long way back into the history of art to find previous examples of grids. One has to go to the 15th and 16th Centuries, to treatises on perspective and to those exquisite studies by Uccello or Leonardo or Dürer, where the perspective lattice is inscribed on the depicted world as the armature of its organization. But perspective studies are not really early instances of grids. Perspective was, after all, the science of the real, not the mode of withdrawal from it. Perspective was the demonstration of the way reality and its representation could be mapped onto one another, the way the painted image and its real-world referent did in fact relate to one another—the first being a form of knowledge about the second. Everything about the grid opposes that relationship, cuts it off from the very beginning. Unlike perspective, the grid does not map the space of a room or a landscape or a group of figures onto the surface of a painting. Indeed, if it maps anything, it maps the surface of the painting itself. It is a transfer in which nothing changes place. The material qualities of the surface, we could say, are mapped onto the aesthetic dimensions of the same surface. And those two planes— the material and the aesthetic—are demonstrated to be the same plane: coextensive, and, through the abyssa and ordinates of the grid, coordinate. Considered in this way, the bottom line of the grid is a naked and determined materialism.

But if it is materialism that the grid would make us talk about—and there seems no other logical way to discuss it—that is not the way that artists have ever discussed it. Open any tract—*Plastic Art and Pure Plastic Art or The Non-Objective World*, for instance—and you will find that Mondrian and Malevich are not discussing canvas or pigment or graphite or any other form of matter. They are talking about Being or Mind or Spirit. From their point of view, the grid is a staircase to the Universal, and they are not interested in what happens below in the Concrete. Or, to take a more up-to-date example, we could think about Ad Reinhardt who, despite his repeated insistence that "Art is art," ended up by painting a series of black nine-square grids in which the motif that inescapably emerges is a Greek cross. And there is no painter in the West who can be unaware of the symbolic power of the cruciform shape and the Pandora's box of spiritual reference that is opened once you use it.

And this brings us back to Scopes and the monkey trial and William Jennings Bryan. For if that trial is a symbol of the absolute rift in the modern world between the sacred and the secular, then we might want to ask: on which side of that split did art come down? And the answer is: it's hard to say. Hard, not because we can't tell the one from the other, but because art seems to have decided for both. In the increasingly de-sacralized space of the 19th Century, art became the refuge for religious emotion; it became, as it has remained, a secular form of religion. Although this condition could be discussed openly in the late 19th Century, it is something that is inadmissible in the 20th, so that by now we find it indescribably embarrassing to mention "art" and "spirit" in the same sentence.

And the peculiar power of the grid, its extraordinary long life in the specialized space of modern art, arises from its potential to preside over this shame: to mask and to reveal it at one and the same time. In the cultist space of modern art, the grid serves not only as emblem but also as myth. For like all myths, it deals with paradox or contradiction not by dissolving the paradox or resolving the contradiction, but by covering them over so that they seem (but only seem) to go away. The grid's mythic power is that it makes us able to think we are deal-

RIDS

th Century Art
Krauss

/ 10022
9, 1979

te
44308

second printing

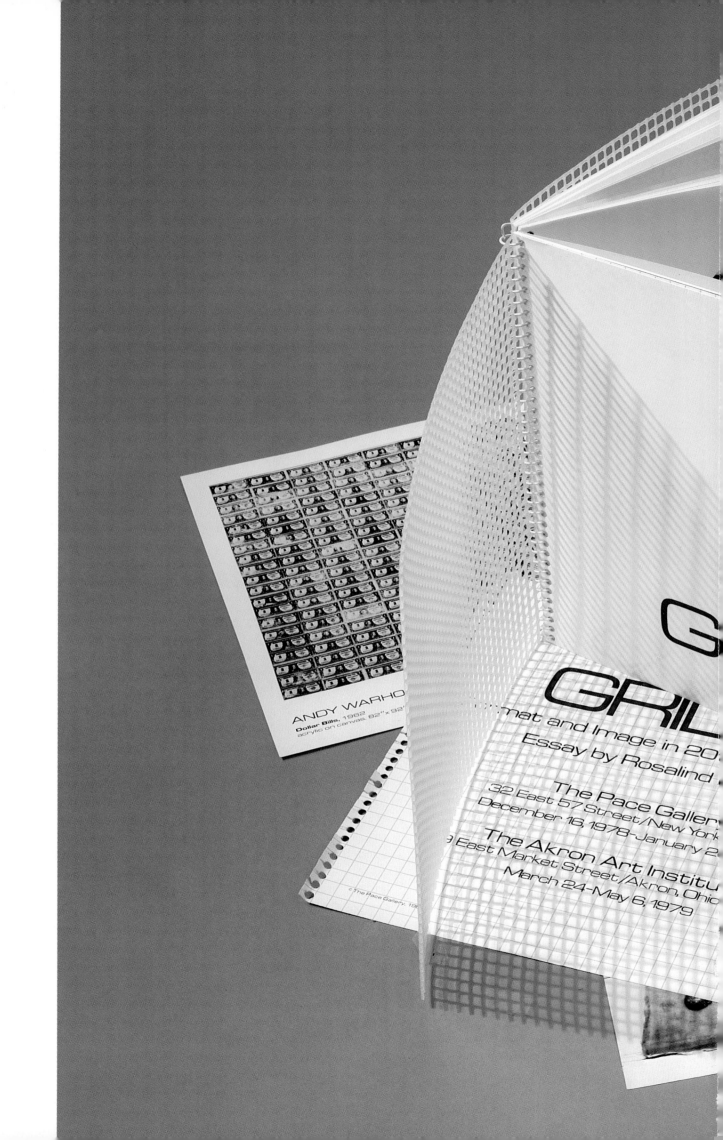

Top: Reinhardt, Mondrian, Johns, Samaras, Reinhardt
Bottom: Stella, Andre, Lichtenstein

In my continuing research for the book Modern Art and Modern Science, *I investigated the grid, the most dominant aesthetic organizing device of the twentieth century. In the process, I conceived and organized the exhibition "Grids," and invited Rosalind Krauss to write the catalogue. It would later become an important part of her work in* The Originality of the Avant-Garde, *published in 1981.*

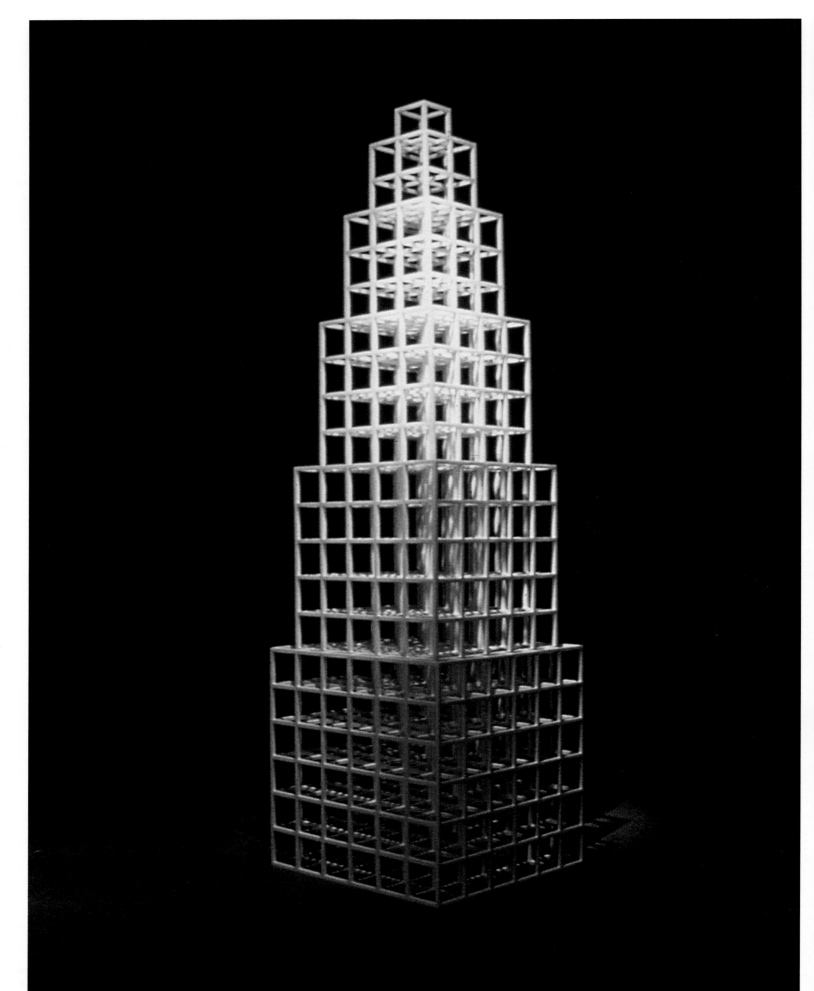

Sol LeWitt, *1 2 3 4 5 6*, 1979
white paint on birch, base 29 × 29"
99¼" high overall

ing with materialism (or sometimes science, or logic) while at the same time it provides us with a release into belief (or illusion, or fiction). The work of Reinhardt or Agnes Martin would be instances of this power. And one of the important sources of this power is the way the grid is, as I have said before, so stridently modern to look at, seeming to have left no place of refuge, no room on the face of it, for vestiges of the 19th Century to hide. . . .

The grid appears in Symbolist art in the form of windows, the material presence of their pains expressed by the geometrical intervention of the window's mullions. The Symbolist interest in windows clearly reaches back to the early 19th Century, and Romanticism.[1] But in the hands of the Symbolist painters and poets, this image is turned in an explicitly modernist direction. For the window is experienced as simultaneously transparent and opaque.

As a transparent vehicle, the window is that which admits light—or Spirit—into the initial darkness of the room. Yet if glass transmits, it also

reflects. And so the window is experienced by the Symbolist as a mirror as well—something that freezes and locks the self into the space of its own reduplicated being. Flowing and freezing; *glace* in French means glass, mirror and ice: transparency, opacity and water. In the associative system of Symbolist thought this liquidity points in two directions. First, towards the flow of birth—the amniotic fluid, the "source"—but then, towards the freezing into stasis or death—the sterile immobility of the mirror. For Mallarmé, particularly, the window functioned as this complex, polysemic sign by which he could also project the "crystallization of reality into art."[2] Mallarmé's *Les Fenêtres* dates from 1863; Redon's most evocative window, *Le Jour*, appeared in 1891 in the volume *Songes*.

If the window is this matrix of ambi- or multi-valence, and the bars of the windows—the grid—are what help us to see, to focus on, this matrix, they are themselves the symbol of the Symbolist work of art. They function as the multi-level representative through which the work of art can allude, and even reconstitute, the forms of Being.

I do not think it is an exaggeration to say that behind every 20th Century grid, there lies—like a trauma that must be repressed—a Symbolist window parading in the guise of a treatise on optics. Once we realize this, we can also understand that in 20th Century art there are "grids" even where we do not expect to find them—in the art of Matisse, for example (his *Windows*), which only admits openly to the grid in the final stages of the *papier découpés*.

Because of its bivalent structure (and history) the grid is fully, even cheerfully, schizophrenic. I have witnessed and participated in arguments about whether the grid portends the centrifugal or centripetal existence of the work of art.[3] Logically speaking, the grid extends, in all directions, to infinity. Any boundaries imposed upon it by a given painting or sculpture, can only be seen—according to this logic—as arbitrary. By virtue of the grid, the given work of art is presented as a mere fragment, a tiny piece arbitrarily cropped from an infinitely larger fabric. Thus the grid opperates from the work of art outward, compelling our acknowledgement of a world beyond the frame. This is the centrifugal reading. The cetripetal one works, naturally enough, from the outer limits of the aesthetic object inward. . . .

Because the centrifugal argument posits the theoretical continuity of the work of art with the world, it can support many different ways of using the grid—ranging from purely abstract statements of this continuity to projects which order aspects of "reality"—that reality itself conceived more or less abstractly. Thus at the more abstract end of this spectrum we find explorations of the perceptual field (an aspect of Agnes Martin's or Larry Poons's use of the grid), or of phonic interactions (the grids of Patrick Ireland), and as we move towards the less abstract we find statements about the infinite expansion of man-made sign systems (the numbers and alphabets of Jasper Johns). Moving further in the direction of the concrete, we find work that organizes "reality" by means of photographic integers

(Warhol and, in a different manner, Chuck Close) as well as work that is, in part, a meditation on architectural space (Louise Nevelson or Lucas Samaras, for example). At this point the three-dimensional grid (now, a lattice) is understood as a theoretical model of architectural space in general, some small piece of which can be given material form, and at the opposite poles of this kind of thinking we find the decorative projects of Frank Lloyd Wright and the work of De Stijl practitioners like Rietveld or Vantongerloo. (Sol LeWitt's modules and lattices are a later manifestation of this position.). . .

In discussing the operation and character of the grid within the general field of modern art I have had recourse to words like "repression" and "schizophrenia." Since these terms are being applied to a cultural phenomenon and not to individuals, they are obviously not intended in their literal, clinical sense, but only analogically: to compare the structure of one thing to the structure of another. The terms of this analogy were clear, I hope, from the discussion of the parallel structures and functions of both grids and myths.

But one further aspect of this analogy still needs to be brought out; and that is the way in which this psychological terminology functions at some distance from that of *history*. What I mean is that we speak of the aetiology of a psychological condition, not the history of it. History, as we normally use it, implies the connection of events through time, a sense of inevitable change as we move from one event to the next, and the cumulative effect of change which is itself qualitative, so that we tend to view history as *developmental*. Aetiology is not developmental. It is rather an investigation into the conditions necessary for one specific change—the acquisition of disease—to take place. In that sense aetiology is more like looking into the background of a chemical experiment, by asking when and how a given group of elements came together to effect a new compound or to precipitate something out of a liquid. With the aetiology of neuroses, we may take a "history" of the individual, to explore what went into the formation of the neurotic structure; but once the neurosis is formed, we are specifically enjoined from thinking in terms of "development," and instead we speak of repetition.

With regard to the advent of the grid in 20th Century art, there is, it seems to me, the need to think aetiologically rather than historically. Certain conditions combined to precipitate the grid into a position of aesthetic pre-eminence. We can speak of what those things are and how they came together throughout the 19th Century, and then spot the moment of chemical combination, so to speak, in the early decades of the 20th. But once the grid appears it seems, I would submit, quite resistant to change. The mature careers of Mondrian or Albers are examples of this. No one would characterize the course of decade after decade of their later work as developmental. But by depriving their world of development, one is obviously not depriving it of quality. There is no necessary connection between good art and change, no matter how conditioned we may be to think that there is. Indeed, as we have a more and more extended experience of the grid, we have discovered that one of the most

modernist things about it is its capacity to serve as a paradigm or model for the anti-developmental, the anti-narrative, the anti-historical.

This has occurred in the temporal as well as the visual arts—in music, for example, and in dance. It is no surprise then, that as we contemplate this subject, there should have been announced for next season a performance project based on the combined efforts of Phil Glass, Lucinda Childs and Sol LeWitt: music dance and sculpture, projected as the mutually accessible space of the grid.

1. See, Lorenz Eitner, "The Open Window and the Storm-Tossed Boat; an Essay in the Iconography of Romanticism," *Art Bulletin*, XXXVII, December 1955, pp. 281–90.
2. Robert G. Cohn, "Mallarmé's Windows," *Yale French Studies*, no. 54, 1977, pp. 23–31.
3. This literature is far too extensive to be cited here; a resentative and excellent example of this discussion is, John Elderfield, "Grids," *Artforum*, X, May 1972, pp. 52–59.

Roy Lichtenstein,
Three Views of the Rouen Cathedral, 1968
oil and magna on canvas, three panels, 63 × 42" each
© Estate of Roy Lichtenstein

5 ACTION PAINTERS OF THE 50s

DE KOONING, KLINE, KRASNER, MOTHERWELL, POLLOCK

September 21 – 13 October, 1979

During the late 60s and into the 70s, with Pop, Op, Minimal, and Conceptual art dominating the New York art scene, interest in Abstract Expressionism, which had brought American art onto the world stage, was declining. Incredulity was the reaction in 1973, when the Australian National Gallery paid $2,000,000 for Pollock's Blue Poles. Late 1979 was a perfect moment to reexamine the protean members of this illustrious group. Among the paintings in the exhibition were Composition No. 19 and Ritual, by Pollock; Spike's Folly I and Woman, 1953, by de Kooning; Yellow Square, by Kline; and Iberia #2, by Motherwell. We republished Harold Rosenberg's classic piece, "The American Action Painters," which also had been neglected since its publication in the December 1952 issue of Art News.

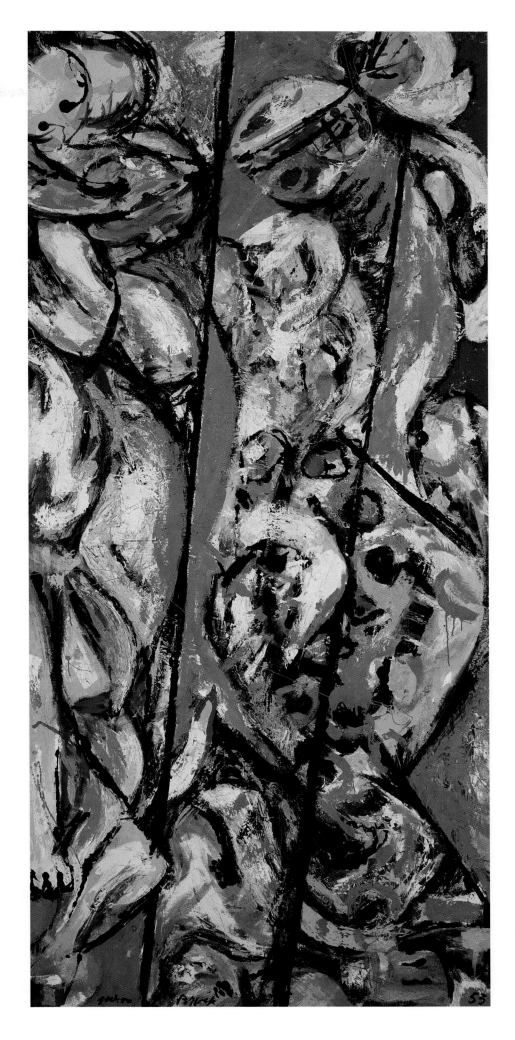

Jackson Pollock, *Ritual*, 1953
oil on canvas, 90½ × 42½"
©2001 Pollock-Krasner Foundation/Artists
Rights Society (ARS), New York

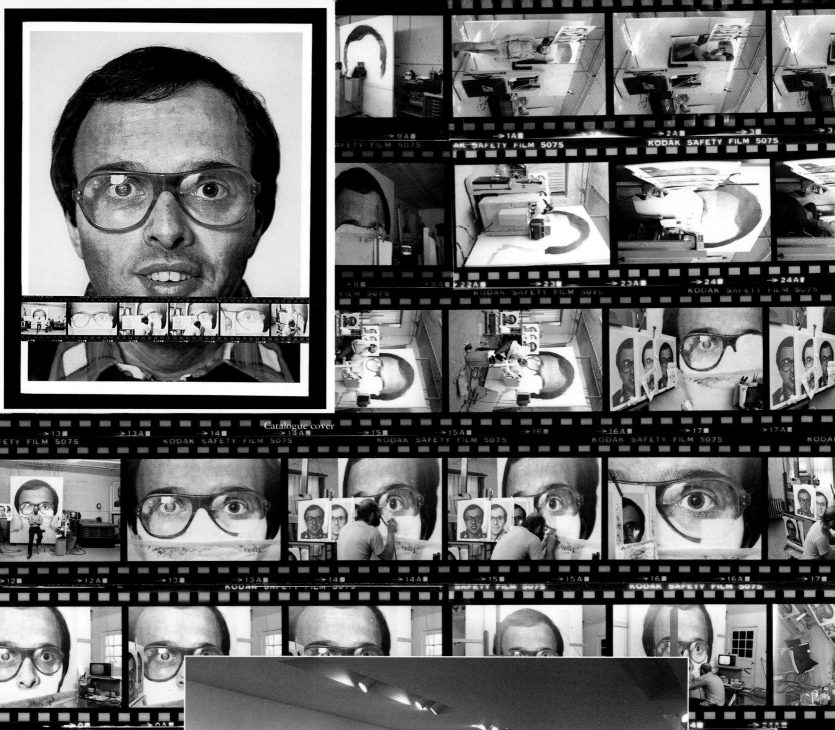

Catalogue cover

CHUCK CLOSE | **RECENT WORK**
October 27 – 24 November, 1979

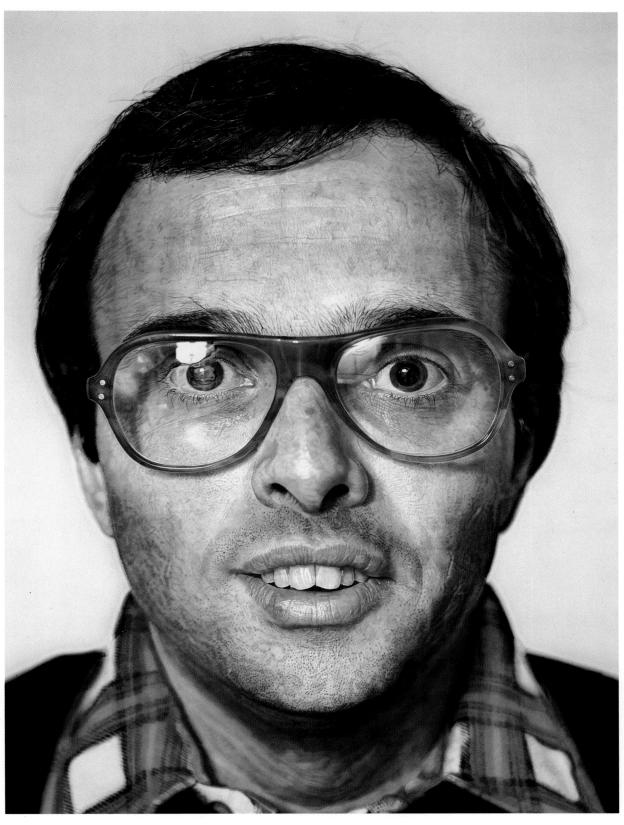

Mark, 1979
acrylic on canvas, 9 × 7'

Catalogue cover

Barbara Rose interviews Lucas Samaras
Excerpt from Pace catalogue

B.R. What started you making the new fabric reconstructions?

L.S. I had a cousin in Greece who had a dress shop. I would go there in the afternoon and I would cut up some paper. But, if I went to touch the fabric, she would say, "now watch it, don't touch the fabric. We're making dresses." She always had other girls around that she taught the business. When I became an adult, or semi-adult, I began using things like pins and wool, and nobody could tell me anymore, don't use them, don't touch them. Even using fabric, in a sense is going back to childhood again and saying, listen, I can cut the fabric, don't bother me. I had the fabrics around, and then I begun cutting them up and sewing them. But, when you take fabrics and you start sewing them, you or I or somebody begins to say, what are you doing? If you're going to make a painting, take some brushes and make a painting. So, you begin to find some kind of justification for what you're doing. The justification either comes from your personal life or else you try to find some historical precedent, or you say this has to be done this way, because I see it that way. The needles are another part of my biography. You see, my father was a furrier. His job was to buy small pieces of fur, sew them into a square plate, wet it, and then nail it to a wooden board until it dried. The hammering and the nails were part of the beauty of that business.

B.R. The colors you use are always the same, but I don't understand where they come from, or how you keep finding them.

L.S. There are expensive colors and there are cheap colors. I think I use cheap colors. It comes from my background. And, they're colors that really didn't exist in this form in art history. When I went to the Metropolitan and to the Modern, I would look around and say, okay, let's see what kind of colors they are. I'd look at the Mondrians, for example, but by the fifties, they had become chic. Well I wouldn't want to use chic colors. These colors come from the five and ten. They also come from my mother's apartment. Let's say, my mother had lousy taste. But, it was wonderful, lousy taste. It was a lousy taste that I could then take and make into grand art. Color or 'chroma' always meant treasure to me as a child. Many of my relatives used to go to different countries for trade. They would take furs there and bring back some kind of silk or satin, sometimes they came at night, on horses with bundles and valises, they would open a suitcase and out would come this wonderful little satin thing or glittering thing with gold and green and blue and perfume. I mean, that was a treasure! I was bedazzled.

Reconstruction #59, 1979
sewn fabrics, 67½ × 92½"

ISAMU NOGUCHI | 75TH BIRTHDAY EXHIBITION
February 16 – 15 March, 1980

by Sam Hunter
Excerpt from Pace catalogue

When Isamu Noguchi was preparing the titles for the sculptures in his concurrent shows at the Emmerich and Pace galleries, he first decided on the rubric *Going Backwards in Three Parts* for one of his pieces. It is an intriguing ensemble of three nubbly, ingenuously shaped boulders which seem to be momentarily arrested from rolling in tandem along a plane. One could readily understand their implied movement to be backward, or in reverse of the accustomed left to right flow, but that notion, which the title supports, also bore unwelcome retrospective associations for the artist. Noguchi substituted the less equivocal title, *Three Linear Pieces*, which now appears in the catalogue. He has always taken an ambivalent view of his relationship to his own past, and to modernist traditions. Even as he acknowledges a continuity with that past in his choice of materials and methods in these new exhibitions, he chooses to avoid the negative inference of looking backwards in time. Today he is once again pursuing the dualities that have long marked his style—renewing an old romance with stone and with *taille directe* methods, but finding fresh avenues of expression in a group of more spontaneous and improvisatory creations made over

> **ISAMU NOGUCHI**
>
> 75TH BIRTHDAY EXHIBITION
>
> 16 FEBRUARY – 15 MARCH 1980
>
> ANDRE EMMERICH GALLERY
>
> 41 EAST 57 STREET, NEW YORK
>
> AND THE PACE GALLERY
>
> 32 EAST 57 STREET, NEW YORK

the past two years. These casually marked, carved, split, and recombined boulders in granite and basalt demonstrate a free and playful spirit entirely unprejudiced by his past achievement in large-scale, formal works designed for public spaces.

Although Noguchi has in his fifty-year career designed gardens, bridges and memorials, created dance and theater sets, and even furniture, and worked in a wide range of sculpture mediums of bronze, aluminum, ceramic, balsa wood and paper, stone has always most deeply engaged him. He is obsessed by his profound, almost evangelical faith in the efficacy of stone, and the host of historical associations that surround direct carving. Stone symbolizes his root life experience, and remains the stable center in shifting currents and vicissitudes of his complex artistic development. . . .

. . . Noguchi is a sculptor who prides himself on eluding hard and fast definitions. If we insist on his Eastern identity, he grows abstract and Western before our eyes; his rationalism in the use of modern materials and Constructivist design only conceals an equally convincing irrational and playful invention. He is an impressive shaper of public environments, and large, isolated sculp-

Binary Practice, 1978
aji granite, two elements, 5½ × 8½ × 6"
and 7¼ × 10 × 9"

Mortal Remains, 1978
basalt, 6½ × 6 × 11"

tures of technical finesse even as he disarms us with his more crude and intimate studio sculptures. The exhibitions with their juxtaposition of sculptural strategies provide fresh insight into one of the most arresting and paradoxical yet consistent artistic personalities of our time. . . .

The current landscape tables are quite varied in their topography, and even in their choice of stone. They range from the soft, feminine, curving mounds in warm pink travertine of *Double Red Mountain* to the severity of the dominant black granite slabs. *Knife in the Rock* evokes the gestural brushstroke of Sumi painting in its single, elongated wave of stone, set on a uniform field of polished granite. The most recent creation, *Radiant Squares*, rotates a rounded cube on its plinth, out of parallel conformation, to give tension to the figure-field opposition in a manner not unlike the helical pylon in Noguchi's most majestic outdoor public space, the Dodge Fountain and Plaza recently completed in Detroit. It is interesting to note that the refinement of his surfaces is countered by the simple blocky slabs with their sides left unfinished, and the grooved channels of the coring tools still visible. . . .

Typically, however, Noguchi resists the distinction between the natural order of stone, casually presented in all its brute expressiveness, and his more artful and finished surfaces. Indeed, the glory of the small new stones is their capacity to revise our notion of just how we are to understand the idea of coarseness, or of an anti-esthetic extremism. They open our eyes to new approaches to the sculptural entity as a scarcely mediated natural object, and lower the threshold of collaboration between artist and nature. By minimal invasions of the pristine stone, taken as it is quarried or found, Noguchi's own presence in the work stops short of a conventional piece of gallery sculpture, judged by current standards of completeness. His process esthetic and the unobtrusiveness of his own interventions in the new pieces link them in many ways to the work of Carl Andre and Robert Morris, which utilizes nature's forms in their preexisting state. Traditional elements rooted in Japanese culture persist in the work, however, and set it apart from an international vernacular of process art. Noguchi's stones can be animistic, and are invariably highly personal and expressive: they also refer to archetypes that may be found in the rock selection of the classical Japanese garden. . . .

8 PAINTERS OF THE 60s

SELECTIONS FROM THE COLLECTION OF BURTON AND EMILY TREMAINE

March 28 – 26 April, 1980

"Eight Painters of the Sixties" should have been entitled "Selections from the Collection of Emily and Burton Tremaine." The Tremaines had donated a group of seventy minor works to the National Gallery in Washington in the process of refining their collection. Peter Ludwig, the German chocolate manufacturer, in addition to his many other collections, ranging from medieval manuscripts to modern paintings, had amassed a great collection of Pop art which he wanted to crown with Jasper Johns' Three Flags *of 1958. Emily Tremaine was rankled by the fact that the works she gave the National Gallery remained in storage and were never shown, but in truth, few warranted exhibition, and were only accepted in the hopes that the National Gallery might become the recipient of the Tremaines' more major holdings. Emily was sure that the museum didn't exhibit them because they hadn't had to pay for them. She felt that the appreciation and exhibition of art could be directly correlated to its value and more directly to the price that the museum paid. The Tremaines were among my biggest clients, and we had become good friends. I began to realize that her logic was a justification for selling one of her greatest paintings for a record price. I saw the Johns painting inching ever closer to the Ludwig Collection, leaving New York for Germany.*

I argued with the Tremaines that this quintessential American painting must stay in New York in the only museum of American art, the Whitney. Emily agreed that if a spectacular price could be achieved, she would sell it to the Whitney. I called my friend Leonard Lauder (then the Vice President of the Whitney) and suggested that the painting could be acquired for $1,000,000. I believe that no work by a living artist had ever achieved that sum and with the exception of the posthumous sale of Pollock's Blue Poles *to the Australian National Gallery, no other American painting had been sold for $1,000,000. Leonard Lauder shared my enthusiasm and put together the Gilman Foundation, the Lauder Foundation, Alfred A. Taubman, and an anonymous donor, together each funding twenty-five percent to make the purchase. The Tremaines agreed to sell the painting, for which they had paid Johns nine hundred dollars. The acquisition made the front page of the* New York Times, *and along with the sale of* Blue Poles, *changed the market for American art.*

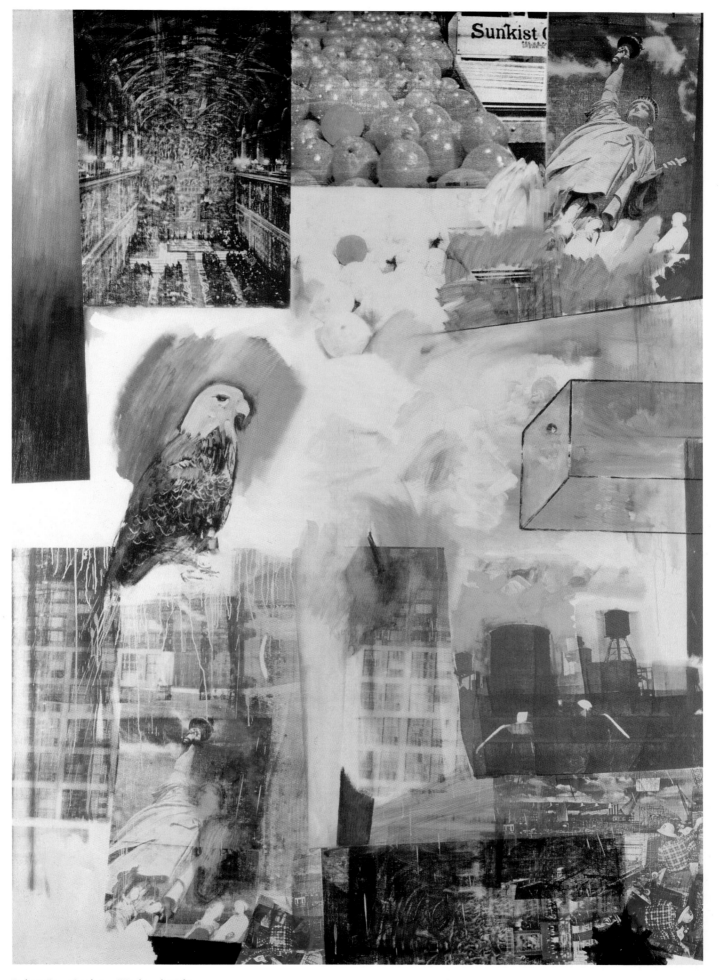

Robert Rauschenberg, *Windward,* 1963
oil on canvas, 96 × 70"
Collection Foundation Beyeler, Riehen/Basel
© Untitled Press, Inc./Licensed by VAGA, New York

205

Roy Lichtenstein, *Femme au Chapeau*, 1962
magna on canvas, 68 × 56"
© Estate of Roy Lichtenstein

The New York Times, Saturday, September 27, 1980

Painting by Jasper Johns Sold for Million, a Record

by Grace Glueck

The Whitney Museum of American Art has paid $1 million for a painting by Jasper Johns, believed to be the highest price ever for the work of a living artist. The 1958 painting, a famous precursor of the Pop Art movement, is "Three Flags." It was sold by the Pace Gallery of New York, acting as agent for Mr. and Mrs. Burton Tremaine of Meriden, Conn., who bought the painting in 1959 from the Leo Castelli Gallery for $900 plus a $15 delivery charge. The artist will not share in the proceeds from the sale.

The painting, which measures roughly 30 by 45 inches, is a triple image of the American flag, painted on three successively smaller canvases, one superimposed on another.

It was hailed yesterday by Tom Armstrong, director of the Whitney, as "without doubt a monument of 20th-century art, a unique statement emerging from the dominance of Abstract Expressionism. Through it and subsequent work the artist has had an influence on the course of art history."

The Whitney had been trying to acquire the work, which appeared in the Jasper Johns retrospective mounted by the museum in 1977–78, for five years, he added, and had made "a very special effort" to get it in conjunction with its current 50th anniversary celebration. . . money to buy "Three Flags" had come from four donors—Mr. and Mrs. Leonard A. Lauder, Mr. and Mrs. Charles Gilman Jr., A. Alfred Taubman, a Detroit businessman, and a member of the Whitney's National Committee, and another National Committee member who asked to remain anonymous.

As far as can be determined, the price surpasses that paid for the work of any artist during his lifetime, a record that Mr. Johns appears to have sustained for sometime. In 1977, another Johns painting, "According to What" (1966) was sold to a collector for a reported $600,000. In 1972, Mr. Johns's "Double White Map" set an auction record for the work of a living American artist—$240,000 at a sale of works belonging to Ethel and Robert Scull.

The record price for a work by a 20th-century American artist, living or dead, is believed to be the $2 million paid in 1973 by the Australian National Gallery of Canberra for Jackson Pollock's "Blue Poles."

Reached by telephone at his house in Stony Point, N.Y., Mr. Johns said he felt "nothing other than amusement" at the price of the painting, for which the Castelli Gallery had paid him $600 in 1959. "I was brought up in the Depression," the fifty-year-old artist said, "and $1 million is a very important figure to one who grew up at that time. But of course, it has nothing to do with painting."

. . .The Tremaine collection, from which the work was sold, is known as one of the outstanding holdings of contemporary art in the United States. Its range is from Cubism through Abstract Expressionism to the works of Pop and Minimal artists, including such names as Picasso, Léger, Mondrian, Rothko, Pollock, Frank Stella, and Lucas Samaras. The Tremaines also own several other works by Mr. Johns.

Until recently, the couple had indicated that their collection of Pop Art plus pre-Pop works by Mr. Johns and Robert Rauschenberg would go to a museum. The National Gallery of Art in Washington, to which they had over the years given a significant number of works, had seemed the most likely candidate.

But they have sold works from the group over the last few years, and last year, 10 paintings, most of them for sale, were shown at the Pace Gallery. From the Pace exhibition, held in conjunction with Leo Castelli, Andy Warhol's diptych "Marilyn" was bought by the Tate Gallery of London for $300,000. The Tremaines were not available for comment.

The artist has been represented by Leo Castelli since 1957, the year Mr. Castelli opened his Gallery in New York. Mr. Johns's first one-man show was held at the gallery in 1958, and Mr. Castelli recalls that he received "Three Flags" from Mr. Johns shortly after that. "In 1959, the Tremaines saw it, and bought it, as they'd bought other Johnses from me," he said. "The price was $1,000, less 10 percent, plus a $15 delivery charge. I must have been poor—I wouldn't make such a charge today."

Recently, he had heard rumors of "Three Flags" being for sale at $1 million, Mr. Castelli said, and in calling Mrs. Tremaine on another matter, told her he had a client for the painting: "She said she would let me know. This week she called to ask me for Jasper's number, and I again inquired about the painting. She said it had been sold. My life blood has been my relationship with Jasper and his paintings—and it has been a faithful, loyal relationship. My selling the work was a matter of principle, not a commercial thing."

Arnold Glimcher, president of the Pace Gallery, said yesterday that he had sold "many paintings to and for the Tremaines over the years," and that the sale of "Three Flags" was his idea. "The Johns work was one of the most important paintings they owned, and this summer in discussing the sale of other works, I urged that it be placed during their lifetime, so they'd know where it was. I suggested the Whitney because it's the quintessential American painting—a masterpiece that speaks of Johns, American painting and the Pop movement. Then I went to the Whitney. Tom Armstrong was exited by the idea, and made its acquisition a priority."

Mr. Armstrong said "Three Flags" would be exhibited temporarily in the museum's lobby gallery Oct. 14–19 and would go on permanent view in a new installation of the permanent collection next year.

"All the News That's Fit to Print"

The New York Times

LATE CITY EDITION
Weather: Mostly sunny today; mostly fair tonight. Partly sunny tomorrow. Temperature range: today 50-66; yesterday 53-72. Details are on page 39.

VOL.CXXX...No. 44,719   Copyright © 1980 The New York Times   NEW YORK, SATURDAY, SEPTEMBER 27, 1980   Events beyond 50 mile zone from New York City. Higher in air delivery cities.   25 CENTS

65¢ FARE CONSIDERED IN TALKS ON COPING WITH SUBWAY CRIME

MORE TRANSIT POLICE SOUGHT

Koch Plans to Meet With Ravitch — Mayor Is Loath to Commit New City Funds to Force

By DAVID A. ANDELMAN

Senior City Hall and transit officials have agreed that New York needs more transit police officers, and Mayor Koch and the agency's chairman will meet shortly to discuss a possible 5-cent fare increase to 65 cents to pay for them.

Mayor Koch said yesterday that he was "prepared to discuss" the issue with Richard Ravitch, chairman of the Metropolitan Transportation Authority. Mr. Ravitch has already held a series of discussions on the matter with other senior City Hall officials.

The city has always assumed all costs of the transit police, and Mr. Koch said that he was reluctant to commit any new city funds to the transit police force while the city's Police Department and other municipal agencies were seriously understaffed.

Solutions Proposed

The principal obstacles to any increase in the transit police force are financial and logistical. To resolve the problems, M.T.A. officials said they were considering the fare increase, economies in other areas of the transit system and the creation of a separate Civil Service list for the transit police designed to avert court challenges on racial imbalance.

On Sept. 19, the M.T.A. board ordered Mr. Ravitch to meet with the Mayor to discuss the problem of subway crime.

Since then Mr. Ravitch has discussed the problem with Deputy Mayor Robert F. Wagner Jr. and Ronay Menschel, the Mayor's executive assistant, both of whom are also members of the M.T.A. board.

The 5-cent fare increase "is a very interesting idea that could be part of the answer," Mr. Wagner said yesterday.

Force Now at 2,895

Most major subway crime categories have increased 70 percent this summer over last summer. Yet the city has cut back the transit police budget from $112 million last year to $107 million—an even larger cutback in real terms when considering police salary increases and other inflationary costs.

Several issues remain unresolved.

It must be determined how many officers can be absorbed by the Transit Police Department. At its peak in 1975, the Transit Police Department had a force of 3,750. Cutbacks and attrition have reduced the force to 2,895, and some officials are said to hope to return the force to its size before the budget cutbacks began.

The increase of the transit fare to 65

Continued on Page 16, Column 1

A Coast Guard cutter towing boats back to Key West, Fla., from Cuba.

Havana Government Unilaterally Cuts Off Refugee Boat Exodus

By STEVEN R. WEISMAN

WASHINGTON, Sept. 26 — The boatlift that has brought 125,000 refugees from Cuba to the United States has been officially ended by the Cuban Government, Federal officials reported today.

White House and State Department officials said that the Havana Government had ordered all remaining boats in the port of Mariel, Cuba, to return to the United States without refugees. American officials said the Cuban action was unilateral and that President Carter had learned of it only after the Coast Guard received word from boat captains returning from Cuba today.

"We had reason to believe there would be such a unilateral action," said Jack H. Watson Jr., the White House chief of staff. "We did not know that it would occur until in fact it did occur."

In an interview, Mr. Watson said the move by Cuba had followed "discussions between representatives of the Cuban Government and representatives of the United States Government" for a period of time. But there had been "no quid pro

Continued on Page 6, Column 2

IRAQ HALTS EXPORTS OF ITS OIL AS RESULT OF DAMAGE BY IRAN

Other Members of OPEC Reported Deferring Plan to Cut Output by an Average of 10%

By ROBERT D. HERSHEY Jr.
Special to The New York Times

WASHINGTON, Sept. 26 — Iraq announced today that it was suspending all exports of oil because it had none to ship.

Iraq, the second-largest exporter in the Organization of Petroleum Exporting Countries after Saudi Arabia, normally ships 3.3 million barrels a day. It told its customers it was declaring force majeure, a legal position under which a party may be excused from a contract because of an unexpected, disruptive event beyond its control. Its oil facilities were apparently badly damaged in the undeclared war with Iran.

As a result of the plunge in shipments from both Iran and Iraq, other OPEC members have deferred tentative plans to cut their production by an average of 10 percent, Britain's Energy Secretary, David Howell, said in Washington.

Blow to Developing Nations

Oil analysts say the drop in oil shipments will be far more difficult for the developing countries, which lack storage facilities, than for the industrialized nations, which have stockpiles. [Page 29.]

There were also reports from Europe that the president of the Venezuelan Congress had pledged that the other OPEC nations would, in fact, step up production to offset the shortfall from their warring partners. A Venezuelan official here, however, said after telephoning Caracas that he could not confirm this plan. "Right now, there is no need for an increase in production," he added.

As a result of Iraq's cutoff, its oil will stop flowing through two overland pipelines to the Mediterranean. These routes remained open after shipments through the Persian Gulf were halted earlier this week, an action that had slashed Iraq's oil shipments by roughly two-thirds.

The Iraqi action prompted France, one of its biggest customers, to bid aggressively for oil in the spot market, where

Continued on Page 39, Column 1

Top Carter Aides, in Policy Shift, Back Higher Plutonium Output

By RICHARD BURT
Special to The New York Times

WASHINGTON, Sept. 26 — In a significant policy shift, senior Carter Administration aides have approved a proposal for increasing United States production of plutonium for use in nuclear weapons.

The agreement in principle by high-ranking national security and foreign policy aides to expand the production of plutonium and other bomb-grade materials at Government nuclear plants was reached at a White House meeting yesterday, Administration officials said. Mr. Carter must now decide how and when it would be done, they said. They said the decision was made after Defense Department officials contended that stockpiles of plutonium might not be sufficient to produce the new nuclear weapons for the 1980's that had been approved by President Carter.

Officials said yesterday's decision meant that plutonium production in the nation would rise for the first time since the early 1960's, when the Government began closing some nuclear weapons plants.

Move Could Deflect G.O.P. Attack

Republicans on Capitol Hill have accused the White House over the last year of neglecting the potential gap in plutonium production, and Administration officials said the decision to increase production could help deflect criticism of Mr. Carter's record in the Presidential campaign.

Both the House and Senate agreed this summer to authorize funds for restarting plutonium production in Government nuclear reactors shut down in the 1960's.

At the same time, however, State De-

Continued on Page 9, Column 3

INSIDE

Bomb Kills 10 at Oktoberfest
A bomb exploded near an exit at the Oktoberfest in Munich, West Germany, as crowds were leaving, killing 10 people and injuring 115 others. Page 3.

Carey to Back Sydenham Move
Governor Carey said he would help the Harlem community with an application to keep Sydenham Hospital open as a full health service facility. Page 25.

An Iraqi soldier near burning oil tanks, part of the complex at Basra.

Shortages and Inefficiencies Plague Industrial Base of the U.S. Military

By WINSTON WILLIAMS

The problem of aging and inefficient industrial plants, which has cost American industry much of its competitive advantage in the world marketplace, is affecting defense-related factories as well, raising deep concern about the nation's ability to respond quickly to a military emergency.

In many ways, the deterioration of the military's industrial base has exceeded the decline in the economy's commercial sector, military experts say. And, they say, because of recurring shortages of materials and skilled manpower in critical trades, military production is facing what some call limited "surge capability" — the ability to gear up production quickly.

How much slack exists in the military production system has become a highly charged political issue as Congress seeks to increase military budgets and Republicans adhere to the military-spending plank in their party platform. But this year's recession has freed enough production capacity to take some of the urgency out of the situation.

"I'm afraid that this time when we push down on the old gas pedal, that

Defense:
Is the U.S. Prepared?
Last of seven articles.

powerful eight-cylinder response we've always received may not be there," said Gen. Alton D. Slay of the Air Force Systems Command.

The military's industrial base is made up of more than 25,000 manufacturers and materials suppliers, plus Government facilities like munitions shops, shipyards

Continued on Page 7, Column 1

IRAQIS INTENSIFYING SHELLING OF ABADAN; REFINERY IN FLAMES

LOSS A SERIOUS BLOW TO IRAN

Baghdad Forces Are Also Driving to Occupy Khurramshahr Port After 'Premature' Claims

By HENRY TANNER
Special to The New York Times

BEIRUT, Lebanon, Sept. 26 — Iraqi troops besieging Iran's oil refinery city of Abadan today set fires raging from one end of the facility to the other with heavy artillery attacks.

Iraqi forces also pressed their assault on the nearby oil port of Khurramshahr, and Baghdad conceded it was "premature" yesterday in announcing its capture. Iran said the defenders were fighting from behind barricades on streets and roofs, and a Reuters dispatch from Teheran, the Iranian capital, said most of the port city's 150,000 inhabitants had fled.

The refinery at Abadan, one of the world's largest, had reportedly been closed since it was first attacked by Iraqi gunners on Tuesday. Today, for the first time, Western correspondents arriving on the Iraqi side of the Shatt al Arab, the disputed waterway between the two countries on which both sides have oil facilities, were able to describe the pounding that Abadan was taking.

The visitors said they could see shells bursting among refinery installations and storage tanks, setting new fires that added to the huge pall of smoke hanging over the city. [Page 4.]

Iranians Firing on Iraqi Sites

Iraq contended that Abadan was about to fall, a statement derided by Iran, which said that only part of the refinery had been put out of commission. The reporters on the Iraqi side of the Shatt al Arab said Iranian gunners, in return, were pounding Iraqi installations.

[Iranian Air Force jets attacked Baghdad early Saturday, Reuters reported from the Iraqi capital. The sound of antiaircraft fire could be heard when the jets attacked the city at about 4 A.M., the report said.]

The increased fighting in the Shatt al Arab area occurred as representatives of Islamic nations decided at the United Nations to send a mission to Iraq and Iran in an effort to end the hostilities. Iraq said it would receive the mission, but the Teheran radio quoted Prime Minister Mohammed Ali Rajai as saying Iran would not accept mediation, although anyone could inspect war damage. Iran's President, Abolhassan Bani-Sadr had requested Islamic intervention. [Page 4.]

Continued Iranian resistance at both Khurramshahr and Abadan added to a growing impression among diplomatic analysts here and in Baghdad that the Iraqis had run into stiffer Iranian resistance than they had expected.

They noted that the Iraqi drive appeared to be slowing down after initial successes earlier in the week, and they speculated that the Iraqi leadership wanted to complete the capture of Khur-

Continued on Page 4, Column 4

Israeli Police Summon Top Official For Inquiry Into Alleged Kickbacks

Special to The New York Times

TEL AVIV, Sept. 26 — The Minister for Religious Affairs, Aharon Abuhazira, has been summoned for police questioning in a case that could threaten Prime Minister Menachem Begin's already tenuous majority in Parliament.

He is to be asked about incidents in the ministry since he assumed office in 1977 and in the town of Ramle while he was its mayor. While officials would reveal no details of the investigation, newspaper reports have said the police were looking into alleged kickbacks from ministerial appropriations to religious schools and bribery in the municipal elections in Ramle, 12 miles southeast of here. The newspaper reports have mentioned grants to nonexistent schools, schools with fictitious enrollments and institutions headed by people close to Mr. Abuhazira.

Three Years of Crises

The affair has already embarrassed the Government, but Mr. Begin, who has survived one crisis after another during his three years in office, is expected to weather this one.

The National Religious Party, Mr. Abuhazira's power base, has stated its continued confidence in him and its belief in his innocence. The party's 12 seats give Mr. Begin's coalition 63 seats in the 120-seat Parliament.

However, the party has not staked its future in the Government on Mr. Abuhazira. For example, if the question of parliamentary immunity for him is

raised, a party leader said, members would be allowed to vote as they pleased. Voting in Parliament on the lifting of immunity is by secret ballot.

Mr. Abuhazira's lawyer, Michael Caspi, said today that he would confer on Sunday with Attorney General Yitzhak Zamir and announce on Monday whether

Continued on Page 5, Column 3

Banks Raise Prime Rate; Stock Market Prices Fall

The nation's major banks, placing the blame on their own higher costs for borrowed money, raised their prime lending rate yesterday to 13 percent, from 12½ percent. The increase sent the prime, the rate charged by banks to their best corporate customers, to its highest level since mid-June.

The Federal Reserve announced that the nation's basic money supply took an unexpected jump of $2.7 billion in the week ended Sept. 17. In moves aimed at discouraging excessive and inflationary growth in money supply, the Federal Reserve has tightened its credit policy on several fronts.

This upward spiral in interest rates, coupled with tensions arising from the hostilities between Iraq and Iran, sent stock prices plunging. The Dow Jones industrial average fell nearly 16 points, to 946.10, marking the biggest drop in almost six weeks. Page 29.

Painting by Jasper Johns Sold for Million, a Record

By GRACE GLUECK

The Whitney Museum of American Art has paid $1 million for a painting by Jasper Johns, believed to be the highest price ever for the work of a living artist. The 1958 painting, a famous precursor of the Pop Art movement, is "Three Flags." It was sold by the Pace Gallery of New York, acting as agent for Mr. and Mrs. Burton Tremaine of Meriden, Conn., who

bought the painting in 1959 from the Leo Castelli Gallery for $900 plus a $15 delivery charge. The artist will not share in the proceeds from the sale.

The painting, which measures roughly 30 by 45 inches, is a triple image of the American flag, painted on three successively smaller canvases, one superimposed on another.

It was hailed yesterday by Tom Armstrong, director of the Whitney, as "without doubt a monument of 20th-century art, a unique statement emerging from

the dominance of Abstract Expressionism. Through it and subsequent work the artist has had an influence on the course of art history."

The Whitney had been trying to acquire the work, which appeared in the Jasper Johns retrospective mounted by the museum in 1977-78, for five years, he added, and had made "a very special effort" to get it in conjunction with its current 50th anniversary celebration. Without con-

Continued on Page 12, Column 1

"Three Flags," by Jasper Johns, sold yesterday for $1 million.

LOUISE NEVELSON

MAQUETTES IN STEEL AND RELATED WORKS

May 2 – 28 June, 1980

The deluxe edition of the catalogue for this double exhibition which took place at The Pace Gallery and Wildenstein Gallery, New York, included a hand-made box which contained the catalogue and a cassette of a conversation recorded especially for this occasion between Nevelson and Barbaralee Diamonstein.

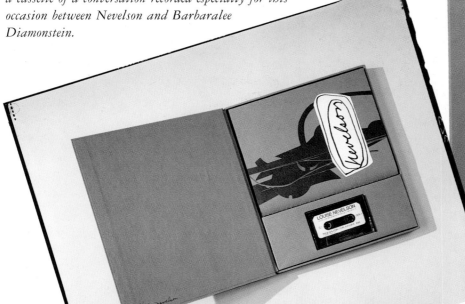

Exhibition catalogue

Excerpts from a conversation with Barbaralee Diamonstein

B.L.D.D. What is the most important thing we should know about your work? Is it a sense of a shadow and light, the mystery, the metaphor, a sense of primitive ritual?

L.N. I think in the end that when one communicates with it, that one should not seek anything, but does it please you? You know it's somehow a love affair, too. Does it please you? Does it gladden you? Now, a lot of people say why do you use black? And, they identify black with death. Now I think it's the Chinese that identify white with death.

B.L.D.D. Why *do* you use black?

L.N. Well, I have claimed that it's the most aristocratic color in the world. Plus, it is not black. Nothing is black. Nothing is one color. There are so many shadows and shades in it that are so subtle that it isn't quite black. But we, for a definition, for a label, call it black. It is very aristocratic. You can take almost anything and once it's black it has another meaning.

B.L.D.D. You've used the materials around you and freed them from their previous associations to make your new creations. Perhaps we should begin at the beginning, and that is, when and how did you get to wood as a medium?

GRIL

...nat and Image in 20...

Essay by Rosalind ...

The Pace Galler...
32 East 57 Street/New York...
December 16, 1978-January 2...

The Akron Art Institu...
3 East Market Street/Akron, Ohio
March 24-May 6, 1979

©The Pace Gallery, 19...

ANDY WARHO...
Dollar Bills, 1962. 82" x 92"...
acrylic on canvas...

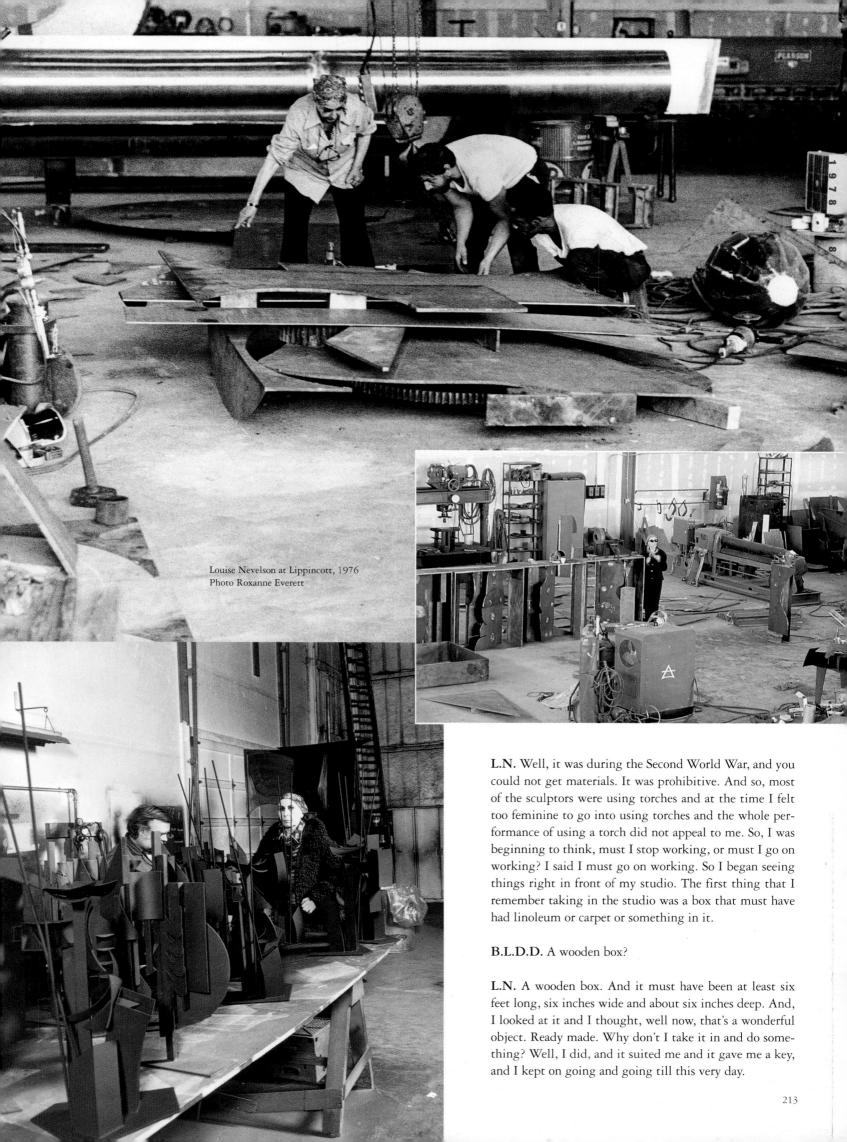

Louise Nevelson at Lippincott, 1976
Photo Roxanne Everett

L.N. Well, it was during the Second World War, and you could not get materials. It was prohibitive. And so, most of the sculptors were using torches and at the time I felt too feminine to go into using torches and the whole performance of using a torch did not appeal to me. So, I was beginning to think, must I stop working, or must I go on working? I said I must go on working. So I began seeing things right in front of my studio. The first thing that I remember taking in the studio was a box that must have had linoleum or carpet or something in it.

B.L.D.D. A wooden box?

L.N. A wooden box. And it must have been at least six feet long, six inches wide and about six inches deep. And, I looked at it and I thought, well now, that's a wonderful object. Ready made. Why don't I take it in and do something? Well, I did, and it suited me and it gave me a key, and I kept on going and going till this very day.

213

B.L.D.D. Could you describe the evolution of your best known form, wooden painted constructions?

L.N. Yes. Now, let's begin from what I have just said about that box. I never wanted to make sculpture. I didn't want to make anything like that. I felt that my great search was for myself, the inner being of myself and that was the best way I knew to project how I was feeling about everything in the world. Consequently, it wasn't that I made anything for anybody. Now, we call it "work" and I don't like to call it work at all. It really is a projection of an awareness, a consciousness. People don't understand that when you project from yourself you are really at the height of your awareness, and that means you're at your best. So I have never moved from the awareness. Now, another thing, for

example, I've never used a yardstick, because I realize that if I stopped to measure a thing my mind would be cut off from a creative living activity. So I'd rather move on to an end and then leave it at that. . . .

B.L.D.D. You have worked in wood, in metal, in paper, in plastics, in terra cotta, in a range of materials. I liken your work on the one hand to an architect, on the other to a collagist. Would you agree with either of those two descriptions?

L.N. I would okay both of them. Yes, it's true. . . . First, we humans walk vertical. Then at night we go to sleep horizontal. Every human being wants a home. It may be a palace, or it may by a hut; it's a home. And so it's as close to us as our skin, you

know. It's necessary to have a home. And so I have always been not only fascinated, but I feel somehow that the laws in my body relate to the laws of architecture, and vice versa. . . .

L.N. If I were writing an essay myself about my work, I would say variations on a theme. . . . [and] that goes right back to what I have said about consciousness and the projection, you see? My awareness is the theme, because you should be able to read the signature in any medium. Now, since I'm a collagist, I've got to tell you this. About a year and a half ago I had a couple of weeks in between going up to Lippincott's to do sculpture and I decided that I hadn't done etchings for some time and I thought, well, I'll go and do an edition or two of etchings. And I decided I didn't want to touch them with a pencil or draw on them or anything. And since I've used laces all my life in my work, that I would use the laces and not touch it. Well, that was quite something. You had to know the weights of the laces and the color of the laces, and then when you put your laces down, you weighed them kind of. And it's in reverse. So you

have to think what you're doing and also what you have done. Well, I got so fascinated that I stayed a year and got about thirty-six editions. Now, if anyone had come to me and given me the world, I wouldn't have stopped. . . .

B.L.D.D. Are shadow and space the most important elements in your work?

L.N. Well, I think so. I think shadow—for me it's a remarkable thing to say—but a shadow to me seems more solid that the object it is a shadow of. Isn't that funny? It's very important. That's where the mystery is, you see. And it's wonderful. That chair isn't so hot. But look at what's around it. It gives you a whole thing, really. I think that shadow, probably, I would put as the supreme thing. It gives you a better definition and it gives you a fourth dimension. . .

Recorded on January 23, 1980, in New York City

Barbaralee Diamonstein is a writer and Chair, Historic Landmarks Preservation Center.

BRICE MARDEN | NEW PAINTINGS AND DRAWINGS
September 29 – 25 October, 1980

Recent Paintings
by Peter Schjeldahl
Excerpt from Pace catalogue

. . . The technique of Dubuffet's recent collage-paintings—including his current series, *Brefs exercises d'école journalière*—is simple, but its formal workings are very complex. He makes a huge variety of abstract patterns in acrylic on paper, cuts them up and glues the pieces in a kind of irregular quilt. . . . Just how disjunctive the quilted field of these pictures is can be appreciated by imagining them without the figurative images that are applied last, like stamps on a package. Without the figures, the fields would be totally chaotic. There is something essential here, I think, about the peculiar feeling that Dubuffet gives us—a feeling of joy in our humanity that might seem strange in being occasioned by human images so distorted, crazy, isolated and oppressed. The esthetic fact is that only by their presence is the abstract dynamic of the field organized and made expressive. The field seems, in fact, to have been made as wild as possible so that its taming by the images may be as dramatic as possible: coherence is withheld in order to arrive at the end all at once, with a bang. One might regard this as a "trick," and in a way it is—a trick grounded in the artificial nature of painting. There is no miracle in the fact that it works, only in the existence of an artist who should have such an authentic and, above all, such an encouraging use for it. To concentrate overmuch on Dubuffet's formal achievement would be like reading a love letter for its spelling. . . .

Only by process of projection and association, not as an art lover but as a person, can one make ultimate sense of Dubuffet's pictures. This is not the same as saying that they are "literary," a dread epithet that he eludes as neatly as he does "merely decorative." Early on, Dubuffet confronted the implications of using figurative imagery in quasi-narrative ways and decided that what it involved, for him, was not an illustrative process but a faithful medium for the reality of the mind, a "language" alternative to verbal language. In his Chicago lecture, he declared that "painting, especially much better than words, allows one to express the various stages of thought, including the deeper levels, the underground stages of mental processes." Obviously he would reject the implication, once widespread, that there is something inherently more basic and original about abstraction than about figuration. And indeed, is it possible, in introspection, to find a *level* of the imagination—not just as a peculiar state of mind—that does not entail some sort of visual imagery? Art for Dubuffet is a question of truth to experience, including the largest one—that of being human. . . .

For all his ferocious rejection of School of Paris tradition, Dubuffet profited from the way in which that tradition normalized the occupation of the modern artist, making possible the sublimely ironic pose of the artist as an ordinary person doing an ordinary job—a kind of bricklayer of the marvelous. Dubuffet never had to heft the burden of existential seriousness, the do-or-die ethos of the Abstract Expressionists, who were obliged to create in a cultural vacuum and to be heroes or nothing. Thus his figures have never had to declare a meaning, a relation to any particular content or to any iconographic tradition. (One is of course free to make any linkages one pleases, but these must be tentative and partial, because the figures are, above all, emblems of the inarticulate.) Dubuffet's figures have no rational reference and no "inner life." Their cartoony eyes, even in fullface, are always abstracted, averted or otherwise oriented to a space other than the literal space of the painting and the psychological space of the viewer. They never meet the viewer's gaze. . . .

My own most informative encounter with Dubuffet's work was the installation, in 1975, of his *Milord la chamarre (Milord of the Fancy Vest)* on the Seagram Plaza in New York. Everyone knows the wonderful group of *Four Trees* at the Chase Manhattan Plaza near Wall Street, but for me the *Milord*, a 24-foot sculpture of polished steel petals painted with a wriggling network of thick black lines, was even better—in fact quite the most successful installation of modern public sculpture I've ever seen. (This is perhaps not as large a compliment as it ought to be.) As its analogue to the patterned or crusted field of a Dubuffet painting, the sculpture had nothing less than the Seagram Building, that masterpiece and talisman of modernist architecture. By being figurative and kinesthetically charming, the insouciant, deracinated *Milord* held scale in its surround as no abstract or formally self-contained sculpture could. (Are we ready yet to face the fact that abstract sculpture has failed as public art?) And by appealing to levels and states of mind suppressed in the ambience of the neighborhood, it made common cause with sheer human vitality beyond architecture, beyond politics and sociology and even beyond art. In my mind's eyes I can still

JEAN DUBUFFET

BREFS EXERCISES D'ÉCOLE JOURNALIÈRE

October 31 – 29 November, 1980

see it standing there, indomitably alive amid that bleak grandeur, and this memory has never ceased to make me happy. . . .

The separation of art from life that is enforced by modernism—and dialectically reinforced by avant-garde attempts to bridge it—is simply ignored by Dubuffet. It is in no elevated or especially acute frame of mind that we best enjoy his work, but just as ourselves, full of the anxieties with which our world invests selfhood. These anxieties become the rhythm of our response, inflected with anger or glee. To imagine this, think of a crippled person with a bad limp, distressing to watch. Gradually, as one watches, the limp is subtly transformed, becoming articulated, purposeful, inspired—a dance! The person is dancing! For the surprising consolation of such moments we are inclined to thank and salute Dubuffet, and to leave him, at age 79, where he has always been, in mid-career.

Voyage en auto, October 15, 1979
acrylic on paper mounted on canvas, 32 × 35¾"

LUCAS SAMARAS

SITTINGS 8 × 10
December 15 – 10 January, 1981

by Carter Ratcliff
Excerpt from Pace catalogue

Are the bodies in these photographs naked or are they nude? I think they're naked—stripped down or, in the case of a priestly-looking man who has kept his eyeglasses, defrocked. Sometimes nakedness glows, blue-green or greenishly red, through a veil of style. Toward the middle of the series a woman appears, calmly seated, her chin tilted up. It's useful for a moment to say she looks Classical. The next moment, she takes on a Courbetian sensuality, thanks to her fullness which is also a variety of sleekness, even slimness. Then there's Egon Schiele. His tortured style is not directly to the point (Samaras has no interest in it), yet auras drift from Schiele's Viennese sensibility to hang like a fog of a familiar unease between us and some of these bodies. Others, seem touched by the Pre-Raphaelite obsession with virginity. Yet even these innocent bodies are naked, not nude, because, after all they evoke an esthetic of Victorian sensuality despite themselves. . . .

. . . Nakedness is Samaras's subject, here and now, just as it always been. In his *Photo-Transformation*, he mapped myriad new lines of human evolution, then traveled them alone, the sole and endlessly mutated survivor of life in the dangerous atmosphere of his art. Naked skin often blistered and peeled away to show naked innards. His talismanic objects, from boxes to chairs, put symbols of obsessive emotion on ostentatious display. And his insistent, sometimes hideous patterns of pins, razor blades, colored yarn and cut paper symbolize *physical* feelings—sensations, not emotions; naked pain, as often as not, but sometimes pleasure.

Certain of Samaras's forms generate odd, suspended states somewhere between physical numbness and sheerly spiritual horror. Samaras has evoked death—his own, never ours. An ultra-Expressionist, a narcissist so extreme he has filtered with the look of his own corpse, Samaras has given himself over, at last, to narcissism's ultimate demand: acknowledgement of the other. During the two years or so which were required to make this latest series of photographs, the artist has led several dozen people to stage center in his art. Samaras remains visible, off to the side. He doesn't look diffident, exactly, but he never competes with any of his star attractions. Once in a while, he even covers his eyes. . . .

The narcissist requires, in his self-absorption, the constant attendance of other selves. They must look, look again, be magnetized. Only then is the narcissist sure he exists with suitable authority. His gaze at himself is only the summary of ours. When we look at images of Samaras's self, we create

him—I mean, we ratify his self-creation. If we were to look away, his vision would fall into a void. And when we join in his rituals of self-absorption, we re-enact our own. . .

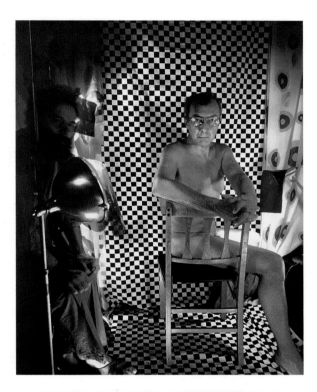

All photos *Sittings 8 × 10*, polaroid photograph, 8 × 10"

221

Homme et femme, 8/17/71
oil on canvas, 76¾ × 51"
©2001 Estate of Pablo Picasso/Artists Rights Society (ARS), New York

PABLO PICASSO | THE AVIGNON PAINTINGS
January 30 – 4 March, 1981

Claude Picasso and I had been casual friends for many years. He lived in New York, working as a very skilled photographer and became a regular at art world parties. After the death of his father and the subsequent success of the law suit that he brought against the French government—which resulted in the recognition of Paloma, Maia and himself as legal heirs—we met again at a party in East Hampton at the home of Linda and Sandy Lindenbaum. Our relationship renewed, we began spending time together in Paris and Claude showed me transparencies from his extraordinary archive of most of the works in the estate. I was most intrigued by the sketchbooks. Even in the few pages of each one that I saw, I recognized new revelations about the process of Picasso's work, as well as previously unknown drawings of great consequence. It was agreed that I would act as agent for Claude, Paloma, and Bernard (Picasso's grandson by Paulo) in presenting a major exhibition from the estate.

The Museum of Modern Art had just presented Bill Rubin's great Picasso retrospective of 1980, and I wanted to make an exhibition that wouldn't seem inconsequential by comparison. What fascinates me about representing the estates of historically significant artists is the challenge of revealing unknown or little-considered aspects of the work, allowing for a new or more complex evaluation and sometimes a reappraisal of their careers. I proposed an exhibition of Picasso's sketchbooks, to be accompanied by a publication that would catalogue most of the other notebooks in the possession of most of Picasso's heirs, as well as others in Claude's archive of notebooks in the estate. The book would be a valuable document.

I began research for the project in 1980 and soon realized that it was such an immense undertaking that I would be unable to present the exhibition for five or six years. Another body of work cursorily represented in the MoMA retrospective was the very late work, shown by Picasso in 1973 at the Palais des Papes in Avignon. The exhibition, mounted in a kind of nineteenth-century Salon style, was Picasso's last great gift. He covered the walls, double and triple hung, with all of the unedited and unframed canvases painted between 1969 and 1972. Critically catastrophic, the exhibition was received as the senile ramblings of a once great painter—as messy and imprecise as the tragedy of old age.

In truth, Picasso was in total control of his powers of precision, as the parallel series of drawings he made in the same years attests. They are confident, precise, heavily worked over or sparsely incisive, and suggested that Picasso had separated skeletal structure (seen in the drawings) from the fleshy volumes that dominated the paintings. In Picasso's paintings, color usually functions as an embellishment of line, but in the Avignon paintings line is practically nonexistent; interdependent broad ponds of paint construct the painting. Furthermore, I knew that the Avignon paintings had already inspired a generation of artists in the seventies, artists as diverse as Julian Schnabel and Georg Baselitz. In the late paintings, Picasso had come full circle as the legatee of the art he influenced from the mid-forties to the early fifties. If de Kooning's post-Cubist images of women, as well as the structure of his landscape abstractions, were influenced by Picasso, Picasso was fulfilling his own legacy in painting and brushwork that looked very much like de Kooning. These were paintings that needed to be shown and reevaluated. I was able to organize a major exhibition in a relatively short period of time since the works, so maligned during Picasso's lifetime, were still largely held by the estate.

Against the advice of my scholar friends and with the full support of my artist friends and Claude, Paloma, and Bernard, we mounted an exhibition of late paintings, which I designated the "Avignon Paintings." It sold out before the exhibition opened to the accolades of the critics. John Richardson graciously told me that the exhibition changed his mind about the late work and in 1988 he wrote the catalogue for the "Late Picasso" exhibition at the Musée National d'Art Moderne and the Tate Gallery. As a result of our exhibition, a series of museums presented shows of late Picasso, including the Guggenheim, and the paintings were celebrated and accepted a dozen years after they were first shown at Avignon.

Baiser, 10/24/69
oil on canvas, 38 × 51"
©2001 Estate of Pablo Picasso/Artists Rights
Society (ARS), New York

Picasso: The Artist In His Studio
by James R. Mellow
Excerpt from Pace catalogue

Nothing can be done without solitude. I've created my own solitude which nobody suspects.

. . .The period about which we know least concerning Picasso's very public private life is the final period when the artist was living in seclusion, first at his Chateau de Vauvenargues near Aix-en-Provence, then at his villa, Notre-Dame-de-Vie in Mougins. Shut off form the world, no longer willing to squander his time on social or business engagements, Picasso was presumably devoting himself to his art. Much has been made of this reclusive period when friends, family, critics, curators and former-hangers-on, were excluded from his company, left to cool their heels at the entrance-gates. Enemies might claim that he was the victim of over-protection by his young wife—(he had married Jacqueline Roque in 1961)—but we know enough of Picasso's character to know that he frequently used others as a convenient blind for achieving his own ends.

A few fortunate individuals managed to break through the isolation barriers that surrounded the artist in his last years—such as William Rubin, Director of Painting and Sculpture at the Museum of Modern Art, who enjoyed some fourteen lengthy visits with Picasso and his wife over a period of two to three years. Rubin found the artist, then in his early nineties, remarkably alert and full of bustling energy—not the morose, misanthropic artist who was the subject of late rumors. He is convinced that Picasso's isolation was self-imposed, a method for avoiding any interruptions in his work-regimen. He claims that Picasso displayed an amazing confidence in his own longevity; at one point, making a passing reference to Titian who reportedly remained active until his early nineties, Picasso made it clear that he intended to outdistance the Renaissance artist and go on creating well beyond the century mark.

Everything we know about Picasso's final phase tends to support the view that he worked as if his talent and his art were an inexhaustible capital against which he could go on drawing forever. But his prolific output also seems to suggest that—consciously or unconsciously—he was in a race with time. Two major exhibitions of his last paintings were held at the Palace of the Popes in Avignon in 1970 and again in 1973. They provide ample testimony of the tremendous surge of creative energy that marked the end of Picasso's extraordinary career. The earlier Avignon show included some 167 oil paintings as well as forty-five drawings—all of them executed within a period of a year. The second showing, which opened in May, 1973—a month after Picasso's death on April 8th—comprised some 201 large scale paintings, produced over a period of twenty months. During this final phase of Picasso's career, moreover, there were three large exhibitions—encompassing some 500 late drawings and prints—held at the Louise Leiris Gallery in Paris. There had been no let-up in Picasso's amazing productivity.

In some respects, Picasso's Mougins studio had become a fortress against the world. But in his isolation, the artist had created an imaginary society in whose picaresque adventures he involved himself from one day to the next. Nothing in Picasso's late career, I think, is so revealing of his tenacity and his ferocious sexual imagination than this final theater of the self with its repetitive dramatis personae. Many of the characters were drawn from his past art while others, presumably, were taken from his private fantasies and his personal life at the moment. It is a society of artists and models, of familiar Pierrots and Harlequins, of pimps and bawds and stalking male and female nudes, of characters dressed in extravagant costumes—matadors in full regalia, musketeers brandishing their swords, poets in ruff-collars crowned with laurels. . . .

Coming at the end of a lengthy career, serving as the culminating variations on long-term themes, Picasso's last paintings can neither be conveniently ignored nor dismissed. They will not, of course, go away; critics who study the broad span of Picasso's work will eventually have to come to terms with them. It strikes me that Picasso deliberately cultivated the ugliness of these works; he seems to have refused to go into retirement by producing pretty and acceptable versions of his past successes. Working in the isolation of his Mougins studio, he evidently intended to leave us with a body of work that would be considered shocking—and even, perhaps, occasionally vulgar—by most acceptable standards; just as his Cubist paintings and his first constructivist sculptures were considered shocking by an earlier audience. Whether Picasso's stratagem works, whether these late paintings can be comfortably accommodated into the canon of his work, only time will tell. Whether the frenzy of his emotions at the close of his life—his love-hate relationship with the female-form, for instance—was too powerful and overwhelming for his artistic style, remains open for discussion. But it is highly possible that Picasso's late, aggravated assaults upon the female nude—that enduring symbol of life in its carnal relation to art—may achieve the same reputable status as the similarly brutalized women of Willem de Kooning's Abstract Expressionist paintings of the early 1950's. At the moment—the moment of their first extensive showing in the United States—Picasso's last paintings seem uncompromisingly raw and unassimilable. . . .

LEE KRASNER | SOLSTICE
March 20 – 18 April, 1981

Excerpts from an interview with Lee Krasner

by Barbara Novak
Boston, October 1979

L.K. Well, I think all painting is biographical. Your input tells a lot in the visual symbols—other than the way we would discuss it verbally. In that sense, I don't think mine is different. I think you can read any artist if you take the trouble to, or if you want to take the trouble to. You can get a good deal of personality through the painting. . . .

I've never understood the fixed image. I've never experienced this state of being where you fix an image and this becomes your identification. I'm forever going through this process of swinging from one place to another. I think it's a very normal state of affairs as long as one's alive. . . .

B.N. When did you begin the process of collaging your own work?

L.K. Around '53. I started tearing up drawings, which led to collaging, and then I went into some of these canvases that had been sitting there a long time and nothing happening with them, and I collaged some of those as well. Consequently, today I can look back and say this seems to be a work process for me: I go back on myself, into my own work, destroy it in some way or reutilize it in some way and come up with a new thing. Now why I do this, I don't know. But this seems to be a work process of mine. I'm constantly going back to something I did earlier, remaking it, doing something else with it and coming forth with another more clarified image possibly. . . .

Crisis Moment, 1980
oil and paper collage on canvas, 69 × 54¼"
©2001 Pollock-Krasner Foundation/Artists Rights
Society (ARS), New York

227

Notes on Rothko's Surrealist Years

by Robert Rosenblum
Excerpt from Pace catalogue

In the beginning was the Big Bang theory of Abstract Expressionism. By the 1950's, everyone on both sides of the Atlantic knew that something so drastic and overwhelming had happened in New York in the late 1940's that "The New American Painting"—to use the Museum of Modern Art's title for it's international traveling exhibition of 1958–59—seemed to have mythical origins, forged of thunder and lightning. The signature styles of the masters of this new art appeared so extreme in their distillations of primordial elements—energy, color, atmosphere, even the brink of nothingness—that they made one gasp in their willingness to jettison, so it seemed, the entire baggage of Western painting. But after absorbing the impact of what first looked like totally unfamiliar art, spectators and historians became more curious about how these heroic images of rock bottom purity came into being. For those who wished to support the stunning visual evidence that the grand tradition of European modernism had suddenly crossed the Atlantic, like an American Athena sprung full-grown from the head of a European Zeus, sweeping new genealogies could be constructed. For instance, the floating, expansive colors of Rothko, Newman, and Still might be seen as belonging to a dynasty founded by such ancestors as Matisse and the later Monet; and the crackling, dark-light structure of de Kooning, Kline, and Pollock might be read as an electrifying transmutation of the scaffoldings that underlay Analytic Cubism. Similarly, in broader cultural terms, the transcendental vistas and breast-beating individuality of many of the Abstract Expressionists could be located as the most recent manifestations of the legacy of Romanticism.

But what was amazingly slow in permeating our view of this new art was the fact that its origins were not the equivalent of a cosmic explosion, but the product rather of a long, slow generative process. So exciting was what looked like the swift emergence of a grand, mature American style that we ignored and were even embarrassed by what was thought of as an awkward incubation period. Checking birthdates alone, it was obvious that most of the major Abstract Expressionists were only a little younger than the century itself, and that in the late 1940's, when their art seemed to be born, they already were in their forties. But what

on earth had they been doing before that? Occasionally, historical surveys would include illustrations of a few "premature" works, in order to fill quickly the gap of decades—the 1930's and the early 1940's—in our knowledge of these masters, but usually they raced ahead to 1947–50, when the action really began. . . .

Nowadays, our view of Abstract Expressionism is also shifting focus. A younger generation of inquisitive art historians and spectators has registered dissatisfaction with the traditional and patently censored legend that would consign to the scrapheap what used to be considered tentative first steps that had better be left unseen. But was it really possible to understand the art of Rothko and his colleagues, if one entered the unfolding drama of their art only at the beginning of the great last act?. . .

But focusing anew on Rothko's Surrealist work of the 1940's, there are still many questions to be asked and sometimes answered. For one, there is the big issue of the timing of these works, which, it turns out, coincide grimly—1938–46—with the immediate eve and apocalyptic aftermath of the Second World War. To live in New York at that time was a strange amalgam of the mythical and the contemporary. The daily chronicle of evil reported in newspapers and on the radio, the living presence in the United States of growing numbers of refugees from hell were ample testimony to the actuality of the Nazis, of the war, of the atom bomb; yet the remoteness and monstrosity of these events in Europe and the Pacific could also give them an unreal, almost symbolic character that only an eye-witness observer could force into contemporary fact. For artists like Rothko, the impulse during those years of dread must have been a familiar one in times of unthinkable terror: an eyes-shut flight to primitive beginnings, to the vital sources of life, art, myth. . .

Rothko's weighty variations upon the cosmic themes of regression existed, to be sure, on an exalted level of 20th-century cultural history; yet it should not be forgotten that there was at least one immensely popular adventure in this primitivist realm which had vast audiences in the 1940's. I'm referring to Walt Disney's *Fantasia* of 1940, which, seen again in a post-Abstract Expressionist world, seems to herald almost every primeval image attained so arduously by Rothko, Still, Newman, or

Gethsemane, 1945
oil on canvas, 54⅜ × 35⅜"
© 1998 Kate Rothko Prizel & Christopher Rothko / Artists Rights Society (ARS), New York

Pollock. Most particularly, the Stravinsky *Rite of Spring* episode provided a spectacular anthology of biological and geological ultimates, in which primeval landscapes, where water, sky, and earth seem interchangeable, were gradually animated by a quivering, microscopic life that unforgettably metamorphosed the biology textbook illustrations of our distant school memories to the territory of myth and art. There, within the huge dimensions of a movie screen, the role of modern men and women in a manmade environment was usurped by oozing, unicellular creatures that throbbed, fed, and reproduced in a life-giving aqueous element, a Darwinian fantasy that, in 1940, coincided precisely with Rothko's first efforts, as in a watercolor of that year, to visualize a primitive universe of protozoic beings that, millenniums later, would take on human configurations.

Disney aside, there are, of course, legions of high-art sources for Rothko's explorations of the 1940's, and many have been pinpointed in general and specific ways. But I should like to add a few which strike me as having been unusually fertile. Miró, naturally, has been often enough singled out as a major inspiration for Rothko's Surrealist period,[4] but one work in particular, *The Family* of 1924—a work included in the Museum of Modern Art's Miró retrospective, of 1941—cast an especially long shadow. Not only does its lucid format—a wide field clearly divided by a horizon line—recur throughout many of Rothko's works, but so, too, does the perpendicular trio of spindly, near translucent creatures who shuttle back and forth in biological and historical time from modern pipe-smoking or bejeweled hominids to ciliated protozoans in urgent need of the life supports of food and sex. . . .

I should also like to point out another particular Surrealist source, a book which, published in New York in 1943 by Curt Valentin, (whose gallery was central to the New York art world's beaten path), must have generated many of the humanoid fantasies of Rothko and his colleagues. This was André Masson's *Anatomy of My Universe*, an illustrat-ed encyclopedia of mythic beings whose race across history and prehistory to create hybrid, imaginary species, within human molds, of everything from plants, trees, insects, and reptiles to demons, astrolabes, and architecture. . . .

But if we are tempted mainly to read these works as evolutionary, embryonic previews of the great Rothkos we know so much better, they are also beginning to look backwards to traditions of modern art much older than the Surrealist movement, which may be claimed as their most immediate source. I am thinking particularly of their many affinities with the Symbolist aesthetic and goals of the late 19th century, which so often attempted to conjure up, as in a seance, the most elusive, mysterious states of feeling through a vocabulary of evanescent shapes, colors, and tones, which equally eschewed any contact with the vulgar realities of the contemporary world and its material contents. . . . Gauguin's anthropological speculations about the common universe of myth and mysticism shared by all distant faiths, whether Christian, Maori, or Buddhist; or Munch's terrifying sense of conflict between the human race in the modern world and the overpowering forces of eternal nature, often symbolized as a sperm cell, an image that Rothko himself, a half-century later, would amplify in his own mediations upon the unicellular origins of life. But doubtless Rothko's Surrealist period will go on disclosing a complex network of connections with its past and its future. Its high seriousness, its search for forms and symbols that could awaken a sense of awe and tragedy not only assured the emotional gravity of the abstract art that, after 1947, absorbed these mysterious hieroglyphs, but also revealed Rothko's place in a long tradition of modern artists who grappled with an encyclopedic repertory of symbols culled from biology and anthropology in a heroic effort to convey the ultimates of life, death, and faith.

4. See especially Gail Levin, "Miró, Kandinsky, and the Genesis of Abstract Expressionism," in Hobbs and Levin, *op. cit.*, [*Abstract Expressionism: The Formative Years*, Whitney Museum 1978] pp. 27–40.

This New Art: To Draw In Space
by Rosalind Krauss
Excerpt from Pace catalogue

In 1932, as he is about to christen the approach to sculpture that he and Picasso have just invented, Julio González's thoughts move backward in time and outward in space to the ancient practice of configuring the constellations. From eight points of light the Greeks and Phoenicians bodied forth the cape of Orion and behind that the phantom presence of the man and his sword; while twenty stars sufficed to suggest the mast and rigging of the ship Argo—although the relation of those twenty to the form of a vessel is just as inscrutable as the eight are to the shape of the hunter and his cloak. With this strange indifference to the look of things, the constellations project the natural world of ships and swans into the heavens, inscribing it there with a drawing that does not stoop to the business of tracing likenesses. To draw with the stars is to constellate, which means to employ a technique that is neither mimetic nor abstract. "In the restlessness of the night, the stars mark out points of hope in the sky. . . ," González writes. "It is these points in the infinite which are the precursors of this new art: *To draw in space.*"

The phrase is taken from the 1932 essay that González dedicated to the work of Picasso: "Picasso sculpteur et les cathédrales."[1] But the domain of thinking from which it emerges has less to do with Picasso's practice with the new sculptural technique than it does with González's own.

By now the Picasso/González collaboration is fixed in the annals of twentieth-century art. . . . González, who had apprenticed in the decorative metal trade under his father, had worked as a master craftsman for over thirty years. Although for fifteen of those years he had also exhibited in Parisian galleries and salons—mostly paintings and small *repoussé* heads in bronze or silver—he identified himself on those occasions as either a jeweler or a decorative artist. This modesty and his expertise in the full range of smithing procedures, including the relatively new technique of oxyacetylene welding, made him the perfect worker of Picasso's aesthetic will. . . .

For in 1929, through Picasso's example, González found himself liberated into an artist of major aesthetic ambition. For the first time he realized that the techniques of which he was master could be pressed into the service of Art—that art was not invariably to be found elsewhere, higher up than the realm of Vulcan, but was to be produced there also, from the mouth of the forge. . . .

That González's maturity as an artist should have been the product of just one year's development, so that from 1930 to 1939 there should have come an almost unbroken chain of masterpieces, is undoubtedly a function not only of the artist's age and experience at the time of his contact with Picasso—he was 52—but also his intimate knowledge of avant-garde production during the decade that preceded their collaboration. Aside from his very close friendship with Picasso and Brancusi, González was connected, by ties that went back to his youth in Barcelona, with Torrès-Garcia, the Argentine artist who arrived via Spain and America in Paris in 1924. Polemical by nature, Torrès-Garcia was voluble in his articulation of the various factions that split the Parisian avant-garde of the 1920s. Needing to take sides (*against* Surrealism, *against* Neo-Classicism), Torrès-Garcia joined forces with Michel Seuphor and formed the association of abstract artists, *Cercle et Carré*. This was in 1929, the year of González's breakthrough. . . . [T]hrough his friendship with Torrès-Garcia, González knew both the issues and the protagonists. Hélion and Vantongerloo had become friends of González's and Mondrian, Arp, Ozenfant and Léger his acquaintances. He was thus at the center of the debate over abstraction—of abstraction as the tool to overthrow the material realm of nature and the means of instituting a reign of pure spirit or intellect. Modern man was thought to be conceptual man, and his art must reflect with greatest accuracy his power of intellection. . . .

González's metaphorical use of the constellations is more eloquent and more precise in defining what it was that had emerged from his own use of direct-metal process than any of his Constructivist cant about body and spirit. For the space defined by González's sculptural drawing is the procedural space of transcription, of the translation of one medium—the sketch—into another—the three-dimensional construction. Abstraction is the almost effortless, because inevitable, product of this method—an abstraction that feels uncanny because the buried memory of the original model seems still to be active within the newly coded forms. . . .

The openness of González's metal drawing is a further product of his method, an openness made possible by the suggestiveness of the "established points." Unlike Picasso, González was not working with the metaphors of bodies—with one object (a bicycle seat) employed because it resembled another (a bull's skull). He was thus not substituting one body for another to produce a sculpture of substantive collage: chains of metaphors fantastically agglutinated. Instead he was employing the baffles of translation, a *process* that would move him further and further from the corporeal object—the collander/head—and closer to a cursiveness that space itself (the space of González's *process:* copying) would render abstract: the deep ambiguity of the W of *Femme se coiffant*.

The kind of drawing in which González engaged—this constellating—with its natural tendency toward the non-physical, without the doctrinaire quality of *Cercle et Carré* abstraction, was shared by a very few of González's contemporaries. And in their hands, also, constellating became a powerful cursive mode. . . .

1. In, Josephine Withers, *Julio González/Sculpture in Iron*, New York University Press, New York, 1978, pp. 131–8. All quotes by González are taken from this text.

JULIO GONZÁLEZ

SCULPTURE AND DRAWINGS

October 2 – 31 October, 1981

Josef Albers
William Baziotes
Romare Bearden
Joseph Beuys
Alexander Calder
Chuck Close
Joseph Cornell
Elaine de Kooning
Willem de Kooning
Richard Diebenkorn
Jim Dine
Mark di Suvero
Helen Frankenthaler
Nancy Graves
Michael Heizer
David Hockney
Hans Hofmann
Edward Hopper
Alfred Jensen
Jasper Johns
Alex Katz
Ellsworth Kelly
Frederick Kiesler
Franz Kline

Lee Krasner
Roy Lichtenstein
Alexander Liberman
Richard Lindner
Agnes Martin
Robert Motherwell
Louise Nevelson
Barnett Newman
Constantino Nivola
Isamu Noguchi
Frank O'Hara
Jackson Pollock
Robert Rauschenberg
Ad Reinhardt
Larry Rivers
James Rosenquist
Mark Rothko
Robert Ryman
George Segal
Ben Shahn
Tony Smith
Saul Steinberg
Clyfford Still
Ernest Trova

PACE GALLERY PUBLICATIONS

Photo © Hans Namuth Ltd.

HANS NAMUTH   ARTISTS 1950-81   A PERSONAL VIEW

HANS NAMUTH

by Calvin Tomkins
Excerpt from Pace catalogue

. . . Taking pictures of artists began as a non-profit sideline in 1950. Namuth and his wife rented a house in Water Mill, Long Island, that summer. One Saturday they went to the opening of an art exhibition at the Guild Hall in East Hampton, where Namuth got up the nerve to approach Jackson Pollock. He had seen Pollock's paintings for the first time a few months before, at the Betty Parsons Gallery in New York, and had not liked them a bit. A subsequent remark by Brodovitch, that Pollock was "one of the most important artists around today," had sent him back for another look, which made him decide he wanted to meet the artist. At the Guild Hall that Saturday, Namuth told Pollock that he would like to come to his house and photograph him, and Pollock agreed. The photographs that he took of Pollock at work helped to change the course of art history. They also gave Namuth his true vocation, although for some years afterward there was little or no market for photographs of contemporary artists.

Over the last three decades Namuth has photographed most of the significant artists of his era, some of them many times. Photographic truth is a partial and particular truth, of course; nobody would claim that these photos reveal more than a fraction of the personality of their subjects. But Namuth's fraction is unusually precise, and often indelible. The reason for this, I suspect, is the trust that is established between him and his fellow artists. Look closely, for example, at the three photographs of Willem de Kooning ("You can never take a bad picture of him," Namuth says). They cover a span of twenty-eight years, and they tell, more dramatically than a novel or film, what sort of toll the furies can exact. To my knowledge, de Kooning has let no one else in this close.

Joseph Cornell kept him waiting for eighteen months, then sat for a portrait that is as strange as the man himself—folded into a chair in the corner of his "music room," holding a copy of T.H.

White's *The Bestiary* to his ear, upside down, as though listening to the sound of its pages. Sandy Calder stumps down a country road in Saché, scowling, dressed in black, as solid and enduring as a French peasant. Joseph Beuys, without his felt hat, looks painfully vulnerable. . . .

In these memorable collaborations, Namuth himself is nowhere to be seen. This is the key, I think, to his achievement. He does not set the stage, he does not interpret, he does not in any way come between us and the drama of an individual life. Namuth is pure catalyst. He precipitates some essential, particular, and precise fact about a personality to which we would not otherwise, unless we are as lucky as he is, gain access. He would have made a superb theater director, and an interesting general. It is a pleasure to share his luck.

Rita, Ad, and Anna Reinhardt, 1958
11 × 14"
Photo © Hans Namuth Ltd.

237

AD REINHARDT

PAINTINGS AND WATERCOLORS 1945–51

December 11 – 9 January, 1982

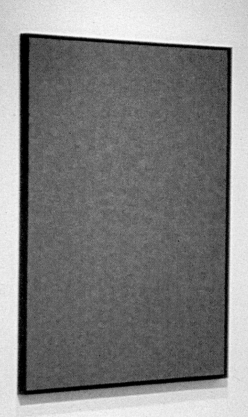

TIMELESS STYLISTIC ART HISTORICAL CYCLES
FIVE STAGES OF,
REINHARDT'S

a. LATE-CLASSICAL-MANNERIST POST-CUBIST
    GEOMETRIC-ABSTRACTIONS
        OF THE LATE 30's

b. ROCOCO-SEMI-SURREALIST FRAGMENTATION
    AND "ALL-OVER" BAROQUE-GEOMETRIC-
    EXPRESSIONIST PATTERNS
        OF THE EARLY 40's

c. ARCHAIC COLOR-BRICK-BRUSHWORK IMPRESS-
    IONISM AND BLACK-AND-WHITE CONSTRUCT-
    IVIST CALLIGRAPHIES
        OF THE LATE 40's

d. EARLY-CLASSICAL HIERATICAL RED, BLUE, BLACK
    MONOCHROME SQUARE-CROSS-BEAM
    SYMMETRIES
        OF THE EARLY 50's

e. CLASSIC BLACK SQUARE UNIFORM FIVE-FOOT
    TIMELESS TRISECTED EVANESCENCES
        OF THE EARLY 60's

ETC.

Cover of catalogue

FROM CHICAGO

From Chicago: A Personal Idiom
by Russell Bowman
Excerpt from Pace catalogue

. . . Chicago Imagism as a movement and a style was born in 1966 with the first show by a group of young students and recent graduates of the School of the Art Institute of Chicago who called themselves the Hairy Who.[2] Perhaps inspired to assume a group identity by jazz or rock groups, and encouraged by Don Baum, then director of the Hyde Park Art Center on Chicago's Southside, who offered them a place to show, the Hairy Who artists, Jim Nutt, Gladys Nilsson, Karl Wirsum, Art Green, Suellen Rocca, and James Falconer, decided to make a frontal assault on art world sensibilities. Although an interest in ads and comics allied them with the then highly visible Pop artists, the work of the Hairy Who drew from grittier, more low-down commercial and urban sources: ads for hair removal devices, trusses and corn plasters, comics, cheap posters and handbills, signs and graffiti. Furthermore, rather than the slick uninflected style of the Pop artists, the members of the Hairy Who worked in a manner reminiscent of the "jamming" of jazz: they freely distorted and reinvented their sources, hyping-up their images with sharp line, fiercely contrasting color, and shiny surfaces. Like the jam musician, they threw in everything they knew and heated the mix; they were hot, *engagé* artists—the "cool" of jazz rather than the distanced, ironical cool of Pop Art. This does not mean that Hairy Who art was without irony, but this irony was reserved for art and the art world rather than their commercial and popular sources. When it came to confronting notions of "high" art and art-world seriousness, the Hairy Who responded with a zany, adolescent humor. They loved word plays, misspellings, puns and malapropisms and frequently incorporated them into their titles and images. . . .

The Chicago Imagists' shared interest in vernacular sources, in the expressive transformation of these sources, in related stylistic devices and in language, narrative and signs, seems sufficient to both define a group style and yet allow for individual differences. But what of meaning; are the personal sign systems developed by the Imagist artists related in content? If a common thread of meaning runs through the various personal styles of the Imagist artists, it centers on fantasy, on paradox and irony, on theater as metaphor, and on psychological expressionism. Chicago Imagism frequently has been associated with Surrealism and with fantasy. It should be made clear that fantasy is a means not an end for the Imagists. Fantasy is a method for unleashing creative power and bringing about direct, unaltered expression but, lacking Surrealism's programmatic Freudian or Jungian seriousness, it allows for memory and play. Thus the Imagists take objects from the everyday environment, often ones imbued with nostalgia, as catalysts for play, for fantasy and invention. They are very aware of the paradoxical elements involved in the attempt to use "low" sources to create "high" art and in the conscious choice of a method to achieve unself-conscious expression. Therefore, they embrace paradox, irony and humor, again, as a method rather than a statement; it is as if by not taking themselves too seriously they might achieve self-expression. . . .

2. This view contradicts that outlined by Franz Schulze. See his *Chicago Imagist Art* (Chicago: Museum of Contemporary Art, 1972) and *Fantastic Images: Chicago Art Since 1945* (Chicago: Follet, 1972). (Exhibition organized with support from the Phyllis Kind Gallery, Chicago-New York).

Top: Reclining Curvaceous II, 1981
gold-plated bronze, 6¼ × 12½ × 8"

Head #48, June 25, 1981
pastel on paper, 17½ × 11½"

Samaras Winged And Wingless, Celestial And Demonic, Anointed And Demented
by Donald Kuspit
Excerpt from Pace catalogue

I

Small, whimsical self-portraits and monstrous lumps of sculpture: Samaras's new work has comic potential. And yet something deadly serious is at hand: the artist and the demons that drive him—the artist again and again trying to capture himself in an interminable process of self-portraiture and the metamorphic demons figured and re-figured, formed and re-formed, adding up to a psychological catastrophe. In its totality the new work is relentless, polemical, at odds with itself, in headlong pursuit of a simple statement of self yet having complex effect—effecting a complex self. It is the work of an artist driven to and fro between the extremes of himself, trying to be in two places at once, caught in a conflict of his own making and yet inescapable, universal. It is the work of an artist who has refined his own narcissism until it bespeaks the condition of the whole of art—the do-or-die reason for being for art as such. . . .

The Byzantine autobiographicality of Samaras's art has long been known. If one takes seriously the Byzantine manner of his imagery, then one must accept the fact that like all Byzantine imagery it is, in the words of one scholar, "created for worship." The self-portraits have a truly hieratic style: they can easily take their place in the cult of worship of the artist's selfhood that has been in existence—more and more blatant existence—at least since 19th century romanticism. The artist's self-worship is supposed to accomplish that miracle of modern narcissism: self-creation. Narcissism, for the modern artist, is the secret of creativity—a secret he was forced to pursue to the extent he was forced back on himself by modernity, with its uncertain patronage because of democracy and its uncertain impact because of its lack of universal ideology. Old-fashioned narcissism wanted the self reflected rather than transformed, confirmed rather than idealized, interpreted rather than revolutionized. Of course, there were glimpses of the new in the old, but never, until the modern period—with the crisis of uncertainty about the significance of being an artist, and by extension of art—the will to implement the new potential in the old actuality of narcissism. The results of the new narcissism are vivid in Samaras's Byzantine style, which not only readily lends itself to the new narcissism but becomes its archetypal expression, its basic method of working. For what one

LUCAS SAMARAS | **PASTELS AND BRONZES**
February 20 – 20 March, 1982

scholar has called the dualism of Byzantine style—its mix of liveliness and solemnity, energetic will to vision and the persistence to hold the vision fast and steady—epitomizes the problem of the new narcissism. It discovers not the old unity of the self—an atavism lost with evolution beyond the old narcissism—but the new, seemingly unresolvable, divisiveness within it. . . .

II

Over the years, Samaras has pushed in two increasingly opposed directions. He leaves the impression that something has to give, that he cannot survive the tensions of his art. It cannot continue to be unremittingly and simultaneously manic and concentrated. It cannot continue to be decoratively centrifugal and imagistically centripetal. It will simply pull itself apart. But in the new works the

decorative and the imagistic are more integrated than ever. This has, I think, something to do with Samaras's new sense of himself as spiritual not only instinctual (aggressively sensual, sensual in aggressivity). . . .

Sculpture Table, 1981
silver-plated bronze, 41¾ × 51½ 35"

SAUL STEINBERG | STILL LIFE AND ARCHITECTURE

April 3 – 8 May, 1982

The Pen In the First Person
(For the Drawings of Saul Steinberg)
by Italo Calvino
Excerpt from Pace catalogue

The first to consider the instruments and actions of his own work as its true subject was a 13th century poet. Guido Cavalcanti wrote a sonnet in which his pens speak in the first person, along with the instruments used for cutting and sharpening them. They introduce themselves in the opening lines:

> [We are the sad, dismayed pens,
> the scissors and the sorrowing knife. . .]

With these verses Guido Cavalcanti opens modern poetry. He opens it, and he closes it. After him, poets prefer to forget that while they write they are writing and not doing something else. . . .

STEINBERG

The pen that Cavalcanti dropped is picked up by Steinberg. It is the pen as subject of graphic action. Every line presupposes a pen drawing it, and every pen presupposes a hand holding it. What lies beyond the hand is a debated question: the I who draws is identified with a drawn I, not the drawing's subject but its object. Or rather, it is the universe of drawing that draws itself, explores, tests, and redefines itself each time. (The physical universe proceeds in the same fashion, I believe).

The drawn world has an aggressiveness of its own: it invades the desk, captures anything alien to it, joins all lines to its own line, overflows the page. . . . No, it is the outside world that enters and becomes part of the page: the pen, the hand, the artist, the desk, the cat; everything is engulfed by the drawing as if by a whirlpool, all the papers on the desk, letters, envelopes, postcards, rubber stamps, postage stamps, dollar bills with the truncated pyramid, the eye over it, and the Latin motto. . . . No, it is the substance of the graphic sign that is revealed as the true substance of the world, the flourish or arabesque or thread of dense, feverish, neurotic handwriting that replaces any other possible world. . . .

The world is transformed into line, a single line, broken, twisted, discontinuous. Man, too. And this man transformed into line is, in the end, master of the world, though he cannot escape his condition as prisoner, because, after many scrolls and curlicues, the line tends to close in on itself and entrap the man-line. But he is surely his own master, because he can construct or dismantle himself, segment by segment, and as a final way out he can commit suicide with two, criss-crossed strokes of the pen, to discover that crossed-out death is made of the same substance as drawing-life, a movement of the pen on the page. Or else we can say that he always retains the supreme freedom of guiding the line in the least expected direction so that the drawing is no longer able to be closed: to draw a cube observing the rules of perspective, and then allow one corner to go off in a direction where it will never join up with the other corners: this incongruous corner contains the real proof of the existence of the I, the *ergo sum*. . . .

Steinberg's irresistible vocation, or let's say the historic mission to which he has been called, is to move in a space of limitless dimensions of the drawn and the drawable, to establish communication between the most contradictory stylistic universes, to make elements belonging to divergent figurative cultures or conventions of perception coexist within the horizon of the same page. A row of houses on the street, each of a different period and style, if it is to be depicted or even looked at, requires the employment of different graphic techniques. Just as the people who pass by on the sidewalk carry, each of them, the style of drawing that can portray their essence, a lighter or heavier pressure of the pen on the paper, the thickness of the ink, or the expanse of white that encloses their secret.

The countless and multiform ways of using pens and pencils and brushes are to be found on Steinberg's page, including the countless and multiform ways in which pens and pencils and brushes can portray pens and pencils and brushes. Until the moment comes when *the* pens make their entrance into the picture, and *the* pencils and *the* brushes in their presence as physical objects, an absolutely modest presence, but absolutely sure of being, of being *there*. Here, then, are Cavalcanti's *dismayed pens* which return to testify in the first person the transfiguration of the artist in the practice of his art. . . .

Translated from the Italian by William Weaver

ROBERT IRWIN
A SUMMARY OF EXHIBITIONS AT PACE
May 14 – 12 June, 1982

PABLO PICASSO

The Sculpture of Picasso
by Robert Rosenblum
Excerpt from Pace catalogue

. . . Sculpture as primitive totem pervades the master's three-dimensional world, from 1907, the time of his first exposure to and absorption of African art, to the monumental commissions of his last decade, when his international renown permitted him to create giant sphinxes for public spaces as far away as New York and Chicago. Already in small figurines of 1907, we feel that the demon spirit of some mythic deity wrenched from distant time and space by modern Western explorers has been reincarnated by a 20th-century witch doctor who had uncanny empathy into a dark world of the occult. A similar breed, this time of eerily tall and commanding goddesses, is spawned in 1931 at the Château de Boisgeloup, which Picasso had just turned into a sanctuary not only for his new young muse and lover, Marie-Thérèse Walter, but for an energetic renewal of sculptural activity in a converted stable on the property. Whittled from frame moldings found at this estate, these small, but uncannily majestic figures, with their prominent breasts, evoke an erotic genius loci, presiding over Picasso's private domain in the country like Stone Age Venuses (such as that from Lespugue, of which Picasso owned two copies). Perhaps most puzzling of these totem deities in Picasso's voodoo world is the *Woman in a Long Robe* of 1943, cast in bronze from body parts taken from a clothes dummy and,

for the left arm, a fragment of an Easter Island sculpture. We can only guess what occult private meanings such a bizarre assemblage of female head, limbs and torso may have had for the master, and turn for speculative answers to his erotic biography, perhaps to the replacement in that year, 1943, of Dora Maar by Françoise Gilot.

If we have ever quavered with genuine fear before the spookily animate stillness and hypnotic gaze of tribal art, whether Oceanic, African, ancient Mediterranean, or prehistoric, we might well do so again before Picasso's resurrection of the magic conveyed by the widest possible range of hexed and hexing artifacts that he seems to have known from every culture. Death looms large in this universe that seems half the product of a learned anthropologist and half the invention of a primitive believer, but nowhere is it more shockingly present than in the famous bronze and copper *Skull* of 1943–44, made in part from inanimate scrap metal that might otherwise have served, ironically, to make German instruments of death. With its rotting mouth and jaw and blindly staring, gun-barrel eye sockets, this impenetrably hard and solid skull evokes the universal specter of death that had become so triumphant in the midst of the war years; yet this public reference has a private side, for we also sense that the man who dared to

Tête casquée, 1933
bronze, unique, 47½ × 27½ × 12"
© 2001 Estate of Pablo Picasso / Artists Rights Society (ARS), New York

create so nightmarish an image as a palpable object might be spared death's ultimate victory for decades to come. Picasso, we learn, had a superstitious reason for expecting to die at the end of the 1940's,[4] and this sculptural black magic may well have been his way of warding off a frightening prophecy of his youth that he would die, after a long sickness, in his 68th year. Even in covert ways, art against death may be, we now know, a subliminal theme of the famous *Glass of Absinth* of spring 1914, whose six painted variations may at first seem only cheerful prestidigitations of the commonplace café still life of a Cubist glass and a real metal absinth spoon (perforated for the straining of water over a sugar cube), a jaunty spiraling of forms whose rakish silhouette could remind Roland Penrose of the period's feminine fashions (angled hats, lace chokers).[5] Yet these Cubist tours-de-force, it also turns out, evoke a multitude of lethal associations,[6] not only through references to the grave public problem of addiction to absinth (responsible for so many deaths in the late 19th and early 20th centuries that it was finally banned in France in 1915), but through still more subtle components (such as the suggestion of black-and-white cruciform patterns) or even personal confrontations with death (such as the passing of Picasso's own father in 1913 or the worsening health of his mistress Eva, who was to die in 1915). And though we are accustomed to thinking of Picasso's Cubist art as impervious to the deathly aura of World War I, there may well be a reflection here, too, of the darkening European clouds of spring 1914 that so often cast their pall over the fine print of the newspaper clippings Picasso chose in 1913–14.

Such implicit reminders of death in life can become far more explicit in many later memento mori still lifes, both painted and sculpted, that often interrupt otherwise cheerful sequences of works. One of these, the *Goat Skull and Bottle* of 1951 may at first seem as theatrically decorative as the *Glass of Absinth* in its rich and bristling array of striped, spiky, and arcing patterns; but the bone-like pall of white and black paint, the symbolic dialogue between the radiant light of the candle burning in the bottle and the desiccated skull of a goat turn this into a macabre meditation on life and death that Picasso had expressed more literally and topically in January 1951 in his painting of the military executions of children and pregnant women during the Korean War. As a memento mori, in the familiar Spanish Baroque tradition, the *Goat Skull and Bottle* recalls continuities in Picasso's work that transcend the period and "ism" categories with which art historians originally compartmented the master's bewilderingly diverse sequences and simultaneities of styles; and in this, it can serve to remind us how today, in ever more distant retrospect, Picasso's total *oeuvre* has become far more fascinating in the unity of its persistently recurrent motifs than in the ostensible disunity of its multiple styles and phases. That the *Goat Skull and Bottle* is actually made from the most ordinary of materials at hand (the blunt horizontals of the pupils in the goat's eyes are made from, and visually equated with, the heads of bolts; the horns, from a child's bicycle handles; the light rays, from nails) is a tribute to, among other things, the continually fertile explorations right into the 1950's and 60's of Picasso's original Cubist collages and constructions in which banal objects could be instantly metamorphosed into complex artistic fictions, just as the dissection of the bottle's volume

Above: Fleurs dans un vase, 1951
bronze, 28¾ × 19¼ × 16½"

by patterns of strong light and shadow echo those in the 1914 *Glass of Absinth*. Such long-term variations throughout Picasso's lengthy career are becoming more apparent every year, so that now, the late work in particular begins to resonate richly with layer after layer of associations in the master's earlier art. . . .

Again and again, both the most modest and ambitious of the late works mirror long and intricate lineages from Picasso's past. Even so unimposing a painted metal cutout as the tiny *Mask* of 1960, we realize, might have been materialized from one of the eyeless, paper-thin mock faces that conceal the material presence of the sinister *Three Musicians* in their dual painted appearance of 1921; and in a work like the carpentered *Man* of 1958, we feel a throwback to other Picasso genealogies, from the wooden Cubist constructions of 1913–14 to the recurrent double and triple images that turn figures into furniture and chair legs into human legs and that can suddenly make us realize that what we thought was only some inert material or abstract pattern turns out to be a brazen display of sexual anatomy. As for the latter, the gawky candor of the ithyphallic young man of 1956 is a simple case; but a more complex one is *Vase-Face* of 1946, which looks like something that, in a more sexually repressed age than ours, might have been kept behind locked doors in an archeological museum. Vase, handle, spout, phallus, nose, mouth, head keep shifting identities and functions with a Rabelaisian humor that conjures up an X-rated inventory of eroticized drinking vessels that range from the Spanish *porrón* to Pre-Columbian pottery.

In Picasso's green-thumbed hands, even leaves and flowers can grow from clay and bronze, burgeoning from vases and figures as they do in his paintings. Real leaves were cast in bronze to make the small but magical *Woman with Leaves* of 1934, in which an uncannily forceful burst of foliage metamorphoses into a birdlike, as well as humanoid head, like that of a forest creature who, in another era, might be an allegory of spring or fecundity. But no sculptural work in this vein is more enchanted and complex than the 7-feet tall *Woman in the Garden* of 1929–31, the subject of a recent study that defines it as first being conceived as a proposal for the monument to honor Apollinaire but then as being transformed into a personal homage to his new mistress, Marie-Thérèse Walter, with images consonant with the paintings of the early 1930's.[7] A paean to Picasso's revitalized powers of love and procreation, this huge bronze tangle fuses woman, nature, and a suggestion of garden furniture in an unruly jungle that looks as if sun and water might make it grow before our eyes. Windswept hair, voluptuously curved body contours, expanding philodendron leaves, throbbing internal organs all quiver and sprout in a furious and joyous explosion of organic energies equaled only in the best paintings of 1931–32. The more rectilinear, lean armatures of the famous earlier models of 1928–29 that Picasso made with González as initial proposals for the Apollinaire monument are here transformed into a kind of vigorous re-

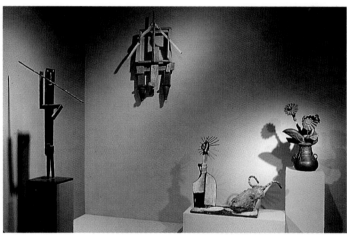

vival of an Art Nouveau vocabulary, with particular parallels to the work of Antonio Gaudí, well known to Picasso from Barcelona. . . .

4. For details of this, and many other penetrating comments, see Leo Steinberg, "The Skulls of Picasso," in *Other Criteria*, New York, 1972, p. 121.
5. Penrose, *op. cit.*, [Roland Penrose, *Picasso: His Life and Work*, (New York 1962), p. 179.
6. For a full account of these matters, see Brooks Adams, "Picasso's Absinth Glasses: Six Drinks to the End of an Era," *Artforum*, vol. XVIII, no. 8, (April 1980), pp. 30–33.
7. See Laura E. Smith, "Iconographic Issues in Picasso's 'Woman in the Garden,'" *Arts*, vol. 56, no. 5 (January 1982), pp. 142–47.

253

BRICE MARDEN
MARBLES, PAINTINGS AND DRAWINGS
October 29 – 27 November, 1982

Hermeticism Made Visible
by William Zimmer
Excerpt from Pace catalogue

. . . Marden has always trafficked in ambiguity, the interchangeability of parts, as a dynamic quality in his art. A clear demonstration of this is the catalog cover of his 1974 Guggenheim retrospective. The painting shown on the front cover is a dark panel between two light ones; the painting featured on the back is its opposite, a light panel flanked by darker ones. On both covers Marden stands to the side of the painting in an identical pose.

Marden's breakthrough painting of 1980, *Thira*, featured rectangles within larger panels arranged into a post-and-lintel scheme. *Thira* means door in Greek. Therefore it is possible to read the central rectangles for all their solidity as passageways. But along with this architectural reading, there is license to read a landscape with the fiery tonalities of Greece. "I have always been interested in the ambiguities of inside and outside," Marden told me. . . .

Brice Marden is deeply absorbed in alchemy, the working system of hermeticism. Alchemy is an area where fools have rushed in, and angels have been known to tread, both hoping to make gold. . . .

Marden's current exhibition contains two new, major paintings. One is *Frieze II* (the first frieze was *Thira*), and the other is *Green Painting*. They are intimately related works, and are wholeheartedly imbued with the alchemical mode of considering existence. . . .

Things of the world, formerly the subjective components of Marden's paintings, are now, paradoxically, both recondite and highly objective. Brice Marden is a made-to-order alchemist slipping us the visions *sub rosa*. . . .

Just as the table of correspondences is a scroll, so is the ground of *Frieze II*. It is the perfectly smooth paper that also constitutes Japanese screens. Brice Marden has never made a painting that isn't a paragon of surface smoothness. However, anyone who is the least acquainted with Marden's paintings will note a pronounced physical change: he has forsaken what has been his signature—encaustic. . . .

Frieze II, 1982, oil on paper mounted on shoji screens, 30 × 135"

As an alchemist in search of "the one thing" Marden is consciously manipulating the four basic elements of the universe: earth, air, fire and water. The corresponding colors of those elements are green, yellow, red, and blue. Marden has always been a master brewer of rare colors and there are some original hues in this painting that fall between "brilliance" at the top of Crowley's color table to "white turning to grey" at the bottom. The blue in the two central panels of *Frieze II* is undoubtedly cobalt blue straight from the tube. It is mottled in appearance here. Cobalt blue is very thin paint and Marden's surface affords it no ridges to hold on to. But since blue equals water, the roiling is effective in this context. The frieze might be the separation of the colors, the marvelous changes an alchemist might observe in his laboratory on the way to gold. . . .

Frieze II has a transparent aspect. Marden considered calling this painting "Window Study." It might be the most well-wrought study in contempo-

rary art. It stands on its own, but is also a doorway *(thira)* opening on a jewel-like *magnum opus,* the stained glass window program conceived by Marden for a protestant cathedral in Basel, Switzerland. . . .

The program is now but working drawings, but Marden's concepts for the windows adumbrate the dynamic investigations in his paintings. He has sought a way to use the alchemical allegory in a Christian setting. He is assigning an elemental color to each of the four sets of windows flanking the center: red, green, blue, and yellow. These colors will weave their way toward the center where they will mesh in the dark confusion that is penultimate to cleansing. Lines that bleed—similar to the lines in his drawings from SUICIDE NOTES onward—will carry the color. Marden's drawing has always been a foil to his painting: solidity breaks down in the drawings. In this context, the bleeding might be a sublime invocation of Christ's passion. . . .

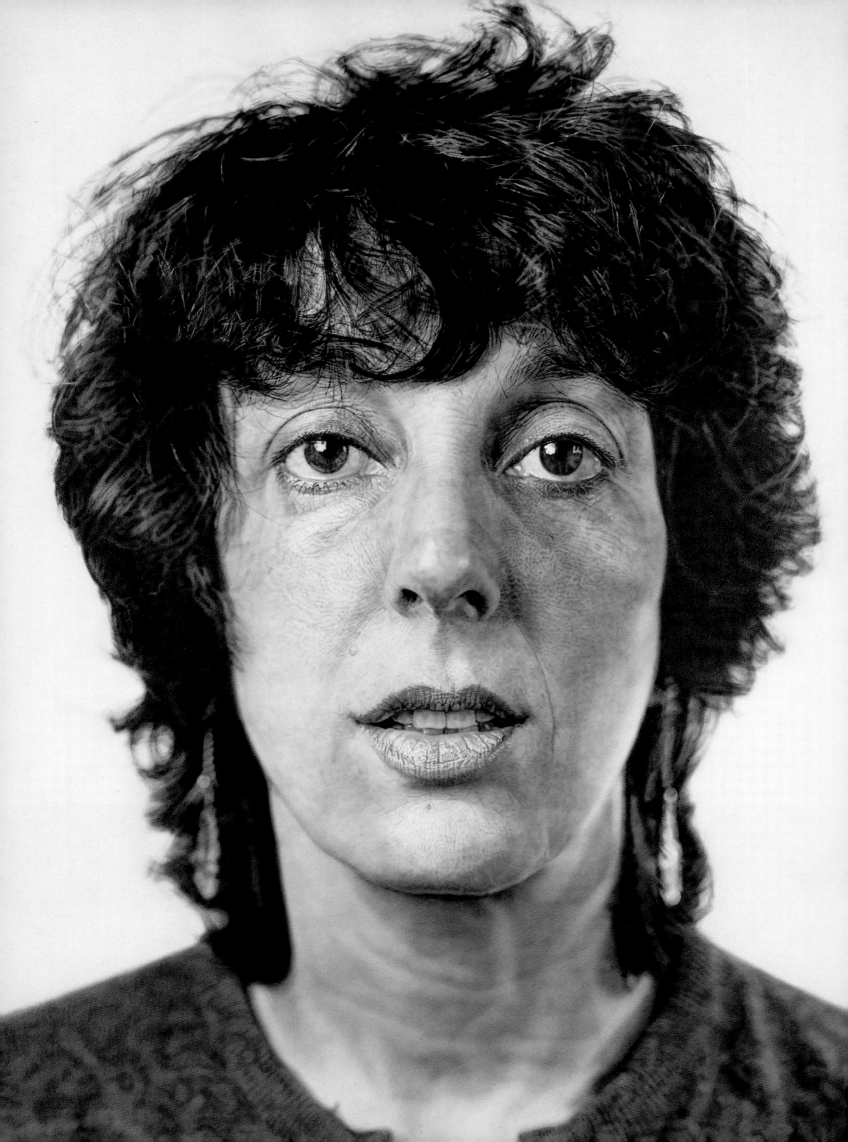

CHUCK CLOSE | **RECENT WORK**
February 25 – 26 March, 1983

Gwynne, 1982
watercolor on paper mounted on canvas,
74¼ × 58¼"

MARK ROTHKO

PAINTINGS 1948–69
April 1 – 30, 1983

Untitled, 1954
oil on canvas, 91 × 59½"
© 1998 Kate Rothko Prizel & Christopher Rothko / Artists Rights Society (ARS), New York

Mark Rothko
(In Memory of Robert Goldwater)
by Irving Sandler
Excerpt from Pace catalogue

Robert Goldwater once cautioned against reading cosmic allegories and other literary fancies into Mark Rothko's nonobjective paintings. Such "program notes . . . relax the visual hold of these canvases, filter their immediacy, and push away their enigmatic, gripping presence."[1] It is noteworthy that even in this warning against the excessive interpretation of their content, an art historian as tough minded as Goldwater should have found it necessary to characterize Rothko's abstractions as "enigmatic"—and also as "apparitional." He obviously could not avoid reporting on his subjective response, a response shared by other viewers, myself included, in sufficient numbers to indicate that inscrutable and preternatural qualities do inhere in Rothko's paintings. Indeed, these ineffable qualities are the source of their distinction, their greatness. But what can be said about them with credibility?

Because Rothko's paintings are enigmatic they have frequently summoned forth the kind of excessive commentary that Goldwater warned against, particularly in the fifties when such art criticism was common. Not surprisingly, the language of Rothko appreciation has been immoderately poetic. Or as Robert Hughes has written, "out come the violins, the woodwinds, the kettledrums, everything."[2] Art critics have churned out inflated rhetoric about Rothko's content, commonly ornamented with quotes from the Kabbalah and the like, although a few have written with insight, relying on their own experience. However, the quality of the prose, even at its best, has not approached the quality of the painting. Rothko has yet to find his Baudelaire or Apollinaire. Maybe he won't or can't, as John Ashbery, perhaps our greatest living poet, suggested. Ashbery remarked that he "had produced a text [on Rothko] containing the words 'shades snapped down against the day,' 'Rembrandt,' 'Dominican,' 'poverty,' 'Spinoza,' and 'the all-importance of fine distinctions.' After having put this paper aside for a few days and come back to it I was infuriated by the inadequacy and silliness of what I had written. Rothko . . . seems to eliminate criticism."[3]

In reaction against the glut of turgid subjective and poetic analysis of content, critics, for example Clement Greenberg, whose formalist approach dominated art criticism during the sixties, dismissed all such analysis as irrelevant. In the name of objectivity, they insisted on dealing exclusively with the formal components of art. Inquiry into issues "external" to art was condemned as disreputable.[4] During the last decade, the formalist approach lost its sway over art

discourse. It succumbed to a surfeit of worldly interpretations of formal minutiae. Critics in increasing numbers and with growing confidence have been investigating extra-aesthetic feelings and thoughts that inhere in the physical properties of works of art, taking care to check their personal responses against the formal evidence, verifying them, as it were, or at least making them understandable. . . .

In 1949, Rothko stopped publishing statements, except for a letter to *Art News* in 1957.[45] He had come to believe that they instruct the viewer as to what to look for and thus stunt his or her mind and imagination.[46] However, in 1958, he felt the need to refute his critics and chose to do so by giving a talk at Pratt Institute.[47] He strongly denied any concern with self-expression, with Expressionism. He insisted that his aim was to formulate a message which transcended self and was about the human condition generally or, as he put it, the human drama. Rothko also denied that his purpose was to make formal innovations, although he allowed that he had "used colors and shapes in a way that painters before have not.". . .

In his talk at Pratt, Rothko confirmed the direction his work had begun to take the year before—toward "a clear preoccupation with death," the sign of which was his growing use of tenebrous browns, deep maroons and plums, grays and black. Rothko had long thought of his painting as essentially tragic. In fact, in the letter to the *Times* of 1943, the only words he himself had written were: "only that subject matter is valid which is tragic and timeless."[48]. . .

In his talk at Pratt, Rothko formulated his self-image as an artist. His function was not that of a formal problem-solver or a self-revealing Expressionist but of a contemporary seer who, on the authority of an inner voice, envisions and reveals new truths about the human drama. He said: "I want to mention a marvelous book, Kierkegaard's *Fear and Trembling/The Sickness Unto Death,* which deals with the sacrifice of Isaac by Abraham. Abraham's act was absolutely unique. There are other examples of sacrifice [that seem related]: Brutus, who as a ruler put to death his two sons [because they had broken the law. Brutus's tragic decision was understandable; the choice was between two known "universals": the State or the Family.] But what Abraham was prepared to do [on God's command audible only to himself] was beyond understanding. There was no universal that condoned such an act. This is like the role of the artist.". . .

interpretation without overdoing it. Rothko greatly admired Goldwater's essay, in part for its reticence.

Confronting the central issue in Rothko's work, Goldwater wrote: "Rothko claims that he is 'no colorist,' and that if we regard him as such we miss the point in his art. Yet it is hardly a secret that color is his sole medium. In painting after painting. . . there are handsome, surprising and disquieting harmonies, and supposedly difficult colors are made to work together with apparent ease. . . . There is a sense in which one is inclined to agree with him, or rather to say that Rothko has been determined to become something other than a colorist. . . [What] Rothko means is that the enjoyment of color for its own sake, the heightened realization of its purely sensuous dimension, is not the purpose of his painting. If Matisse was one point of departure. . . Rothko has since moved far in an opposite direction. Yet over the years he has handled his color so that one must pay ever closer attention to it, examine the unexpectedly joined hues, the slight, and continually slighter, modulations within the large area of any single surface, and the softness and the sequence of the colored shapes. Thus these pictures compel careful scrutiny of their physical existence . . . all the while suggesting that these details are means, not ends."[62]

1. Robert Goldwater, "Reflections on the Rothko Exhibition," *Arts* (March 1961) : 44.
2. Robert Hughes, "Blue Chip Sublime," *The New York Review* (21 December 1978) : 16.
3. John Ashbery, "Paris Notes," *Art International* (25 February 1963) : 73.
4. See Clement Greenberg, "Art : How Art Writing Earns Its Bad Name," *Encounter* (19 December 1962).
45. See 42. [Mark Rothko, "Editor's Letters," *Art News* (December 1957) : 6.] See 47. A few statements attributed to Rothko were published after 1949. See 26. [Mark Rothko, statement delivered from the floor at a symposium on "How to Combine Architecture, Painting and Sculpture," The Museum of Modern Art, 1951, published in *Interiors* (May 1951): 104.] Seldon Rodman, in *Conversations with Artists* (New York: Devin-Adair, 1957), 93–94, recorded what he remembered of a swift, unfriendly encounter with Rothko. See also Dore Ashton, "Art: Lecture by Rothko," *The New York Times*, 31 October 1958, 26.
46. Katherine Kuh, "Mark Rothko," *The Art Institute of Chicago Quarterly* (15 November 1954) : 68.
47. Mark Rothko lectured at Pratt Institute, New York, on 29 October 1958. The talk was not taped. I took detailed notes on the lecture which have not been published. Dore Ashton's notes on the same lecture appear in "Art: Lecture by Rothko." Unless otherwise identified quotes are taken from my notes.
48. Gottlieb and Rothko, "Letter to the Editor." [Adolph Gottlieb and Mark Rothko (in collaboration with Barnett Newman), "Letter to the Editor," *The New York Times*, 13 June 1943, sec. 2,9.]
55. Thomas F. Mathews, "The Problem of Religious Content in Contemporary Art," a lecture delivered to the International Congress on Religion, Architecture and the Visual Arts, New York (30 August 1967). Mathews' thesis was that the painting of Rothko, Still, and Newman was the valid religious art of our time.
56. Gottlieb and Rothko, "The Portrait and the Modern Artist." [Adolph Gottlieb and Mark Rothko, "The Portrait and the Modern Artist," broadcast on "Art in New York," Radio WNYC (13 October 1943).]
60. Kuh, "Mark Rothko."
62. Goldwater, "Reflections on the Rothko Exhibition," 43–44.

What was to replace conventional subjects? The answer to this question, as Rothko viewed it, was his own self-transcendent experience as revealed through art, through painting and, above all, color, the inherent expressiveness of color. Such experience, personal though it is, possesses intimations of The Transcendental, "of the presence of God, the all-holy."[55] In this sense, it is religious or, because it is not based on any established dogma, quasi-religious. To put it another way, transcendental experience generated through the creation and apprehension of art is analogous to that generated through religion. Because such experience is "real and existing in ourselves,"[56] it is human. Because it is intense, it is dramatic. Because it calls to mind death, it is tragic. And when it promises nothing beyond, it can be unbearably tragic. Rothko's talk at Pratt was studded with the words "human," "drama" and "tragic.". . .

Rothko stopped publishing statements in 1949 because of his "abhorrence of . . . explanatory data."[60] Let the viewer be! But art criticism would not cease.

But there was rigorous writing, above all Goldwater's review of the retrospective, which stretched formal analysis to the point where it evoked poetic

Mark Rothko, ca. 1983
Photo Regina Bogat

TONY SMITH | PAINTINGS AND SCULPTURE

September 23 – 22 October, 1983

ALFRED JENSEN

THE LATE WORKS
December 2 – 7 January, 1984

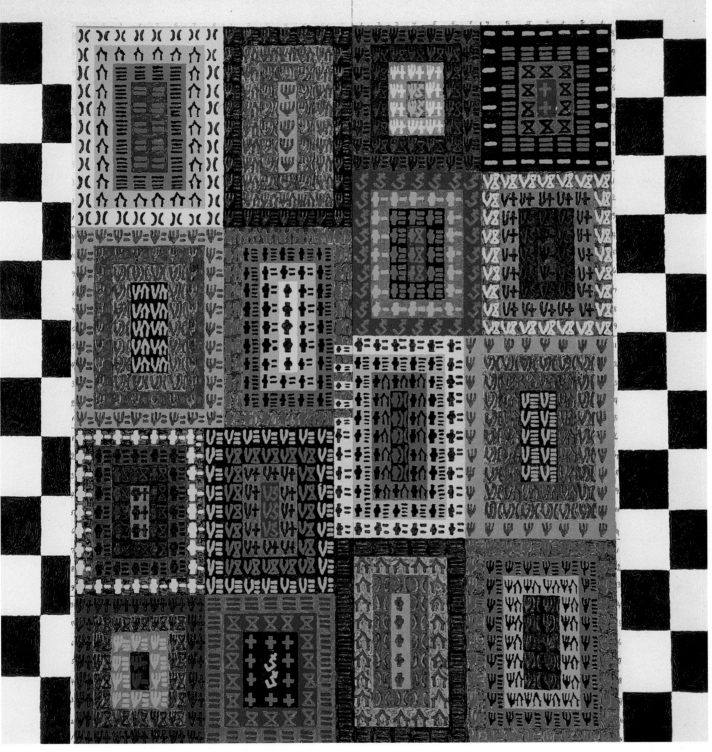

Research in a Growth Hormone, 1978
oil on canvas, two panels, each 114 × 48", overall 114 × 96"

AGNES MARTIN | **PAINTINGS**
January 20 – 11 February, 1984

Untitled #4, 1983
acrylic and pencil on canvas, 72 × 72"

JOAN MIRÓ

THE SCULPTURE OF MIRÓ
April 27 – 9 June, 1984

Toward A New Miró
by Peter Schjeldahl
Excerpt from Pace catalogue

. . . The large majority of Miró's sculptures fall within a broadly contemporary frame: since 1968. Unlike Picasso, Miró was not a periodic sculptor throughout his career, but a painter increasingly preoccupied with sculpture late in life. With no disrespect for his beautiful late paintings and prints, I regard Miró's sculpture as easily the crowning achievement of his old age. He had one comparably intense previous involvement with three-dimensional work: the "poetic object" assemblages of the 1930s. But those works (few of which survive) may be seen as outriggers of his development in painting. A foursquarely sculptural inspiration reigns in the late torrent of "Personages," "Women," "Birds," and combinations of these highly non-standardized motifs—with the frequent found object or monumental project or other tour de force, typical of Miró's endlessly supple inventiveness.

Apart from proximity in time and high quality, Miró's sculptures have a potentially large artistic significance, a significance bearing on the currently confused and debilitated situation of sculpture in general. Indeed, the considerable trouble we are apt to have in appreciating Miró's sculpture is very much of a piece with the daunting problems confronting young sculptors in the '80s: 1) how to give serious credence to modeled sculpture in the round after the success (and exhaustion) of "pictorial," either relief-based or "drawing-in-space" modernist aesthetics, and 2) how to reinvest sculpture with mimetic, representational, and symbolic functions after the triumphant scorched-earth policy of Minimalism.

Now, that may seem a terrible lot of theoretical baggage for a body of work usually described, if at all, as "playful." But I am convinced that, in

269

his always intuitive and spontaneous, non-analytical way, Miró the sculptor reached an advanced and even radical understanding of his medium—such that to comprehend his work in it is to discover keen issues of theory, and vice-versa. One must be cautious, of course, to respect the historical peculiarities of Miró's style, its rootedness in Surrealism and, for want of a more exact term, classical modernism. Considered stylistically—for its look, its signature—his sculpture is indeed of the past. But then, isn't the making-present of pastness the supposed keynote of postmodernism? There is such a thing as being too cautious—timidly pious and clerkish—in the ways we use art. And Miró's integrity is equal to any use of his art, especially since, in this case, our aim will be not to change him, but to change ourselves. . . .

The dominance of surface in Miró's sculpture, as in his paintings, renders his composition of forms and parts lyrically casual, almost random.

There is a quality of "here and there," of "this and that," of "why not?"—making composition as ineluctable and as unimportant as a pattern of stars reflected in water. Also, strangely enough, this dominance of the surface acts to short-circuit "tactile" response (a desire to touch), despite the sculptures' often seductive textures. The materiality of Miró's surfaces launches a giddy ascension of meaning: up from the physical through the psychological into the transcendently imaginary. We have little impulse to fondle the skin because it is a skin without insides and without otherness—not a skin that feels but a skin that *is* feeling. Truly experienced, Miró's sculptures, like his paintings, induce a sense of disembodiment: not anti-sensually, as in Mondrian or Kandinsky, but with a sensuality freed of all particular relations, raised to a state of oceanic self-identity and self-enjoyment. . . .

Our problem in appreciating Miró's sculpture and in imagining a newly mimetic contemporary sculpture is—to give it a name—the problem of the "personage." A basic theme of sculpture between Surrealism and Minimalism, the personage expressed a modern fascination, partly inspired by primitive art, with the ineffaceable integrity of the human image: how even the slightest cue, the least suggestion of head or leg or breast, can and does trigger the perception of a whole figure. The personagist plays at associating to the most abstracted and degraded figures a range of individual qualities—qualities not just of a figure but of a person, not only of an objective creature but of a subjective "character." This fundamental operation of Miró's sculpture is in an aesthetic blind spot for us, subject to reflexive disbelief.

Why? The revulsion against mimesis of formalist and Minimalist sculptors was too powerful to be explained merely in terms of aesthetic principle. I think the cause is a trauma affecting our entire civilization. It reflects a drastic loss in the significance of the individual human—a desacralization, if you will, inflicted by the periodic horror of mass murder and the quotidian terror of nuclear weapons. The notion of a distorted—say, a "melted"—human face is all too eloquently referential for us. We feel less tyrannized by the ordinary aspect of things than desperately anxious about its survival. The personage may strike us as a joke in unwitting bad taste. (I ignore, here, the expressionistically distorted figure, which apostrophizes anxiety and is in bad taste on purpose: This trope was alien to Miró.)...

In seeking a contemporary relevance for Miró's sculpture, I am aware of difficulties other than stylistic and other than those produced by our own discontents. The most insidious—because of the authoritative line of Miró's modernist champions—is a tendentious identification of him with conservative styles and values, from "pure" abstraction to anti-cosmopolitanism. Such bullying is futile in the long run, but in the short run it can daunt the unsure—those, that is, who have not built hysterical defenses against the vivifying contradictions of history and life. If Miró's art, or that of any past master, is to live, it must speak to our changing needs, not rebuke us for having them. Some people cannot leave off using the past to beat the present, never mind damage done to the past in consequence. They would rather kill everyone's pleasure in one of their heroes, it sometimes seems, than take a chance that he will please riff-raff.

On their own terms, our contemporary mossbacks might well fret about Miró, who seems open to a charge of affinity to some of the urban primitives of the post-graffiti movement. Not only the anarchic element in Miró but also the formalistic is instinctively echoed by these up-and-comers, natural-born "field" painters since their earliest, train-yard nights and days. Certainly Miró makes a better precedent for them than the often-cited Dubuffet. Sociological assumptions to the contrary, much of their work shows a fastidious love of order and an aspiration toward beauty, not the "brut." Obviously the comparison founders on a lot of differences, but it is a legitimate example of the tricks of parallax that history can play—and must be allowed to play, if art is served by constant refreshment of vision.

CONSTRUCTION

July, 1984

Pace Editions and The Pace Gallery shared the new second floor, although the gallery's primary exhibition space continued to be the third floor gallery at 32 East 57th Street. The second floor space had 14 foot ceilings, and as the size of paintings began to increase significantly during the 80s, the works themselves demanded a more commodious environment. The second floor was rebuilt into a more flexible gallery that would become the gallery's primary space. Pace Editions, now called Pace Prints, took over the third floor, which was used as additional space to mount more comprehensive exhibitions, and for offices and viewing rooms for the growing inventory of multiples and editions that were being published by contemporary masters, under the direction of Dick Solomon. Within the next few years, Pace, including the gallery, Pace Editions, Pace Primitive and Pace/MacGill (photography), would expand to occupy seven floors at 32 East 57th Street.

BRICE MARDEN

RECENT WORK
September 28 – 27 October, 1984

17.1.84
KoH Samui
Thailand

Dear Anne,
To bring you up to date on this painter's
meanderings. Hydra, Athens, Basel, Freiburg, Bern, Zurich, Thaila[nd]
The window samples were completed in mid December
I enclose my only reference photos, taken somewhat
crudely, as notes, just before I left Freiburg. The stay
there was dry and full of work. Siegfried Bauser, the
head of the glass firm was a warm, concerned and
marvelous host ... was told to rid me of
my "a... ...s and be dirt. The
...corner of the upper
...work because t...
...most problematic
...ass factor. We
...to explore an bro...
...linger as to putt...
...is being the
...ying over the
...the four col...
...s to be operable on pain...
medium did not seem disturbing

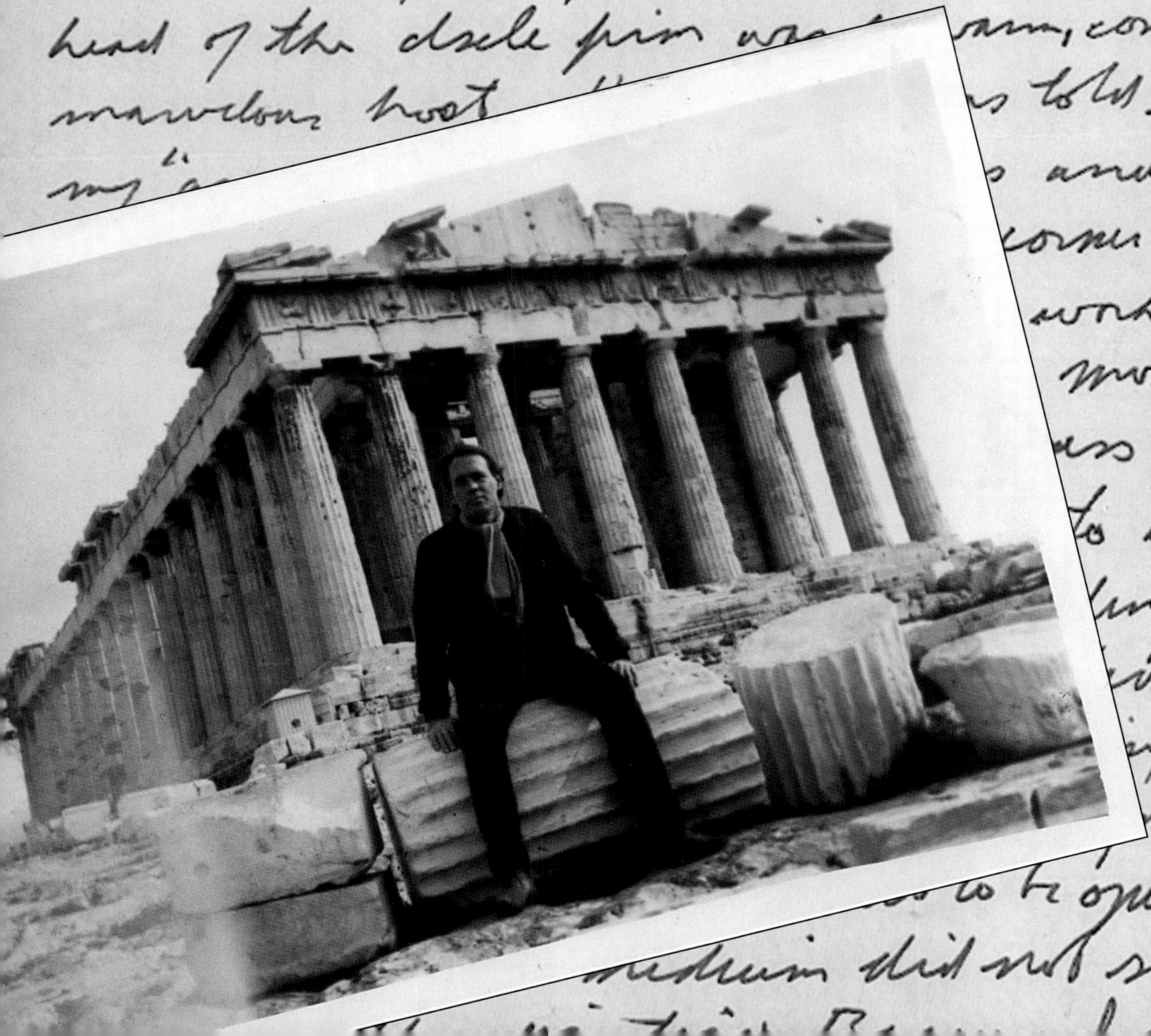

17–1–84
Koh Samui
Thailand

Dear Arne,

To bring you up to date on this painter's meandering. Hydra, Athens, Basel, Frieburg, Bern, Zurich, Thailand.

The window samples were completed in mid-December. I enclose my only reference photos, taken somewhat crudely, as notes, just before I left Frieburg. The stay there was dry and full of work. Siegfried Hauser, the head of the firm was a warm, concerned and marvelous host. He says he was told to rid me of my "angst" about stained glass and he did. The first sample is the low right corner of the upper yellow window which is shown to work because the yellow window could prove to be the most problematic in terms of the light entry or blindness factor. We toned that down and were able to explore a broad range of yellows but thoughts do linger as to further options in situ; the prime option being the application of opaque black drawing over the upper yellow window alone amongst the four colours. Control of the colours worked out to be operable on painterly terms. The medium did not seem disturbingly different from painting. Because of structure factors drawing of shapes has been altered but that opens up compositional possibilities within windows that I find exciting. We didn't fully explore the more erudite possibilities of technique but we touched on the ones I had thought of using enough so that I can have *working* ideas rather than conceptual ones. I think the green window works well. The yellow is still off and hard to judge. Large areas would nullify some of the somewhat difficult colours.

The samples will be delivered to the committee at the end of January 1984. Steel frames have to be built, glass painting must be cooked in the oven and, they have to be permanently puttied. The committee knows of this further work that had to be done before delivery. The committee should be informed that I will be back in Europe in the early part of March and that at that time I can meet with them to answer any further questions they may have. One reason given for my making samples is that they now will have a better idea of approximate workshop cost, I don't think any money should be discussed until you and I have met again. . .

Thailand is beautiful, distant, not too mysterious and filled with believably beautiful houses and simple wood furniture. The wood, lumber, impresses me the most. The landscape is one that would produce Buddhism. With this travel I become more convinced that the art comes out of the landscape. It always looks just like it. Rocks in the sea look like reclining buddhas etc.

A lot of Noguchi reminders here in the south where rocks fall in to and out to sea, softly. Limestone formations, small eruptions that become mountains. Sculptural scale. The clouds do not flow along the horizon but move independently of it, turning in convolutions that surprise this western eye. . . .

– B.M.

275

JULIAN SCHNABEL

Julian Schnabel and the
Mythography of Feeling
by Gert Schiff
Excerpt from Pace catalogue

Julian Schnabel's achievement is in constant danger of being obscured by his success. His sudden rise to fame, the fact that at 32 he has, in the words of one of his European defenders, the status of a "classic" of the new painting—such are the considerations that have politicized the man to the detriment of a fair evaluation of his work.

Much has been written about Schnabel's use of materials, about how the plates relate to human scale, about his borrowings. Critics have discussed, time and again, his position vis-à-vis Minimalism, Expressionism or the combine paintings of Rauschenberg. There seems to be a consensus in only one respect: "Schnabel's paintings block attempts at decipherment . . . and so impel the viewer to locate his relationship to the painting viscerally."[1] . . .

There is, of course, in any iconographic endeavor a temptation to explain away the mystery, to narrow down the plurality of reference to a neatly manufactured set of "messages." One is but too easily led astray by one's own tendency to project. "Although my work is about meaning," Schnabel says, "it is not necessarily your meaning."[2] However, Schnabel's own personal signs and symbols are invariably joined by borrowings from every possible source in high art, low art, and non-art. One must have seen the billboard which forms part of Schnabel's open-air studio. On it, pinned and pasted and exposed to the elements, hang clippings from German pre-WWI magazines; reproductions of details from Goya's Black Paintings; Mexican playing cards; illustrations of racial types from an old ethnographic publication; turn-of-the-century advertisements; a line engraving from a nineteenth-century tract on mythology; a nude from a physique magazine; devotional pictures; a depiction of tephillim; old postcards and heaven knows what other grist for his omnivorous mill. When incorporated into Schnabel's paintings, such images stand out like glyphs preserved intact on a weathered, overgrown tablet, allowing the beholder to divine at least part of the runic text. . . .

One-Figure Plate Paintings:
Ghosts, Puns and Passions
. . . Much of the emotional impact of the plate paintings derives from an antagonism between the integrity of a painted face or body and the brokenness of the surface upon which it is painted. An example is *T.T.* Here, Schnabel creates a pattern-upon-pattern effect reminiscent of Gustav Klimt's portraits of Viennese society ladies. While the surrealist horse-skull on the tabouret corresponds, by way of a visual pun, to T.T.'s bony frame, the only intact plate to the right bears the image of a Louis XVI lady, her eighteenth-century prototype. In *800 Blows,* a near-identity of surface structure and representation is achieved: the broken shards render the ravages time has wrought on an antique marble head.

Schnabel prepares his shard-covered supports with no particular composition in mind. He can fit almost any subject to their jarring, strained surface rhythms. *Vita,* an almost El Greco-like woman, tall and lithe, is rendered in the attitude of the crucified Christ. The plates both enhance and disrupt the articulation of her body. Directional brushstrokes invest the background plates with a downward tendency, like a blizzard of giant snowflakes. An ornate yellow plate, broken in four, replaces the traditional motif of solar and lunar eclipse. We all know the real "Vita": Veruschka, the world-famous fashion model who was also one of the first practitioners of body art. Schnabel uses the crucifixion metaphor to show the pain and sorrow that may lie at the root of such glamour. In the secularized vocabulary of modern painting, the Passion of Christ has long been used as synonym for Everyman's passion. Ensor, Klinger, Grosz and Beckmann provide examples. But by rendering Vita's hands as being not nailed to the cross but held by two straps, Schnabel stops short of a total identification of an individual with a universal symbol. Instead, he depicts Vita's hands like the helpless wings of a wounded bird. Quite generally, he treats religious symbols not as absolutes, but as mythopoeic structural elements. . . .

Paintings on Velvet II: Ethnic Types
Schnabel at the beginning of his career was living for some months by himself in Mexico, dividing his time between surfing and looking at Zapotec artifacts. Without any contact with other whites, and unable to speak native languages, he experienced with his own isolation the radical otherness of the Indians. This turned his thoughts towards mankind in all its ethnic variety, especially to those tribal societies which,

Resurrection: Albert Finney Meets Malcolm Lowry, 1984
oil and molding paste on velvet, 10 × 9'

I was introduced to Julian Schnabel's work by Chuck Close, who asked me to meet him at Mary Boone's gallery to see Julian's first plate painting show. Chuck's enthusiasm was infectious and I was very impressed by the sheer power and originality of Julian's enterprise. Artists are the best divining rods for a dealer to follow. Lucas Samaras had brought Chuck's first portraits at the Bykert Gallery to my attention in the same way.

I followed Julian's shows, always impressed with his fecundity and saw the many works that Charles Saatchi had amassed. Through a series of events that included Saatchi's endorsement and a visit to Schnabel's tennis-court-turned-studio in Bridgehampton with Leslie Wadding-ton, I learned from Julian how influential my 1981 show of Picasso's Avignon *paintings had been on his work. Beguiled both by his innocence and the scale of his ambition, and impressed with his ability to keep exploring new avenues of his talent, I asked Julian to join Pace. The time was right for both of us.*

281

The King of the Wood, 1984
oil and bondo with plates and bronze
casting of spruce roots on wood, 10 × 19'6"

untouched by civilization, still live according to those prelogical modes of existence that took shape during the nameless millennia preceding historical time.

Two paintings, *Ethnic Types #15 and #72* and *Ethnic Type #14*, are offshoots of this continuing preoccupation. The first one includes images of a Malay and a Kaffir; the second, a Papuan Chieftain, all taken from an old ethnographic magazine. These are random choices; and so are the numbers, which do not refer to an (as yet unpainted) encyclopedia of human races, but hint at the vast number of possible alternative selections. . . .

Epiphanies: The Sacred and the Profane

. . . Finally, there is that tour-de-force of a monumental, tripartite plate painting, *King of the Wood*. . . .

Every feature of Frazer's narration has its precise counterpart in the painting. In large areas, the plates are so heavily overpainted that they are no longer perceived as separate entities but become subservient to the rendering of surface flicker. Yet there is a constant dialectic between their function as carriers of illusion, and as "molecular" structural elements. In a few instances they determine outline and modeling as, for example, in the face, where one eye is modeled by the convex rim of a plate, the other one by the concavity of another. The fact that the plates stand out in relief and are at the same time "flattened" by cohesive areas of color solves a representational problem: to let the figure appear immersed in the landscape and nevertheless assert itself in all its barbaric splendor. Add to this the perfect necessity of "extraneous" elements—the branch to the left that slurs over the figure's hand, the tangled roots to the right which echo the top of the willow tree—and you catch a trifle of the consummate art with which Julian Schnabel handles a method entirely his own.

Of all the painters of his generation, he has the widest range both in formal means and invention. If the return of emotion, imagination and meaning is what is called for in art today, he has already had a royal share in the work of bringing this about.

1. David Robbins, in *Julian Schnabel* (exhibition catalogue), Waddington Galleries, 1983, p. 3.
2. Julian Schnabel, *"The Patients and the Doctors,"* Artforum, February 1984, p. 56.

JEAN DUBUFFET

MIRES
December 7 – 12 January, 1985

INSTALLATION DUBUFFET
MIRES   DEC 7 - JAN 12 1984

THE PACE GALLERY

Mire G 111 (Kowloon), August 4, 1983
acrylic on canvas, 79 × 78¾"
© 2001 Artists Rights Society (ARS), New York/ADAGP, Paris

MARK ROTHKO

Rothko's Endgame
By Brian O'Doherty
Excerpt from Pace catalogue

Rothko's dark paintings of 1969 are still an open question, one of the few pieces of unfinished critical business of the abstract expressionist era. How many of them are there? The number is uncertain, probably around twenty-five. All are on canvas, in vertical and horizontal formats. Seven are in the Rothko Foundation, seven are in the estate. The rest are in private collections in Europe and elsewhere. The year of his death, some were first shown at Marlborough which represented his work at that time. . . .

Whatever the dark paintings' ultimate value, they were not taken seriously by many. And the least we can do is examine them with a seriousness commensurate with Rothko's when he made them. Never an artist of trivial emotions, and always suspicious of easy gains, he was stretching himself here, taking what he realized were large risks, courting further misunderstandings—painful for a man who placed communication as one of his highest artistic goals. . . .

These paintings prowl around a single question. Formally it can be expressed as how to keep a unitary image in dialogue with its dialectical parts—a problem with all paintings, but here reduced to its fundamentals. This question is, I think, resolutely answered, though the changes in size and format of the dark paintings may indicate some doubts on Rothko's part. As minimal paintings, self-referential and generating their own critique, they are to my mind convincing in their relationship to the monochrome paintings by younger artists of the sixties. Most monochromes then left themselves very few options; the emphasis was on edge, margin, surface. The dark paintings never define their terms so narrowly that there is nowhere to go. . . .

But Rothko was never a formalist painter. Content obsessed him. Yet he was too sophisticated to bring into his discourse those two mutually dependent cripples, form and content, criticism's Lucky and Pozzo. Implicit in these last works—the exact sum of their means—is an answer to the question that the entire oeuvre circles around; like most answers in art, it poses another question. That oeuvre, if we run it through chronologically, alternates between dark and bright. The earlier dark works tend to be monumentalized in series. Often wine-colored, maroon, or dark purple, they are richly sensual, and our cultural associations, since Nietzsche, tend to cue them toward the Greeks and tragedy. They deal, perhaps, as much with the myth of the tragic as with the tragic itself. They are elevated in feeling, rhetorical, and grounded in the sensual. If we speak of their formality, it is the formality of ceremony donated by the frontality and the

hypnotic intimacy inescapably forced on us by color and large scale. The ceremony is gone in the last paintings, which is why, I think, they are his most modern pictures.

The richness of the tragic as a cultural idea has been replaced by a barer, more impoverished definition. A contraction has occurred, but the result is far from negative. The removal of the sensual leaves works that, in their extraordinary reductions, attempt to preserve in the spareness and calm of the image a trace of the transcendent in the face of the tragic, which is of course antagonistic to it. The two areas in their dialogue and fusion with the overall image summon the cultural implications of dark and bright; but the eloquence of the means that so summons them withdraws to leave a question that can be posed according to the viewer's scenarios of "meaning.". . . These works are about a more abstract idea than any of those previous to them. They thus imply a different mode of thinking about the spectator, a spectator deeply considered in this painter's mature works. The options are left to us; like some of the best poetry, the last paintings offer rewards with effort but do not solicit attention. The strategies of these works trap a different definition of the author, of an artist who is not there. For the artist is indifferent to whether the spectator comes or goes. The transcendent self has been largely replaced by a secular void. Again this is a more modern conception of the artist, who previously seemed a third party anxious but unable to introduce the spectator and the work.

Now these paintings pose another question that would not have been asked twenty years ago. Can abstract painting possess the meanings here ascribed to it? How odd to find oneself asking that question after seventy heroic years of abstract art. Yet it must be asked, now that the post-modern reaction devaluates the achievements of classic modernist painting, and indeed of modernism at large. It is a question that some minds—and they are often sophisticated literary minds—welcome now that abstract painting is no longer fashionable. Abstraction seemed to be equally idealistic and subversive of "reality," and by implication of man's place in the world. A quasi-political content was thus forced upon it, and its gratuitousness became suspect. Aside from the usual changes of fashion, there is something slightly sinister about this. It is now time to represent the evidence to refute the facile charge that abstract art is somehow handicapped in its reach. The dark paintings, Rothko's most stringent and modern pictures, are in my view an irrefutable part of that evidence, should they be seen as they are. . . .

Untitled, 1969
acrylic on canvas, 100 × 80"

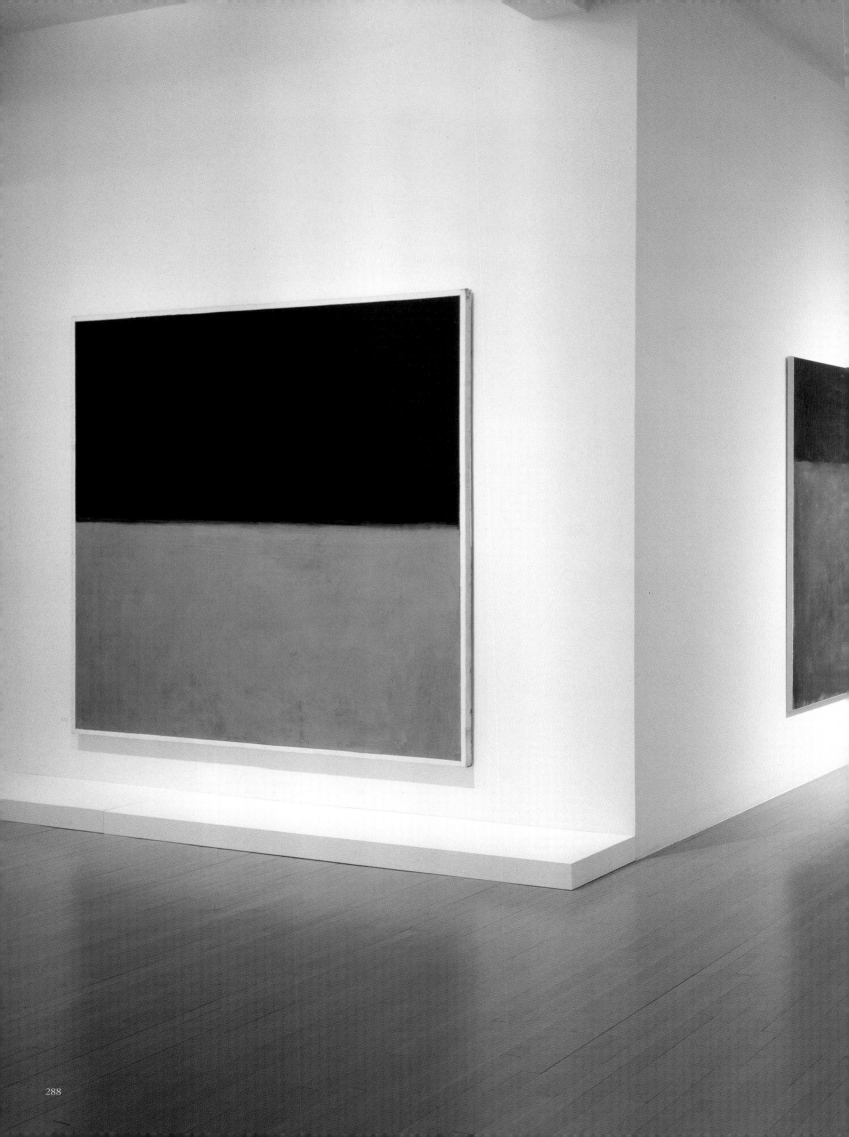

Sandy Says. . .
by Jean Lipman
Excerpt from Pace Catalogue
Reprinted from *Calder's Universe*, 1976

Sandy has always had a remarkably uncomplicated view of himself, his work, life and family, and a way of succinctly stating his values—though he repeatedly makes it clear that he just wants to work, not talk about it. His autobiography contains the sum of what he has wanted to say. . . . [Following are] comments from interviews and statements and, above all *Autobiography with Pictures* by Calder.

Sandy has said that he had "a big advantage" in that he was "inclined to be happy by nature." Indeed, from his earliest years, his life has been filled with a series of pleasant events and people. . . .

Asked by a *Life* reporter if he ever experienced sadness, he answered, "No. I don't have the time. When I think I might start to, I fall asleep. I conserve energy that way.". . .

About his work: "I feel an artist should go about his work simply with great respect for his materials . . . simplicity of equipment and an adventurous spirit are essential in attacking the unfamiliar and unknown. . . . Disparity in form, color, size, weight, motion, is what makes a composition. . . . It is the apparent accident to regularity which the artist actually controls by which he makes or mars a work.". . .

"I have a cardboard visor. I put it down and look for it when I arrive in the shop. That ties in with what I was doing yesterday."

"Sometimes I intend to destroy one of my works, but then I improve it." "If I don't like a piece, it's no good. That's my only criterion. . . .

"I have developed an attitude of indifference to the reception of my work, which allows me to go about my business."

Calder deliberately uses the word "work" instead of "art," and he usually calls individual pieces "objects" because "then a guy can't come along and say, no, those aren't sculptures. It washes my hands of having to defend them." In early catalogues there are few titles; Calder was inclined to use the generic term mobile, and over the years he has invented other general titles, such as Towers, Gongs, Totems, Crags, for series of related works. Specific titles can be convenient, he admits: "A title is just like the license plate on the back of a car. You use it to say which one you're talking about." "Sometimes it's the whole thing that suggests a title to me, sometimes it's just a detail." Often his titles are purely descriptive (*Red, Black and Blue*), but many refer to animals or other natural phenomena (*The Crab, Snow Flurry*). The title of his great mobile for Kennedy Airport, *.125* (the thickness of the metal from which the elements were made), reflects his background in engineering. Calder always loves puns or a play on words (he named the stabile *Gwenfritz* for the woman who commissioned it, Gwendolyn Cafritz, much to her dismay). . . .

Elephant, 1936
sheet metal, wire, lead, and paint
27½ × 33 × 35"
© 2001 Estate of Alexander Calder /
Artists Rights Society (ARS),
New York

293

ROBERT IRWIN

September 13 – 12 October, 1985

During the previous decade, Irwin traveled continually, while maintaining a dialogue with educators, students and public officials, concerning his ideas about the perceptual, contextual, and experiential nature of art. At the same time he created permanent "site-conditioned" works in public places and temporary installations in museums, galleries, and universities. This exhibition was comprised of plans, maquettes and photographs of both his completed projects, as well as some proposals not yet realized. In addition, he made two temporary installations in the gallery space, one involving the window that faces 57th Street and the other concerning itself with the spiral staircase that linked the gallery's two exhibition floors.

Arne Glimcher with Chuck Close:
A Conversation
Excerpt from Pace catalogue

A.G. The affinities that your work has with the reductionist or minimalist concerns prevalent in the '60's and '70's are well known. Your analytical investigations of the properties of perception and visual information processing itself are documented. Although the new work continues to build images out of a single incremental mark, something different, more expressionistic is happening. In addition to transmitting information of a perceptual sense, I'm also responding to psychological information especially in the portrait of "Fanny", which seems to mark a major extension of the work. The fingerprint itself, from which it is constructed, begins to suggest the possibility of a looser treatment.

C.C. I think there are several things going on at once, but I don't think the paintings are really looser. The tool is clumsier. My fingers are not capable of certain kinds of

nuances. And I rather like that. I like the physicality. I like playing with the feeling of the pigment, feeling how much I'm picking up, feeling how much I'm putting down. The fingerprint is a very personal mark; even though it's more personal and physical, the way I'm working is still similar in the way the paintings are construct-

ed or "built." I still work incrementally. The increments are now fingerprints. There are still limitations, the size of my thumb and my forefinger, and the various ways I can manipulate them to make the marks. That attitude stays the same—the activity is different.

But I think there is a change in attitude on my part, towards the nature of the image itself. I feel that something of this physicality has gotten through and changed the way the paintings feel. I feel more engaged in the actual making of the painting than I did when I used to spray stuff. There was some kind of intellectual distance. The way I'm working now feels more intuitive and more physical. You're actually touching. . . . It's less like magic. In the spray paintings, I would wave this spray gun, which was sort of like a magic wand, in front on the canvas. And I couldn't even believe that it was happening. In this, I'm much more actively involved in building the image. The paint is still very thin, the least amount of pigment possible to make the painting, but that deposit of paint is more manipulated. Some people have compared my work to minimal art, which is perhaps understandable because I came out of the same time and the same conditions that produced minimal work and process sculpture. The same influences influenced me, I suppose.

A.G. How would you describe those conditions?

C.C. A notion for trying to purge the work of certain conventions that were associated with abstract expressionism. The need to find other ways to make a painting. And then, the drive to make very personal art, to back yourself into your own particular corner. For example, the people who used to take rubber and stack it up, or lead and roll it, were involved in an attempt to find a material that didn't have any baggage; nobody else had used it. There are a number of conditions that were at play at the time. But even though I came out of the same conditions which were operating with those people, I also always wanted to make the antithesis of minimal painting. Yet, at the same time, my paintings were maximal. I always tried to put in unbelievable amounts of detail and information. And these are not paintings that you can have an assistant make. These are not paintings that can be ordered over a phone. I was always very interested in—I

Fanny/Fingerpainting, 1985
oil on canvas, 102 × 84"

hate to use the word because of its negative associations— a certain aspect of craft that I thought was necessary to make a product to which you had a certain kind of personal emotional commitment as an artist. If I didn't put that kind of time and energy into it, I didn't feel like I had done my job. And that was a very different attitude from either the pop or the minimal. A commitment over a long period of time is essential to the method of building something incrementally. (Which is why I've always had a greater affinity for my friends who are writers rather than those who are painters.)

A.G. We were discussing change. Can you elaborate on that?

C.C. The other thing which I think has changed recently is that initially I wanted to make big, aggressive, confrontational images. I chose to portray myself as the angry young man, the James Dean period of my life, with the cigarette hanging out of my mouth. I didn't try to purposely make those paintings ugly, but I think there was a certain kind of theatricality, in the sense that you present an image that you want to have dealt with in a certain way. On the other hand, they were also made in a very cool and detached way. So there was a nice kind of dichotomy between those two issues. I think what's happened is, as I've gotten older and mellowed, I've become more at peace with who I am as an artist and as a person, I realize that it's people who make art. I think I'm more in touch with who I am as a person. I have greater awareness and insight as to what makes me tick. I don't feel I need to pose in a certain way as much as I have posed myself and tried to pose other people. I feel much more sentimental about the images. I've chosen most recently to paint the people who really I am the closest to. I always painted my friends and I was looking for a particular kind of image. Grandma Fanny is my wife's grandmother, my children's great-grandmother, the only surviving member of her family—of ten brothers and sisters and mother and father, and all her aunts and uncles killed by Hitler. She's the only existing member of this huge family. And she's an incredible person.

A.G. In the portrait of *Fanny*, the fingerprint itself is used like a brushstroke, building up an emotionally sweeping image. It's as though it were made of fall leaves blown across the sidewalk, fixing into this image. It's very spontaneous.

C.C. I like that metaphor. In a way, I want it to look like it just happened, even though the progress takes a long time. I've always wanted my work to look like it just happened. People shouldn't have to think how much it must have taken to make that thing. I want those leaves to blow across the canvas and just congeal into an image, like magic.

A.G. *Fanny* isn't an impersonal passport photograph. It doesn't have the anonymity of a passport photograph that some of your other earlier images have. Fanny's photograph conveys a life filled with emotion, and the painting intensifies this feeling in an overwhelming way. And unlike my response to pictorial information, I seem to be responding to an extraordinary story unfolding.

C.C. Her face is a road map of her life. And, to a certain extent, everybody's face is. If you laugh a lot, you have laugh lines. If you frown a lot, you have furrows. But it's unbelievable what this woman has experienced.

A.G. In the same way, I think it was courageous and interesting to make drawings of the baby.

C.C. Well, you know, it's funny. I never allowed myself to paint old people or babies, because I didn't want to use *The Family of Man* notion. When I was a student, *The Family of Man* show at the Modern was an incredibly important show, because it happened when abstraction reigned supreme. And then, there was this nagging quality that that show had, and really, all we wanted to look at was paint and drips and splatters and stuff. So I think that throughout my whole career there's been a kind of love-hate relationship for photography. I've found it very seductive as well as something I felt I really needed to keep at a certain distance, but my paintings always transcended the photograph, even from the beginning. . . .

ISAMU NOGUCHI | SEVEN STONES

March 28 — 26 April, 1986

MANIFESTO

I am challenged by the unknown, by accidents, from which to extricate something beyond preconception. My effort has been to expand this area of challenge.

Looking for rocks to make the UNESCO Garden (in 1956-68), I started to carve granite boulders. I had returned to Japan some years previously with a Bollingen Fellowship on a search for the meaning of sculpture. This I had found in the rocks of gardens as the essential projection of time. Trees pass, the rocks remain, erode. How else may the enduring be manifest? Or sculpture reveal its secret?

Marble was something else again, which comes form water and its chemistry. The tradition of sculpture as I first knew it derived from marble, or more correctly, clay and its reproduction in marble and bronze casting. Both are an artisanage of indirection. With sheet metal came a diagrammatic sculpture which I carved with dissatisfaction in marble and slate.

It was in revolt from all this that my questioning began, that which led me through the many gardens I subsequently made larger than sculpture, environments – sculpture to walk through, a passage of time.

No matter how much time it would take or beyond duplicating, I wished to find out something about sculpture; that which I found missing.

I was fortunate in that my time has coincided with the rapid development of tools. Within our destruction or our saving would be found the needed scope of sculpture – its enduring to define the space of our garden, the earth.

If in a time of triviality such a course seems implausible, all the more reason. Seek the dead center of gravity, seek out of our difficulties the enduring.

–Isamu Noguchi, February 18, 1986

Stone Embrace, 1985
basalt, 67¾ × 41 × 4½"

PABLO PICASSO

JE SUIS LE CAHIER / THE SKETCHBOOKS OF PICASSO

May 2 – 1 June, 1986

The catalogue for the exhibition was a significant addition to the Picasso literature, published by Atlantic Monthy Press. The volume included a descriptive listing and image of each of the 175 sketchbooks in the estate. In addition, the following scholars wrote about one of the sketchbooks: E.A. Carmean, Jr. – The Saltimbanques, *1905; Robert Rosenblum – The* Demoiselles, *1907; Theodore Reff – Sketchbook No. 59, 1916; Rosalind E. Krauss – Sketchbook No. 92, 1926; Sam Hunter – Sketchbook No. 110, 1940; Gert Schiff – The* Sabines, *1962. Claude Picasso and Françoise Gilot wrote memoirs.*

The following texts are all excerpts from that book including Arne Glimcher's Preface which follows.

. . . Picasso considered all of his works to be entries in his diary; he excluded nothing. The sketchbooks are generic chapters inextricable from his oeuvre. In Picasso's paintings the spontaneity of gesture is deceptive since the manner in which he leaves his tracks visible superficially suggests minimal preparation. Although most of Picasso's solutions appear to be immediately worked out on the canvas, this was far from the fact. Many paintings sprang fully formed as the fulfillment of preconscious models, but very often others were the product of the process of trial solution and discovery through drawing. There are eight sketchbooks for *Les Demoiselles d'Avignon*, five for the *Saltimbanques*, four for the *Luncheon on the Grass* series, and two for *The Rape of the Sabines*. In sketchbook No. 171, Picasso inscribed: "La peinture est plus forte que moi elle me fait faire ce qu'elle veut" ("Painting is stronger than I am; it makes me do what it wants"). The sketchbook itself is the statement's validation.

"I am the sketchbook"—"Je suis le cahier"— appears in Picasso's own hand on the cover of sketchbook No. 40, and also serves as the title and cover of this book. That assertion of identity is crucial to an understanding of the sketchbooks as vital and interdependent parts of the development of Picasso's work. Conversely, we might say the sketchbooks are Picasso. They are the legacy by which we may decipher the process of Picasso's creativity and understand the cohesive totality of his lifework.

Some of the sketchbooks are small enough to have been carried in Picasso's pocket to cafés, bullfights, and on outings, to record events, responses to the environment, and interpretations of what he saw. Larger sketchbooks, sewn or spiral-bound, were used in his studio; these are volumes of preparatory and intermediary drawings in the service of picture-making as well as statements complete in themselves. Often they contain after-sketches based upon completed paintings and sculptures, such as sketchbook No. 140 which has images of the sculpture *The Bathers*. On occasion there are depictions of paintings that appear to be records of completed works functioning like inventory photographs of pieces that may have been lent to exhibitions. This kind of image exists in sketchbooks No. 96 and No. 99. . .

The sequence of drawings within a given notebook is important to an understanding of the creative process. It is, therefore, crucial that these sketchbooks remain intact. Unfortunately, some have been dismantled since Picasso's death, and, in at least one instance (sketchbook No. 24), the pages have been sold separately. Occasional, serial images, each so obsessively similar to the others that they might have been traced, are interrupted by a drawing that, at first, appears anachronistic (for example, sketchbook No. 59, p.12). Sometimes the relationship is clarified later in the series, but often the drawing appears to have functioned as an oasis for refreshment before Picasso continued his analytical investigation through the end of a series.

There are 175 known sketchbooks, created between 1894 and 1967. Picasso kept most of them intact, occasionally removing a page to be released as a single drawing. After 1964, however, Picasso sold complete sketchbooks of drawings to his dealer Kahnweiler at the Galerie Louise Leiris, where, with Picasso's agreement, they were dismantled and the pages exhibited as separate drawings. In these particular sketchbooks, though, the drawings were most often conceived as individual works, elaborate in color and complexity.

This book is an attempt to document Picasso's development through his sketchbooks and to provide a reference book for scholars. It is the direct result of five years of planning and research that culminated in the first exhibition of Picasso's sketchbooks, held at the Pace Gallery in New York, May 2 to August 1, 1986, with this book as its accompanying catalogue. . . .

– Arne Glimcher

The *Saltimbanques*
Sketchbook No. 35, 1905
by E.A. Carmean, Jr.

"Chronologically we are entering the unknown," wrote Pierre Daix and Georges Boudaille of Picasso's rose period, in their classic volume of the artist's early years, published in 1966.[1] And with good reason. These eighteen months, from the end of 1904 until May of 1906, not only gather Picasso's saltimbanque and circus themes, they also mark the transition from the youthful blue-period works to the classicizing and abstracting pictures made at Gosol, works created, so to speak, near the border of cubism. Furthermore, this period embraces Picasso's first clearly major undertaking, in the central painting of this period: the *Family of Saltimbanques*, the very large picture now at the National Gallery of Art, Washington.

In 1980, the rose period gained some new clarity. In that year, I requested the conservation laboratory of the National Gallery to make a complete x-radiographic record of the *Family of Saltimbanques*.[2] The resultant photographic images, combined with other, subsequent laboratory examinations and an extensive review of the rose-period works and the accompanying art historical literature, showed that the *Family of Saltimbanques* had evolved through three very different stages, and that key elements of the initial two were still extant beneath the final surface. Almost like archaeological strata, these successive layers in the painting recorded the developments in Picasso's art during this period. Moreover, as each layered work was very different in imagery, composition, and feeling, they create a trio of artistic magnetic poles, and around one or another, many of the other rose-period works can be clustered.

Now other works from this key transitional period have emerged. These are the drawings and notes contained in three Picasso sketchbooks of 1904–1906, No. 33, No. 35, and No. 36. Together, they further clarify Picasso's evolution of the *Family of Saltimbanques* and add new insights into his pictorial thinking during this crucial time. And, as always seems to be the case when unknown works of Picasso come to light, we find revealed in these notebooks further evidence of the depth and richness of the artist's imagination. . . .

Perhaps the most exciting is sketchbook No. 35, where the young Picasso recorded the beginning of his first grand painting.

No. 35 is a very small sketchbook—actually more of a pocket notebook in size, measuring only 14.5 by 9 cms, or approximately 3½ by 5¾ inches. With a total of fifty-one pages, it contains thirty separate drawings. The remaining pages are given to various notes and other written passages, including two laundry lists. This latter material, in addition to its notebook size, suggests that Picasso carried sketchbook No. 35 around outside the studio, using it for practical as well as artistic purposes.

Of course, in sketchbook No. 35, as well as in the other two sketchbooks, we cannot say with certainty that the sequence of drawings from front to back is the order in which Picasso actually created them; but the extant chronological ordering we do already have from other works suggests that such a first-to-last-page sequencing is indeed the case, and it is followed here in the discussion of the drawings.

Seated Figures

Sketchbook No. 35 begins with a set of six drawings in pen and ink of a seated boy. Nude and placed on a stone cube, this figure is studied in right profile, two back views, left profile, a frontal placement, and finally in a three-quarters position. Such a series suggests that Picasso was working with an actual model, rather than his imagination. This observation, in turn, suggests that Picasso had a stone cube in his studio for posing such models.

The seated figure comes as something of a surprise at the beginning of this first saltimbanque sketchbook. However, it does provide a transition—among Picasso's lost blue-period works in Paris in the fall of 1904 is the watercolor *Old Man with a Child*, where the elderly figure is shown seated on a similar cube.[10]

The theme of the figure seated on the stone cube, and occasionally the representation of just the cube itself, appears throughout this period. Its most fully realized form is in the sizable painting *Young Acrobat on a Ball*, now in the Soviet Union. This composition—also known in a related drawing—shows a male figure seated on the cube (or upon a drum in the study) watching the young girl on the ball in the near background. Interestingly, in this drawing (location unknown) Picasso appears to have a suggestion of possible color on the male's costume. Such a testing accords with the passage of brownish red Picasso has washed over the seated boy in the first of the six notebook studies. . . .

1. Pierre Daix and George Boudaille, *Picasso: The Blue and Rose Periods* (Greenwich: New York Graphic Society, 1966), p. 67.
2. See E.A. Carmean, Jr., *Picasso: The Family of Saltimbanques* (exhibition catalogue, National Gallery, Washington D.C., 1980).
10. See Daix and Boudaille, p. 248, D.XI.3.

JE SUIS LE CAHIER

THE SKETCHBOOKS OF

PICASSO

Throughout his long and prodigious career, the sketchbooks were always a part of Picasso's creative process. They functioned as a forum for the development of ideas, the analysis of images and the examination of his surroundings.

The sketchbooks of Picasso are the last unknown works by the greatest artist of the 20th century. Dating from 1894 to 1964, the one hundred and seventy-five sketchbooks include over 7000 drawings, notations and even shopping lists.

Apart from containing many of Picasso's greatest drawings, the sketchbooks serve as a vital historical tool. The development of images from famous works such as the *Family of Saltimbanques*, *Les Demoiselles d'Avignon*, the *Crucifixion* and *The Rape of the Sabines* can be traced through the pages of these sketchbooks. The precise sequence of drawings is another important asset unique to the sketchbooks, providing a greater understanding of Picasso's creative process.

In the light of these personal and spontaneous expressions, many facets of Picasso's work take on new and richer meaning.

The international tour of *Je Suis Le Cahier: The Sketchbooks of Picasso* will be sponsored by American Express.

The *Demoiselles*
Sketchbook No. 42, 1907
by Robert Rosenblum

It was appropriate to the most superstitious of twentieth-century artists that I myself harbored an utterly silly superstition about Picasso, which was brusquely shattered on April 8, 1973. On that day, some six and a half months before what would have been his ninety-second birthday, he unbelievably revealed his mortality by dying, whereas I had always had a crazy hunch that if anybody in the history of the human species might forever outwit Death by a truly supernatural creative energy, it would be that diabolic Spaniard. Of course, I was wrong, but only partly. Since 1973, Picasso has gone on living the afterlife of a canny pharaoh, whose buried tomb treasures, one by one, are turning up in the form of an unending succession of unknown paintings, sculptures, and drawings that oblige us to think about him not in the past but in the present and future tenses. From his teens to his nineties, he still seems to be making art posthumously, and everything we thought we knew about him remains tentative and alive, subject to the changes effected by the next disclosure of this or that startlingly unfamiliar work or by a flurry of smaller bits of new visual and documentary evidence that may either underscore or subtly alter some moment or some masterpiece of his eight decades of frenetic productivity.

It is in the latter category that this fresh rain of Picasso sketchbooks falls, a group of highly individualized *carnets* that, as exhibited and presented here, may set off yet a whole new sequence of interpretative events in the never-ending career of Picasso. The year of the sketchbook of pencil drawings I am introducing, 1907, is the most epochal of his first maturity; and the specific season is apparently the spring months, from about March to May, when he was involved in the early phases of *Les Demoiselles d'Avignon.* The sketchbook offers a variety of visual and written evidence to enforce and to expand our knowledge of Picasso's ever more breathtaking inventiveness in creating a strange new human race that would soon be shattered in the pictorial earthquake of the *Demoiselles.* . . .

. . . Primarily . . . the sketchbook is populated with studies of the female nude, an open-ended exercise generating a humanoid species that regressed to some archaic form of anatomical imagery and of regained magical powers. Here, the Darwinian evolution of a nineteenth-century realist art—which had attained, by the time Picasso was born, an infinite virtuosity in making painted and sculptured facsimiles of the human body in motion—is reversed, with the master pushing backward to imaginary origins that may glimmer, in passing, in figures such as those on pages F and G, who evoke an archaic Mediterranean world where women, like caryatids or peasants, carry baskets on their head or stride forward with ritualistic vases in hand. But such figures, which hark back to an abundance of similarly archaizing motifs painted largely during Picasso's sojourn in spring and summer, 1906, at the Catalan hill town of Gosol, can revert to even more elementary distillations of form, as if a primeval vocabulary were being invented for the making of new idols to serve a religion still to be codified. Pages A and B, for example, appear to be the same goddess seen both head-on and from behind in an image of absolute frontality associated with exotic tribal arts or with the origins of Western sculpture in Egypt or archaic Greece. Moreover, this austere and rigid creature will serve as a model for other paintings of the period. Other pages, such as 19 and 20, demonstrate more informal variations on this manufacture of hieratic icons, with the former offering frontal and dorsal views and the latter, two lateral elevations of a deity cut from the same symmetrical mold. . . .

. . .[W]ithin the context of the sketchbook, this image of aggressive female sexuality becomes a kind of Galatea to Picasso's Pygmalion, a creature who can shift from the role of a timeless, immutable idol to that of a shrill modern harlot and who provides, so to speak, a rehearsal for the major drama of the *Demoiselles.* It is no surprise, then, to find interspersed in these pages two studies for that scene in a brothel parlor that began with a kind of stage setting in which a sailor draws back a curtain to enter the inner sanctum of what the French call a *maison close* and that ended, in July 1907, with that quintet of furies who confront the spectator head-on as if to draw him into their tumultuous theater of sexuality. . . .

Picasso at the Crossroads
Sketchbook No. 59, 1916
by Theodore Reff

Initially, it is through the quality of its drawings that Picasso's sketchbook of 1916 exerts its fascination. They project forms of a monumental power and scale with a boldness of vision altogether exceptional for an object of this kind. Over nine inches wide and twelve high, this is the largest of the ten sketchbooks Picasso used in the years of the First World War; but more important, most of its pages are filled to the edges with a single image, giving it an expansive power well beyond its actual size. The larger format evidently also encouraged Picasso to work more deliberately, for there are many signs of revision and of reworking in another medium—in black chalk or soft pencil over the harder pencil he began with—yet no signs of a softening or blurring of that fierce clarity which is this sketchbook's essential characteristic. The whole is in fact in excellent condition, as if it had not been opened in the seventy years since Picasso last closed it sometime in 1916. Close examination reveals that eight pages have been removed—the perforations near their inner edges made it easy to tear them out—and this was most likely done by Picasso himself, perhaps to give them away. Three of the missing drawings, two of them signed, are probably among those published separately in the Zervos oeuvre catalogue.

The artistic quality of the individual drawings is matched by the historical value of the sketchbook as a whole. In its pages we observe in miniature that simultaneous cultivation of two opposed styles, cubism and naturalism, which was the most striking feature of Picasso's art throughout the war years. The two styles not only coexist here, but are at their greatest distance apart: the severely rectilinear "crystalline cubism" of the studies of a seated woman (pages 5–11), whose flattened, largely abstract forms seem like exercises in plane geometry, could hardly be more remote stylistically from the suavely curvilinear "Ingresque naturalism" of the sketches of a sugar bowl and of the artist's own hand (pages 12, 37), whose foreshortened, fully rounded forms seem like experiments in perspective projection. Obviously delighted by his mastery of the two styles, Picasso deliberately compared them in different drawings of the same subject. In studies of a seated harlequin playing a guitar, for example, light, curved strokes describe the skillfully foreshortened forms on one page and dark, rigid lines define the boldly patterned shapes on the next (pages 35, 36). Two drawings of a full-length standing nude, one smoothly outlined and subtly shaded in the Renaissance manner, the other reduced to a sys-

tem of strongly contrasted lines and planes in the cubist manner (pages 13, 29), provide another example, equally striking if less intentional.

For all their obvious differences, however, the two styles share certain features—perhaps inevitably, as products of the same vision at the same moment in its development. With a few notable exceptions (pages 3, 4, 13, 17, 21), there is little suggestion of local color or modeling in the drawings in this sketchbook; line alone is used to define form and space. And this line is consistently thin and uninflected, without the graceful mannerisms seen in Picasso's drawings of a decade earlier or the nervous intensity of those he made one or two decades later. It is a deliberate, almost impersonal device for creating form, suggesting in most cases an incisive certainty and in others a slight hesitancy as the artist's hand gropes for the right direction. Besides this purely graphic unity, however, there is a unity of vision in the sketchbook that reveals itself in the cubist devices employed in naturalistic images, and vice versa: in the tilting up and flattening of the fruit in a powerfully sculptural still life (pages 2–4), for example, and in the vivid rendering of the table leg and chair in a largely abstract still life (page 21).

Although Picasso had already been working simultaneously in the two styles since the summer of 1914, he had employed the naturalistic one almost exclusively for drawings, especially for portrait drawings of friends such as Jacob, Vollard, and Apollinaire; the only major example among his paintings, *The Painter and His Model*, begun that summer, remained in his studio, unfinished and entirely unknown. In the summer of 1916, the period in which he most likely used this sketchbook, Picasso was preparing to reveal this recently developed naturalism on a grand public scale in the overture curtain he designed for the Diaghilev company's ballet *Parade*. His first thoughts about that project can be found in this very sketchbook, in the many drawings of a harlequin of the type already discussed. Thus, the historical significance of the sketchbook is obvious: in its pages we witness Picasso, not only employing and consciously comparing the two styles that so fascinated him at the time, but also beginning to plot that *coup de théâtre* in which they would be brilliantly juxtaposed in public for the first time. . . .

. . . Through this first venture into the theater, and the others that soon followed, Picasso was able "to go from the public of laborious though friendly exegetes to that of snobs, from Bohemians to society women, from Kahnweiler's narrow shop to the international stage," in short, "to open the doors that the uncompromising austerity of cubism had maintained shut against him."[1] It was in August that he took this momentous decision, which accelerated his movement away from the cubist style he had worked in almost exclusively, at least in painting, for the past nine years. And appropriately, it was in July that he chose for the first time to exhibit *Les Demoiselles d'Avignon*, the revolutionary work in which he had begun to explore that style in the spring of 1907.[2] The two events may not have been associated in Picasso's mind, but in retrospect they seem to symbolize the crossroads at which he found himself that summer. It was not unlike the crossroads at which the young Hercules had found himself in the well-known myth—an analogy made all the more compelling by the famous photographs of Picasso, taken in 1915–1916, showing the compact, muscular artist as a modern Hercules, stripped to the waist or in a workman's overalls.

In stylistic terms, it would be wrong to describe Picasso's art simply as moving from cubism to naturalism in these years. The movement we observe in the sketchbook of 1916 is not a progression from one to the other but an oscillation between them; and as he himself later said, "Different motives inevitably require different modes of expression,"[3] though we have seen that he could treat the same motive in entirely different modes. In psychological terms, however, it would certainly not be wrong to see a progression from the static and hermetic works of the "cold" or "crystalline" cubism of 1915–1916 to the more dynamic and accessible works of the "classical" cubism and naturalism of 1917–1919. As always with Picasso, such a change reflected changes in the circumstances of his life. . . .

1. Pierre Cabanne, *Pablo Picasso: His Life and Times,* translated by Harold Salemson (New York: Morrow, 1977), pp. 176–177.
2. Pierre Daix, *La Vie de peintre de Pablo Picasso* (Paris: Seuil, 1977), p. 151.
3. Statement of 1923, cited in Cabanne, *Pablo Picasso*, p. 197.

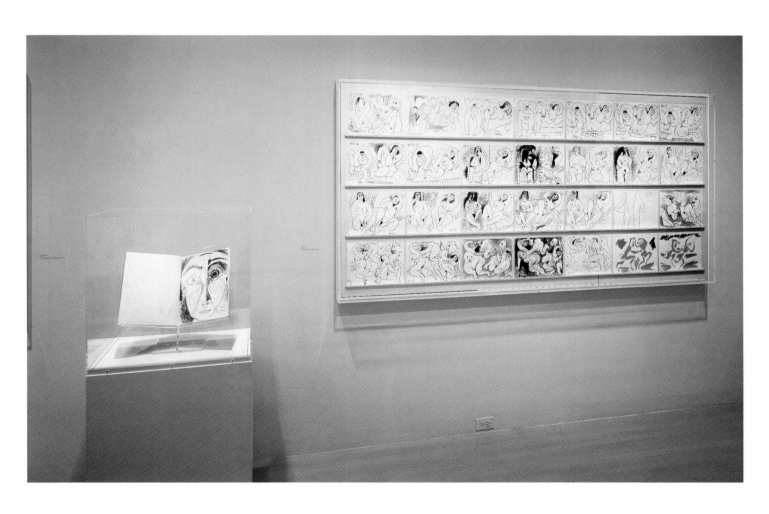

LOUISE NEVELSON

MIRROR–SHADOWS
September 19 – 25 October, 1986

Louise Nevelson, ca. 1979
Photo Balthazar Korab

Beyond Simulation?
by Wilfried Dickhoff

Now let us talk about death, about freedom, love, transcendence, magic, and soul—about all the things that seem to have been lost in a time of postmodern simulation culture, but that, as ever, constitute the thematic and spiritual core which is played on by the "visible presence" of painting. When I see a picture, I want to "see" what it has to "say." That is, I want to "take in" an experience sublimated to form. The constellation made up of color, composition, line, and light must stay in my pupils like an abstract heart. This visual analogy to spiritual and magical (re)cognition is what is still at issue. It is already clear that all of this is impossible, that art is now merely a structured nexus of artificial signs, that the artist is merely an art performer, and, thus, that the whole thing is a simulation model which serves as its capitalistic exchange rate. This is the situation from which today's artist must proceed. S/he must also understand that there is nothing outside the structure of the signifier and the omnipresent simulation of identities. But if art has any meaning at all beyond fashion, that is, beyond the eternal recurrence of the new as a parody of colorful corpses, it is when art begins where the affirmative garbage of nostalgic products of simulation ends.

It is no longer enough to be satisfied with the fact that everything is a mere mock-up of itself, in order to then reproduce (with a halfhearted, intelligent, concept-design aesthetic) just that art replacement sign from which one fancies oneself to be at an oh-so-smart distance. What is called for is a certain anachronistic unreservedness, a displaced autonomy, a putting oneself at risk, a spiritual and formal venture; pictures that hold the presence of death at bay, that speak from love, a spiritual and formal gamble: the pictorial presence of an individual universality that is quasi deducted from the structure of the signifier and in this way attests to a difference, a deviation. At issue is the picture as a "formulation of silence,"[10] full of "life," existing in between the system of language that we do not speak but that speaks us. At issue is the art of painting that doesn't imitate the visible—especially not the hyperreal—but "renders visible" the imaginary texture of reality by making an emotional fact visible. Whenever this kind of painting is attempted today, there is the danger that it will get screwed by its own simulation. That is, today every kind of painting is "romantic," since it must feel that to desire the impossible is perfectly rational. An art of authentic visibility is imaginable only as a paradoxic simultaneity of simulation and the romantic strategy of raising it to a higher power:

> The world must be romanticized. In this way you again can find its primeval meaning. Romanticizing is nothing but a qualitative raising to a higher power. . . .[11]

That is, a doubling of illusion *(Schein)*, a potentiation of the number of art signs, a multiplication of

JULIAN SCHNABEL

allusions, a diffusion of the self, and a perfecting of seductive art until this series of potentiation shifts to a simple, formally clarified, non-signifying utterance of magical presence. Where such romanticizing succeeds, the hyper-real interchangeability of the exchangeable art-ersatz is not invalidated. And even the autonomous artwork remains today in paradox.

Julian Schnabel's painting is no more and no less than a small alteration in this paradox, a counterfactual romantic breakthrough in painting, which from the beginning stood at odds to every aesthetic discourse, especially to modish postmodernism. Paradox in his pictures is accomplished in the facial structure. Simulation is in no case cached behind the illusion of pseudosubjectivity. On the contrary, it is openly visible. Material filled to bursting with potential meaning such as truck tarps, linoleum floors, or theater backdrops are used, for instance, to build up the backgrounds and foregrounds. Chains, bronze ornaments, picture quotes, antlers, and found objects of all kinds are only some of the means Schnabel helps himself to in order to construct a counterfactual magical surface. His large formats and sculptures arrive on the scene as if it were no problem to re-create the magic of African sculpture from "the mysteries in our culture." In other words, the simulacra are there, but so superficially and offensively overdone as to withdraw behind the (ir)real presence of the picture. Schnabel's battleground of materials breaks through the modish handiwork of the ingratiating, epigonic art now found everywhere, as well as through the conceptual design of postmodern paint appliers. All the talk about the impossibility of any positive placement *(Setzung)* in painting is serenely left behind by his pictures. By driving the picture as a "panel of meaning" to the extreme, he ventures onto the terrain of romantic yearning, where nothing looks like art anymore and everything becomes a question of the poetic (dis)harmony of soul and form. The involuntary methodic basis of these pictures is made up, on the one hand, of an irrealization of all meanings and, on the other, of a deliberate form sublimation and a calculatedly "ungainly" displacement. There are

systems of irreconcilabilities that draw your gaze in fascination, such as I have experienced with few other painters these last years. The instant *(Augen-Blick)* of fascination is that in which content rushes into form, in which the seen realizes the point of view of its perception and the picture raises its gaze, so that you no longer see it "before you" but see "with it." The crucial factor is then not so much in the forms and themes as such but in the forces, densities, intensities by which the inner equivalent of things gains a visible existence. Painting functions as a soulful and soul-inspiring magnet from which a rational idiocy rings out like willful self-determination *(Eigen-Sinn)* in the (heart)beat. It avoids the reality impact of themes and contents and acquires the reality impact of the imaginary. Schnabel's artwork thrives on the magic of painterly "visibility" for invisible spiritual realities. Like all great painting, it celebrates the riddle of visibility "in that it unfolds its dream world of carnal essences, actualized resemblance and mute meanings."[12]. . .

10. Jean-Paul Sartre, *Was kann die Literatur?* (Reinbek, 1969).
11. Novalis, "Fragmente und Studien 1997–98," in *Novalis Werke* (Munich, 1981), p.384.
12. Maurice Merleau-Ponty, *Das Auge und der Geist* (Hamburg, 1984), p. 22.

Excerpt from an essay originally written for Pace catalogue, later revised and entitled "Julian Schnabel's Intensity Program" with a new translation by Jeanne Haunschild, in: Wilfried Dickhoff, *After Nihilism: Essays on Contemporary Art* (Cambridge University Press, New York, 2000), pp. 97–108.

JOSEPH CORNELL | BOXES

December 5 – 31 January, 1987

Catalogue cover

Joseph Cornell
by Brian O'Doherty
Excerpt from Pace catalogue
Reprinted from *American Masters,
The Voice and the Myth*

Themes of innocence and the vernacular, of voice and myth, of Europe and America, of, indeed, Europe in America, offer themselves so plentifully in Joseph Cornell's work that they can obscure the reading of its quality. For this marvelous art is perhaps the most perfect any American artist has produced.

Cornell is as much a major figure as his contemporaries, Rothko and de Kooning. He is presented here as their peer, a figure large enough that history must inconvenience itself to rearrange its priorities. Not that Cornell has been neglected. Among American artists he is perhaps the greatest stimulant to "poetic" art writing. Everyone has done his exquisite Cornell paragraph, to the point that putting writers in boxes is one of his involuntary specialties. Serious attempts to place him in twentieth-century art are few indeed, and his isolation seems to survive his critics' best intentions. Lacking the aggressiveness of the historicizing thinker, he has come to stand for all that is marginal and eccentric. Once so relegated, he can be patronized like some obscure violin maker of inexplicable genius.

As an outsider of a peculiar kind, like Ryder and Poe, Cornell had a sense of European culture that is one of his art's strongest underpinnings. In the larger historical picture this will eventually bring him, as it has them, to the center of attention. He is one of those rare artists whose universe is, like theirs, so imaginatively authoritative that it corrects the narrow views we accept without question from the official "art scene" itself. Certain Americans, without ever seeing Europe, have re-enacted it in a way central to American experience; not only Europe but its fabulous culture which, in Cornell's case, narrows down to a part of it so intensely understood—Symbolist France—that it becomes a lens through which all the rest is seen. . . .

The range of territory covered by Cornell's art— epicurean and vulgar, sacred and profane—is astonishingly matched by the fact that his art includes all the others. Music, dance, theater, visual art itself, are incorporated not out of some Wagnerian desire to fuse them into an imperial synthesis, or from some modernist itch to conquer realms of experience inaccessible to particular arts, but by virtue of the most discreet modesty, which also extends itself to his means. His genre—the box which is not collage, not sculpture, not painting—seems to have evolved from a desire simply to give his objects room to breathe, so that they can etherealize space, make it purely metaphysical, and give to it the elasticity of the imaginative faculty.

Cornell fed not so much on the energy of the New York scene, with which he was well acquainted, but on the community of tradition, the spiritualism—if we may call it that—of culture. Communication is the key word in his universe, but his attempts to link present and past are devoid of the least competitiveness, of that egomaniacal self-assertion that is one of modernism's afflictions. Lacking any desire to subdue culture, Cornell makes the New York scene seem small in its range and grubby in its ambitions. Laughable though it may seem at first, Cornell bestrides American culture in a way none of his colleagues did. Nonetheless, a number of his contemporaries seem to fall within the scope of his interests. Stuart Davis and Rauschenberg in their orientation to the city and its vernacular; Andrew Wyeth in his pursuit of intimate sensations in a transcendental rural context; Edward Hopper in his relentless tracking of fugitive echoes through the stage sets provided by the deserted city; de Kooning in his obsessive connections between past and present—though in terms of mastery; above all, Rothko, whose desire, not just for an historical position but for an ideal culture, is similar to Cornell's. . . .

Untitled, mid-1950s
mixed media, 15 × 9½ × 2⅝"
© The Joseph and Robert Cornell Memorial Foundation/Licensed by VAGA, New York, NY

JEAN DUBUFFET

1943–1974 Wildenstein Gallery
1975–1985 The Pace Gallery

Jean Dubuffet:
Towards An Alternative Reality
by Mildred Glimcher

It was impossible to be unchanged by an encounter with Jean Dubuffet, for the electricity of his passionate confidence in his beliefs, and his articulate conviction in expressing them, pervaded his conversation as well as his written and painted *oeuvre*. And so, the last time I saw Jean Dubuffet in early April 1985, I was filled with sadness. He was bent almost in half by the deteriorated vertebrae that had tormented him for the last ten years, but more telling, the impish laugh, the ironic sense of humor were scarcely in evidence. He said he was finished painting: "I've been painting every day for forty years and I think that must be unhealthy for anyone!" There were no plans on his table for future projects—exhibitions, monuments, books—nor was he interested to discuss (as he

Wildenstein Gallery

always had been) the reception his work had occasioned in various parts of the world.

Dubuffet produced such a wealth of statements, responses, instructions, clarifications and manifestos that he himself warned: "If I chose to paint to express myself, it is because I do it better through painting than through writing. Trust my paintings and not my writings."[2] Shortly after his death, in the summer of 1985, Hubert Damisch wrote: ". . . No one was better than he at commenting on his works, reporting on their evolution, defining their aims, and setting forth their objectives, all with such an unwavering ease of expression, such a persuasive eloquence, and such authority that the reader was sorely tempted to flow into this mold and slip into the theater the painter had fabricated for his own personal use, at the risk of playing the minor roles and being reduced to borrowed postures, if not of being enthralled to the point of echolalia."[3]. . .

In 1968 William Rubin stated: "Dubuffet, in my estimation, the only major painter to emerge in Europe after World War II, stood outside the main trends of French art . . . ."[4] Throughout his life, Dubuffet remained always a subversive, a *provocateur*, within the cultural landscape of the mid-twentieth century. He sought, in his life and through his art, to liberate himself as well as the rest of us from all forms of intellectual oppression, which he believed could only be accomplished through the elimination or transformation of the mental habits and attitudes from which this oppression springs. . . .

The Roots of Jean Dubuffet
. . . As a result of the post-war devastation of the psychological, cultural and actual landscape, . . . the decade following World War II saw the flowering of a climate of repudiation of received values, and a simultaneous passion to return to origins both nationalistic and primal. . . . The search for authenticity and purity led the artists Fautrier, Wols, Michaux and Chaissac. . . to look outside Western culture, and within man, for new sources of inspiration. . .

It was in a similar spirit that Jean Dubuffet began in 1945 the systematic collection of what he called *Art Brut* (Raw Art). The collection, which today is composed of more than 5,000 works by those at the margins of art history—the insane, prisoners, mediums, isolated provincials—is informed by the position that the authentic moment of creativity must be captured in its savage purity and that intellectuals and culture have reduced the creation of art to an anemic, meaningless exercise of imitation and empty transformations. . .

Throughout Dubuffet's career the collection remained an ongoing source, a kind of personal history, and there are many aspects of *Art Brut* which resonate in and unify his work. . .

Dubuffet in America

. . . Dubuffet had nine solo exhibitions at the Matisse Gallery between 1947 and 1960. Throughout the fifties he was seen in several yearly group shows at the Matisse, Kootz, and Janis galleries. Represented by Daniel Cordier in America during the early sixties, his relationship with The Pace Gallery began in 1967 and continued to his death. Americans were therefore aware of Dubuffet from the beginning of his career and received his work with greater enthusiasm than their counterparts in Europe. One might expect this was the result of a less tradition-bound and more adventurous "culture" but in fact, it was the commitment of a few interested collectors who enthusiastically labored for the dissemination of his work.

Fascinated to see for himself this "uncultured" America, and curious about the collectors of his own work, Dubuffet made his first trip to America in November 1951, accompanied by his wife Lili and Alfonso Ossorio. . . . Ossorio relates that upon his arrival in New York, Dubuffet found a studio immediately, along with sources for materials, and was at work within ten days.

Dubuffet was particularly interested to meet the fiercely independent Chicago collectors, led by Maurice Culberg, whose dedicated enthusiasm for his work was born of their historical commitment to Surrealism, tribal art, and figurative painting. Journeying to Chicago for a few days in mid-December, Dubuffet had an exhibition at the Arts Club and on that occasion presented the provocative and influential lecture on his *Anticultural Positions*. The lecture was attended by only the most dedicated group of artists and collectors as it took place during a typically severe Chicago snowstorm. . . .

His February 1952 show at the Matisse Gallery exhibited the cycle of works, begun in Paris and finished in New York, entitled *Landscaped Tables, Landscapes of the Mind,* and *Philosopher's Stones.* He returned to Paris in April, disappointed with what he had found here and told Barbara Rose in 1979: "I came to America believing I would find non-conformism, but I was mistaken."[51] He continued to have regular gallery shows of recent work

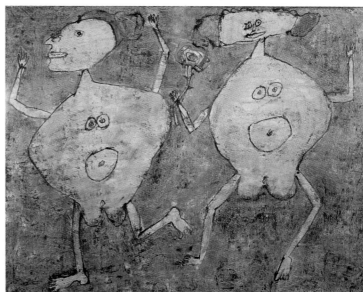

Gambade à la rose, December 1950
oil on canvas, 51 × 63¾"
© 2001 Artists Rights Society (ARS), New York/ADAGP, Paris

Wildenstein Gallery

323

until his death as well as retrospectives in 1962 at the Museum of Modern Art, the Art Institute of Chicago and the Los Angeles County Museum; a significant exhibition in 1966 at the Guggenheim Museum; and in 1973 a major retrospective at the Guggenheim which included the first presentation of his spectacle, *Coucou Bazar.* He returned to the States for two week periods in September 1966 and October 1968 and then for a few months in the winter/spring of 1973 to prepare the sets, dancers and music for the presentation of *Coucou Bazar* at the Guggenheim Museum.

His substantial exposure in America enables one to examine the question of his place in relation to his contemporaries in the United States. His European roots clearly established, one first must address the tantalizing question of the effects of that first six month visit in 1951–52 when the groundswell of Abstract Expressionism was washing over the New York art world. One is startled to realize that, with the exception of the subject matter of the *Bowery Bums* there is nothing to indicate he had ever left Paris. The drawings of the denizens of the Bowery are informed by the same agitated linearity and brutal dematerialization of the *Corps de dames* drawings done in Paris and it is impossible to establish without identifying labels, which *Landscaped Tables, Landscapes of the Mind* and *Philosopher's Stones* were done in New York or in Paris. . . .

Other Considerations

Dubuffet's work is suffused with an interior dialectic which engages culture and anti-culture, exteriority and interiority, graphism and the *informel,* high color and monochrome, figure and ground, relief and flatness, the natural and the synthetic; in fact all the issues raised by painting in the twentieth century. . . Fostered by his pursuit of constant revolution, the work was driven by this interior dialectic as a source of spontaneity. The artist strove, not for unity or logical development but rather the ambiguity, confusion and impermanence of real life. In order to avoid the ever-present danger of 'acculturation' Dubuffet committed himself to self-renewal through changing pictorial effects, materials and aims; remaining available to the unexpected as it might advance the direction of his work.

Yet the apparent self-consciousness of that renewal has sometimes troubled his audience. They see a contradiction between the discipline and consciousness which marked his life-style, his writing, and his careful craftsmanship; and his call for amnesia regarding culture and received values, in order to abandon himself to chance and the spontaneity of the materials. He was an artist who,

except when physically unable, worked every day for forty years. With the exception of Picasso, no artist of this century has produced more works and none, except Klee, has documented himself more fully. . . He lived in the most austere manner, shunning society, remaining in the same studio from 1944 until his death. But no effort or expense was spared to enable the accomplishment of his work, whether it was the collection of *Art Brut,* the establishment of the Secretariat, a lithography studio to produce the *Phénomènes,* or the *Cartoucherie* of Vincennes to effect the monumental *Four Trees* and the universe of *Coucou Bazar.* For Dubuffet, none of this bore on artistic creativity, which sprang from the work, the materials and the man. He believed this control over his environment permitted him the freedom to pursue his work on his own terms. He knew he remained part of the culture, and could not completely escape from it, but the purity of Art Brut was an ideal toward which he strove. . . .

2. Gaëton Picon, *Le travail de Jean Dubuffet.* (Geneva: Skira, 1973), p. 155.
3. Hubert Damisch, Catalogue introduction for 1985 retrospective at Fondation Maeght, Vence, France.
4. William S. Rubin, *Dada and Surrealist Art.* (New York: Harry N. Abrams) 1968, p. 409.
51. Barbara Rose, "Jean Dubuffet: The Outsider as Insider," *Arts,* April 1979, p. 146ff.

This text and the two following are excerpted from Jean Dubuffet: Towards an Alternative Reality, *Abbeville Press and Pace Publications, New York 1987.*

Notes For The Well-Read, 1945
by Jean Dubuffet

This early example of his more formal polemic style establishes most of the issues that concerned Dubuffet throughout the length of his career. . . .

Starting with the Unformed

Your starting-point is the surface that you have to give life to (a canvas or a piece of paper) and the first spot of color or ink you throw on it; the resulting effect. The resulting adventure. It is this spot that, as you enrich it and guide it, should direct the work. A painting is not built the way a house is built, according to the architect's blueprints. On the contrary: you turn your face away from the outcome, you grope your way backwards! You won't find a method for making gold just by looking at gold. Alchemist, hurry to your retorts. Boil some urine, gaze, gaze eagerly at the lead. That is your task. And you, painter, spots of color, spots and outlines. Look at your palettes and rags. There you'll find the clues you're hunting for. . . .

The Forgotten Native Soil

So-called artistic painting (which claims an exclusive patent on that title) has no dealings with the activity that more modestly dubs itself housepainting or interior decorating. They don't know each other anymore, they don't even greet one another. A bad state of affairs. What! Two men slave all their lives with the same paints, thickening them, thinning them, trying all sorts of things with them—and they don't even share information with each other? Can it really be true that they don't meet? I witnessed the beginnings of one artist, his very first steps. He walked past the house-paint store without even glancing at the cans and vats of coloring matter in all hues, and drawers full of the most dazzling powders—he just hurried on. At the art supply store, he bought six tiny tubes of artist's paints—smaller than the tubes used for lip balm or vaseline. Returning home, he squeezed a pea's worth of color out of each tube and sat down in front of an apple. Beneath his windows, a worker, armed with several cans of paint, was working out a life-sized illustration of an innkeeper presenting a menu. But the young artist saw neither the worker nor the work. I ran into him twenty years later. He was still painting apples with paints from his tiny tubes. I spoke to him about the picture of the innkeeper on the front of his building. It had never even crossed his mind to look at it, he told me. I also spoke to him about the colors of his studio walls; but he said artists are moody, absent-minded people, deeply absorbed in their work, so he had never taken notice. . . .

Material is a Language

Never say that the concern with technical means puts art on a sensual level or a craft terrain where it does not belong. That isn't true. Naturally, it's not hard to find examples of paintings that rely solely on those technical means—without the help of inspiration or the involvement of the mind—but the technical means used in these works are poor and inadequate. Art should be born from the material. Spirituality should borrow the language of the material. Each material has its own language and is a language. There's no need to adjoin a language to it or make it serve a language. . . .

Teaming Up with Chance

Start a painting: an adventure that could lead you almost anywhere. It wouldn't be very interesting for the artist if he already knew the ultimate destination, if he were to paint a picture that already existed fully in his mind. Nothing of the kind. The artist teams up with chance. It takes two to tango, not one; chance always joins in. It pulls to the right, to the left, while the artist leads as best he can, but always flexibly, and he makes a point of utilizing any fluke that happens to crop up, making it serve his ends, which he will never hesitate to change at any time. But we should not, strictly speaking, be speaking about chance. Here or anywhere. There's no such thing. Man calls chance anything that comes from the big black hole of unfamiliar causes. The artist is not pitted against just any kind of chance, but against a particular kind, one that fits the nature of the material employed. The term "chance" is inexact; it would be better to speak of the whims and aspirations of the baulky material. . . .

A Big Spree

There is no art without intoxication. But then: wild intoxication! Let the mind seesaw! Let it rave! The highest degree of delirium! The depth of burning insanity! Further than any alcohol can go! Art is the most passionate orgy within man's grasp. Can you encounter people who speak coolly about art, who tell you, "I'm seeing a painting soon," without their teeth chattering? As though it weren't the most intimate and most total profligacy imaginable, a witches' sabbath which you can't go to without your heart pounding wildly, without your simply confiding to someone: "I'm seeing the wizard soon. I want him to change me into a mouse.". . .

Translated from the French © Joachim Neugroschel
Original title, *Notes pour les fins-lettrés*
© Editions Gallimard, 1967 and 1995

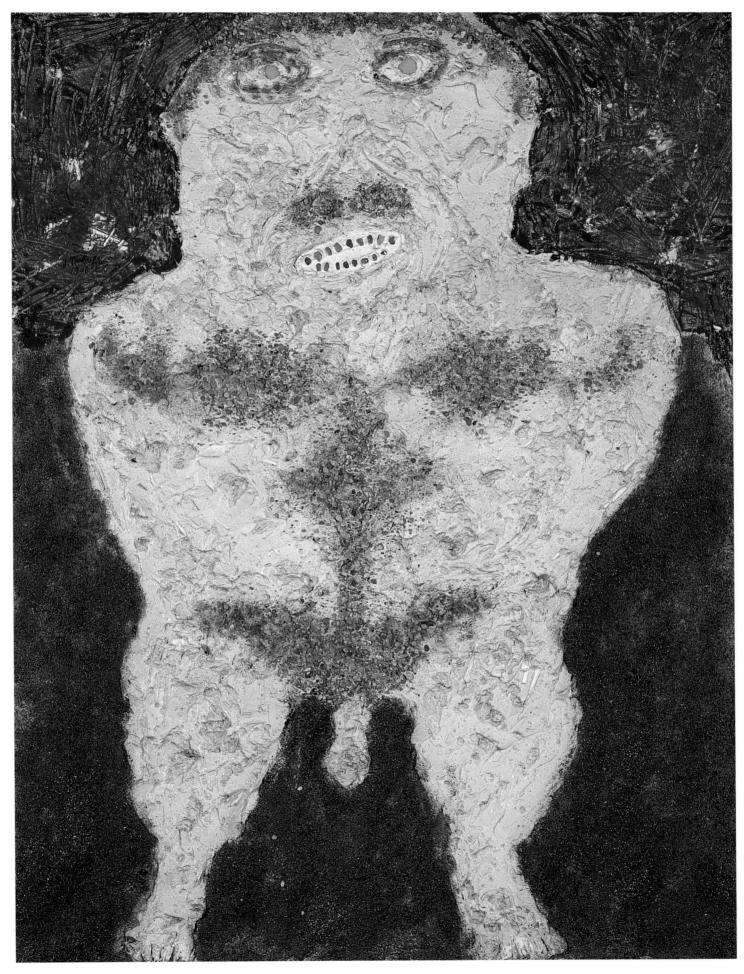

Volonté de puissance, January 1946
mixed media on canvas, 45¾ × 35"
Collection Solomon R. Guggenheim Museum, New York
© 2001 Artists Rights Society (ARS), New York/ADAGP, Paris

Perceiving
by Jean Dubuffet

From the catalogue of the 1960–61 Dubuffet retrospective at the Musée des Arts Décoratifs in Paris.

Attention kills anything it touches. It is a mistake to believe that watching things attentively will help you to know them better. For your gaze, like a silkworm, spins so well that it envelopes you in an opaque cocoon, leaving you sightless. That's why the painters who gawk their eyes out at models capture nothing at all.

Attention runs a whole gamut of degrees. You can see a huge number of things in an instant, a sputtering. Some you do not notice, you glimpse them casually, almost askance, at an oblique angle. Your eyes may rest more perpendicularly on other things, perhaps a wee bit longer. In the first set of things, you have perceived next to nothing, but at least your gaze has had little time to alter them. Whatever it dwells on, it spoils utterly. It burns and wipes out as it lights up. It's not easy to see something! And the slightest thing you see is instantly digested by your brain, which attacks it with its gastric juice, changing it totally. The glimpse is over! Nothing's left.

Your eyes are very mobile, darting very quickly from object to object, blazing up and dimming out a thousand times a second, cutting off and then resuming. Endlessly inverting themselves, turning inward, taking and giving, giving and taking, secreting their thread nonstop, a thread that breaks and reforms, with its fibers dangling everywhere.

This thread can also be painted. It is magnificent.

Painting can easily restore everything at once: the fleeting phases of the inattentive eyes, what the sights project upon those who perceive them, and what the perceivers project upon them, what the sights return to the eyes. You can blend all these things together. A painting can arrest such plays of mobile and evanescent phenomena.

Understandably, such an enterprise is enough of a challenge—we don't have to complicate it by assigning an exceptional soul to the person who looks at things and then digests and transcribes them. I personally am not interested in the exceptional in whatever area. My fare is commonplace. The more banal it is, the more I like it. Fortunately, I don't feel that there's anything exceptional about me. What I want to find in my paintings is the gaze of the average man in the street. Thus, without adding to the simple means available to any ordinary person's hand (I don't want anything but the rudimentary techniques of the layman, they seem quite good enough for me), I've tried to produce huge, high celebrations. Festivities are lot more worthwhile when we stick to everyday life rather than going to areas foreign to it. That is the only way the intrinsic virtue of festivities—to commute our workaday life into a wondrous celebration—can truly function. I am referring to celebrations of the mind. Please understand: I mean celebrations achieved by moods and deliriums.

Art addresses the mind, certainly not the eyes. Too many people think that art addresses the eyes. What a poor use of it that would be!

Likewise, in regard to sights, I am drawn to the simplest and most common. No need to go far afield, seeking rarities. Everything is right there, in front of your nose or on the ground, right at your feet. There, you'll find everything you're looking for, you won't have to go anywhere else. I am a very special kind of tourist: anything that's picturesque makes me feel squeamish—the less picturesque something is, the more it arouses my wonder.

And besides, is there such a thing as an exceptional soul? I very much doubt it. I have my qualms about the alleged superiority of the erudite savant, the refined and precious aesthete, over any old farmhand. Perhaps, what they gain at one end, they lose at the other.

Many people imagine that because I stubbornly run things down, I enjoy showing miserable things. What a misunderstanding! I wanted to show them that things they consider ugly and have forgotten to see are really sublime wonders. We must avoid that misunderstanding. We must stop talking about "humor" or "satire" (as some people foolishly do) or "gloomy bitterness" (which I have also been accused of). I am actually trying to rehabilitate objects regarded as unsightly (do not, I beg you, deprive those vilified objects of all possibilities). I present my works in a posture of celebration (incantation). It is a lucid celebration, with all smokescreens and camouflage eliminated once and for all. A painter must be honest! No veils! No ruses! Everything has to be naked at its worst; presented at it's worst.

Translated from the French © *Joachim Neugroschel*
Original title, *Apercevoir* © Editions Gallimard, 1967 and 1995

The Pace Gallery

SAUL STEINBERG | RECENT WORK
October 31 – 28 November, 1987

by Adam Gopnik
Excerpt from Pace catalogue

Saul Steinberg is a natural. Like the shortstop who gets to balls other players can only watch, Steinberg has always been gifted in a way that enables him to do well what other people can only do poorly or not at all. Steinberg, one of the most popular of modern image-makers, has the kind of gift that in the past has been associated only with "eccentric" or isolated artists, like William Blake: Steinberg can make the life of the mind visible—he can take metaphors and abstract ideas and turn them into drawings. But because of the exceptionally public and openhearted way with which Steinberg has conducted his career—because his work isn't merely the monologue of a visionary but a dialogue between a natural gift and a cultural moment—it's been possible to see his work primarily as an inspired form of art criticism. Harold Rosenberg and E.H. Gombrich, the two best critics of his art (comparable in ability only to each other, and divided on every subject about modern art except for the importance of Saul Steinberg's drawings), have shown how knowing Steinberg's work is as a philosophical commentary on the nature of modernism, and on the dialogue between representation and abstraction—we've come to think of Steinberg as a kind of umpire in the game of modern art. But as his work has continued its extraordinary evolution, the foundations of Steinberg's art are increasingly coming to seem not magisterial but romantic—rooted in the belief that the imagination can reveal things hidden to plain sight, and expressed in a set of original and obsessive images. The real subject of his art—the struggle between our urge to retreat into a private, ordered world of our own making, and the constant counterpoised allure of the world of glamorized violence—are not the subjects of a semiotics major concerned primarily with the nature of representation but those of a poet concerned with the nature of modern life: a cosmopolitan traveler whose shifting experiences are given form by an innate imaginative gift.

We can isolate Steinberg's gift—the basic natural imaginative ability, like the shortstop's agility, on which all the more complex intellectual triumphs of his art rest—fairly precisely. Saul Steinberg is one of the most remarkable natural "synesthetes" in the history of art. Synesthesia is the name psychologists give to what we do when we unconsciously associate something we perceive in one "sense modality" with something we perceive in another—when we think of one kind of musical pitch as red, or think of the name "Martha" as colored apricot, or associate particular moods with certain sounds and certain colors with certain smells. It is an ability that all of us have to one degree or another, and that seems, typically, to decrease as we grow older.

In a few rare cases, however, this gift not only doesn't decrease, or disappear, in maturity but seems to extend and become more and more complex, until it has become a complete system of what the early twentieth century Russian psychologist A.R. Luria called "extended reference"—where every visual image immediately summons up an abstract idea, and every abstract idea is immediately seen as an image. . . .

At its simplest and most scherzo-like, Steinberg's work has always depended on the exploitation of this remarkable synesthetic gift, the gift of "extended reference." Synesthetic images occur not in any single period but as a recurring ground bass in Steinberg's career, and they are the basis of his popular reputation. He still makes occasional presentations of such images and insights in his work. The set of "Country Noises" that appeared in *The New Yorker* in 1978—matching country sounds with typography—is a particularly elegant recent work of this kind.

At the same time, Steinberg, far more than any other gifted visual metaphor-maker, is not merely a maker of metaphors but an analyst of them, too. He has never been content simply to exploit his gift. He has also become its own best observer, both the patient and the psychologist. Along with his visual analogies for abstract ideas, therefore, the other pillar of Steinberg's work has always been his studies of the creative process itself, his drawings about the process of drawing.

I suspect that Steinberg's self-awareness about the process of drawing began as a form of self-analysis. Steinberg has a skeptical intelligence at least as large as his visionary genius. "What I draw is drawing, and drawing derives from drawing. My line wants to remind constantly that it is made of ink." Most artists with a gift like Steinberg's tend to become their own rhapsodists—they become convinced that they are visionaries or mystics. Steinberg has a much drier and clearer sense of the conditions of communication. He has never fallen for the notion that anyone's art, including his own, can simply be a transcription of a pure, original mental experience; he knows that art can no more simply "transcribe" an image in the unconscious than it can simply "transcribe" an image in the world. A gift is private; art is public. All representation, of what we see outside or of what we sense inside, has to employ the shared codes and conventions of other representations. Steinberg knows that the search for pictorial metaphor, however specially gifted the searcher, passes, of necessity, not just through the unconscious but also through the Louvre. Steinberg is aware that his search for a private language of symbolism is always meditated by other people's styles—to represent its own processes, the mind must pick and choose among the codes that history supplies. . . .

If the new drawings represent one aspect of what Steinberg sees around him, the new objects that Steinberg has made represent the other pole of values in his imagination: the world of the studio and drafting table and library. There is a basic recurring dialogue, in all of Steinberg's work, between inside and outside, between the ordered world of books and drawings and the sexy, alluring world of the violent and perplexing street. Perhaps most beautiful and touching of all of these works is Steinberg's "drawing in wood" of his own bookcase, where books from his childhood are represented by found pieces of driftwood, carefully inscribed with their classical titles. Steinberg's bookcase, with its row upon row of ordered books, interrupted by the driftwood books, which are clearly ghosts, is like an eighteenth-century grotto; at once a refuge from perplexity, and a kind of *memento mori* to lost time.

The violent street on the one hand, the ordered studio on the other; if Steinberg's gift is romantic, in the sense that it believes that imagination is a power

of vision that reveals things hidden to plain sight, the values in his work have become, in the end, entirely classical. The dialogue between indoor and outdoor, between the studio and the street, has been made to echo the classic Horatian juxtaposition of the world the artist has made outside the capital—the grotto or villa—with the world the artist is forced to confront in the urban capital whose presence haunts his retreat.

What is finally best, and most moving, about Steinberg's work is the clarity and generosity of its morality. The choices that Steinberg presents—for all that he perceives them in an incomparably heightened form—are still the moral choices that modern experience offers almost all of us. On the one hand, the ordered, self-made world of the studio and drafting table and bookcase, serene and beautiful but touched with a kind of Chekovian pathos; on the other hand, the world of the street with all its sexuality and glamor, and its violence and horror and morality. Steinberg sees and records both, the hypnotic beauty of the violent world outside and the serenity and sadness of the measured world we make, and draws no conclusion. This unsentimental articulation of our moral dilemma is Steinberg's gift to us. Saul Steinberg is the spy we have set on ourselves.

Overpass at 58th Street, 1983
graphite and colored pencil on paper, 14½ × 23"

ROTHKO AND MIRÓ

MAGNETIC FIELDS AND MURALS

December 4 – 2 January, 1988

CY TWOMBLY

WORKS ON PAPER
January 8 – 30, 1988

Top: Roman Note 3, 1970
oil and crayon on paper, 27½ × 34½"
Bottom: Roman Note 4, 1970
oil on canvas, 27½ × 34½"

JIM DINE | NEW PAINTINGS

February 5 – 5 March, 1988

For People Who Don't Know, I Am the Wife of These, 1987
oil on canvas, 66 × 60"

GEORGE CONDO

PAINTINGS AND DRAWINGS
March 11 – 2 April, 1988

BARNETT NEWMAN

PAINTINGS
April 8 – 7 May, 1988

On his birthday, January 29, 1948, he prepared a small canvas with a surface of cadmium red dark (a deep mineral color that looks like an earth pigment—like Indian red or a sienna), and fixed a piece of tape down the center. Then he quickly smeared a coat of cadmium red light over the tape, to test the color. He looked at the picture for a long time. Indeed he studied it for some eight months. He had finished questing.

Thomas B. Hess, *Barnett Newman* (The Museum of Modern Art, New York), 1971, p. 51.
Quoted in Yve-Alain Bois, "Perceiving Newman" (The Pace Gallery, New York), 1988.

Barnett Newman at Betty Parsons, 1952
Photo © Hans Namuth Ltd.

Perceiving Newman
by Yve-Alain Bois
Excerpt from Pace catalogue

To Annalee Newman,
for her love and loyalty to Barnett Newman

. . . I would like rather to concentrate, in conclusion, on a third solution to the figure/ground question which appears for the first time in one of the elongated "shaped canvases" of 1950, the fourth untitled painting of that group. The canvas constitutes an obvious commentary on *Onement I*: it uses the same colors and is ostensibly symmetrical. Two dark red "zips" of equal size, each limited by a different side of the canvas, flank a lighter and wider field of double width; or one might also say: a bright red "zip" divides a field of dark red whose extension is drastically cut by the limits of canvas. The zip has become a plane, and in doing so has rendered utterly undecidable the very terms of the opposition figure/ground. The sequel to this positive/negative aporia will be *The Way I,* in which the lateral symmetrical "zips" themselves have gained so much width that their existence as zip is wholly undermined, and Newman will be interested again in this obtrusively ambiguous structure until the end of his life (from *Primordial Light* (1954) to *The Way II* (1969), via *Profile of Light, Voice of Fire* and *Now II* (1967), among other works). But I find it quite remarkable that in this case too Newman felt a definite urge to depart from symmetry. It all started, according to him, with the painting of *Who is Afraid of Red, Blue and Yellow I* (although one could say again that this is already announced by the lateral displacement and the widening of the zip in *Abraham*: in a sense *The Gate* (1954), which uses the type of displacement of bilateral symmetry seen in *Abraham*, but this time with planes, as in the works just mentioned, would point to such a filiation). "I did have the desire that the painting be asymmetrical and that it create a space different from any I had ever done, sort of—off balanced," writes Newman.[35] He then became immersed in a coloristic problem which led, as is well known, to his discovery that he could at last confront without fear Mondrian's dogma of the primaries. But, if we want momentarily to leave aside the issue of color (not that I think we should take too seriously Newman's anti-coloristic stance—the famous "I am always referred to in relation to my color. Yet I know that if I have made a contribution, it is primarily in my drawing"[36]—but for the sake of clarity), we will have to turn to other canvases deriving from this new shift in his work, namely *White and Hot* (1967), an untitled painting of 1970, and above all *Anna's Light* (1968), which combine with this new structure the huge size of *Vir Heroicus Sublimis* (it is, in fact, the largest painting Newman ever realized, measuring nine by twenty feet).

Those three paintings have in common a central field of color flanked by two asymmetrical white areas respectively bordered by the right and left limits of the canvas. One of these white areas is narrow—if it were not at the edge one would see it as a zip, and even as it is one is tempted to do so—while the other is larger but nevertheless infinitely narrow in comparison to the color field it delimits, hence denied any definite status for our perception (its narrowness or width is measured against the two other elements of the canvas, which give simultaneous and contradictory answers). The fact that those white areas are on the border of the canvas and are asymmetrically displaced (unlike what happens in *Now I* and *II*, for example) raises immediately the issue of our ability to take in limits of the canvas. This is an important issue for Newman, whose large size canvases emphasize that we do not cease to incorporate those limits in our perception even when they cease to be in our visual field (seeing *Noon Light* in a restorer's studio, unstretched and pinned flat on a board like frog bound to be dissected, I realized there is no way to be able to look at a Newman without interiorizing those limits). In fact, looking at those three canvases, we immediately start to work on trying to define, for ourselves, their beginning and their end. In doing so, of course, we try to compute instinctively their center, but that is precisely what their asymmetry will forbid us to achieve: the off-centered color field will jump with our gaze either on one side or the other, will either try to push over the narrow white area with the the help of the large one, or vice versa. We try then to compute the center of the colored field alone, but here it is the non-identity of the white areas, each pulling towards it or away from it the virtual axis we are trying to define, which will undermine our attempt: the lack of coincidence of those two centers prevents us from being able to grasp either of them. In the end, we will only be left with the sheer sense that this color area occupies a space with the solidity of a metal plate, but will have to renounce finding out *which* space exactly: we see that it is there (or rather "not there—here"), it confronts us forcefully, but we have no way of virtually absenting us from this *hic et nunc* to be able to conceptualize the nature of this confrontation.

It would seem at first that the red and white *White and Hot* and the blue and white untitled painting of 1970 function like a pair: in one canvas the larger white area is to the right, in the other to the left. Yet the different sizes of the two paintings indicate clearly that it would be altogether wrong to exhibit them as pendants (this would mean an attempt to reestablish some kind of symmetry, an attempt which would be doomed to failure). In fact, it is not by chance that *Anna's Light* was painted in the lapse of time that separates the two, for here Newman reverted to his greatest ally (largeness of scale) to give a final blow to the very possibility of a part-to-part relationship—that is, to achieve asymmetrically what he had achieved in *Onement I*, to address the spectator in the physicality of the present tense, as an "I" to a "You." But here Newman achieves this without resorting to the type of indexicality he had so successfully called upon in his "conversion" piece: the field is not simply declared by a zip which measures it for us. On the contrary, the colored field seems to move with us, to follow our gaze as a dog follows his master or the shadow our walking body. And, precisely because we cannot find its center (a situation which is almost opposite to what happens in *Onement I*), and hence do not manage to constitute it as a figure, it "moves" without ever leaving its base, reaffirming its instantaneous blast each time we try to distance ourselves from it.

The handling of color plays the same role in the three paintings (undercoats applied with a roller, final coat applied with a brush), but it is in *Anna's Light* that its function is most apparent: this last coat of red is shiny but slightly darker, which makes the hue modulate according to our distance from the painting and the way it is lit (the last coat is not evenly applied and there are areas where it does not seem to have been applied at all: when the canvas is brightly lit, those areas look darker from close up—as they are not shiny—and lighter from further away). These modulations are opposed to the sensuous color modulations one can find in the large canvases of the 1950's (think of *Vir Heroicus Sublimis*, whose unique red is constantly shifted by the color accents of the numerous zips, or of *Cathedra* and its deep blue). Those were part of the strategy of fixation/perception which I described earlier: like the zips, the modulations were constantly singularized but their singularity

was constantly denied by the lateral spread of our perception. But here this opposition of fixation/perception seems abolished: we cannot even attempt to focus on anything but are constantly obliged to deal with the mere vastness of the whole red field, as a whole chunk of color. The modulations do not perform any more, as it did in the 1950's, like subtle accidents within a field, like a discrete solicitation of our gaze or an intimation to accommodate further, even if in the end we were denied this possibility. The shiny gloss, here and there, forestall any desire for this sort of accommodation, and our gaze is not authorized to ever attempt to go beyond the surface of the canvas: as such, those modulations function as a sort of internal respiration of the field of color which has become as indivisible as one's own body. *Anna's Light* seems to me like the last major step Newman took in order to achieve the wholeness he wanted to achieve. In a way, this canvas is a direct answer to the puzzle raised by *Onement I*: how to free oneself entirely from part-to-part relationship without reverting to the pure laying out of the axis of symmetry, how to convey the essential discovery represented by the "conversion," that of the anchoring of perception within the "pre-historical" knowledge of our body without referring to the originary condition of its orientation in space. The red wall of *Anna's Light* shows that disorientation is as essential as orientation to our perception—and that disorientation could be achieved even without setting various levels of perception in mutual opposition. As such, it is one of Newman's most abstract canvases, and also one of his "fastest." Like *Onement I*, but with utterly different means, it assumes the existence of the instant, strives to suspend duration (which is impossible): such was, it seems to me, what separates most of Newman's art from Minimalism (for what would his attachment to the word "zip" mean otherwise?). If *Onement I* represents the break of origin, *Anna's Light* expresses the flood of life made possible by this single flash.

35. Statement for *Art Now: New York*, vol. I, no. 3, March 1969, n.p.
36. In Seckler, op. cit., [Dorothy G. Seckler, "Frontiers of Space," *Art in America*, Summer 1962], p. 87.

ISAMU NOGUCHI

BRONZE AND IRON SCULPTURE
May 13 – 17 June, 1988

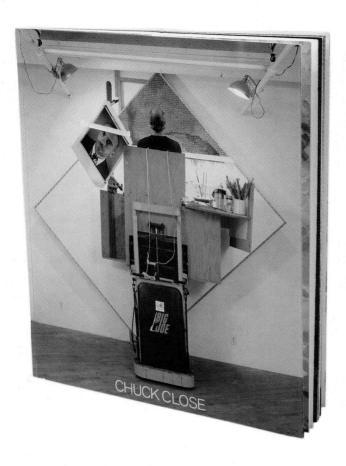

The Rewards of Middle Age
by Klaus Kertess
Excerpt from Pace catalogue

De-portraiture as much as portraiture has been the subject of Chuck Close's art. In the twenty some years of his artistic maturity, he has compulsively constructed hyper-real images of faces that have employed the sitter's likeness to mine and undermine the differences between abstraction and figuration, painting and photography, craft and mechanical and electronic reproduction, style and technique, content and information. Photography, the very medium that helped liberate Western painting from its mimetic imperatives, has itself become the subject of a painting enterprise that has enlisted Modernism's own strategies to retrieve the figure from exile. Beginning with the overall deployment of a uniform dot module in a group of drawings done in 1973, Close has increasingly faced and defaced his portrait heads with a variety of radically restricted, mark-making codes, often ruled by a grid. An ink dot, a diagonal line, an inked fingerprint, a circle or oval of collaged pulp paper, a Ben Day-like painted dot—each has become a visually self-evident module of process that turns the physiognomy of the photographed face

into the topography of a painted (or drawn) plane.

Close's technical virtuosity, perversity, and acute formal intelligence have continually renewed themselves to create dazzling literal and figurative tours de force of the issues that have ruled abstraction since the 1950s. Yet under the surface of the multiplicity of increments pulsing with a cybernetic delirium lurks a far less neutral program, one that includes the processes of Close's intuition and the nuances of the interaction of his personality with those of his portraitees. The breakdown of the barriers between abstraction and figuration that Close's work has been so crucial to has engendered a renewed tolerance for, and interest in, the lapsed subject matter of earlier painting. Emotional and purely aesthetic concerns seep through the highly restricted artificiality of the formalist grid. Close's own earlier insistence on his relationship to his Minimalist and Process Art peers has given way to the somewhat mellower mode of his maturity. His new group of paintings of four artists who are self-portraitizers more willingly relaxes—and even risks compromising—the

Cindy, 1988
oil on canvas, 102 × 84"

CHUCK CLOSE

NEW PAINTINGS
September 23 – 22 October, 1988

willed neutrality of the hand that has drawn so many conclusions in the art of the recent past. . . .

The monumental scale of Close's cinematic blowups not only emphatically insists upon the subject as impalpable image derived from a photograph, but also looks back through Rosenquist, Katz, and Lichtenstein to the scale of Abstract Expressionism. But unlike most gestural painters, Close deploys marks that decrease with, rather than increase with, the size of his support. The tiny pointillist dots seem to deny all invention because of their near mechanical and neutral repetitiveness and labor-intensive monotony—here is the Protestant work ethic *in extremis*. The dots reinforce the disembodied photo-mechanical nature of the image and ensure a homogeneous overallness; but, within the infinitude of this minuscule restrictiveness, Close has made room for unpredictability and surprise. The dots and blips of the new paintings are now more complexly layered, varied, and interdependent—they are woven into veils of flickering light. The pale backgrounds of both *Francesco I* and *Cindy* hark back to the diaphanous walls of light in the paintings of Vermeer that Close

has so avidly admired. Close constantly reinvents his means rather than predetermining them as he works through each painting. A color is put down arbitrarily and intuitively and then requires a response. Depending upon its neighbors, an orange dot may not require a complementary purple but rather a green—because he needs more yellow. A shadow or a reflection may begin to assume an independent form that is then encouraged. A configuration resembling the biomorphic forms in de Kooning's *Pink Angels* insinuated itself into the flow of dots that built a cheek in *Lucas I*. Close knows where he is going but not how he is going to get there. The process is self-evident, the technique rigorously reductive and seemingly simple, the result incredibly complex. Close's virtuoso mastery of tone and the unending chain reaction, from mark to mark in layer upon layer, sets each painting in a tension of shimmering motion. If the method and the paint application are very dry, the result is, nonetheless, very rich.

The viewer moves backward through Close's procedures until he or she is face to face with the canvas and the dizzying confetti of Close's tech-

shot into paint, Close's hand brings with it information and feelings not seen in the photographs. Each of these four self-portraitizers has a meaning for Close that insinuates itself into the paintings. All four artists are admired by Close. Two of them (Alex Katz and Lucas Samaras) made their entry on the art scene prior to Close; the other two (Francesco Clemente and Cindy Sherman) are younger artists whose continuing presence and accessibility make the escalating cruelty of New York City still bearable for Close. . . .

With these paintings, Chuck Close has extended his formal and visual vocabulary into a richer and more nuanced language. The emotional traps risked by the more open dialogue with his portraitees (already evident in the previous group of portraits of members of his family) is paralleled and punctuated by Close's more open dialogue with his procedures. He has achieved a new depth without sacrificing the old clarity.

nique. The lack of full resolution of the images made with an incremental technique sacrifices the more powerful immediate impact of the earlier, seamlessly toned and defined works; what is gained is a more visceral and seductive envelopment of the viewer in the process of the image's solution and dissolution. Even at some thirty feet, the heads of the large paintings waver on the edge of closure. As the viewer approaches, the face becomes camouflaged with a pulsating veil of marks, and then finally dissolves into the plane of the canvas and the fizzing dance of gridded dots. The move from the depth of illusion to the flatness of the canvas, from the blur and the sharp focus frozen by the monocular vision of the camera lens to the flat handmade marks that translate an instant into painterly duration, unfurls in an unending panoply of visual and perceptual orchestrations.

The topography of the human face—photographed in a blunt frontal pose pushing out of a reduced depth of field—has since 1967 provided Close with an endless variety of visual information and configurations, and has freed him from the vagaries of invented composition. The use of photographs of four artists whose faces are largely or partially already known as images of their own works, moves these subjects even further into the realm of neutral hyper-reality. However, in the process of translating the seemingly insistent and banal factuality of the snap-

Lucas, 1986–87
oil on canvas, 100 × 84"
Collection The Metropolitan Museum of Art
Purchase, Lila Acheson Wallace Gift and
Gift of Arnold and Milly Glimcher, 1987

Catalogue cover

LUCAS SAMARAS

BOXES AND MIRRORED CELL
October 28 – 26 November, 1988

A Conversation:
Malcolm Morley and Arne Glimcher
Excerpt from Pace catalogue

A.G. I perceive the violence that underlies everyday life as a dominant characteristic in your work. In the post-cards or the boat paintings of the early sixties or the most recent painting in progress, *Black Rainbow Over Oedipus at Thebes*, or even in the bucolic beach paintings, there is a sense that the images are about to be blown apart as they are barely stuck together, and it is that imminent tremor that walks the fine line between bliss and disaster. Is this only my response or is it your intention?

M.M. This is a hell of a statement you just made. I translate violence into another realm, which really has to do with the process of painting itself. And the idea of it flying apart or coming together is the fight against the idea that I basically think that I'm a very clumsy painter. I've always felt that. What happens is the fight against my own clumsiness.

The process itself allows those things that you're talking about, the idea of things splitting apart, and the idea of violence about to happen. I don't really know physics, but matter itself is violent. If you look at it under a microscope, there's nothing solid.

A.G. So your view of the universe is violent.

M.M. Well, it's only a word that we're using for a process, for a state of being. So in terms of what you call violent, I might call painterly.

A.G. Or evolution?

M.M. Or evolution. The keystone of everything is that it's painterly, but painterly according to my temperament at that moment. There is an evolution going on.

The key is that I keep having to come back to the idea that it's the process that I've worked out in making these paintings, that allows so many different ways of doing it. What you might call a violent painting, I might call a careless painting or a casual painting or a "non-careful" one. Then, suddenly you can start talking about genital organization and polymorphic perversity. I mean, you can start bringing in a lot of stuff.

A.G. I'm not suggesting a Freudian interpretation of the pictures. I'm more concerned with universal truths. I think you're an extraordinary observer as well as a participant.

M.M. I'm a sponge.

A.G. I think you arrest forces at critical junctures.

M.M. I'm a sponge.

A.G. There's a duality in all of your work, whether it be a duality of excess and opulence or something ephemeral and spectral. So very often I have the sense, while I'm looking at the work that I'm about to grasp it, and just then it changes.

M.M. That comes back again to the process, really. The anchor in all of it is its realization on a two-dimensional surface. By that I don't mean just the idea of a painting as something flat, but rather the mental image in your mind, is two-dimensional. The imagination is either two-dimensional or it has no dimension. Imagine the projection of the imagination being almost flat, having no dimension at all.

The idea of projecting everything side by side allows for its perception which is experienced holistically. It comes into a tremendous conflict rather than violence—there's really a conflict between the idea of perceiving the parts in relation to the whole. That's the way the painting is constructed; there is a holistic image appearing in relation to the format, the outside format of the canvas. You can't hold the whole picture for very long because the vector of the parts, the tracking so to speak, is coming counterpoint to the image.

For example, the image is constructed in cross section. The cortex, in terms of the center of perception, is very confused about how to read this image. There's a pulsation going on between the whole and the part. I've actually timed it to a heartbeat. The gyration of how long you can hold the whole of it, is the length of the heartbeat.

There's a very visceral connection I don't even have to think about; it's a given. If I go through the process of the painting any which way I want, I don't need to connect the parts as much as I used to think I did. In fact, the less connected they are, the more I exaggerate that beat between the whole and the part, the more painterly it becomes.

A.G. The most recent work kind of insinuates the image. Fragments or insinuations of figures and landscape seem to be provided for completion in the cortex.

M.M. Yes.

A.G. I find this process cinematic.

M.M. Yes, frame by frame, the viewer connects them together. The viewer is painting the picture, in terms of his temperament as well. I don't want to steal the experience from the viewer. I've had my experience making them. The viewers, depending on where they're coming from, are going through a process of self-discovery by constructing the images themselves. . . .

A.G. Let's talk about the cathedral painting that began from a drawing you made in Barcelona. The model was not Gaudi's cathedral. But the painting is Gaudi-like in that the invention of the color is almost like taking shards within reach that have come automatically, using the first ones on the palette. Sections of the painting have totally different chromatic schemes and seem totally alien from one another with different psychological overtones.

M.M. Yes. Yes.

A.G. And they still manage to create a unity. Was that a deliberate process?

M.M. I wouldn't say the word "deliberate." Let's think about the word "de-liberate." D-E . . . De-lib—liberate. Liberation? Deliberation?

A.G. Was that a liberating process?

M.M. Yes. I mean, the whole idea is to die a free man.

A.G. Do you think that's possible?

M.M. Yeah. You can die real happy. You can get very happy. Some sages have just been in a state of ecstasy as they're dying. One can imagine the highest form of pleasure that a human being can have is to die; which is a form of surrendering.

A.G. Which is a form of acceptance of the nature of the universe. . . .

AGNES MARTIN

Agnes Martin
Photo Donald Woodman

JOHN CHAMBERLAIN

NEW SCULPTURE
February 24 – 25 March, 1989

by Donald Judd
Excerpt from Pace catalogue

November 1988

Chamberlain's work is not sufficiently known, even among artists, since the situation in art has both grown and declined in the last decades. As I've said before, art is the only activity, beyond plain work, in which the producers have no say as to what happens to the product. It's an activity with no integrity as an activity; as knowledge, as information, as discussion, as education and as commerce, its parts have been cannibalized. Chamberlain had a show at the Guggenheim Museum in '71. Otherwise he has had a hard time. Discussion and interest are always at fault. Criticism in New York, where he showed at the Castelli Gallery, is impenetrably parochial from decade to decade. But since the art dealers have more influence and at least some sense of reality, depending on which ones, they are consequently more at fault. These matters shouldn't be glossed over. Also in regard to art criticism in New York, although its style has changed several times since the forties, a gloss is always there hiding the real activity, the best artists, and the reality that the artists are particular people doing something, something of interest to others now and to others later. The opposite of this is the assumption by most critics and museum people, many dealers, that art is a scene, a continuum of expendables. Only when Xavier Fourcade began to sell Chamberlain's work did it and his fortunes change. The change seems to be permanent. In other words what should be the equivalent to the availability of a scientific paper in that activity is completely dependent on the market, which neither museums, criticism nor education modify, question, supplement or extend.

Chamberlain's work is great and diverse. He's a very intelligent guy, verbally, and of course in his work. As I wrote, the earliest pieces were influenced by David Smith; the subsequent ones in the early sixties were very much Chamberlain's. Throughout '64 he made eight reliefs, possibly one or two more, four feet by four each on masonite, which I described in '66, as well as many small paintings about a foot square. Very few people were interested in these reliefs and paintings. I said affectionately and conservatively at the time that I thought painting was probably finished. The prediction assumed a decline in what was being done; instead there's a debasement of everything that has been done. Now there is only one fine painter: Agnes Martin. I wrote in '66 that Chamberlain's paintings and reliefs suggested alternatives to all the dead ideas of what to do with a discrete flat surface. They still do. Chamberlain is right: "sculpture" should be three-dimensional, voluminous and spatial, and painting should be flat. In this case Michelangelo was wrong, saying that painting should be sculptural. In this he didn't follow classical precedents, which are very three-dimensional and very flat.

In '66 Chamberlain made the constructed pieces which I wrote about then. I haven't seen any since and I'm not sure any exist. A deliberate attitude suits me but I don't think it suits Chamberlain. The balance is different. In being deliberate he broke the ordinary appearance which the crushed metal provided and the lack of intention which it, as well as the scheme and lacquered surfaces of the reliefs, provided. In fact the apparently deliberate reliefs are what the constructed pieces should have been. But these were too intentional, in structure in a way usual in sculpture, and in color and surface, which was unusual. In general Chamberlain's use of color is amazing.

In '67 Chamberlain made pieces out of foam rubber tied. In '70 he made pieces of Plexiglas folded and coated in Larry Bell's fabulous vacuum coating machine. In '73 he wadded foil into balls and sprayed them with lacquer. Throughout he made work of painted metal. There is a great variety. The Plexiglas pieces have some of the fault of the

Chamberlain's Studio, Sarasota, Florida
Photo Peter Foe

constructed pieces. The foam rubber pieces were very fine. The material deteriorates very quickly and people were careless with them, as usual, so that I assume few exist. Chamberlain also cut couches from blocks of foam rubber. Since '70 most pieces have been made from automobile scrap, usually with the color left as is, sometimes partially painted. There are a great many fine collages, prints and monotypes. It's an amazing amount of work.

As I said, Chamberlain's color is great and this is conspicuous in the three movies that he made, two of which were shown at Hunter College, one whose name I don't remember and *The Secret Life of Hernando Cortez* (Fernando Cortés is the correct spelling). The unnamed movie had no plot and was primarily the color of interiors. The plot of *Cortez* was pretty casual: what to do next, having arrived in Veracruz. Like the reliefs the movies suggest ways out of old ideas or simply enforcement of the medium. Movies are usually meager visually. There's not much to see in black and white and little in color. This doesn't have to be so. And then, like painting, they retain the tiresome stories. No story is better. At any rate the usual story is one idea of existence; there are others.

I looked up the movies. *Cortez* was made in '68. Earlier in '68 John made *Wedding Night*. The unknown movie is *Wide Point*, projected on seven screens.

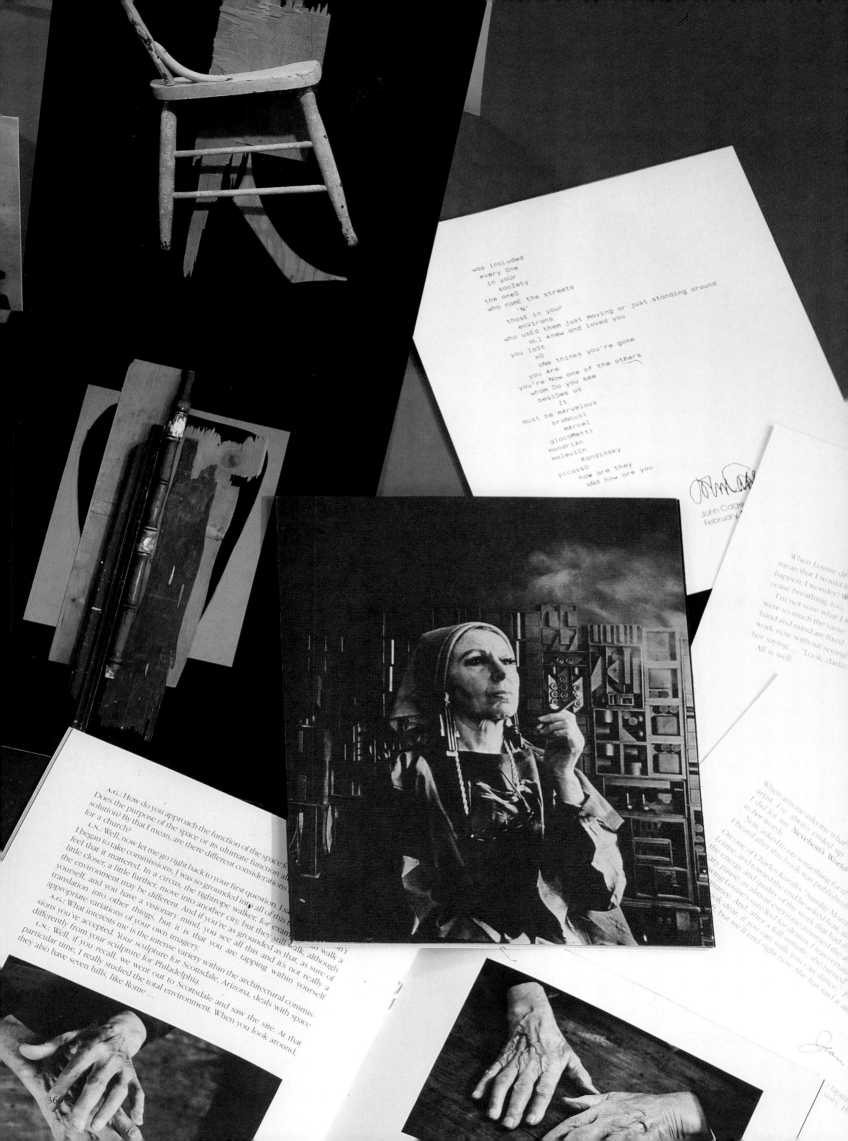

was incLuded
 every One
  in yOur
   socIety
 the oneS
 who namE the streets
    'N'
    thosE in your
     enVirons
 who usEd themm just moving or just standing around
      aLl knew and loved you
 you laSt
    nO
     oNe thinks you're gone
  you Are
  you're Now one of the others
   whom Do you see
    besiDes us
      It
 must be mArvelous
      broNcusi
      mArcel
    giacoMetti
    mondriAn
    maleviCh
         Kandinsky
   picassO
      how are they
      aNd how are you

                    John Cage
                    February

When Louise d...
mean that I would ...
happen, I wonder? ...
cease breathing, too, ...
  I'm not sure what I ...
were so much the same ...
hand and mind are fixed ...
work now without seeing ...
her saying.... "Look, darlin...
All is well."

When anyone asks me what ...
artist, I've always ended up ...
I did for my *Newton's Worl...
in *New* words.
  Now, asked to say something for ...
I heard after this book was publishe...
  On one of *Charles Kuralt's "Sunday Mo...*
Louise, and toward the end he asked how...
the energy, and quality of the work that had...
ary pause, as almost everyone assumed she had...
"loving Louise," sure feel for drama. I was cert...
"romance. And after a full minute, she turned t...
"Look, dear, if you can walk you can dance...
it's true," but we'll end right now. She has said it ...

A.G.: How do you approach the function of the space f...
Does the purpose of the space or its ultimate function a...
solution? By that I mean, are there different considerations...
for a church?

L.N.: Well, now let me go right back to your first question. I sa...
I began to take commissions. I was so grounded into all of this t...
feel that it mattered. In a circus, the tightrope walker, for exam...
little closer, a little further, move into another city, but they still walk a...
the environment may be different. And if you're as grounded as that, although...
yourself, and you have a visionary mind, you see all this and it's not really a...
translation into other things, but it is that you are tapping within yourself...
appropriate into other things, but it is that you are tapping within yourself...
A.G.: What interests me is the intense variety within the architectural commis...
sions you've accepted. Your sculpture for Philadelphia...
differently from your sculpture for Scottsdale, Arizona, deals with space...
L.N.: Well, if you recall, we went out to Scottsdale and saw the site. At that...
particular time, I really studied the total environment. When you look around...
they also have seven hills, like Rome ...

LOUISE NEVELSON

Louise Nevelson and
Arne Glimcher,
ca. early 1970s

Louise Nevelson's life was such an intricate pattern of fantasy synthesized with reality that separation of myth and fact is nearly impossible. Nevelson rejected the ordinary and conjured her own history, eliminating what was beneath her notice and amplifying the most important. A chronology of her life provides the barest skeletal outline of incidents to which she reacted. These reactions, evident in their residual products, or art works, are only the visible and tangible evidence—the key—to the realization that Nevelson's life itself was her greatest work of art.

I sincerely wish to thank Mike Nevelson and Diana MacKown for their constant support and Edward Albee, John Cage, Merce Cunningham, Barbaralee Diamonstein-Spielvogel, Jim Dine, Willy Eisenhart, Emily Genauer, Bill Katz, Hilton Kramer, Jean Lipman and Lucas Samaras for their contributions to this publication.

Arnold B. Glimcher
February, 1989

```
was incLuded
  every One
   in yoUr
     socIety
 the oneS
 who namE the streets
       'N'
    thosE in your
       enVirons
  who usEd them just moving or just standing around
       aLl knew and loved you
  you laSt
      nO
        oNe thinks you're gone
     you Are
  you're Now one of the others
   whom Do you see
     besiDes us
       It
 must be mArvelous
      braNcusi
       mArcel
   giacoMetti
  mondriAn
  maleviCh
      Kandinsky
  picassO
    hoW are they
     aNd how are you
```

John Cage
February, 1989

When anyone asks me what Louise Nevelson was really like besides being ... artist, I've always ended up by telling them something *she* said. That's ... I did for my **Nevelson's World** book, to tell about her work as best I ... in *her* words.

Now, asked to say something for this portfolio, I thought of a bit of an inte... I heard after this book was published, that I would have liked to have inc...

On one of Charles Kuralt's "Sunday Morning" TV programs he was interv... Louise, and toward the end he asked how, at her age, she could possibly ma... the energy and quality of the work that had made her famous. There was a ... scary pause, as almost everyone assumed the answer had to be "you can't... knowing Louise's sure feel for drama, I was certain that the pause was part... performance. And, after a full minute, she turned to Kuralt and said, lou... clear, "Look dear, if you can walk you can dance." He said, "We've got s... minutes left, but we'll end right now. She has said it all."

Jean Lipman
February, 198...

June 6, 1986

Dear Louise:

You are receiving the Compostela award from the Cathedral of St. James in Brooklyn for your work and your life and your gift of both to others. I am most happy to have been asked to congratulate you this way. What would New York be without you!

You have spoken many times about your love of the City, all of it. About the mix, the mixture of peoples and the spirit, the diversity and the plain cure it holds.

Here is a part of New York saluting you for your energy and spirit, your dedication to your work and certainly your love.

Louise, dear, we love you.

Yes.

Merce

She came from Russia to Maine, from Maine to New York—the natural place for her. Her father was a builder and she became a builder too, an "architect of light and shadow," she said, her blueprint inborn for her life. "If you want a kingdom, you have to build it."

Her material of choice was wood, old wood that resonates with its past uses by human hands and minds. She liked its intelligence, its cast-off beauty. And in New York, constantly tearing down and building, renewing itself, reaching upwards, the evening streets were full of pieces waiting to be collected into that big black station wagon and taken back to the studio.

In the middle of the night she worked in the quiet and the darkness, the queen of the night, ordering and placing what she had gathered, working as the dawn came up, surrounded by the black array of forms: chips and spools, chairs and table tops, organ pipes and house beams, all ready for composing.

At the end of the day, relaxing, sitting in the dining room, perhaps ready to go out, she talked of friends, the news, and metaphysics. And as she talked about people and things and events and their relations, she was arranging the table precisely, stacks of papers, letters, books and magazines, pens and pencils, cups and glasses, placing these things too, always composing. The light shone between the slats of the wooden shutters, gilding the table and its objects, patterning light, dark, light, dark as twilight fell on the always-changing order.

The architect of light and shadow. Her book is called **Dawns + Dusks**, for the mysterious in-between times of the day, of long shadows, of change from dark to light, light to dark, the beginning and the end of it. Her mind, her life, her work were all of a piece, a piece with many facets.

She searched all her life, a question mark always placed there in her awareness. And with geometry of form she built her own reality, the kingdom in which to lead a total life, a life of creation with all its labor pains. She reveled in the livingness of life. For Louise there was fulfillment, *l'chayim*.

Willy Eisenhart
February, 1989

ALL IS WELL

When Louise died I thought my response to her work would alter. I do... mean that I would like it less, or more—just differently. What did I think w... happen, I wonder? Would the absence of the artist turn art into artifact? Wou... cease breathing, too, become mythic?

I'm not sure what I thought, but I needn't have fretted. Louise and her w... were so much the same thing—were such an extension of each other—tha... hand and mind are fixed in each piece in a permanence, and I cannot look a... work now without seeing her mouth move into its furtive half-smile and ... her saying.... "Look, darling...."

All is well.

Edward Albee
February, 1989

February 14, 1989

Dear Louise,
Having had the privilege
of working and living with
you for twenty six years, it meant
a great deal to me when Arnold
asked me to assist with this show.

I have lived with the work,
seen it unfold and have been a
part of its creative effort, and it
is a joy to see it out in the world,
as you intended it to be.

This show will have its own
magnificence, and I know the work
will cross continents of awareness, as
always.

Diana

Diana MacKown

In the middle of the 1950's Nancy and I came to
New York City from Athens, Ohio where we were
students. I remember Louise's Black Environment
at Grand Central Moderns. We stepped into the blackness
of her room and the forms revealed themselves slowly.
It was just the way I thought art would be in New York.
She seemed to be so accurate in her depiction of darkness.
To be confronted by this intense idea was terribly
important to me as a young artist. I thought she
understood the void better than those minimalists and I've
reserved a special thank you to her for this specific revelation.

Jim Dine
February, 1989

When I think about Louise nowadays, it is not to the glamorous artist-celebrity
of her later years that my mind tends to turn, but to the virtually unknown artist I
first met in the nineteen-fifties. Louise was then at the beginning of the major
phase of her work. She had been living and working for some time in that
strange townhouse on East 30th Street, which had so little in common with the
studios of other artists I knew or with the kind of upperclass residence one
might have supposed a house of that type in that location would be. It looked, if
anything, like the refuge of a mad collector. The legend of the Collier Brothers
was much on people's minds in those days, and it was natural to think of clutter
on this scale as slightly demented. Objects and debris, which only gradually one
perceived to be art objects already made or in the process of being made,
crowded most of the very capacious space, and even on the brightest days the
light tended to be fugitive and fleeting. One got used to encountering a bathtub
filled with sculpture, to the rooms filled with discarded, broken furniture and
other objects Louise had picked up in the street, and to the fact that there were no
comfortable chairs on which to sit. (Had she, one wondered, turned them all
into sculpture?) Until one looked closely at what she had made, or was in the
process of making, a spirit of excess and disorder seemed to reign everywhere.
But soon, when one was able to make out what was really going on, one came to
understand the discipline and ambition and vision governing the creative life
that was harbored in this enchanted house.

It was a house of shadows and high spirits, of much laughter, much drinking,
and much hard work. The shadows weren't only physical, either; Louise had had
her share of unhappiness, and had no doubt been the cause of unhappiness in
others, as we all are. The people who came to know her later, when the house on
East 30th Street had long been demolished and she had become the much-
photographed and much-quoted media and benefit-party empress of the art
scene, were often surprised at how funny she was, and how serious and hard-
working. She put on a great act for this new public and fitted easily into its image
of the art world as a place of glamor, money, and power. But the truth is, she was
remarkably undeceived about life and about the ways of the world, including the
art world, and as hard-headed in dealing with fame and success as she had been
for so many years in coping with obscurity and failure. Her emergence as an
artist belongs, in any case, to a period when artists' reputations were not yet
calculated in terms of money and fame.

It was in the house on East 30th Street that Louise changed the scale of modern
sculpture. Out of all that clutter and romance, this was her crucial achievement,
and it is what she will be remembered for when the glamor is forgotten.

—Hilton Kramer
January, 1989

Dear Sola:
The deep dark
stark dangerous aroma
of your work and passions
continues to bedevil
and caress me.

Lucas

Lucas Samaras
February, 1989

ALEXANDER CALDER | STABILES
May 5 – 17 June, 1989

CALDER
STABILES

Catalogue

JOSEPH CORNELL

DOVECOTES, HOTELS AND OTHER WHITE SPACES

October 20 – 25 November, 1989

La Strada, 1956–57
box construction, 16 × 10⅞ × 5½"
© The Joseph and Robert Cornell Memorial Foundation/Licensed by VAGA, New York, NY

JULIAN SCHNABEL

FOX FARM PAINTINGS
December 1 – 6 January, 1990

Read This
by Thomas McEvilley
Excerpt from Pace catalogue

. . . Schnabel's work, while not primarily theoretical in intention, responds sensitively to shifts in the theoretical situation. At an early age he had achieved what, supposedly, any ambitious artist (or careerist of any kind) wants: a signatured style that is bankable—meaning primarily the plate paintings of 1978 and after. He was not alone in his generation in this achievement. But two or three years later he *was* alone, when he decided to abandon or de-emphasize that style and move on to another—and then, a few years later, another, and another. He has not been afraid to experiment, and even at times to look bad because experimentation is bound to come up empty some of the time. He has risked what he has gained. . . .

Changing Style
This increasing rate of stylistic change has been a sign of the growing conceptualism in Schnabel's work. In general, neo-Expressionist painters have not radically altered famous and signatured styles—anymore than the Abstract Expressionists did in their day. There is a reason for this. According to the Kantian theory, the essential aesthetic reality does not change; an artist who radically revises his or her style is at the same time rejecting his or her earlier style and denouncing the works that embodied it. Since the new work evolved out of the old, invalidating the old by radical change, rather than slow aesthetic development, may invalidate the new also. Schnabel's tendency to abandon aesthetic territory already won, and move unpredictably into new modes, has led him partway out of the realm of neo-Expressionism and brings up a limited but visible comparison with the oeuvres of artists such as Gerhard Richter, Bruce Nauman, Yves Klein, Jannis Kounellis, and others whose work is making a conceptual point by its wild variation.

Schnabel's work started out the decade perceived as more or less pure painting—meaning Expressionist painting with overtones of existentialist ideology. There was talk about the emotionality of his brush stroke (which he was driven to publicly deny). His oeuvre ends the decade as a decidedly impure painting, anti-aesthetic and conceptual impulses prominent alongside the ever more perverse pleasure of the brush or the spray can. There is no doubt, of course, that Schnabel's work involves expression, but his mercurial or even quixotic shifts of expressive mode imply a relativization of expression—almost a critique of it. . . .

A Cure for Culture?
Another sign of the breakdown of the Kantian theory is the introduction of chance elements into the work, a process which Duchamp began early in the century. Randomness is, in effect, a part of nature, a way we perceive it to work; it signifies unpredictability and inaccessibility to control. Introducing it into the artwork erodes the barrier between nature and culture which, on the Modernist view enunciated by Hegel, is the bulwark of civilization—its way of keeping its head above the ocean of chance. To introduce chance into the project of civilization is to confound it. At the end of the second millennium of perhaps five millennia of civilization, chance shoots through the fabric of things. Nature intrudes. The barrier between nature and culture becomes a joke. What then become of the ideas of humanity and history?

"There is No Place on this Planet More Horrible than a Fox Farm during Pelting Season" is a phrase that arose at random, a found phrase, written in red ink on a ten dollar bill given as change. Perhaps the notation of an animal rights advocate, it seems to criticize the fur industry. For Schnabel, it signifies humanity, and the plague of AIDS. A sadness which derives personally from the multiple deaths of friends from AIDS is projected outward as a lament or dirge for humanity in general at the present social moment. The emphasis on red in these paintings extends the idea of paint as bodily fluid. The amorphous, fucked-up compositions and the sometimes grinding intersections of red and blue distance any light or decorative reading of the works, which seem to invite a sombre, even horrified response. . . . Culture was supposed to be a force that would protect us from nature, from the cold and the storm and the famine and so on. Now we look helplessly to nature for some cure for culture.

But nature may not be there to give a cure. It has been proposed recently that the natural world is no longer nature, because it has been so altered by cultural interventions that nature is now a part of culture. . . .

Untitled, 1947
oil on canvas, 53½ × 39⅝"

MARK ROTHKO | MULTIFORMS
January 12 – 10 February, 1990

by Mark Stevens
Excerpt from Pace catalogue

. . . By the late 1940s, Rothko had already banished many elements from his art, including the representational imagery of his Surrealist years. His pictures were abstract in form (though he himself continued to take subject matter seriously and hated the term "abstract") and were moving toward the concentration of the classic works. During these three years, I think his essential search, in formal and spiritual terms, was for gravity—and *gravitas*. Much as he admired Surrealism, he seemed to have found it too light, with its emphasis on automatic writing, individual quirkiness, and go-with-the-flow imagery. He desired something more weighty and grand, an art that could express not just the unconscious of an artist but the spirit of mankind.

In the Multiforms we can see Rothko beginning to reconcile lightness and immateriality with something heavier. He does this most successfully with color. On the one hand, Rothko remains interested in an openness, even looseness, before the various upwellings of the unconscious, which is characteristic of one aspect of Surrealism. Hence his color retains much of the fluidity of watercolor. Often it has the cloud-like delicacy, the random freedoms, that water brings to paint. Form cannot quite contain it: the edges blur. Luminous patches are floated across the canvas with confident daring. The surprising harmonies are luscious. Sometimes Rothko will apply one color on top of another, not quite covering up the earlier one, so that the color behind glimmers out from the edges, adding a kind of halo. In common with many Abstract Expressionist paintings of the late 1940's, Rothko's color during this period occasionally has a slightly gray ashiness about it, which probably owes something to the tough urban environment that surrounded these painters before they became famous. . . .

He does something similar to his shapes. One can still sense a freedom in their evolution, a spontaneous feel for what a line or a rectangle must do under the impulse of the moment, which is characteristic of some Surrealist art. He retains the Surrealist impatience with boundaries. He has a way of dissolving the rules of geometry. At times he even lets the movement of the brush show. In a few works, there is some scribbling, bits of calligraphy and a messing around with uncharacteristic shapes, such as the little horizontal lozenge forms that, in one picture, gather up like a small herd. However, Rothko's feeling for shape is also becoming more settled. He will almost never surrender entirely to spontaneous cloud swirls or biomorphic imagery. He knows that a rectangle weighs far more, in our mind's eye, than a looser form. In the Multiforms there may be no pure rectangle or square (with a couple of odd exceptions, when the artist tried floating some hard-edged rectangular forms against a misty background) but neither does randomness preside. In the Multiforms, a balance is being struck between form and dissolution, the permanent and the impermanent, the eternal and the momentary.

In Rothko's treatment of color and shape, this balance is lovely, mature, and fully in keeping with the artist's later work. Where Rothko's impatience still shows—where he has probably not yet arrived at the balance that suits him—is in the composition of the picture as a whole. It is not that any particular painting is "unresolved" or indifferently composed. Many artists have been content to play freely across the field of a canvas, while trying to make inspired visual rhymes of various kinds. In that way, Rothko often succeeds. . . .

MARK ROTHKO

MULTIFORMS

JIM DINE

DRAWINGS

February 16 – 17 March, 1990

Self-Portrait, 1989
watercolor, pastel, charcoal, pencil and ink on paper, 31 × 22¼"

No one of his generation has made a greater commitment to the art of drawing—or drawing as an art form—than Jim Dine. Over the years it has gradually become the raison d'être in all he does. In a definitive discussion of Dine and drawing it would be necessary to exclude little, if any, of his work. He draws on canvas and paper; on stones, plates, and printing blocks; in Plasticine and on ceramics. . . . Line, which he sees as a drawn line, is even at the heart of his sculpture. "Drawing is," as he says, "what I do."

Constance W. Glenn, *Jim Dine, Drawings*, (New York, 1985) p. 9.

Untitled, 1989
watercolor, pencil, charcoal, oilstick and oil paint on paper, 18 × 16¼"

Self-Portrait, 1989
mixed media on paper, 30½ × 22"

ROBERT RYMAN

Surprise and Equanimity
by Yve-Alain Bois
Excerpt from Pace catalogue

. . . **R.R.** I think all painters are somewhat isolated. Even though they are aware of what's going on and what's been done, they're not concerned with that so much. Little things that you pick up here and there trigger insights. It's only afterward that you can look at a number of different painters from the same period and pick up the threads of what people were thinking at the time. And that doesn't always work either. They can be misinterpreted.[13]

No grand scheme, no positioning. The only possible relationship to history is fragmentary, limited by one's own standpoint, uncertain. Bits here and there. Narrative can eventually come after the fact, but even then it is likely to be deceptive. Ryman wants to have no part of it. (When I asked him if there could be any relationship between a certain "return" to his problematics of the late '50s, in some works of the current show—for example, *Roll, Match, Locate*—and the fact that he had just had a retrospective at the Dia Foundation, for the preparation of which he must have spent a long time revisiting his past production, he simply told me that he had not "thought of it that way." A typical answer of his: firm in its matter-of-factness, yet again, nonemphatic, nonviolent.)

The same casualness pervades his beginnings. Born in Nashville, Tennessee, in 1930. Came to New York as a jazzman in 1952, as soon as he left the Army. Discovered museums. Worked as a guard at the Museum of Modern Art (I accepted anything I saw. . . . I felt that anything in a museum was worthy of being there").[14] Decided one day to try it out:

> There was a little art-supply store on the corner. I went there and bought a couple of canvasboards and some oil paint . . . and some brushes, and I thought I would try and see what would happen. I wanted to see what the paint would do, how the brushes would work. That was the first step. I just played around. I had nothing really in mind to paint. I was just finding out how the paint worked, colors, thick and thin, the brushes, surfaces.[15]

The most anticlimactic "first step." No painful and glorious initiation, no dramatic conversion: Ryman became a painter by impregnation and sheer curiosity. He was in the middle of paintings all day, and wanted to find out what it was like to paint. Yet this simple, unpretentious "playing around," this child-like enchantment before an unknown universe, led to one of the most sustained careers of a New York painter. Not to "express oneself," according to the traditional program of the period, but to find out how things worked: Ryman's motto was entirely given in his very first handling of the brush.

Because he withdraws from tragedy, because he avoids metaphors like the plague, because he discards images, Ryman is seen by some of his critics as an iconoclast, a reductionist, a Calvinist champion of purity. His work is often read as based on exclusion.[16] On the contrary, no work seems to me more inclusive; that everything counts in a painting has been his unbending position for more than thirty years. If he preferred not to fuss with colors and shapes, that is, if he wanted to prevent hierarchical relationships, it was only to render explicit this fundamental "democratism." Herein lies Ryman's lesson: nothing is insignificant in the institutional gestures of the pictorial practice, anything can become an integral part of the work. It may be the signature (displaced to the middle of the canvas, enlarged, multiplied, or affixed on the edge) or the date (as in the recent *Correspondent*); it may be the stretching of the canvas, or the choice of the brush and the quantity of pigment it can hold (in the *Winsor* series, the horizontal bands which fill up the canvas in an all over manner are rhythmically divided by brushstrokes methodically indicating this quantity); or it may be the frame, or the mode of fastening to the wall (increasingly so since 1976 and in *all* the canvases exhibited here); in could be the choice of the support (Ryman paints on the wall, on papers of all sorts, on cardboard, fiberglass, steel, plastic sheet, you name it, and, of course, on cotton canvas—"probably still the best surface," he said at one point);[17] sometimes it is the choice of the pigment itself (oil, casein, pastel, enamel, all the variations permitted by acrylic); or again, it might be the lighting, or the whole architectural environment of the painting (Ryman does not make environmental or, properly speaking, site-specific works—he likes his paintings to travel, to be exposed to different lights—but he insists on the interaction between the painting and the actual space where it is shown as part of the aesthetic experience. This space can vary and the nature of the interaction can change, but its fact remains as an aesthetic fact.) . . .

Ryman liberated all the "little simple things that are not generally considered," that we take for granted, that are plainly common. He liberated them, deinstrumentalized them, retrieved them, gave them an active function. One example: the fasteners. In certain cases, like the conspicuous pins in some of Picasso's *papiers collés*, they end up right in the middle of the work (see the recent *Condition*, for example). "The thinking for the fasteners has to do with the way a painting hangs on a wall; usually paintings, particularly if they're pictures, hang invisibly on a wall, because we're not so interested in that. It's the image that we're looking at in the confined space."[22] *Usual*, invisible through the force of habit, taken for granted, "naturalized," made into clichés: such are the numerous pictorial codes and procedures to which Ryman gave a fresh look, and patiently reinvented for us through de-

familiarization. But habit can also, in Ryman's dialectics, become an instrument of displacement: the trick, again, consists in a certain availability. The most striking features of *Initial*, for example, (one of the smallest paintings in this show), are the tiny cubic wooden pegs on which the painted surface rests. Asked about them, Ryman simply notes that they were holding the painting while he was working on it, that he got so accustomed to them that they became inseparable from the work, they became part of the work. . . .

Context, 1989
oil on linen with steel, 117 × 111"

1990

GREENE STREET

When Leo Castelli decided to close his auxiliary space at 142 Greene Street, we took over the lease, because our artists wanted to show their work in SoHo, where they lived. We then embarked on a plan to create a new identity for the venue by extending our exhibition program.

Leo's last exhibition was of an immense steel work by Richard Serra, whom we jointly represented at the time. During the disassembly of the piece, a mechanical failure caused it to fall and hit a column, destabilizing the entire building and permanently crippling one of the movers. Not only did the building have to be made secure before we could begin renovation, but the landlord refused to allow us to ever show Serra's sculpture in the space again.

In May 1990, in a new interior designed by the architect David Acheson, Pace opened its auxiliary gallery at 142 Greene Street with Julian Schnabel's first sculpture exhibition. Several of the gallery's artists found the new exhibition space better suited to the scale of the works they were producing. Others preferred Greene Street because they considered it a less commercial venue than the 57th Street gallery.

As SoHo evolved, the art world attracted the fashion world. Clothing and furniture boutiques proliferated, creating the most hip and, ironically, the most commercial shopping mall in New York. Taking advantage of the escalating value of property, the art dealers who owned their buildings began to take the profit on their real estate and move their galleries to the underdeveloped area of the city known as Chelsea. Under the directorship of Susan Dunne, we continued to present exhibitions at Greene Street for a decade, ending with Robert Rauschenberg's Apogamy Pods. The gallery closed in January 2001 and at this writing, our new space in Chelsea is under construction, designed by Robert Irwin and scheduled to open in the spring of 2001.

JULIAN SCHNABEL

RENÉ MAGRITTE
PAINTINGS, SCULPTURE AND DRAWINGS
May 11 – 29 June, 1990

Magritte by Magritte
Excerpt from Pace catalogue

Resemblance, an issue in everyday language, is attributed to things that have or do not have a common nature. The idiom goes: "They're as alike as two peas in a pod," and people say that the false resembles the genuine. This so-called resemblance consists only in a relationship of similitude discerned by a mind that examines, evaluates and compares.

Resemblance is identified with the essential act of thinking: the act of resembling. Thought resembles by becoming that which is offered to it by the world, and by restoring what it is offered to the mystery without which there would be no possibility of a world and no possibility of thought.

Inspiration is the event that gives rise to resemblance. Thought resembles only if it is inspired.

The art of painting—not conceived as more or less innocent mystification—would not be able to state ideas or express feelings: the image of a weeping face does not express sadness—since a feeling or an idea has no apparent form that could be visibly represented. A circle drawn on a painting is equivalent to a "round thought," but does not represent the idea or the feeling of the circle, which can be defined only by philosophy.

The art of painting—which really deserves to be called the art of resemblance—allows us to describe, by means of painting, a thought that is capable of becoming apparent. This thought understands exclusively the figures offered to us by the apparent world: people, stars, furnishings, weapons, solid bodies, inscriptions, *et cetera*. Resemblance spontaneously unites those figures in an order that directly evokes mystery. The description of such a thought does not endure originality. Originality or imagination would only bring weakness and misery; the charm and precision of an image of resemblance are reduced for the mediocre benefit of an original way of describing resemblance. Different ways do not exist for representing the inspired thought that resembles the apparent world.

The act of painting resemblance must limit itself to spreading colors on a surface in such a way that their actual aspect recedes, allowing an image of resemblance to appear. . . .

Inspiration gives the painter what he ought to paint: resemblance, which is a thought capable of becoming visible through painting: for example, the thought whose terms are a pipe and the inscription "this is not a pipe," or else the thought constituted by a nocturnal landscape under a sunny sky.

Such thoughts evoke mystery *de jure*; while mystery is evoked only *de facto* by a pipe placed on an ashtray or a nocturnal landscape under a starry sky.

It should be noted that any image that contradicts "common sense" does not evoke mystery *de jure* if that image is nothing but a possibility of contradiction. Resemblance does not worry about tallying with or challenging "common sense." Resemblance spontaneously unites figures of the apparent world in an order given by inspiration.

Translation © Joachim Neugroschel

Tentative de l'impossible, 1928
oil on canvas, 45½ × 32"

Les droits de l'homme, 1947–48
oil on canvas, 56⅝ × 45"
© 2001 C. Herscovici, Brussels/Artists Rights Society (ARS), New York

GEORGE BASELITZ

THE WOMEN OF DRESDEN / 57TH STREET

October 19 – 24 November, 1990

58½ × 29¼ × 16¾"

Photo Benjamin Katz

Besuch aus Prag (Die Dresndner Frauen), May 30, 1990
ash painted with cadmium yellow and egg tempera
58½ × 29¼ × 16¾"

DE KOONING/DUBUFFET

I first proposed this exhibition to Jean Dubuffet ten years ago. He was approving and enthusiastic but each time I fixed a date, Dubuffet postponed it, preferring to show his most recent works. Ultimately, it became clear that Dubuffet expected me to show only his contemporary work, implying that in the future I would be free to make thematic exhibitions.

Willem de Kooning, *Woman*, 1953
charcoal on paper, 10⅝ × 8¼"
© 2001 Willem de Kooning Revocable Trust/Artists Rights Society (ARS), New York

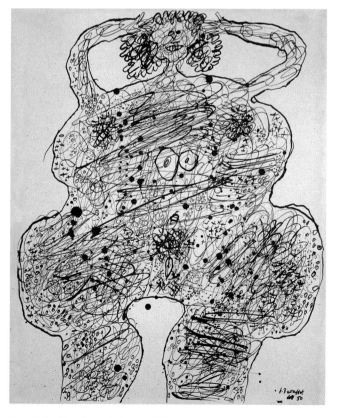

Jean Dubuffet, *Corps de dame*, 1950
ink on paper, 10⅝ × 8¼"
© 2001 Artists Rights Society (ARS), New York/ADAGP, Paris

The Women
by Mildred Glimcher
Excerpt from Pace catalogue

Paintings exist in multiple spatial and temporal contexts. They are artifacts of the time and place of their making, but have another life as well. They have actuality as contemporary images affecting the present-day audience and its discourse.

It is perhaps not surprising that this is the first full-scale confrontation of these two powerful series of *Women* painted almost simultaneously in postwar Paris and New York.[1] These are difficult and shocking pictures: difficult within the context of postwar modernism, which is marked on both sides of the Atlantic by the passionate opposition of abstraction and figuration, shocking in the ferocity and transgressive power of these images of women. Their juxtaposition should encourage the recuperation of issues neglected in much of the current discourse which has focused on Abstract Expressionism as a "Weapon of the Cold War."[2] We would hope that this confrontation will provide an opportunity for feminist art historians to enlarge their discourse as regards images of women and "woman as sex object."

Who are these women? They are certainly not our mothers, sisters or wives. De Kooning's women have been called Black Goddesses, harridans and whores, while Dubuffet's were named "manifestations of the Great Mother-Whore."[3] How did these two painters, so different in their means and ends, come to paint these disturbing images? Are the paintings emblematic of a shared postwar ambivalence and alienation? Do they reflect each man's personal anxiety towards women? How can they be located within the present art discourse?

. . . This confrontation does not imply in any way a question of "influence" in either direction, as these images evolved at the same time in each artist within the practice of his own work. Although women had been a dominant thread in de Kooning's work since 1940, the earlier works did not prepare his public for the six *Women* shown at the Sidney Janis Gallery in March 1953. The female form appeared from time to time in Dubuffet's oeuvre but, by his own declaration, we know the *Corps de dames* were all painted between April 1950 and February 1951. They were preceded by the *Paysages grotesques* which might be regarded as meditations on his 1949 sojourn in the Sahara.

In these works man and nature are one. The figures are part of the earth, defined solely by the trace of the incised lines. This non-hierarchical unification of man and nature is continued in the *Corps de dames* paintings where the ladies' bodies become a metaphorical landscape.

This confrontation should serve as a lynchpin in a discussion of the similarities and differences in the cultural milieu of this period and the possible relations between the two artists. On both sides of the Atlantic, World War II was perceived as a point of new beginning. The widespread influence of Existentialism was a reflection of the dissatisfaction with old solutions. Conventional answers would no longer do as artists sought to throw off the constraints of tradition. The mood towards this *tabula rasa*, however, was very different in the two cities. Paris was devastated and demoralized by the war. The work made there during the second half of the forties has a grimness and grittiness that reflects the physical condition of that city. Whereas, in New York, artists not directly touched by the horrors of war and its aftermath were demonstrating an optimism quite distinct from their French colleagues.

There was a growing disillusion with the ideals of Communism and its dominant aesthetic form, Socialist Realism, which contributed to the denigration of the tradition of realism. This politicization heightened the intensity of the ongoing debate between the advocates of figuration and abstraction.[6] As a result, the immediate postwar period saw the renewal of abstract painting in both cities: Abstract Expressionism, Action Painting in New York, and *L'Art Informel, L'Abstraction Lyrique* in Paris. Each group had a coterie of defenders: the artists themselves who often wrote, writers, critics and dealers, and in America (but not in Paris), curators and museum directors. The *Women* of de Kooning and Dubuffet encompass a new attitude toward the figurative within the domination of abstraction. . . .

Images of Women
Scopophilia, the sexual pleasure of looking, has been amply discussed in feminist literature, especially in connection with cinema.[50] Scopophilia implies the passive woman as object, receptor of the male gaze. But Dubuffet and de Kooning turn this pleasure on its head as all their images of women confront the viewer with their own active gaze. These two groups of extraordinary paintings are the heirs of a complex visual and iconographic tradition. Throughout the history of art, male artists have used the image of Woman to carry universal allegorical meaning, be it the *Nike* of Samothrace, the Virtues and Vices on medieval cathedrals or Delacroix's *Liberty Guiding the People*. On the other hand, the tradition of the female nude, the passive object of desire of the male gaze, be it by Titian or Velázquez,

de Kooning

dubuffet

was inflected and deformed by Manet's *Olympia* and the foreground figure in the *Déjeuner sur l'herbe* who both refuse to participate in this convention and confront the viewer with their own gaze. In fact, in many of the paintings by de Kooning and Dubuffet, the bodies themselves confront our gaze as breasts can be read as eyes, genitalia as mouth. In 1965, Loreau noted the relationship between several *Corps de dames* and Dubuffet's *Portraits* of 1947.[51] . . .

Personal Reflections

The paintings should be understood as each artist's personal manifestation of refusal to be enclosed in any system of rules or tradition, be it the "tradition of the new" (abstraction) for de Kooning or what Dubuffet perceived as the totality of outmoded western intellectual aesthetics. The schematic primitivism of Dubuffet's figures must have appeared more radical as they seem to come from nowhere, except perhaps from sources in his own work or *Art Brut*. They project a gritty rawness that reflects the despair of the French postwar condition. Their big-city crudeness was an important model for Oldenburg and other artists, especially in Chicago, who were coming to maturity at the end of the fifties and trying to escape the self-conscious elegance of second generation Abstract Expressionism. In Dubuffet's use of the image as sign, their grafitti-like scrawl and emphasis on non-art materials, the *Corps de dames* speak directly to the art making and audiences of the eighties. They may appear coarse and raw but the care lavished on making, in the use of glazes and the careful buildup of the *matière* give them a revolutionary kind of "finish."

De Kooning's method is antithetical to Dubuffet's as he lays down, scrapes away and even refuses to "finish" many works. His high-key color and vigorously active surface reflect the more optimistic milieu of postwar New York. While the paint in the *Corps de dames* takes on the hardened and dessicated quality of the earth, in de Kooning's *Women*, paint is juicy and alive, like flesh. While Dubuffet rejected all art history, de Kooning made clear in his statements and the paintings themselves his unwillingness to cut tradition loose in his work. This is particularly true for his Dutch forebears, Rembrandt, Van Gogh, Mondrian. His reverence for tradition was always married to an equal attraction to his own lived experience. His introduction of the banal and the vulgar into American high art is probably the most long-lived contribution of these works. Their afterimage could be seen almost immediately in the Rauschenberg Combines of the mid-fifties and on into the sixties in the works of Lichtenstein, Rosenquist, Warhol and Wesselmann.

Reflection upon this confrontation can lead in multiple directions, only a few of which have been sketched here. The focus has been their situation within the contemporary landscape and their personal dialogue with tradition as they perceived it. For all their differences, there were several basic viewpoints they shared. Process, chance and the introduction of a dialogue with non-art materials is privileged in most of their works.

Both men insisted upon the connection between art and life at a moment when the proponents of formalism were succeeding in removing life entirely from art. Both sought inspiration within themselves and their contact with life but, by virtue of location, their experiences and the resulting images were quite different. The Paris of 1950 had not yet fully recovered from the decay of the war with its crumbling walls and sober sense of deprivation. On the other hand, New York, with its pinup girls advertising everything from cigarettes to cars, had just inaugurated its role as the progenitor of a new consumer society. Dubuffet and de Kooning sought not only to escape the restraints of tradition but to find a "new image of man" that would be

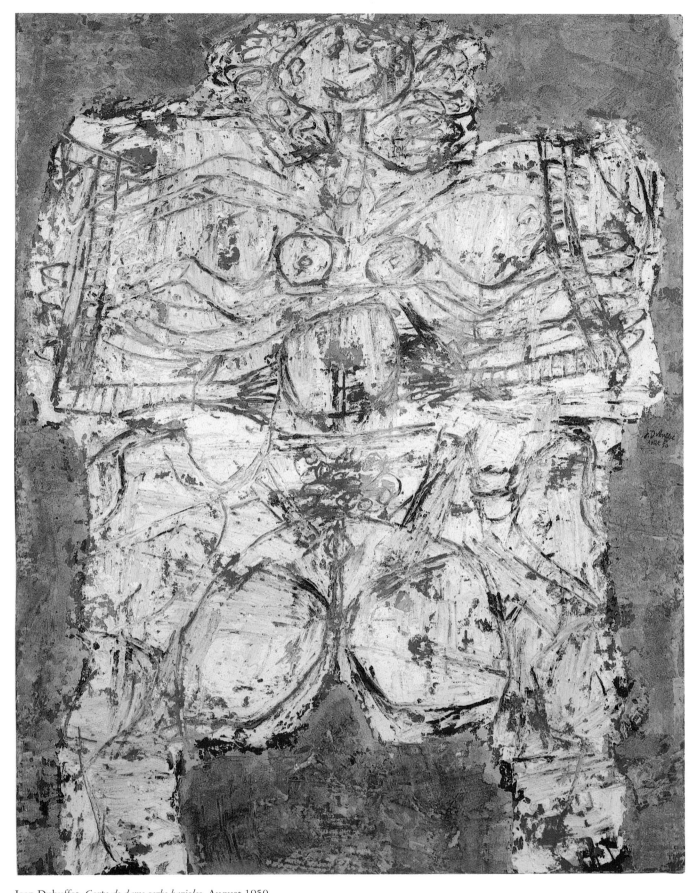

Jean Dubuffet, *Corps de dame gerbe bariolee,* August 1950
oil on canvas, 45¼ × 34¾"
© 2001 Artists Rights Society (ARS), New York/ADAGP, Paris

Woman and Bicycle, 1952–1953
oil on canvas, 76½ × 49"
Collection Whitney Museum of American Art
© 2001 Willem de Kooning Revocable Trust/Artists Rights Society (ARS), New York

commensurate with the societal transformations brought about by the spiritual and physical devastation of war, as well as the elation and optimism of a victorious America.

The desire for a *tabula rasa* is not a new phenomenon after a global catastrophe, but their perception of the meaning of tradition and the character of the *tabula rasa* that evolved was quite different. Whereas Dubuffet and his circle insisted on a rejection of *all* forms of culture with a return to primitivism and to art in its ante-cultural stage, the Americans, especially de Kooning were not yet prepared to throw out all of western culture. In order to prove they were ready to "play with the big boys" and win, the Americans had to remain on the traditional European playing field, striving to find new answers to old twentieth-century questions. They were unaware that their French colleagues had already left the field and were beginning a new game with a new set of rules. It is for this reason that de Kooning's *Women* are clearly the progeny of Picasso's *Demoiselles* and Dora Maar portraits of the late thirties, while Dubuffet's remind one either of some imagined primitive cave paintings or the graffiti of the "common man" on a city wall.

1. I would like to thank Arnold Glimcher and Elinor Klein for their help in realizing this essay.
2. See Max Kozoloff, "American Painting during the Cold War," *Artforum* 11, (May 1973) pp. 43–53; Eva Cockcroft, "Abstract Expressionism, Weapon of the Cold War," *Artforum* 12, (June 1974) pp. 39–41; Serge Guilbaut, *How New York Stole the Idea of Modern Art*, trans. Arthur Goldhammer, (Chicago 1983) Among the publications refuting this position see Ann Gibson and Stephen Polcari, eds., *Art Journal* (Fall 1988) and Michael Auping ed., *Abstract Expressionism: The Critical Developments*, Albright-Knox Art Gallery and Abrams, (New York 1987).
3. James Fitzsimmons, "Jean Dubuffet: A Short Introduction to his Work," *Quandrum* IV, (1957 27–50) p. 36.
6. Germain Viatte, [translation from *Aftermath; France 1945–54*, Barbican Art Gallery, (London 1982)] p. 12.
50. The originary piece on this subject: Laura Mulvey, "Visual Pleasure and Narrative Cinema" *Screen* 16, 1975. Mulvey notes: "Originally, in his *Three Essays on Sexuality*, Freud isolated scopophilia as one of the component instincts of sexuality which exist as drives quite independently of the erotogenic zones." Quoted from the reprint in: Laura Mulvey, *Visual and Other Pleasures*, (Bloomington 1989) p. 16.
51. Max Loreau. Fascicule VI, (Paris 1966) p. 11. *Catalogue des travaux de Jean Dubuffet*, Paris 1966–87.

The Inflection
by Yve-Alain Bois
Excerpt from Pace catalogue

. . . There is much that could be said about Judd's recent evolution, in particular his increasingly free use of color and his new casualness with respect to composition (about which he as recently as 1987 remarked to Catherine Millet that he has "not thought about it for years"),[24] his less and less exhaustive use of systems of formal generation with more and more parameters (as Jochen Poetter remarked concerning the 1989 Baden-Baden exhibition, which included twelve pieces constructed on an identical module, even without taking color into account, it was clear that the possibilities offered by the system far exceeded those that had actually been exploited);[25] and finally, his current sense of ease with respect to systems of classical proportion, whose dependence on Greek rationalism or Renaissance humanism had long repelled him. Overall, it would seem that, having broken free of his beginnings as a painter (which for a good while he had actually insisted on, in order to mark himself off from the whole sculptural tradition), and after a frontal attack on notions that are ontologically foreign to the pictorial tradition ("real" time, "real" light and "real" space), Judd was thenceforth able to return to it in the most emancipated way.

But, in order to conclude, . . . I'd like now to explore one of the least evolutionary aspects of his work, namely his perpetual reworking of earlier pieces, employing different materials (as is the case, in the present exhibition, with one of his very first works, the box with pipe from 1963). To be sure,

this practice can be interpreted precisely as a refusal of linear history (a refusal to be found in a good number of the artist's statements), but for me this is not its most important feature. Given all the recent hubbub concerning Panza's unauthorized reconstructions or even "reworkings" of Judd's works, I shall start by quoting the artist himself: "Obviously to Panza, only the configuration of a work is real, the configuration sketched on paper. He just makes the sketch in three dimensions. . . . Since to Panza the shape only has to get off the paper, the nature of the material and of the surface and the details of the construction are all irrelevant. Panza does not even bother to inform himself of the intervals between parts. . . . Consequently Panza makes mock-ups, fakes."[26] Or again: "Panza constantly repeats the word 'project.' I never made 'projects.'"[27] And lastly (as one of his assistants puts it): "The meaning of the works is achieved only through the quality of its fabrication and the correctness of its installation."[28]

Judd's position is clear, and perfectly congruent with his declared empiricism: even if their structure is identical, none of his stacks, none of the works related to the Wallraf-Richartz piece, none of the mural progressions, no work is ever the same as another. It's just like Albers's *Homage to the Square*, a painter for whom Judd, in basing a large part of his work on the potential gap between a "factual" form or color and its "actual" perception (as Albers put it), very early felt a certain elective affinity. Just as the latter's obstinacy in

sticking to the same configuration during the last two decades of his career as a painter was often interpreted as a poverty of inspiration (the same stupid argument can be found here and there applied to Reinhardt's "black" canvases), in the same way, observers have often been thrown off by the stubbornness in Judd's work. There is no need for long philosophical preambles, however, in order to see that seriality is just another aspect of the dialectic of identity and difference I mentioned earlier: it is partly because it can be measured by a morphological constancy that the unicity of the works stands out so much in each series. And Judd has been taking pains for some considerable time now to state the ineluctable character of this unicity, *hic et nunc*, through an infinite variation in his materials, and by exploring, for our delectation, their specific possibilities.

It has to be said, though, that his intentions haven't always been terribly clear on this point. Not that he has ever deviated from his empiricist position, but his early casual attitude to the material side of his pieces, or his presentation of diagrammatic drawings at the Whitney exhibition in 1968 (even though they were done after the sculptures to which they refer) has given rise to some confusion. Certainly, he has never made a conceptualist fuss about the "impersonal" production of his works by others (he doesn't distinguish between the manufacturer in the factory and the studio assistant), but, in my view, his ever-increasing concern for precision in the physical appearance of his pieces goes hand in hand with a growing awareness of the potential gap between a "project"— a word of low repute—and its realization. (In Glaser's 1966 interview with both him and Stella, Judd discusses the fact that one can never know in advance what a piece will actually look like;[29] to which I would add that, if, for essentially economic reasons, he at the time feared unpleasant surprises, today he is in the fortunate position of being able to look forward to the pleasant ones).[30] In any case, more than ever before, Judd refuses to consider matter as an inert given awaiting form; it is now less than ever possible to comment on even the slightest of his pieces without actually having it in front of you, without being able to judge in each case the special way that light is reflected by his polished metal or colored plexiglas surfaces, or, on the contrary, is absorbed by the more rustic dullness of the wood he uses (which, by the way, is why I haven't said anything about the works featured in the present exhibition, works which, as I write these lines, are yet to emerge from the various studios and factories on various continents in which they are being fabricated). . . .

24. Catherine Millet, "La petite logique de Donald Judd," *Artpress*, November 1987, p. 7.

25. Jochen Poetter, "Hermetic and Open – Precision and Beauty," in *Donald Judd* (Baden-Baden, op. cit.), p. 35. As Judd has often noted, it is enough to be aware of the fact that there is a system (and thus that the work is not compositional): there is no need to cross all the t's and dot all the i's. Here again, we find everything that separates him from LeWitt, for whom the exhautive and obsessional implementation of the system is paramount.

26. Donald Judd, "Una stanza per Panza," op. cit., part two (July 1990), p. 12. On the Panza affair, apart from Judd's diatribe, see Susan Hapgood, "Remaking Art History," *Art in America*, July 1990, pp. 115–122 and 181.

27. Ibid., part three, (September 1990), p. 4.

28. Ibid., part four, (November 1990), p. 10. This last point is tainted by naïveté and I'm not sure that Judd would subscribe to it entirely. No meaning can ever emerge without a context in which it is posited and to which it is opposed, and in the case of a work of art this context does not consist only of the "installation." It also consists of a vast network of institutional, aesthetic, socio-political and strategic relations that it is the historian's task to examine.

29. In discussing two works consisting of the same number of identical elements but set out differently, the author of the *Catalogue Raisonné* notes with a certain surprise tinged with naïveté that Judd sees them as two different pieces (cf. no. 323); it is hard to see how it could be otherwise.

30. Cf. Glaser, op. cit., p. 162. Judd has often spoken of his disgust for mockups, and of his negligible investment in sketches: such modes of notation give a false idea of the work and "teach him nothing"; it is only once it has actually been produced in the material or materials for which it was conceived that a piece can be judged. As far as "pleasant surprises" go, a recent example is furnished by the pieces he did for the Baden-Baden exhibition, where the colored reflections form a kind of column of virtual color in mid-air: "I knew the blue [piece] would do that. But I didn't think about the others in that way." ("Back to Clarity," op. cit., p. 99).

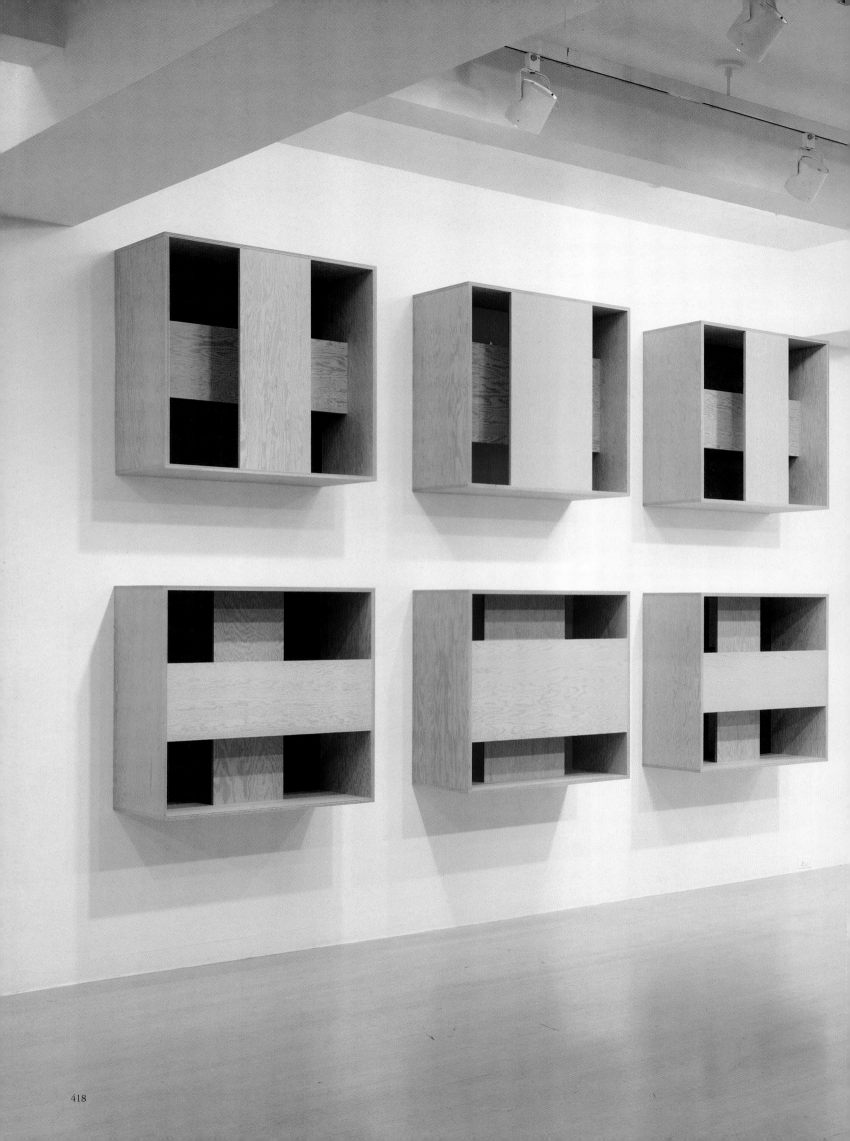

JIM DINE | NEW PAINTINGS AND SCULPTURE

September 21 – 26 October, 1991

Wheat Fields

by Martin Friedman

Excerpt from Pace catalogue

In 1989, Dine began constructing a landscape, as he terms it, based on objects he found during his summer sojourns in Walla Walla. For many years, a prime source for such scavenging has been the junkyard adjacent to the Walla Walla Foundry. Its contents include discarded tools, household objects, and rusted farm machinery. The junkyard, in Dine's words, is "quite inspiring to see." For the sculpture, *Wheat Fields*, the land surrounding the foundry became his studio. He preferred to work on this piece in the late afternoon because of the quality of light at that time of day. Seated on a chair in the middle of a field, he studied the results of com-

bining the large elements that would constitute the piece. These included a sixteen-foot long wood beam connecting a pair of tractor wheels in a quasi-symmetrical composition, whose dominant central element was a massive skull.

All components of *Wheat Fields* underwent the Walla Walla alchemy. Each was transformed from its original state—whether wood, plaster, or rubber—through being cast in bronze. These facsimiles were then painted illusionistically by Dine to faithfully replicate their original appearance. In addition to the diverse unrelated objects, *Wheat Fields* boasts,

what is particularly distinctive about this sculpture is its linear, horizontal configuration.

Although its wheels are cast in bronze and firmly fixed, the overall configuration of the piece implies movement. This bi-wheeled structure's agricultural allusions—it suggests tractors, wagons, and harvesters—are reinforced by Dine's inclusion of a rake, a pick, shovels, and axes. Juxtaposed among these artifacts of the field are a number of improbable objects that he gleaned along the roadside and then had cast in bronze. These include a multi-hued parrot, a headless Jesus, and a duck.

Dine, long addicted to junkyards and roadside curio shops, is ceaselessly on the prowl for shards of contemporary Americana. He has no problem combining fragments of kitsch culture with forms fabricated by his own hand. A prime example of the latter is the massive skull he chain saw carved in wood in 1987, two summers before the *Wheat Fields* project began. Nor is he reluctant to combine references to art history and his personal life in such sculptures. A truncated figure of the Venus de Milo, a portrait head of his wife Nancy, and a Giacometti-like visage mounted on a pole are part of this frontal sculpture's polychromed vocabulary.

Wheat Fields, 1989
painted bronze with patina and pigment, 80 × 172 × 99"

421

CHUCK CLOSE | RECENT PAINTINGS
November 2 – 7 December, 1991

Angels of a New Baroque
by Peter Schjeldahl
Excerpt from Pace catalogue

Few rooms in this world are big enough to afford sharp perception of the images in Chuck Close's new paintings. In most spaces one simply cannot get far enough away to lose sight of the work's facture, its bravura shatter of visual information, in the representation it cunningly makes up. Looking through the wrong end of binoculars would probably help. When I viewed Close's new self-portrait at his studio, I hit on two other stratagems for seeing better by seeing worse. Retreating as far as possible, I removed my glasses. Then I asked for a floodlight on the painting to be turned off. Immediately the great gray face—cobbled of gridded marks of black, white, gray, blue-gray, and umber—snapped into sufficient focus for me to make out its expression of open-mouthed avid gazing. The image came through the dim loft to my slightly blurred eyes with a tigerish pounce, the roughly eight-foot-high face taking on at a distance of perhaps fifty feet the optical scale of a life-sized face shoved into mine. I felt less that I was looking than that I was being benignly but very aggressively looked at. Replacing my glasses, then, and walking forward, I watched the face loom and disintegrate back into its constituent pieces—thousands of little square compositions like thousands of discrete minipaintings, row on row—and was again a looking subject rather than a looked-at object, but a subject awed. I knew myself to be standing in a field, radiating from the canvas, of representation-in-action. It was a Baroque sensation, physically enveloping and at once blatantly artificial and almost punishingly lively. It felt very grand. Thinking about it put me in mind of something about Velázquez. . . .

Is painting paint or image? It is both, and more than both. Paint itself becomes an image in the eye, and images complexly meaningful can seem to the mind as ductile as any pigmented stuff (such images constantly changing in aspect, always a jump ahead of comprehension). In the half-century since a general collapse of easel-painting conventions ruled out standard finesses of the image/paint conundrum, making self-consciousness about it mandatory, most strong painters have gravitated temperamentally toward one or the other pole. (Weak painters either fail to notice the conundrum's existence or, as with much color-field abstraction and mannered painterly realism, vacillate blandly in the middle.) Willem de Kooning is paint-as-image; Andy Warhol is image-as-medium.

It is the rare painter—Jackson Pollock, Jasper Johns, Gerhard Richter, or Close—who revels in the conundrum itself, devising new ways to energize its opposite extremes simultaneously. Such a painter seeks a state of perception thoroughly incoherent, bollixing rational expectation and understanding, on all grounds except the formal order of painting, which by surviving the violent test strikes the mind with an effect of majesty. The formal order of painting, for such a painter, is never given in advance. It is what is left, an obdurate residue, when there is no other way to explain why some determinedly bizarre deployment of paint on canvas is not a mess. Close's violent test is an imposition on painting of mere orderliness: geometric (grids), scientific (optical formulas), and technological (photography). In terms of the subjective truth that is painting's cynosure, those objective systems don't make for order at all, but for chaos and entropy, a chill in the heart. Close's taciturn processes leave human interest and human feeling just two utterly disjoined refuges: the interest of somebody's face viewed in the fleeting instant of a snapshot and the feeling of a hand distributing paint over an incredibly long period of time. Between them, the lightning vision and the snail's-pace touch generate an artificial, impersonal, stunning effect: a revelation of the formal order of painting or, to use the old-fashioned term for it, beauty.

Beauty is a mental breakdown. It is a brick wall the mind runs into. I had a jostle with it at the recent Whitney Biennial when first glimpsing Close's wonderful *April* in the distance, through two doorways, upon entering the museum's second floor. *April* spilled across the intervening space its tawny and roseate effulgences, a complicated soft chromatic explosion in which, like the Rouen cathedral in a *Rouen Cathedral* by Monet, some substantial worldly entity ungraspably but powerfully asserted its reality. The face of April Gornik seemed less to take form on the canvas than, by its expression, gently to will the painting into existence, modulating a dancing emission of color in order to have eyes, a mouth, and hair. Even at the distance, the image was somewhat blurred, just verging on distinctness—but actively verging, in a moment of becoming. This impression, like most experiences of beauty, was over in a flash. . . .

As with art of the Baroque, Close's new works are paintings for palaces. They have a mission to en-

hance and expatiate on the grace and justice of privileged spaces, which in our day are definitively museums and museum-like venues. Close plainly works with such venues in mind. On an obvious level, only rooms engineered for optimum display of large works can meet his art's voracious space requirements. Lots of artists are similarly oriented, competing for the big rooms, but scarcely a handful possess Close's comprehension of the gestalt required by the contemporary palace: the exact balance of matter-of-fact physical presence and outer-directed dazzle, a blend of the imposing and the engaging that is convincingly infused with somebody's inner necessity. . . . Simply, Close wants to make paintings that are satisfactory, up to the job that

any painting must perform to justify itself now. That job, rigorously and subtly conceived, is his subject. The fantastic—the preposterous, the dumbfounding—labor-intensiveness of his style announces it, the more thrillingly because the effect attained is so light and clear, frictionless as sailing on a glassy sea. It is as if Close were driven by a titanic ambition to be responsible and modest, exalting little virtues. (I think again of Velázquez, who more or less gave up painting for the more desirable job of court decorator.) . . . In the scintillating force-field of his new work you know where you are: in some sanctuary of a civilization that still hungers for epiphany and has not yet lost the capacity for producing people who can deliver it.

Eric, 1990
oil on canvas, 100 × 84"

April, 1990–91
oil on canvas, 100 × 84"

AGNES MARTIN | RECENT PAINTINGS
December 6 – 4 January, 1992

Beauty Is the Mystery of Life

When I think of art I think of beauty. Beauty is the mystery of life. It is not in the eye it is in the mind. In our minds there is awareness of perfection.

We respond to beauty with emotion. Beauty speaks a message to us. We are confused about this message because of distractions. Sometimes we even think that it is in the mail. The message is about different kinds of happiness and joy. Joy is most successfully represented in Beethoven's *Ninth Symphony* and by the Parthenon.

All art work is about beauty; all positive work represents it and celebrates it. All negative art protests the lack of beauty in our lives.

When a beautiful rose dies beauty does not die because it is not really in the rose. Beauty is an awareness in the mind. It is a mental and emotional response that we make. We respond to life as though it were perfect. When we go into a forest we do not see the fallen rotting trees. We are inspired by a multitude of uprising trees. We even hear a silence when it is not really silent. When we see a newborn baby we say it is beautiful—perfect. The goal of life is happiness and to respond to life as though it were perfect is the way to happiness. It is also the way to positive art work.

It is not in the role of an artist to worry about life—to feel responsible for creating a better world. This is a very serious distraction. All of your conditioning has been directed toward intellectual living. This is useless in art work. All human knowledge is useless in art work. Concepts, relationships, categories, classifications, deductions are distractions of mind that we wish to hold free for inspiration.

There are two parts of the mind. The outer mind that records facts and the inner mind that says "yes" and "no." When you think of something that you should do the inner mind says "yes" and you feel elated. We call this inspiration.

For an artist this is the only way. There is no help anywhere. He must listen to his own mind.

The way of an artist is an entirely different way. It is a way of surrender. He must surrender to his own mind.

When you look in your mind you find it covered with a lot of rubbishy thoughts. You have to penetrate these and hear what your mind is telling you to do. Such work is original work. All other work made from ideas is not inspired and it is not art work.

Art work is responded to with happy emotions. Work about ideas is responded to with other ideas. There is so much written about art that it is mistaken for an intellectual pursuit.

It is quite commonly thought that the intellect is responsible for everything that is made and done. It is commonly thought that everything that is can be put into words. But there is a wide range of emotional response that we make that cannot be put into words. We are so used to making these emotional responses that we are not consciously aware of them till they are represented in art work.

Our emotional life is really dominant over our intellectual life but we do not realize it.

You must discover the art work that you like and realize the response that you make to it. You must especially know the response that you make to your own work. It is in this way that you discover your direction and the truth about yourself. If you do not discover your response to your own work you miss the reward. You must look at the work and know how it makes you feel.

If you are not an artist you can make discoveries about yourself by knowing your response to work that you like.

Ask yourself: "What kind of happiness do I feel with this music or this picture."

There is happiness that we feel without any material stimulation. We may wake up in the morning feeling happy for no reason. Abstract or non objective feelings are a very important part of our lives. Personal emotions and sentimentality are anti-art.

We make art work as something that we have to do not knowing how it will work out. When it is finished we have to see if it is effective. Even if we obey inspiration we cannot expect all the work to be successful. An artist is a person who can recognize failure.

If you were a composer you would not expect everything you played to be a composition. It is the same in the graphic arts. There are many failures.

Art work is the only work in the world that is unmaterialistic. All other work contributes to human welfare and comfort. You can see from this that human welfare and comfort are not the interests of the artist. He is irresponsible because his life goes in a different direction. His mind will be involved with beauty and happiness. It is possible to work at something other than art and maintain this state of mind and be moving ahead as an artist. The unmaterial interest is essential. . . .

– A.M.

ROBERT MANGOLD | THE ATTIC SERIES

February 14 – 14 March, 1992

Thinking Walls

by Klaus Kertess

Excerpt from Pace catalogue

For nearly thirty years, the lean grace of Robert Mangold's art has sought to embrace an autonomy of the radically pared down components of painting itself: form, color, line, and surface. In most of his works, the interdependence of the irregular geometry of the interior figure with the dissimilarly inclined, irregular geometry of the physical plane of the painting's support presents itself with the immediacy, self-evidence, and economy of a mathematical equation. But the seeming empirical certainty of geometry yields an uncertainty. Mangold's precision conflates the edges that distinguish the perceived from the conceived just as it conflates the edges that distinguish the interior from the exterior of the painting. Like all consequential art, his confounds the known with the unknown.

In his most recent work, Mangold's laconic eloquence explores color's propensity for atmospherics and stretches his drawn edges toward perspectival dimensionality—making it ever clearer that his geometries are not so much figures of objectivity as they are figures of intuition reflecting the flux and play of mental processes. The insistent planar flatness and self-evidence that has been so endemic to his art is not violated but rather becomes host to a new dimension, both literally and figuratively. Step by step, Mangold's extreme reductiveness has retrieved lapsed conventions of abstract painting, as he has moved from an almost virtual materiality toward a panoply of optical allusiveness.

The blankness that has inhabited Mangold's painting since its beginning in the mid-1960s is, of course, a hallmark of the Minimalism that he played such a seminal role in charting. The exaltation of emptiness and silence pervaded much of the culture of the 1960s: the pursuit of primary states of consciousness varied in intent from the purely analytic to the Zen ecstatic, from the drones of Lamonte Young's and Ravi Shankar's music to druggie rock'n'roll to the neutralized grids and monochromes of Minimalism. Mangold's intentions were, and remain, purely secular. He sought to retrieve the matte wallness and abstract rhythmic clarities of Western art's pre-Renaissance fresco and panel painting—before the invention of oil paint and mimetic illusionism. Indeed, in their determined flatness, wall dependence, and light-suffused dryness, Mangold's paintings relate to fresco. But his frescoes, like his culture, are nomadic (portable) and fragmentary. . . .

The rules for these paintings are as follows: A vertical format—if it is wider than tall, a physical break must be made at that juncture; the bottom edge is parallel to the floor; the irregular quadrilateral may be rectilinear or have one curved side; if there is a curved side, the interior figure must be rectilinear; if all four exterior sides are are rectilinear, the interior figure must be curved; the interior figure must touch all four sides of the exterior shape. Like the simple linear strategies of a game plan, Mangold's strategies are given body by the idiosyncrasies of his unique dexterity and instinct. Rationality coordinates intuition and vice versa. Mangold's longtime penchant for simple self-evident and self-contained rule-making is shared with such peers as Sol LeWitt but is open to the flexibility and unexpectedness found in the maneuvers taking place within the skewed square field of the sport of baseball, of which Mangold is a major fan.

As in his previous work, he starts with a pencil sketch, then moves to a colored drawing, then makes a small, painted study and finally the full painting. The solution is not a priori; it unfolds with slow and open deliberation. In general, the Attic paintings are roller painted with more restraint and homogeneity than the more aggressively variegated surfaces of the related Irregular Area paintings made between 1985 and 1987. Now the thinly layered paint is often more saturated in hue than were previous paintings; and the color is more prone to atmospherics. Many of the Attic paintings explore the realm of red, suggesting another, then still another. Some of these reds approach the heated lushness of Mark Rothko's zone, but they are never allowed to vaporize the plane.

The fulsome elliptical contour of the interior figure of *Attic Series I* encloses the majority of the area of the irregular plane and is firmly anchored to its exterior, physical edges. In its more visibly hand drawn line and in its configuration, this painting looks back directly to the paintings started in 1985. In the subsequent Attic paintings, the ellipse is more distended; the edges meet the exterior shape at the extremities of its corners—more of its contour floats freely within the plane. The greater independence of the interior figure, together with its more extreme distension, which has the appearance of a diagrammatic perspectival distortion, propels the figure to torque in and out of flatness. In the paintings since *Attic Series VII*, Mangold has frequently introduced a twisted interior figure of an ellipse or quadrilateral that draws the space into still further vacillation. This ambiguity becomes the linear counterpart to the spatial ambiguities now encouraged by color and surface; it is literally and figuratively underlined by the tensile grace of Mangold's precise, objectively ruled but minutely fluctuating hand. Geometric precision and objective materiality and the resonant imprecision of intuition and abstract painting become one. . . .

Attic Series XVIII, 1991
acrylic and black pencil on canvas, 96 × 96"

DAN FLAVIN | **RECENT WORK/GREENE STREET**
February 15 – 14 March, 1992

Untitled (for A.C.), 1992
pink, green, blue and yellow fluorescent light, 96 × 96 × 9"

433

Elch Kaum, 1990
oil on canvas, 114⅛ × 114⅛"

GEORG BASELITZ | RECENT PAINTINGS
March 20 – 18 April, 1992

[T]he pictures build up and break down before our eyes, a deposit of forms, of thoughts, of feelings. They place together in time and space what would immediately have covered itself in an exteme vision. The heroes in *Bildzwei* do not so much look like reclining figures as like a reversible and symmetric dimension of the experience.

Eric Darragon, *Le Palimpsest des Grands Amis*. Taken from the English translation in *Louisiana Revy*, 33, Argang Nr. 3, May 1993, p. 67.

Bildzehn, 1991
oil on canvas, 113½ × 180¼"

CLAES OLDENBURG

Claes Oldenburg interviewed
by Arne Glimcher
July 2, 1992
Excerpt from Pace catalogue

A.G. How did objects as disparate as a harp, sax and perfume bottle come together in your mind as a sonata?

C.O. Oh, I meant that the subjects are put through several variations of metaphor, and material action, changes of technique and scale, all kinds of transformations—like the melody or theme of a sonata.

    Since several of the subjects are musical instruments, it seemed an appropriate analogy. The perfume bottles were in the show as well, so I just included them.

A.G. All of the instruments and objects, including the perfume bottle, are dependent upon wind. The harp vibrates, the saxophone uses forced air, the perfume bottle's action is powered by air— in fact it creates its sound by air. Other works created at the same time, such as the *Leaf Boat* are also driven by wind.

C.O. The soft harp, too, can stir in the air like a sail. In fact, it can be raised and lowered like a sail.

A.G. The leaf in the boat also becomes a sail.

C.O. In the case of the harp, the wind is very delicate, but in the case of the notebook pages—which have also become involved in the exhibition—the wind is stormy. The saxophones show a kind of twisting motion which makes one think of a spiral or tornado. And the spiral is a very important element in the notebook pages. Though torn apart, they're kept together by a spiral.

A.G. Do the objects in this sonata have specific gender?

C.O. This show began with thoughts circulating about certain experiences in France, where gender is an unavoidable part of an object. But gender is associated with objects everywhere, such as the harp, usually shown being played by a woman, or female angel. Even Harpo Marx seems to change gender when he plays.

    This can start a line of thought which, in my work, results in a combination of two or more objects in the final result. Like the literal renditions of a metaphor. The harp suggests a wing, for example, and that suggests a sail, which is confirmed by associations of women such as sirens or Lorelei playing instruments in a watery setting.

    Perfume bottles tend to be more exclusively female, and some female stereotypes are invoked in developing the sculptures, like the boudoir associations of pillows or pink. The saxophone is more ambiguous. For a long time it was a man's instrument, but this is changing, and the form has a voluptuousness which I associate with a female torso.

A.G. Your large saxophone is positioned as a seated odalisque in a decidedly seductive female pose.

C.O. The problem is that a saxophone is always held by someone. Here it supports itself by "sitting," and the sax has something in common with a torso. The result, together with its particular scale, is rather anthropomorphic. It reminds me of *La Grande Baigneuse* by Ingres, though the "costume" is more from Delacroix. . . .

A.G. There is the sense that these objects, with the exception of the *Leaf Boat*, are interior images that bring you back to the sensibility of *The Street*. During the last decade, large formal transformations of common objects often found themselves in the streets configured as sleek formal monuments. These naturally sleek objects (musical instruments, perfume bottles) have been transformed into gritty, messy street images. The saxophone seems to be dancing like a snake charmer's snake, the object of a street bazaar. Do you feel this relationship to the street?

C.O. Yes, the scale and technique required in the fabrication of larger works doesn't favor the disheveled, detailed look of *The Street* or *The Store*, but that sensibility hasn't gone away. It was set aside in 1977 when Coosje and I decided to concentrate exclusively on large public works.

In 1984, at Coosje's urging, I returned to working in cloth and paint with the props for the performance of *Il Corso del Coltello* in Venice, Italy. This stimulated a return to intimate works and a continuation, with certain variations, of the aesthetic established in the 1960's.

The linear progression of art that had so dominated the 50's and 60's had evaporated and it was possible to do almost anything. For example, a "happening" was no longer a doctrinaire form; you could mix up "happening" ideas with *commedia dell'arte* and whatever. This freedom showed up in all the props which were done for the *Coltello*, with enthusiasm for the performance, without thinking a lot about art history. That attitude persisted after the performance.

A.G. You're legendary as a great draftsman. Unlike you, most of your generation of artists became draftsmen late in their careers. Learning how to draw was like on-the-job training, as drawing was not the major concern of the image-makers of your generation or the generation of Abstract Expressionists before you.

How much do you have to fight this facility that is not typical of your peers? You can make anything look like art. Is there a conscious battle going on for you to strip the drawing of facility?

C.O. It's very hard to define drawing. For example, I find it almost impossible to obtain a likeness. My drawing seems to be the projection of a world inside me, shaped by gestures naturally produced by my body. I censor the work not in the doing so much, but in discarding what I don't like. Facility can be all right, if it fits. Every drawing has its own rules.

Drawing should be uninhibited. Some may be art, some may just lead to art, some may not be art at all and still be interesting. I think of Picasso's remark that if he were locked in a prison cell without any tools, he would be compelled to draw in the dust on the floor with his tongue. . . .

A.G. Your drawings take place before, during and after the completion of the work. Are the drawings part of the process of transforming these images?

C.O. Certainly. The drawings begin on a very small scale as the setting down of an idea.

A.G. Are they made in a notebook?

C.O. The notebooks are the place where all my ideas appear at first. The procedure with the notebooks is that every two weeks, whenever they're filled, I go through them and take out the things that seem worth developing. I glue these up on 8½ × 11 inch sheets and I put them in a binder. The remaining notebook is torn in half and discarded, which produces the form that is used as the basis for the *Torn Notebooks*. . . .

So that's how it starts, these notes are gathered. After that there are different kinds of larger drawings. There's a sort of architectural, schematic drawing which enables me to get the subject to the proper scale and ultimately leads to the construction of the sculpture. . . . As with the *Leaf Boat*, it's a drawing of the sculpture in different contexts, such as floating in the sea.

A.G. Does the sculpture then serve as a model for drawings?

C.O. Yes, for the situations depicted in the drawings.

A.G. So the saxophone as odalisque could then become a model to draw from, not unlike life drawing?

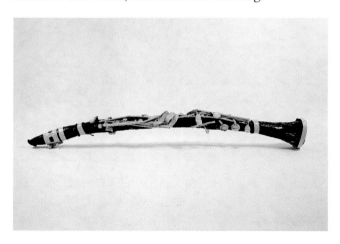

C.O. The sculpture itself becomes the subject in the later stages of a theme. These drawings can be rough, impressionistic, or carried to a high degree of finish if they're going to be posters or prints. The subject may be repeated many times in variations until it fades out.

Previous page: Saxophone, Scale A Hard, 1992
canvas, wood, cord, resin and latex print, 32 × 12½ × 15"
Above left: Perfume Bottle, Pink, 1992
muslin, wood, clothesline, dacron, resin, and latex paint, 14½ × 9¾ × 38½"
Above: Clarinet Bridge, 1992
canvas, wood, clothesline, urethane foam, resin, and latex paint, 14½ × 11¼ × 98"

The New York Times, September 25, 1992

Matter Turned Into Light and Space
by Roberta Smith

Robert Irwin is an optical magician who doesn't believe in fooling the eye. For more than two decades, this 64-year-old maverick West Coast Minimalist has been known for creating installation pieces whose mysterious (and beautiful) visual effects are also utterly comprehensible.

Mr. Irwin, whose impressive installation work at the Pace Gallery in SoHo is his first New York City exposure in seven years, began his career in the late 1950's as a maker of streamlined abstract paintings with roots in Abstract Expressionism. But in the 60's, his art performed a kind of disappearing act. By the late 60's he was making pale cast acrylic wall pieces that were almost invisible, except for the shadows they cast. In 1970, he dispensed with the art object entirely. As in the work of several other artists working in Los Angeles, including James Turrell, Maria Nordman, Douglas Wheeler and Larry Bell, light and space had become his primary materials, visual experience his main subject.

Mr. Irwin's installation pieces—the first was executed in a small, unmarked, skylighted gallery at the Museum of Modern Art in 1970—usually immerse the viewer in a soft, grainy light that sets off subtly disorienting visual illusions. Space expands or contracts; whole chunks of architecture momentarily disappear in the light; walls or corners pop into focus with unnatural sharpness. But almost invariably, Mr. Irwin creates these effects without tricks. If you look hard enough—and looking hard is exactly what his work is about—you can't help but discern the modest, rather honest means with which he works his magic.

Mr. Irwin's untitled installation at Pace, one of the best and most elaborate indoor pieces he has made, is no exception. On a physical level it consists quite literally of almost nothing: five white, translucent nylon scrims that run from floor to ceiling across the space in layers; several rows of fluorescent lights covered by colored gels that run wall to wall on the ceiling behind the scrims, and six big black horizontal rectangles. Four of these are spray-painted onto four scrims; the fifth is painted on the gallery's back wall, and the sixth, made of black adhesive plastic, covers much of the gallery's front wall, an expanse of big French doors and windows with etched glass that shield two shallow offices.

Ward Ackerman and Robert Irwin

In true Irwin form, what all this amounts to in visual terms is at first beautiful and mysterious: a kind of levitating vision that dominates, and darkens, the entire gallery.

The floating see-through black rectangles recede toward the final, opaque one like a series of deep, echoing visual chords. It is as if Mr. Irwin is trying to coax the motifs of his modernist ancestors into real, everyday postmodernist space. The piece brings to mind the resonating squares of a Josef Albers painting, as well as the geometries of Malevich and Mondrian, and the dark floating rectangles of Ad Reinhardt and Mark Rothko, the Abstract Expressionists whose art seems to have meant the most to Mr. Irwin.

The rectangles occupy an ambiguous space, which could be as little as 10 or as much as 50 feet deep, and is cast in further doubt by faint tints of pink, green and yellow emanating from the fluorescent lights overhead, coloring different layers of the work.

Fortunately, all this mystery is easily dismantled, for Mr. Irwin has made real a kind of pictorial space that is usually reserved for the eye alone. At the far right, a series of small doorways enables you to walk through the odd visual sandwich he has created, examining its effects layer by layer, bottom to top.

Yet moving through the zones measured off by the scrims also makes the work quietly kaleidoscopic and in some ways even more optical. The colors cast by the fluorescent lights become more or less tangible: from the fourth and final section, the second section reads as a volume of pinkish light, the third is paler, but both yellow and green. Edges and corners disappear and re-emerge;

ROBERT IRWIN

1°2°3°4°/GREENE STREET
September 19 – 17 October, 1992

people walking through other parts of the piece become hazy silhouettes, like figures in Seurat's drawings. And the rectangles change enormously. From certain angles they are almost opaque; from others they nearly evaporate, even as their cumulative darkness fills the atmosphere.

These visual shifts multiply as you spend time with the piece. A final surprise comes in the last section, from which, as you look back through the layers, the black rectangle on the windowed office is most clearly defined. Suddenly it seems as if the entire work might have been inspired by the narrow, often overlooked offices that buffer the exhibition area from the street. They seem to form the original layer of see-through space that has generated all the others.

It makes perfect sense that the subtle, multi-faceted experience of vision that Mr. Irwin has orchestrated at Pace might have been set in motion by a simple architectural given already in place in the gallery itself. The ultimate message of his work, simple yet profound, is the more you look, the more you see. . . .

... In one sense, every life is the history of simple discoveries, a progress of cognitive additions as we learn about the contents of our world. After a while, we discover all we need to know about our lives as defined by external cognitive boundaries: the life of home, village, neighborhood. Reading, education, travel, may widen these boundaries past what we need to know merely in order to live our lives, but curiosity is a powerful motive, in human beings as in cats, as urgent as the search for power, according to Hobbes, and in a certain sense an enhancement of it. It is possible to view Saul Steinberg's discovery of America in this way, as a series of simple discoveries of what American cities and villages are like, how Americans memorialize and enshrine, what their government buildings look like—all drawn with a somewhat comical line, postcards of things seen, for the educated amusement of sophisticated recipients. As a matter of biographical fact, Steinberg, born in Romania, European to the core, was shaken loose from a form of life that was altogether congenial to him by the turbulence of politics and war, and cast ashore in America after a certain number of adventures. This was no desert island, but Steinberg really was a Robinson Crusoe, and he set about exploring this extravagant culture, making a certain number of simple, useful discoveries on his various expeditions by bus, train, and motorcar, learning from the outside what ordinary Americans took for granted as the fabric of their lives. As Steinberg did not come in the service of some latter-day Ferdinand or Isabella, he more or less left things as he found them, simply transcribing

them as images. But in this spirit of simple discovery, he saw the most ordinary of ordinary things as marvelous. In the sense of simple art history, with its narrative of priority, Steinberg led the Pop artists to the discovery of the commonplace, the exoticism of the ordinary.

... But as Harold Rosenberg was to say, "The United States was made to order for Saul Steinberg," and so his probes into the American landscape were undertaken in the spirit not merely of curiosity, but as in Crusoe's case, of finding what he needed to make this world his own: learning, item by item, as a stranger and an adult, what native children learn as a matter of course. . . .

Arthur C. Danto. Introduction, *Saul Steinberg: The Discovery of America.* (New York 1992)

The South, 1955

SAUL STEINBERG

THE DISCOVERY OF AMERICA/GREENE STREET
December 5 – 9 January, 1993

JOHN CHAMBERLAIN

RECENT WORK/GREENE STREET
October 24 – 28 November, 1992

Interview with John Chamberlain
by Henry Geldzahler
Excerpt from Pace catalogue

H.G. At some point, you didn't use the pieces as found and then merely crushed them, but you added color and then crushed them. When did that start to happen?

J.C. Adding color? That was '61. . . . I used the color I found, up to about 1961, and then I started messing around. . . . When you look at the formula for the paint they used on automobiles, you find that there are five components to the formula. You can look at a book, a paint catalogue. . . . You can find 1,800 variations of white that are listed and there's more, the Pepsi Cola "white" or the postal service "white," there are all different whites. It's amazing. . . .

For the last two years, the only materials I've been using are van tops and chrome—chrome bumpers. The van tops are tops of vans that have been cut away when they've been replaced with bubbles. . . .

So the van top—and it's the complete top, too, when they take it off—I buy at three bucks apiece.

H.G. They're not too similar?

J.C. They're all similar. What we do is make two cuts lengthwise, so we have three strips. And each of those strips is painted by the painter on both sides . . . and I tell him what I want him to do for a while and he does that. We cut templates, and he uses the templates to paint. He makes up a sort of palette. For instance, this particular piece was sandblasted. I got tired of the colors that were on things at the time. They were my paint jobs. I thought, I've seen enough of them. I wanted to get rid of the color and I thought: "Well, let's see what it looks like if we just take all the color off." Well, it went matte, didn't shine. And so, what we did was, well, listen to this— we tried making roadways with the paint and things like that, and you could tell when he was in a hurry. . . I mean, there were some days when the lines would be thin, he would be in a hurry. Some days they'd be thick when he wasn't in a hurry. This stuff was painted—everything's painted. They were laying around, just parts in a pile. So, the paint would drip down and through. . . .

It's just like I take this pile and start painting . . . you know, dripping paint back and forth. Then it would go down through and mix up that way. The pouring is all right, but the weight of it coming out of the can hits things and goes this way, goes this way and it goes that way. It does things you wouldn't get unless you did it like this. . . .

445

ROBERT RYMAN | **VERSIONS**
December 4 – 9 January, 1993

"To me, what is very important in painting is not to think when you paint. You can think before you paint, you can think after you have painted, but while you are painting, thinking is the worst thing that you can do. It is like a typist whose fingers are moving across the keys automatically, without thinking of the letters on the typewriter. The typist just knows what to do, and probably could not even tell you how he or she is doing it. It comes through the knowledge of the typewriter. In the same way that the typist would not be thinking about the typewriter, the painter would not be thinking about painting or about art or about what could be done with the painting. The artist just does it. I think that can only come about, of course, when you understand your materials and do not have to think about the technical aspects. Like the typist would have control over the typewriter, the painter has control over the brushes and the manner in which these technical aspects work. If, of course, you have to struggle with the technical aspects, you cannot be free to let the painting come about."

– R.R., April 1992

Versions V, 1991
oil and graphite on fiberglas with wax paper, 45 × 41"

COENTIES SLIP

Indiana
Kelly
Martin
Rosenquist
Youngerman
at Coenties Slip
by Mildred Glimcher
Excerpt from Pace catalogue

Until it was razed during the mid-1960s to make way for the encroaching high-rises of the adjoining Wall Street area, Coenties Slip evoked the romance of a New York long past. Almost at the southern tip of Manhattan, near South Ferry, Coenties Slip had been part of the city's earliest harbor complex, stretching back to the era of wooden sailing ships. It is significant that the area elicits associations with Charles Demuth, Walt Whitman, Hart Crane and Herman Melville. Robert Indiana reminds us that on the opening page of *Moby Dick*, Melville writes: "There now is your insular city of the Manhattoes, belted round by wharves as Indian isles by coral reefs . . . Circumambulate the city of a dreamy Sabbath afternoon, go from Corlears Hook to Coenties Slip, and from thence, by Whitehall, northward . . ."[1]

The familiar photograph of Robert Indiana, Ellsworth Kelly, Agnes Martin, Jack Youngerman, his wife, the actress Delphine Seyrig and their small son Duncan, taken by Hans Namuth in 1958 on the roof of 3–5 Coenties Slip, also expresses a romantic nostalgia for a world that, in 1992, seems almost as distant as that of Ishmael and Ahab. Familiar to many, but meaningful to only a handful the photograph is a curious icon of the American postwar art scene. The aim of this exhibition is to illuminate this time and place by engaging some of the artists who lived and worked there during the period between 1956 and 1967. We focus on Indiana, Kelly, Martin, Rosenquist and Youngerman who were part of a larger, rather fluid community that included Fred Mitchell, Charles Hinman, Lenore Tawney and Ann Wilson, as well as writers, filmmakers and actors.

The slip was a three-block-long funnel-shaped space that opened toward the East River, facing Brooklyn and its beautiful bridge. At its wider end, closer to the river, was the small Jeanette Park, built in the 1880's, whose ginkgo and sycamore trees provided, along with the river itself, a welcome sense of nature in the city. Before it was torn down, "the Third Avenue El . . . continued down the Bowery and made a notorious snake curve on Coenties Slip painted by Stuart Davis."[2] Its entrance

at 25 South Street, on the northeast corner was the Seaman's Church Institute, an important asset for the artists who often used its cafeteria and showers. The artists were drawn to the abandoned sail lofts and ships' chandleries by very low rents and the luxury of large spaces in which to live and work. But the abandoned buildings often lacked the basic amenities of hot water and electricity, and actually were, in many cases, illegal residencies.

Although these artists are diverse in age, background and aesthetic outlook, the location and physical character of the slip fulfilled common needs. Several consciously sought to separate themselves from those under the influences of Jackson Pollock and Willem de Kooning. Coenties Slip was a place apart, physically and spiritually distant from the Abstract Expressionist power center of Tenth Street and the Cedar Bar. But these artists were not the first to venture below Greenwich Village. By 1954, Robert Rauschenberg and Jasper Johns were working on Pearl Street, and Barnett Newman had a studio on Wall Street. Deserted in the evening and on weekends, with fresh air, a water view, the trees of Jeanette Park, and the human scale of 19th-century buildings, the slip was unique. As the buildings were at an angle to the river, all of the windows had river views.[3] But, "if one looked landward instead of seaward, one could see the solid cliff of stone that . . . Wall Street makes . . . . Here this heady confluence of all the elements—the rock, the river, the sky, and the fire of ships and commerce—created a natural magnetism that drew a dozen artists to the slip."[4] If, for each of these artists, the studios on the slip were not their first in New York,[5] it was in those studios that each made the work that would bring them to the attention of the rapidly evolving art world of the late 50s and early 60s. As we survey their personal experiences on Coenties Slip, we will discover their unique responses to the place and the community that evolved there.

Ellsworth Kelly returned to America from France in 1954, scarcely knowing anyone in New York. He paid a visit to Fred Mitchell, who he had known in Paris and

who had settled at the water's edge (26 Water Street) when he returned from Rome in 1951. . . . Through Mitchell, Kelly found his first loft on Broad Street, one block from the slip. In 1956, he moved onto the slip itself. Attracted by the skylights and the space, he took the top floor of 3–5 Coenties Slip, which was actually two buildings joined by a central staircase. . . .

In 1956, when Robert Indiana struck up a conversation with Kelly at an art-supply store near the Parsons Gallery, he inquired if Kelly knew of any studios for rent. As Fred Mitchell had recently vacated his top-floor loft at Number 31, it was through Kelly that Indiana arrived at the slip in June[9]—a move that would have a tremendous impact on his work. Although intensely private while making his work, Kelly's presence on the slip was important for many other artists there. . . . Of all these artists, Indiana was most affected by both the history and the physical reality of his new studio. Almost immediately, inspired by the ginkgo trees in Jeanette Park, he began his first "hard-edge" painting, based on the doubled form of the ginkgo leaf[11] which would reappear in *The Sweet Mystery*, 1960–61.

When Number 31 (where the rent was $30 a month) was torn down in 1957 to enlarge the adjoining parking lot, Kelly moved to 25 Coenties Slip (which rented for $45 a month) where he remained until 1965. He was, in fact, the last to leave the slip. . . .

Moon and *Duncan's Column* were assembled from the beams of the demolished buildings in his neighborhood and from "carefully selected 'junk' with a profoundly associative past,"[13] like rusted wheels and drain covers. These sculptures are immensely important within the evolution of his work. . . .

It is a curious historical conjunction that, like Indiana, many American artists were descending into the street (Louise Nevelson, Robert Rauschenberg, Claes Oldenburg, and Jim Dine, to name a few) to gather materials for their work. Protesting the "academization" of Abstract Expressionism, they sought to endow their work with material reality, thereby connecting art and life in a new way.

Betty Parsons was a frequent visitor and important presence on the slip. In 1956, Kelly had his first solo New York show at her gallery, and the same year, indirectly through Kelly, she visited Jack Youngerman in Paris. Youngerman and Kelly had been in Paris together, members of the group of young expatriate American painters who had settled there after the war to study. Parsons promised Youngerman a show if he agreed to move to New York. Married, with a baby, Youngerman had never actually lived in New York. He wanted to return, but needed a reason to "step into the unknown."[15] Parsons' promise of a show gave him that reason and Youngerman credits her with his move to New York. (He did have his first show at Parsons' Gallery in 1958.) Upon his return, it was through Kelly that Youngerman found his way to Coenties Slip, moving into Number 27 in 1957. . . .

For [Youngerman], the importance of the slip was that "it was completely apart from the New York art scene. Down there, one of the things we were very conscious of, without talking that much about it, was the fact that we all knew that we weren't part of the de Kooning/Pollock legacy in art which was centered around Tenth Street." Youngerman describes the artists in this exhibition as "intensely individualized" having lived much of their lives in a solitary fashion and he points out that he is the only one still working in New York. "You know, there's a movie by Godard called *Band of Outsiders* . . . It was a little bit like that."

This sentiment is shared by all the artists. It was not a question of regarding themselves as a group, like those who gathered at The Club to conduct formal discussions about aesthetics or problems they confronted as artists. They were individuals drawn to Coenties Slip by the physical qualities of the place itself. Many became friends, sharing meals or early morning rides on the Staten Island ferry, especially in the heat of the summer. In 1958, Hans Namuth was commissioned to photograph Kelly as part of a pictorial essay about the artists who were to participate in the Brussels World Fair. The now-famous image of the group on the roof was, in fact, the climax of a day in which Namuth followed Kelly and his friends to a lunch in his studio, a visit to Youngerman's studio, and a bicycle tour around lower Manhattan. Kelly fondly recalled the "civilizing" influence of Youngerman's wife, Delphine Seyrig, a French actress who would soon receive international acclaim for her role in Alain Resnais' now classic film, *Last Year at Marienbad*.

During the early years money was short, so the support and encouragement of the group was important. Indiana paid homage to Jesse Wilkinson, who became a kind of "den mother"[18] who sustained them when times were tough. The cafeteria and hot showers of the Seaman's Church Institute were essential for their survival. More than 30 years later, many remember the generosity of the place. Kelly recalls a visit from Alexander Calder, whom he had met in France through Delphine Seyrig's parents. Calder was enthusiastic about Kelly's work, and subsequently wrote letters on his behalf to Alfred Barr and James Johnson Sweeney. When Calder left the little party, Kelly found a check on the table which was meant to pay the rent.[19]

In 1957, in an effort to make a little money, Indiana and Youngerman tried to open a small workshop for life-drawing classes on the first floor of Youngerman's building at 27 Coenties Slip. The cover of the brochure, *Paint on the Waterfront*, "featured Indiana drawing on a pier head emerging from a typical Youngerman motif."[20] The venture was a failure as the space was "impossible to heat adequately for nude models and later became Agnes Martin's first loft on the slip."[21]

When Betty Parsons saw Agnes Martin's work in Taos, New Mexico, in 1957, she made the same promise to Martin that she had made to Youngerman in Paris; she would give her a show if she moved to New York.[22] When Martin (who had been in New York at Columbia Teachers College in 1941, 1951 to 1952 and briefly in 1954)[23] returned to New York in 1957, Parsons introduced her to Kelly, Youngerman and Coenties Slip. She took a floor in Youngerman's building at Number 27. The location at the river's edge, with various views of water and sky was important to her. . . .

As she has repeated many times, she rejects the concept of "influence" and therefore strongly believes that her work was not influenced by the slip and that she would have made the same paintings, wherever she lived.[28]. . .

With the waning dominance of the Abstract Expressionists, and as the artists began to achieve recognition and more financial stability, there was a change in the atmosphere on the slip. It began to replace Tenth Street for those in search of the avant-garde. Kelly remembers a visit from Antonioni and Monica Vitti at the time of the opening of *L'Avventura*. The visit was arranged by Sophia Loren's secretary because Antonioni expressed an interest in meeting some artists.[35] Whereas Betty Parsons and Eleanor Ward were the earliest dealers to visit the slip, after 1960, as more artists began to settle in this area, it became a destination for dealers and the hungry new collectors hot on the trail of the "new art." During 1961 Rosenquist was visited by the dealer Allan Stone, followed by Dick Bellamy, whom Rosenquist met "hanging out" at the Cedar Bar. Bellamy brought Robert Scull, Henry Geldzahler and Ivan Karp— who brought Leo Castelli.[36] By the opening of his first solo exhibition at Bellamy's Green Gallery in February 1962, the exhibition was sold out.[37]

By the early 60s, the artists on the slip had begun to make their mark on the New York art scene. Their exhibitions become too numerous to recount in this short space. In 1959 Jack Youngerman designed the sets for an off-Broadway production of Genet's *Deathwatch*. He and Kelly were included in Dorothy Miller's ground-breaking "Sixteen Americans" at the Museum of Modern Art in 1959. Kelly moved away from the slip in 1963 but by then, besides his shows at Parsons and the Museum of Modern Art, he had been included in the Carnegie International and other important international exhibitions. After three shows with Parsons, Martin joined the Elkon Gallery in 1962, where she had four exhibitions until returning to New Mexico in 1967 when her building was torn down. During these years, she, too, was included in the Carnegie International and exhibitions at the Whitney Museum, Guggenheim Museum and Museum of Modern Art as well as many others worldwide. . . .

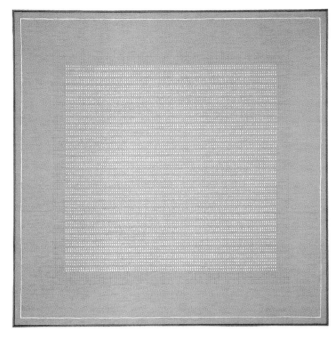

Agnes Martin, *The Islands*, 1961
acrylic and graphite on canvas, 72 × 72"

By the mid-60s, most of the buildings on the slip were marked for destruction by developers in order to make way for "progress," in the form of office towers that ironically still remain partially empty. The slip itself no longer exists and only Number 3–5 remains, solely because it shares a block with the historic Fraunces Tavern.[38] It is fascinating to realize that by a chance conjunction of circumstances, Coenties Slip became a seminal locus, a "*bâteau lavoire*," for the development of a new generation of American painting. The artists themselves carry that time and place into their contemporary lives with varying degrees of importance.

The shared experiences of Coenties Slip remained solely in the memory of those who had been there until 1973, when Bobby Buecker and Fred Mitchell made an exhibition which reunited most of the inhabitants. The show at the Buecker and Harpsichords Gallery inspired several young members of the Whitney Museum Independent Study Program to present an expanded version in 1974 at the downtown branch of the Whitney Museum on Water Street, not far from the original location of Coenties Slip.[39] Their show included the work of Charles Hinman, Indiana, Kelly, Martin, Mitchell, Rosenquist, Lenore Tawney, Ann Wilson and Youngerman. We, in turn, have been able to reveal only a portion of the richness of our subject. As many of the artists in our exhibition were committed to the concept of the fragment, so should this exhibition be viewed—as a fragment of this highly diverse era. The "band of individuals" on Coenties Slip, striving to express the American experience through their own vision and language, should be understood as emblematic of a new American pluralism.

1. Carl J. Weinhardt, Jr. *Robert Indiana.* (New York 1990) 35.
2. Statement by Robert Indiana to the author, December 13, 1992.
3. Conversation with Agnes Martin on December 1, 1992.
4. Robert Indiana. *Early Sculpture: 1960–1962.* (Salama-Caro Gallery, London 1991) 11.
5. It was Youngerman's first studio in New York.
11. Indiana, *Early Sculpture.* 49.
13. William Katz, 'Introduction' from Indiana, *Recent Sculpture.* 13.
15. This and following quotes are from a conversation with Jack Youngerman, November 25, 1992.

18. Conversation with Robert Indiana, December 14, 1992.
19. Conversation with Ellsworth Kelly, December 15, 1992.
20. Statement by Robert Indiana to author, December 13, 1992.
21. Indiana statement.
22. Barbara Haskell. *Agnes Martin.* Exhibition catalogue, Whitney Museum (New York 1992) 100.
23. Haskell, *Martin.* 97–98.
28. Conversation with Agnes Martin, December 1, 1992.
36. Judith Goldman. *James Rosenquist: The Early Pictures 1961–1964.* (New York 1992) 30.
37. Goldman, *Rosenquist: The Early Pictures.* 7.
38. Conversations with Ellsworth Kelly, December 15, 1992.
39. We would like to acknowledge the research of the participants: John Beardsley, Denise Bratton, Barbara Flynn, Jane Kleinberg, Richard Marshall and Judith McCandless. The photograph on the cover was from the Seaman's Church Institute.

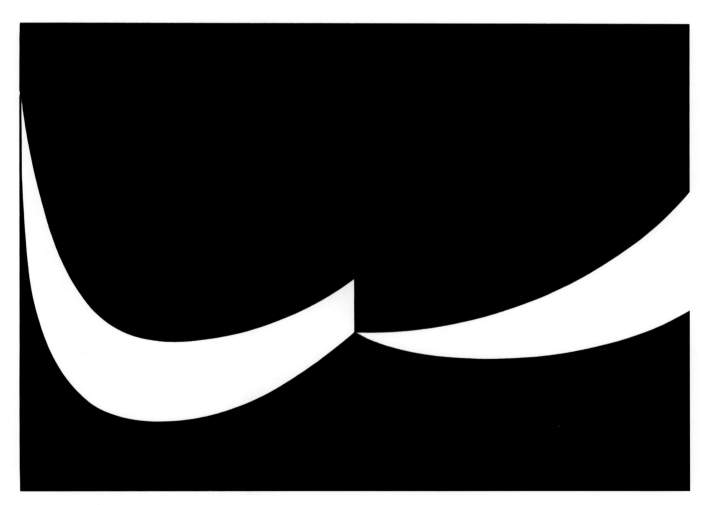

Ellsworth Kelly, *Atlantic*, 1956
oil on canvas, 80 × 114"
Collection Whitney Museum of American Art

ANTONI TÀPIES

RECENT WORKS
February 19 – 20 March, 1993

Language and Desire: Textual Practice in the Art of Antoni Tàpies
by Robert S. Lubar
Excerpt from Pace catalogue

> I have always believed that a painting doesn't represent things but is a thing; a kind of talisman that even through touch can exert an influence on us.[1]
>
> – Antoni Tàpies

It has been 40 years since Antoni Tàpies celebrated his first show in New York at the Martha Jackson Gallery. Having exhibited at the prestigious Carnegie International in 1950, and at the Venice Biennale in 1952, the 29-year-old Catalan artist came to America with a respectable curriculum of critical accomplishments. Although the press responded to Tàpies's first exhibition with little enthusiasm, the artist would earn the respect of American critics over the next four decades, even if his work was narrowly defined. Indeed, with the exception of an early show of paintings at the Guggenheim Museum in 1962, a traveling retrospective in the United States and Canada organized by the Albright-Knox Art Gallery in 1977, and a comprehensive exhibition of prints at The Museum of Modern Art last year, Tàpies's work has still not received extended consideration in America. The dominant reading of Tàpies has typecast him as a "matter" painter, exploring the telluric mysteries of the material world. . . .

My aim is not to dispute specific interpretations of Tàpies's work in America,[6] but merely to observe the pervasive character of a criticism that has failed to address the polyvalence of meaning in his art. Characteristic of this criticism is a tendency to reduce Tàpies's painting to a form of protest against the repressed consciousness of the totally administered society[7] (a leitmotif of criticism in the late 50's and early 60's, when Tàpies's reputation was at its zenith in New York), without considering the ways in which this protest is constituted through language.[8] This kind of interpretation limits Tàpies's project by denying the core of his art as a form of textual activity, "perceived and received," to quote Roland Barthes, "in its integrally symbolic nature."[9] I want, therefore, to turn to a different kind of reading of Tàpies—one that will come to terms with the sheer quantity of letters, numbers, signs, ideograms, and hieroglyphs in his work within the framework of a radically symbolic signifying practice. I want to investigate the ways in which Tàpies's much discussed "walls" are . . . opaque fields that transfer the project of reading from an inner mimesis to a form of textual play. It is through this linguistic operation, I will argue, that Tàpies's paintings declare themselves in the most profound sense as social sites of production within the (unrepressed) realm of desire.

While critics have long proposed elaborate readings of Tàpies's signs and symbols according to an iconographical index,[11] the artist himself has never insisted upon stable interpretations of his paintings: "There is some kind of repertoire that I use as my brand mark, but in which each sign has a variety of interpretations."[12] When questioned about his work in series, Tàpies emphasized the need to read his work intertextually: "I do not work in series in the sense that a theme is started, then developed and then completed. But I do use motifs or elements that repeat in different works, a little bit in the sense of musical variations. Themes which in a moment mean something specific may in another moment

mean something else. I do different readings of my motifs according to the context."[13]

. . . [His] comments on the
"unconscious" formation of his
signs locate Tàpies's method in the
broad framework of Surrealist automatism. . . . Tàpies's art denies
the idealist content inherent in the Surrealist project.
Tàpies's incisions, inscriptions and imprints refuse to open
onto a transcendental signified; they are bound to the surface of his paintings as physical presences, and when they
appear to reach closure, they return to that surface as a condition of their polyvalence. The artist has explained:

> When I paint a sign, an X or a cross or a spiral, I experi-
> ence a certain satisfaction. I see that the picture receives
> a real force with this sign . . . However, I set down let-
> ters with very diverse significations: The A as beginning
> and limit; the T as the stylization of the crucifix and as
> the initial of my last name; and also as the meeting place
> of coordinates, etc. Together, the A and the T may sig-
> nify the union of my first and last names, or my last
> name with that of Teresa, my wife.[16]

Although Tàpies works within an open process of
signification, his approach is deliberate and methodical,
with clear roots in the Modernist languages of Miró and
Klee, among others.[17] Working in the tradition of the
painter-poet, Tàpies's exploration of the resources of image
and text also corresponds to a wider cultural field. We need,
for example, to consider Tàpies's sustained interest in the
linguistic sign from the earliest days of his career, and his
close collaborations with poets in his native Barcelona (most
notably, Josep Vicenç Foix and Joan Brossa). . . .

Tàpies surrenders himself to the full materiality of
the sign. His paintings are not representations, but inscribed surfaces. Their objective character—their solidi-
fied, ritualized content—is always in evidence. It is in this
sense that Tàpies speaks of his paintings as weapons or tal-
ismans, whose "function" is to enter into direct and active
communication with a user. They are sites of dialogue
rather than the spaces of contemplative immersion. . . .

Because meaning is mobile in Tàpies's art, the viewer is placed in a position of expectation or anticipation. It is
precisely this deferral of meaning that allows us to speak
of Tàpies's textual and linguistic project as an exploration of

the realm of desire. . . . This is in large measure what Tàpies
means when he says that his work doesn't represent
"things," but *is* a thing. But a true consummation (of
meaning) cannot take place; it is always projected onto an
object, satisfied by proxy. As sites of desire, Tàpies's en-
crusted and viscous surfaces attest to the sensual and carnal
embodiments of a pure, unrepressed experience that has
yet to be realized. Surfaces of communication, sites of repression and fulfillment, Tàpies's paintings chart a passage
through the labyrinth of language and desire.

I would like to thank Patricia Berman of Wellesley College for her many
helpful suggestions in the preparation of this essay. Unless otherwise indicated, all translations from the Catalan, Spanish, and French are by the author.

1. Antoni Tàpies, interview with Lluís Permanyer, conducted on March 18
   and 25, and April 1 and 8, 1973; reprinted in Antoni Tàpies, *El Arte con-
   tra la estetica* (Barcelona: Ariel, 1978): p. 213.
6. For an excellent overview, see Manuel J. Borja-Villel, "The Changes of
   Taste: Tàpies and the Critics," in *Tàpies: els anys 80* (Barcelona: Ajunta-
   ment de Barcelona, 1988): pp. 246–256.
7. For a discussion of the interpretation of the "wall" in Tàpies's art as the site
   of protest, see Borja, "Antoni Tàpies: The 'Matter Paintings,'" pp. 74–77.
   For a recent analysis, see Serge Guilbaut, "Material for Reflection."
8. For French interpretations of Tàpies's project as working with the language of oppression from the inside of art in order to deconstruct its operations, see Borja, "Antoni Tàpies: The 'Matter Paintings,'" pp. 82–83.
9. Roland Barthes, "From Work to Text," in Roland Barthes, Image-Music-
   Text (New York: Hill and Wang, 1977): p. 159.
11. See, for example, Borja's discussion of Juan Eduardo Cirlot's interpreta-
    tions of Tàpies's work in the early 1960's, in "Antoni Tàpies: The 'Matter
    Paintings,'" pp. 71–72. More recently, Victòria Combàlia has proposed
    elaborate, if suspect, interpretations of individual paintings, advancing
    specific art historical references. Victòria Combàlia, "Comments on Some
    Works in the Exhibition," *Tàpies: els anys 80*, pp. 237–241.
12. Antoni Tàpies, in Borja, "Antoni Tàpies: The 'Matter Paintings,'" p. 224.
13. Ibid., p. 224.
15. Antoni Tàpies, in Barbara Catoir, *Conversations: Antoni Tàpies* (Paris: Edi-
    tions Cercle d'Art, 1988): pp. 74–75.
16. Ibid., pp. 74–75.
17. For an extensive examination of Tàpies's artistic dialogue with the work of
    Miró, Klee, Ernst and Dali, see Manuel J. Borja-Villel, "Writing on the
    Wall," in *Tàpies: Comunicació sobre el mur*, pp. 290–303.

Catalogue

Sergei Eisenstein
Alfred Hitchcock
John Huston
Fred Zinnemann
Akira Kurosawa
Orson Welles
Federico Fellini
Robert Benton
Terry Gilliam
Martin Scorsese
David Lynch
Rainer Werner Fassbinder
Tim Burton

DRAWING INTO FILM

DIRECTORS' DRAWINGS
March 26 – 24 April, 1993

The role of process in the plastic arts has been one of the great revelations of the 20th century and has in many instances served as subject. When Picasso painted *Les Demoiselles d'Avignon*, he left different areas of the painting in various stages of development, never bringing all of the areas to the same level of completion. As such, the painting became a chart of its own progress and emblematic of the trajectory art would take in the 20th century.

Unlike painting, process in film making is less readily visible as technological or surface perfection is required to allow the viewer's unencumbered entry into the film's reality. Although the use of the medium as language is integral to the completed film, process remains largely unrevealed and henceforth, undocumented. The concept of this exhibition is to chart the flow from annotated idea to completed scene.

– A.B.G.
(Catalogue introduction)

Drawing Into Film

by Annette Michelson

Excerpt from Pace catalogue

. . . The storyboard, adapted from the technique of animation cinema, proved, . . . so useful a device in establishing the parameters of production design conceived in its largest sense that the film industry eventually developed professional practitioners and standardized conventions of the form. For the director, the storyboard offered a way of planning on several levels: the composition of shots, their size, and their interrelation within the flow of the narrative. It allowed one to determine needed equipment and location sites. It represented an intermediate stage between the script and the editing process; it could, in fact, be seen as a form of pre-editing. It facilitated communication between director and producer, on the one hand, and between director and technical crew, on the other. The pictorial schema was often, though not always, supplemented by written instructions as to direction of movement within the shot, duration, camera movement. And since it can, in addition, specify lens changes, dissolves, and the projected use of other optical effects, the range of detail and accuracy of the storyboarding process is, therefore, very wide.

Although it is claimed that the storyboard can, in its most detailed and technically sophisticated instances, actually be read much as a musician reads a score (involving the use of especially scored paper, written specifications, and color coding), the storyboards here to be considered represent the freer, more flexibly conceived plans articulated in drawings from the hands of directors. These have served as basic plans and points of reference, subject, when necessary, to modification or amplification.

Such is the case of Scorsese's *Taxi Driver* (1976), for while the drawings project an accurate sense of the shot sizes, rhythm, and directionality of the sequence's editing pattern, the film as shot and edited shows the intercutting of a few additional shots of De Niro in close-up. The storyboard for the brilliantly composed sequence of the La Motta-Robinson fight in *Raging Bull* (1980) offers confirmation of the mastery of editing technique that links Scorsese to the tradition of cinematic montage epitomized in the work of Hitchcock. For despite the evident and radical differences of sensibility and thematic concerns, that link is clearly manifest. Scorsese's earliest work, such as *The Big Shave* (1967), indicates the manner in which the beginning filmmaker had studied the lessons of the magisterially edited shower sequence in *Psycho* (1960). The work of the mature Scorsese demonstrates, as in the 1980 fight sequence, the extreme care and precision with which he had by now absorbed and mastered the technique of assertive editing as represented by the British master's work. It discloses an awareness of the manner in which the rhythm and rapidity of montage could reinforce the effect of risk, relentlessness, and physical violence in this crucial episode.

Of Hitchcock's own work, the sketches made in preparation for the penultimate sequence of *Saboteur* (1941) propose the penultimate and climactic sequence of pursuit and capture of the villain, set in the Statue's hand holding aloft the torch of Liberty in New York Harbor. Virtuosic in its own right, the suspense generated through contrasts of scale, close-ups and long shots, and high and low camera angles anticipates, as well, the more celebrated episode of the chase over Mount Rushmore in *North by Northwest* (1958). . . .

While many directors continue to produce their pictoral outlines, whether on storyboard or in individual sketches, in black-and-white, thus scanting the cinematic role of color, Kurosawa's drawings for the *Crows* episode devoted to Van Gogh in his film *Dreams* (1990) articulate the manner in which solar radiance and coloristic exuberance drive the narrative itself.

This series of drawings, done as full-page sketches, represent that other central line of preparatory representation of film narrative, that the director as draftsman or illustrator, working more freely and offering a more elaborate linearity or chiaroscuro than the sketches of the storyboard format provide. Drawings of this kind do not offer a detailed and general plan as such; rather, they make visible the phantasmatic dimension of filmmaking. . . .

Fellini's work, particularly that of the 1960s and '70s, appears as the most evidently carnivalistic in the contemporary cinema, and not least in his portrayal of what Bakhtin termed "the grotesque body," exemplified in literature by Rabelais, who found it "important to demonstrate the whole remarkable complexity and depth of the human body and its life, to uncover a new meaning, a new place for human corporeality in the . . . spatio-temporal world." In Fellini's films, "the human body becomes a concrete measuring rod for the world, the measurer of the world's weight and of its value for the individual." And there is a sense, beyond the individual sensual effect of the woman's body that "it is not the individual body, trapped in an irreversible life sequence, that becomes a character—rather it is the impersonal body, the body of the human race as a whole, being born, living, dying the most varied deaths, being born again, an impersonal body that is manifested in its structure, and in all the processes of its life." It is as if Fellini had wanted "to return both a language and a meaning to the body, return to it the idealized quality it had in ancient times, and simultaneously return a reality, a materiality, to language and to meaning."[1] . . .

1. M.M. Bakhtin, *The Dialogue Imagination*, ed. Michael Holquist, trans. Caryl Emerson and Michael Holquist, University of Texas Press, 1981, pp. 170–171

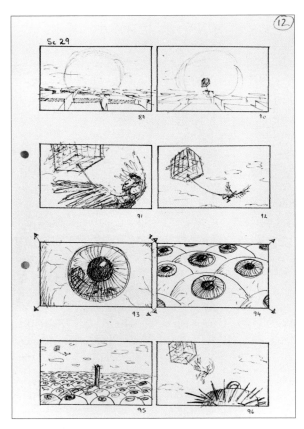

Terry Gilliam, storyboard panels,
a dream (never realized), *Brazil*, 1985
felt pen and pencil on paper, 11¹¹⁄₁₆ × 8½"

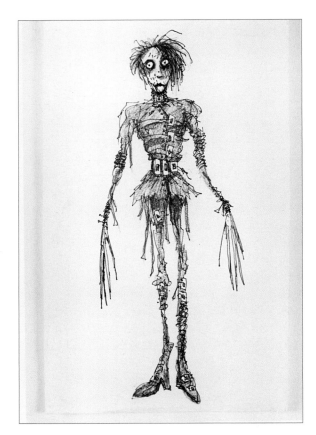

Tim Burton, drawing of Edward for
Edward Scissorhands, 1990
pen on paper, 15 × 9"

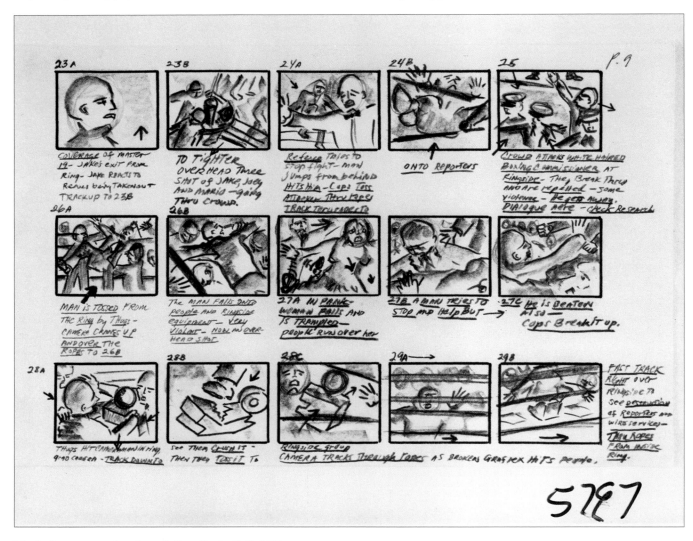

Martin Scorsese, storyboard panels from *Raging Bull*, 1980
pencil on paper, 8 × 14"

Akira Kurosawa, *Crows* sequence, 1989
pastel, watercolor and graphite on paper, 9¾ × 14"

Frederico Fellini, script cover *La Strada*, 1954
pen and pencil on paper, 13½ × 9½"

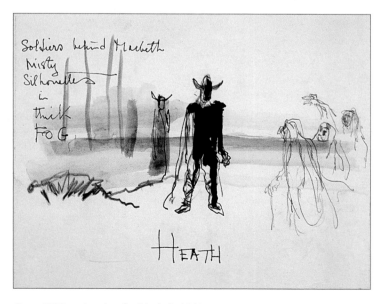

Orson Welles, drawing for *Macbeth*, 1948
pencil and black ink wash on paper, 7 × 8¾

461

JOEL SHAPIRO | SCULPTURE AND DRAWING

April 30 – 18 June, 1993
57th Street (Illustrated)
April 30 – 5 June, 1993
Greene Street

Joel Shapiro Now

by Peter Schjeldahl

Excerpt from Pace catalogue

One recent Joel Shapiro sculpture that does not appear in the present show sheds a distinct radiance on the occasion. It is the two-part monument, installed in February, outside the United States Holocaust Memorial in Washington, D.C. I will start my look at Shapiro's new work by describing this remarkable piece, which suggests a turning point in the artist's career. It is that rare phenomenon, a really successful example of public art, making a seamless fit of collective, rhetorical meaning and individual, aesthetic conviction. Shapiro's art has always been humanly communicative in addition to formally inventive. Advancing on both fronts, he now amplifies former tones of public engagement while, very notably in work with cylinders and spheres, initiating subtle researches that are full of promise for the future.

The main component of the Washington piece is a twenty-four-foot-high structure of nine rectangular bronze blocks differently sized and abruptly jointed, the whole seeming to describe a figure violently collapsing. The image varies according to viewpoint. From some approaches it appears entirely abstract; from others it can hint at two figures or perhaps an expressionistically gnarled tree. But the dominant impression, always returning, is of something drastic happening to an individual, who thrusts an arm skyward, flailing for balance, in a losing battle with gravity. . . .

The sculpture's other component is a bronze house-shape. Eight feet high as installed, the house rests upside-down on one of its rooftop angles, the topsy-turviness unmistakably evoking domestic catastrophe. As with the figure, there is a dancerly quality to this geometry of disaster. It can suggest the odd grace of a flying fragment in some high-speed photograph of an explosion—depending, again, on point of view. . . .

Taken together in context, house and figure are harrowing to the mind while buoying the heart. The Holocaust, which destroyed so much and so many, is gravely remembered and fiercely opposed in this mute declaration of invincible human energy. Besides silent, the declaration is simple, like a child's understanding. The sculpture does not presume. It does not preach. It creates a place beside the Potomac River, facing cherry trees and watched by the nearby Washington Monument, hospitable to the personal reflections of visitors whose approach to the Memorial it accompanies rather than dominates. It is a triumph of tact and abounding eloquence. . . .

Shapiro shared with other ambitious younger artists in the late 1960s and early '70s a sense of artistic crisis that had to be confronted at close quarters, with something like hand-to-hand combat in the studio. The crisis arose in part from art's very success during the preceding wild decade, a flimsy, journalistic glamour remote from the inner necessities modeled by great art of the then still recent modern past. At once goaded and antagonized by the world's expectations, Shapiro and his more trenchant colleagues set out to reinvent fundamental senses of what an artist is and does. For him, the challenge seemed to dictate a process and a performance based in *making* and true, at all costs, to some emotional reality dramatically engaging to himself. . . .

Joel Shapiro's sculpture today is changing more rapidly than at any time in over a decade. His new work deploys three distinct formal orders, individually and in combination. One of them, using spherical shapes, recalls the artist's early work with hand-formed balls and other varieties of ground-hugging form. Another, a leap into verticality employing cylinders, is almost unprecedented in his career or anyone else's, for that matter, and brings with it the excitement of aesthetic revelation. The third order is Shapiro's familiar lexicon of blocks, but assembled with novel, audacious spontaneity and touched with a new grandeur. . . .

The present figures bear familial resemblances to the Washington piece. Most of them likewise "fall," though each with a different attitude. A seven-foot-high horizontally oriented bronze, its limbs splaying to a length of eleven feet, seems seized amidst taking a terrible header by a frantically hopeful notion. Maybe it is not falling, after all. Maybe it is flying! The thought seems lodged in the slightly upward diagonal of the torso, urging the arms to consider that they are flapping rather than flailing. The instant of hapless surmise is tragicomic, and in its aspects inexhaustible. (I focus on this reading of the work as the most insistent. Another might see the element on the floor as a lower leg knee-

joined to a thigh. In a flash, the figure is flopping over sideways and backward.)

This figure is a noble object, meanwhile, a grand formal congeries of generous masses begging to command some architectural site. Though wonderful in galleries, Shapiro's work increasingly seems less arrived than parked in them, eager to be off to congenial worldly environs. To be at once physically impressive and imaginatively enthralling has always been the ambition of Shapiro's art. He now throttles up both terms to higher and higher intensity with a nearly offhanded, fast-and-loose grace.

Joel Shapiro has not yet performed many public commissions, but I suspect that will change. He may be the ideal public artist for an age of uncertainty about where the private ends and the public begins, an age of personal conscience invaded by political standards and group politics couched in terms of individual suffering. His art makes common cause with states of divided, tentative feeling, even as it fulfills architectural requirements for objects of formal authority, accessible meaning, and elegance. With something like perfect pitch, he avoids the twin errors of much recent public work that either grovels to ingratiate or overbearingly snoots the populace. His art is rigorous and companionable, and its capacity to speak secrets of the heart in a splendid language of form is growing before our eyes.

Photo Todd Eberle

DE KOONING/DUBUFFET

THE LATE WORKS

September 17 – 16 October, 1993

The Patriarchs

by Peter Schjeldahl
Excerpt from Pace catalogue

. . . De Kooning and Dubuffet leave no successors, only survivors, in the tradition of the easel painting. From the *Mona Lisa* to *Woman I*, that tradition was a touchstone of Western arts. It became the proving ground especially of modern art, which wrote finis to rival traditions of architecturally integrated painting for church or palace. The easel painting has functioned in language as a symbol of creativity in general. To apostrophize the creative, it used to be sufficient to mention Rembrandt or van Gogh; and you don't have to be very old to remember when the words "art" and "painting" were more or less interchangeable in common speech. (I wonder if an etymologist could trace the lifespan of that curious conflation.) Today "art" is apt to connote an academic department or a business, at any rate a professional field. "Painting" may

evoke an awkward vocation, both grand and wanting: the speciality of a meritocracy exiled from significance. What happened?

There are more than enough answers to that question. One answer is simply that modern art happened, an acid bath of self-consciousness that ate away dispensable conventions until finally it dissolved paintings's indispensable, bedrock fictions. "The only certainty today is that one must be selfconscious," de Kooning wrote in 1949. Like Dubuffet, de Kooning embraced the destructiveness of the modern even as he gave it something toughly resistant to work on. To put it another way, these two potlatch chiefs munificently squandered painting's historic capital, which could not be saved. As their working lives ended, they were still

feeding painting and themselves into their ceremonial bonfires, now in solitude.

It will not do to yoke de Kooning and Dubuffet too tightly. They are mutually antagonistic figures, all the more so for their numerous similarities: born three years apart at the start of the 20th century, both "northerners" by heritage who gravitated to "southern" abandon, both individualistic late bloomers in their careers, both abstractors magnetized by the figure, both competitive males fiercely ambivalent toward the feminine. Nor do their most obvious differences account for the acutest discrepancy between them. De Kooning is the more classical painter, one of the all-time masters of the craft. Dubuffet ironized painting, identifying it with the God-touched ineptitude of the primitive, the insane, and the renegade. The Dutch-American cultivated the flowers of his extraordinary gift. The Frenchman ripped his own extraordinary gift out by the roots. But these are incidentals in our present story.

The true distinction between the two is a matter of temperaments assigned opposite roles by culture and history. De Kooning played the Apollonian modernist in the youthful revolution of American postwar painting. Dubuffet played the Dionysian rascal in the weary devolution of the School of Paris. History counts in our comprehension of artists of this magnitude. They worked with culture at their backs, peering over their shoulders at the decisions they made. . . .

"Why do I keep doing this?" de Kooning said to me wonderingly when last I saw him. He was gesturing at his studio crammed with work in progress. "I don't need the money!" He shook his head in antic disgust. Of course, he kept painting because it was what he did, what he was. Out in the world, the climate for painting grew ever more inclement. He couldn't help that. He couldn't help himself. Nor could Dubuffet help himself, whose boundless worldly ambition increasingly went unrequited but whose spirit never succumbed to bitterness.

When Willem de Kooning would stand before a blank canvas, that was a moment of Keatsian "wild surmise" marvelous to conjure up: the medium of Titian about to be taken for yet one more exquisite ride. As for Dubuffet, it is hard to imagine any canvas staying blank for more than an instant in his vicinity. He plowed through the muddy world bespattering every accessible surface with manic glory. Like Lear, these patriarchs outlived themselves, at last speaking luminous monologues in paint without use or call and defenseless to a shortsighted art world that responded, if it responded, "Take them away."

JIM DINE | **APE AND CAT**
October 22 – 27 November, 1993

CHUCK CLOSE

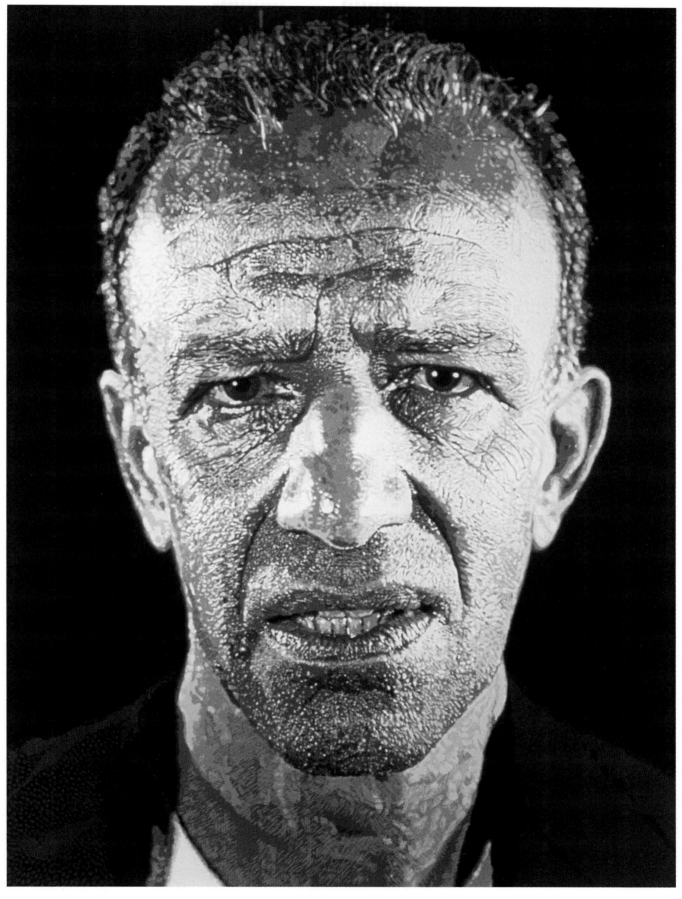

Alex/Reduction Print, 1993
screenprint from linoleum, 79⅜ × 60⅜"

To Draw and Paint in and on Wood:
Georg Baselitz's New Sculptures
by Donald Kuspit
Excerpt from Pace catalogue

Baselitz's carvings have a mission: to make sculpture that honors the organic and instinctive in a world that believes in the artificial and mechanical, and thus to renew sculpture, which has become trivially modern. His painted carvings convey the truth: that there is no escape from the organic reality and instinctive life of the body, despite the modern tendency to regard it as a machine. Their primitivism rebels against the constructivism and conceptualism that have dominated modern sculpture and symbolize the modern attitude to being. They never told the whole truth about the lifeworld, and never served human vitality. They are not expressions of inner necessity. The modern belief in the primacy of technological reason, and the modern assumption that any object can be "philosophized" into art—made to serve an abstract idea of art, increasingly obscure because of its perversion into a text about itself—have come to seem absurd and inhumane. (Today, philosophy, in its senility and decline, seems to have no other purpose than to problematize everything—take everything down with it. The art attitude this fosters results in a pseudo-practice similar to its own.)

. . . Rejecting [constructivism], Baselitz renews the expressionist revolt against its overintellectualization—overphilosophizing it—and the expressionist concern with the lived body and interior life. For the expressionist, to seriously live the body is to experience its inseparability from inner life. It is to experience primordial humanness. German Expressionism has always resisted modern reason, not in the name of irrationality, as has been claimed, but for the sake of a certain experience of the body, which is restorative of an elementary and elemental sense of self. It believes that without an intense experience of the fundamentality of the body there can be no sanity and integrity. It has resisted the rationalization of art to suit the needs of technological society, which reduces the body to a manipulable machine, and even worse has no use for a strong sense of self—for a subject that resists objectification as an instrument. Thus Baselitz's expressionist sculptures defy what Ludwig von Bertalanffy calls the robot model of humanity, which has dominated science as well as modern society. It is "demonstrably false" according to him.[8]

Thus, Baselitz's sculpture makes us aware of the vicissitudes of the body, and of life in general, which sometimes creates a Sonderling. His sculpture makes us aware of the inescapability of what Freud called the body ego. Even more profoundly, Baselitz's activated, excruciating gestural surfaces make us aware of the more fundamental skin ego, as Didier Anzieu calls it. Seemingly mutilated, or at least scarred by experience, the skin ego nonetheless survives intact, suggesting a defiant integrity—a strong self.

Aesthetically, Baselitz's sculptures reconcile the masculine whittling away which carving is and the feminine building up which modeling is. In so doing, they collapse the difference between the realized figure and the matrix of process that is the ground out of which it emerges—the Apollonian and Dionysian, if one wishes. By putting destructive peeling, as Kirchner called it, to constructive use, Baselitz's sculptures achieve a new intensity of "rapid content"—the term Stokes used to describe Rodin's sculpture[9]—emblematic of the plasticity of imagination itself. Imagination is the fundamental "plastic agency, fashioning its products with fragments,"[10] imprinting them with its own "associative and transitional qualities,"[11] thus making them signs that concretize its process. The genius of Baselitz is to have restored plastic imagination to sculpture by rearticulating the neglected idea of organic wood sculpture, and giving it fresh significance by making it emblematic of the plastic imagination itself, which creates forms that are primordial and all too human, carved and molded at once. Thus he rescues sculpture from modern attitudes that have become obsolete and obstacles to creativity. He uses a neglected mode of sculpture to articulate truths neglected by and transcending modernity.

8. Ludwig von Bertalanffy, *General System Theory* (New York: George Braziller, 1968), p. 188.
9. Adrian Stokes, "Stones of Rimini," *The Critical Writings of Adrian Stokes* (New York: Thames and Hudson, 1978), vol. 1, p. 235.
10. Ibid., p. 230.
11. Ibid., p. 235.

Henry Moore
a sculptor's drawings

HENRY MOORE
A SCULPTOR'S DRAWINGS
December 3 – 15 January, 1994

by Bernice Rose
Excerpt from Pace catalogue

Henry Moore began with drawing and always drew. His drawing was about sculpture: he was unable to think of form in anything but three dimensions, and he drew as a help toward making sculpture, as well as toward generating ideas for it and reflecting upon it. In retrospect, it is clear that Moore initially used drawing to develop a flexible formal vocabulary—one that was original to him alone, although characteristic of its time. But over the years, whether in a sketch or in a drawing rendered for its own sake, Moore's remained a sculptor's drawing in its emphasis on three-dimensional form, even as he treated the sheet as a two-dimensional surface to be elaborated. . . .

Although Moore drew incessantly throughout most of his life, this exhibition concentrates on his drawings of the 1930's and 40's, when his lifelong occupation with the human form, and most particularly the female form was already clear. During the 1930's his drawings were almost solely concerned with the making of sculpture. In classic studio poses and archetypal subjects, one can see the development of his characteristic themes: the Seated Figure, often transformed into the Madonna with Child, which leads to the Family Group; the Reclining Figure, which resembles the recumbent figures on Etruscan funerary sarcophagi; and that classic monolith, the Standing Figure. In sketch after sketch, Moore continued to explore the figure. By 1934 he opened it up with his now famous "holes" to allow space to move through it. He also explored the relationship of body parts to one another, inside and outside, contrasting bone and viscera with flesh. Finally, he broke the figure into monolithic segments. . . .

As Moore was developing a sculptural vocabulary through his study drawings, he also engaged in a parallel study of drawing itself as both art and science. In the 1920's and 30's, he had developed a style and technique that combined fine-line drawing with areas of deep shadow, often achieved through hatching, and arrived at a flexible, varied language with intimate ties to his sculpture, although independent of it. In the 1930's, Moore experimented not just stylistically but technically as well. There were occasional experiments with color, but Moore was not interested in color as such. He wished to create atmosphere and space around his forms, which he placed in a drawing as a sculpture is placed in a setting. . . .

Before returning to the making of sculpture in 1943, Moore had already prepared the way with his study drawings. However, by the 1950's he found drawing to be of diminishing importance in the development of his sculpture. To study the complex relationship of forms in his new multi-part monumental sculptures of that decade would have required too many drawings, and he turned to working out his ideas directly in clay or plaster maquettes. By this time Moore had, in any case, developed his characteristic formal vocabulary, and no longer relied on drawing for that purpose. He was familiar enough with its variations to be able to manipulate them directly from idea into three-dimensional form. The interdependence between drawing and sculpture continued, however; drawing seems to have become a means for releasing the constant flow of ideas and for choosing among them.

As Moore had become more involved in drawing as an activity for its own sake, he had developed a working pattern that remained unchanged for many years. Ideas that particularly interested him among his initial exploratory sketches were pursued and transformed into larger, more finished drawings. Sometimes he made a maquette from a rough sketch and then would draw from the sculpture as an aid in realizing the final drawing. The finished drawings extracted new information from the sculpture. The continuing reflection on sculptural forms in settings appropriate to them in his finished drawing seems to have interacted with the conception of his monumental sculptures, aiding in their ongoing development. . . .

Two Women Winding Wool, 1948
pencil, white wax crayon, pen and ink, colored crayons and gouache on paper, 22¼ × 25½"

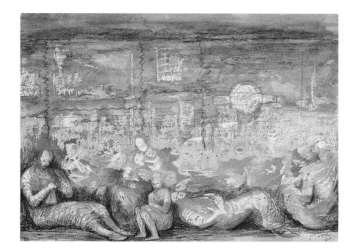

Study for the Grey Tube Shelter, 1940
pencil, chalk, crayon and watercolor on paper, 11 × 15"

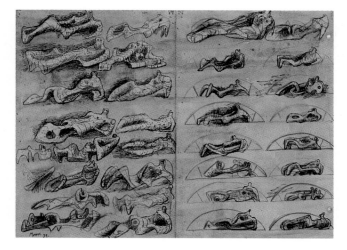

Ideas for Sculpture: Reclining Figures, 1939
pencil, wax crayon, wash, pen and India ink on paper, 11 × 15"

1993

PACE/WILDENSTEIN

We had just finished the 1973 installation of Dubuffet's monumental sculpture Four Trees *at Chase Manhattan Plaza and I was enjoying the aerial view of it from David Rockefeller's office. David had said there was something he wanted to discuss. He congratulated me on the progress my gallery had made but said that only one gallery was preeminent above all others and that was Wildentstein. I was surprised to hear that his friend Daniel Wildenstein was interested in my gallery and wanted to meet me, as I didn't think that Wildenstein was even aware of my existence. A meeting was arranged in Paris chez Wildenstein, and during our lunch Daniel explained that the Wildenstein inventory had been built by three generations, in a revolving acquisition, sale and reacquisition of a finite group of paintings. Although Old Masters and Impressionist paintings were the gallery's strength, in the early part of the twentieth century, Wildenstein had been Picasso's dealer and, in the fifties, had acquired the major portion of the Bonnard Estate. Daniel's plan was to bring Wildenstein into the second half of the twentieth century through an association with Pace.*

We discussed the concept of a family business, and he assumed that my two children would join the gallery. Although at the time they were both planning careers in the sciences (that was before Marc joined the gallery), Daniel insisted that they could study whatever they pleased but that they should eventually have a career in the gallery. Explaining that I had no sense of dynasty, I said, "If my father had insisted on my joining his business we wouldn't be having this discussion." "What did your father do?" he asked. "He had a cattle ranch," I said—to which he responded "Yes, but not the King Ranch."

Over a period of several years, a friendship developed among Daniel, his sons, Guy and Alec, and me. Eventually we made acquisitions of art together and presented two landmark exhibitions; Nevelson at Wildenstein in 1980, and a Dubuffet retrospective at both galleries in 1987. When my son Marc joined the gallery in 1985, Daniel again raised the idea of a merger. A few years later, the time and conditions were auspicious, and PaceWildenstein was formed in 1993. Together we had a complementary group of collectors. Some of our collectors were interested in acquiring Impressionist works, and some of the Wildensteins' clients were interested in extending their collections past Impressionism and Bonnard to contemporary art. The merger enabled us to provide our collectors with works from the Renaissance to the present.

SOL LEWITT | WALL DRAWINGS
January 29 – 12 March, 1994

DONALD JUDD | SCULPTURE
September 16 – 15 October, 1994

"The new work seemed to be the beginning of my own freedom, with possibilities for a lifetime.
The possibilities and lifetime are now well along."

– D.J. 1993

"In our western world, art has been whatever a self-identified artist thinks it is. Communication of such thought is democratic and unnecessary. Therefore motions of quality are also extra."

– D.F. 1993

DAN FLAVIN | **SCULPTURE/GREENE STEET**
December 3 – 15 January, 1994

JOHN CHAMBERLAIN

RECENT SCULPTURE/GREENE STREET
September 17 – 15 October, 1994

Urban Garlic, 1994
painted steel, 73¾ × 89½ × 78¼"

BARNETT NEWMAN

THE SUBLIME IS NOW: THE EARLY WORK OF BARNETT NEWMAN

October 21 – 26 November, 1994

Enacting Origins

by Jeremy Strick

Excerpt from catalogue

On August 9, 1955, Barnett Newman addressed a letter to Clement Greenberg in response to the critic's landmark essay "American-Type Painting," published earlier that year. Newman stated: "I first created my concept and developed my present style in 1944–45. By 1946 I had already done a series of pictures which culminated in the picture I called *Euclidean Abyss*."[1]

. . . "It is too bad that you were not as acutely aware of my work during these important years as you are now, because you would have had a more correct picture of my history and my work and you would not now be putting both under a cloud."[2]

. . . Newman asserts the unity of his artistic project, tying his work of the mid-1940's directly to that of the mid-1950's. The concept and the style that distinguished Newman's art in 1955 were invented by the artist a decade earlier. . . .

The importance of Newman's claim only becomes fully apparent when seen in relation to the specific shape of his artistic career. Newman began attending courses at the Art Students League in 1922 at age 17, when he was still in high school. He continued taking courses at the League through much of the 1920's, and in 1931 began teaching art as a substitute teacher in the New York City high schools. During the 1930's, he formed friendship with Milton Avery, Mark Rothko and Adolph Gottlieb, among other artists, but he did not exhibit his work.

Sometime around 1939–1940, when he was about 35 years old, Newman virtually stopped making art. He did not begin again until 1944. All the work he had made prior to 1944 he destroyed.

The years 1944–45, then, those Newman points to as marking the origin of his style and his concept, mark as well the time at which the artist again began to produce works on paper and on canvas. Most significantly, perhaps, these years mark the time at which Newman chose to preserve his work.

. . . "I recall my first painting—that is, where I felt that I had moved into an area for myself that was completely me—I painted on my birthday (January 29) in 1948. It's a small red painting, and I put a piece of tape in the middle, and I put my so-called 'zip.'"[3]

The painting Newman describes here is *Onement I*. This is, indeed, the first painting Newman made that displays the essential features that would largely define his painted oeuvre. Here, an unmodulated monochrome field is divided vertically by the Newman "zip," which proceeds uninterrupted from the bottom to the top of the canvas. The zip is painted with feathery orange strokes over a strip of masking tape. The tape was initially set down in order to keep the canvas beneath it blank—in reserve—as Newman painted the red fields on either side. His intention was to paint over the red fields with a second color, and the orange stripe brushed over the tape was begun as test color (in most, but not all, of his subsequent paintings Newman removed the tape before painting his zip in the reserved area).

The textured zip in *Onement I* contrasts with the unmodulated field that it divides, while its rough edges contrast to the strict geometry of the canvas edges. Despite these contrasts, and the contrast of color, the zip somehow seems to stand neither in front of nor behind the field. The field, despite its division, remains unified. For Newman . . . this was the crucial feature of *Onement I*. . . .

The discovery of *Onement I* amounted to a reversal of the procedure that Newman employed for his drawings and that he had sought to replicate in his paintings. The field was painted a solid color, and the zip was irregularly brushed in over a dividing strip of masking tape. No longer the reserve, the zip all at once achieved equality with the field—it became a positive presence in the painting rather than an absence. At the same time, Newman was able to establish the field as an absolute, unified entity by stripping it of the veils of painterly

atmosphere in which he had earlier enshrouded it. One measure of the significance of *Onement I* to Newman can be gathered from the fact that, for 10 years after he painted it, he made only six drawings.

With *Onement I*, Newman found the means to state clearly and decisively in painting the ideas he had begun exploring in drawing several years earlier. That statement, and the works which followed it, allowed Newman to take his place as one of the most crucial painters of his generation. The statement was achieved through a repeated process of re-examination and re-consideration of his own work that took place in the years between 1944 and 1949. The frequently stated theme of those years, expressed in Newman's essays and his titles was that of origin. But it was through continually reassessing and re-enacting his own artistic origins that Newman moved his art forward. For Newman, the search for the subject about which he wrote was ultimately just that:

the search for himself as a maker of art. Newman's art of the future was located through an intensely focused process of rediscovery and artistic reenactment of his own recent past.

1. Barnett Newman, "Letter to Clement Greenberg" in *Barnett Newman: Selected Writings and Interviews*, ed. John P. O'Neill, first paperback edition University of California Press, Berkeley, California, p. 204. The present exhibition is the first of Newman's paintings and drawings to be organized subsequent to the publication of Newman's selected writings by Alfred A. Knopf, New York, in 1990. That publication has already had a significant impact upon Newman studies, enriching our knowledge of Newman's thought, and allowing us to track with far greater precision how certain of Newman's key ideas emerged and were developed over time.

2. Ibid. Greenberg's essay, despite Newman's specific objections, was highly supportive of the artist's work, and marked a crucial turning point in its reception. Greenberg curated a one-man show of Newman's work in 1959, at French and Company, the New York gallery.

3. Barnett Newman, "Interview with Emile de Antonio," in *Barnett Newman: Selected Writings and Interviews*, p. 305.

Included in this exhibition were models for large-scale projects that were documented in the contemporaneous publication Claes Oldenburg Coosje van Bruggen: Large Scale Projects.

Clothespin—45 Foot Model, 1976–79
Cor-ten and stainless steel, 60 × 24 × 19⅝"

CLAES OLDENBURG
COOSJE VAN BRUGGEN

LARGE SCALE PROJECTS
December 2 – 7 January, 1995

ISAMU NOGUCHI

BEGINNINGS AND ENDS/GREENE STREET
December 3 – 15 January, 1995

Untitled (Black Waterfall), 1994–95
mixed media, installation dimensions variable

ROBERT WHITMAN

BACKTRACK/GREENE STREET

March 11 – 15 April, 1995

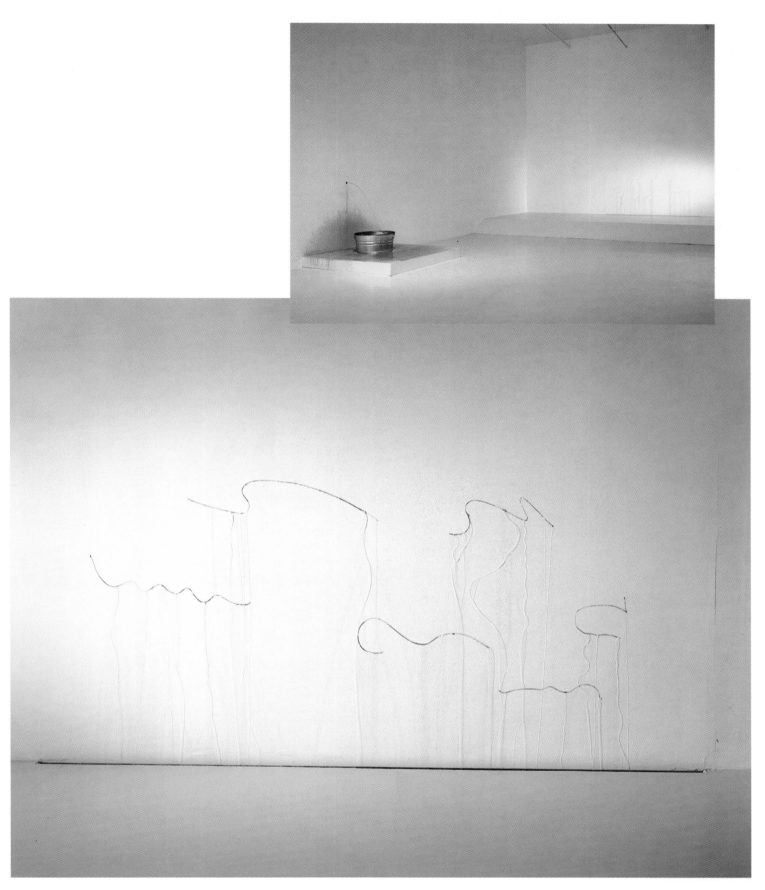

Untitled (Leaking Wall), 1994–95
mixed media, installation dimensions variable

JOEL SHAPIRO | WOOD SCULPTURE
March 24 – 22 April, 1995

Untitled, 1994
oil paint on wood, 47 × 13 × 18½"

"I think paint makes them more abstract, and removes the material or the form—*the material of the form*—from its source. If your have a chunk of wood, and you cover it with paint, you're disguising the material. And you're presented with a chunk of color, or a chunk of paint. Of course we know that it's painted wood or it's painted bronze or it's painted canvas. But the fact is, it denies its materiality. It might make it a more real idea, or a more realized idea."

—J.S.

"Picasso and Drawing," over 100 works spanning nearly 70 years, focuses on Picasso's use of line as the driving force of his art in different media. Paper, canvas, board, and metal rods became the support for Picasso's drawings. In the 1956 film Le Mystère de Picasso *by Henri-Georges Clouzot, Picasso even drew with light, demonstrating his complex use of drawing as an instrument of invention.*

Picasso and Drawing

by Bernice Rose
Excerpt from Pace catalogue

1933. The Sleeper. A woman lies sleeping, her arms cradling her head. Only a patch of blue in the upper corner suggests place; otherwise she floats, her only home the flat canvas that she fills with the swelling, voluptuous forms of her body. Light emanates from the bare canvas—the blue paint supports the illusion that the space of the canvas is an infinite universe saturated with light. The woman is depicted half-length and is seen up close. She is soft and yielding, an image brought to life by a lover's gaze. She is a creature made of a singular kind of magic, an apparition of her own shadows, as the charcoal line moves to describe and caress the contours of her body. . . .

In choosing to distill this woman's form, the artist rejected conventional distinctions between painting and drawing; medium and finish ceased to be defining factors. Instead he appropriated the scale and the canvas support that normally belong to painting, while the faint traces of former lines and the smudgy shadows left behind in their erasure, a technique that belongs properly to drawing, are the painterly essence of the work. . . .

1904. Debienne Watching Fernande Asleep. A man gazes at a woman asleep. The drawing is composed in two zones: she is bathed in light, the focus of all reality; the man in deep shadow, thin, head bowed. His hungry gaze fixed on her, he is a surrogate for the artist, who is the real watcher. The light glowing from the sheet is warm, as if from a gas lamp. In this, the first statement of a lifelong theme of watched women in Picasso's art and the first in a group of watched sleepers, the artist has created an intimate and hermetic world. . . .

Between this drawing and *The Sleeper* of 1933 lies an investigation into the nature of form in which nothing mastered is ever discarded. The years 1904 through 1907 represent the deconstruction of convention—of art as it was known up to that time—through a series of discoveries outside the Western canon. Yet despite Picasso's revolutionary breakup of traditional artistic devices—of the act of looking itself—his style is rooted in those very academic conventions, which he had learned years before, initially from his father, a drawing master, and later from the study of Ingres. Ingres' work was thought to exemplify the academic principle that the ideal form was sculptural, man was the measure, and that the ideal drawing was made according to a refined linear system that expressed that form. . . .

The system that Picasso recognized as a common thread through these varied styles and that he used as he rationalized and reconciled them was the academic drawing system. Drawing, as taught according to academic principles, was a highly conceptual system; it seems even to have had pretensions to scientific objectivity. Such drawing took line for granted as the first element of a language for the imitation of reality. . . .

The new structure of twentieth-century art was not only scientific but as compelling as any prior scheme in the history of art in its power to signify the most profound emotions and social upheavals. Until his death in 1973, Picasso's extraordinary linear inventions and his manipulation of them in phantasmic combinations and recombinations of abstract and representational, organic and geometric forms, continued to produce one of the most fertile and moving bodies of work in the history of Western art.

Portrait de Mme. Picasso, 1912
oil on canvas, 51¼ × 38½"
© 2001 Estate of Pablo Picasso/Artists Rights Society (ARS), New York

1903-1910

La dormeuse, March 13, 1932
oil and charcoal on canvas, 51¼ × 63¾"
© 2001 Estate of Pablo Picasso/Artists Rights Society (ARS), New York

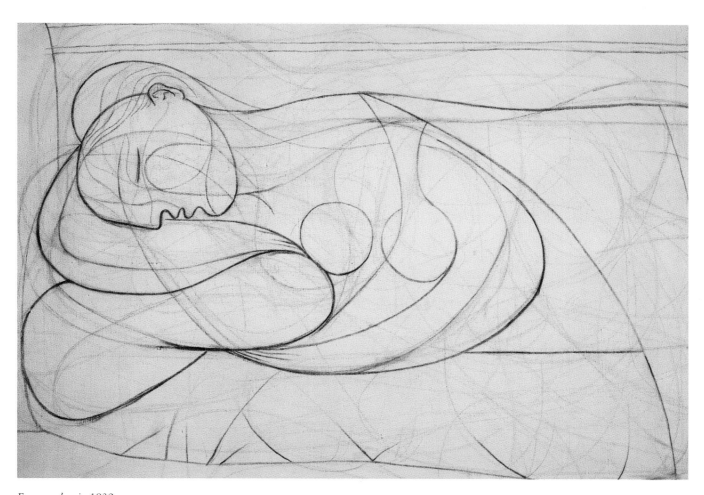

Femme endormie, 1932
charcoal on canvas, 38¼ × 51¼"
© 2001 Estate of Pablo Picasso/Artists Rights Society (ARS), New York

KIKI SMITH | NEW WORK/GREENE STREET
September 16 – 21 October, 1995

Untitled, 1995
patinated silicon bronze with palladium leaf, 48¾ × 16 × 10"

Lilith, 1994
silicon bronze and glass, 33 × 27½ × 19"

1995

LOS ANGELES

In September 1995, we opened our Los Angeles branch of the gallery at 9540 Wilshire Boulevard in Beverly Hills. In celebration, a tent was erected on Rodeo Drive, adjacent to the gallery. Over 600 people, including the mayor of Beverly Hills and celebrities from the worlds of art and entertainment, attended the party.

The gallery was comprised of a space for photography, a drawing gallery and a large exhibition space for paintings and sculpture. Often Los Angeles galleries were the legatees of works left over from New York exhibitions. To change that perception the gallery opened with an exhibition of new work by Chuck Close. Sending exhibitions to Los Angeles before they opened in New York became a customary practice, as well as designing exhibitions especially for Los Angeles including Pablo Picasso: Works from the Estate and Selected Loans.

CHUCK CLOSE | RECENT PAINTINGS

September 29 – 28 October, 1995
Los Angeles (Illustrated)
December 1 – 13 January, 1996
Greene Street

Self-Portrait I, 1995
oil on canvas, 72 × 60"

Following pages: Gala opening of the gallery in Los Angeles
Left to right, top row: Alan and Marilyn Bergman with Jim Dine;
Arne Glimcher, Mark Johnston and David Hockney;
Dustin Hoffman, Arne Glimcher and Chuck Close
Middle row: George Condo; Ivan and Genevieve Reitman with
Arne Glimcher; Close and Michael Ovitz;
Blair Underwood and Lucas Samaras
Bottom row: Michael Ovitz; Hoffman, Glimcher and Close with
Bernard Ruiz Picasso; John Chamberlain,
Prudence Fairweather and Julian Schnabel; Natalie Geary and
Marc Glimcher; Joel Shapiro and Schnabel

ROBERT MANGOLD

CURVED PLANE/FIGURE PAINTINGS/GREENE STREET

October 28 – 25 November, 1995

Visual Dialogue and the
Acknowledgement of Particularity

by David Carrier
Excerpt from Pace catalogue

Often, much can be learned about an artist's work from his titles. Titles of many Abstract Expressionist artworks, evoking heroic struggle, suggest a very different view of artmaking than do Robert Mangold's always literal titles. *Distorted Circle within a Polygon (yellow-ochre)*, 1972, says a great deal about that early Mangold, identifying the shape of the support, and describing both the distorted circle drawn within that polygon and the polygon's color. However, it would be a mistake to conclude that such a description is prosaic. Is there not aesthetic pleasure in economy, in telling much about an artwork in so few words? Since Mangold's three elements are the shaped canvas, the drawing which creates interior structure, and the color of that canvas, this title is pretty complete.

His titles can be interestingly elaborate, as *A 1/4 Circle not Totally within a Rectangle and a Square (yellow)*, 1976, or sly, as *Untitled Frame Set B (green-brown)*, 1970, which, after claiming that this painting is untitled—normally a way of refusing to give the information a title provides—identifies the shape, its place in a series, and its color. The *Attic Series*, begun in 1990, may seem an exception to this generalization. But, in fact, that title is an elliptical way of giving the construction rules for these paintings, rules akin to those employed on some Greek pottery Mangold admired in the Metropolitan Museum of Art. . . .

Mangold's artworks are large enough almost to fill the field of vision in a normal studio or gallery situation, and so, when setting individual ones in sequence, inevitably we turn away from one painting to other related works. Since aesthetic experience involves focus on particulars, on the here and now, on that magic moment when all merely distracting thoughts fall away, this procedure ought to seem surprising. Nothing whatsoever is hidden in any of Mangold's works, which contain within themselves all that is necessary to appreciate them. What then justifies discussing interrelationships among the different paintings of the *Curved Plane / Figure Series*? What sanctions bringing *Unfinished Dance Mural* and *Madonna del Parto* into this account?

Robert Mangold in 1992 wrote something that for a long time puzzled me very deeply: "I often sit for hours, looking at paintings I have done, or am doing." What is happening? How is it possible for artworks with no narrative, with no explicit political meanings or symbolic content, to be so utterly absorbing? He goes on to ask a further question which also interests me a lot: "What am I looking at? What is the kind of dialogue I am having with the work?" A dialogue requires two partners. When looking at his paintings, with whom would Mangold talk? How, to press the point, does his looking differ from schizophrenic Becketesque staring at a blank wall?

To answer these questions, I am forced to speculate. Robert Mangold entered the American art world near the end of the golden age of dialogue, an era, today utterly vanished, when lively verbal intercourse amongst artists was highly important. What I think he has incorporated within his own recent works is the potential for ongoing conversation, preserving in his art something of great value to him which in the real world has disappeared. This dialogue starts within individual paintings. In the *Curved Plane / Figure Series*, the several ellipses define a dialogue. And line and surface enter into dialogue. When we go further, we can look to Matisse's dancers and the curtain held by Piero's angels. Mangold is using drawing neither as a tool for mensuration nor a vehicle for making visible transcendence, as did Piero; unlike Matisse, he is employing the shaped canvas neither as a setting for depicted forms, nor as embellishment for an architectural setting. Searching for affinities between very different kinds of things, he seeks identification of relationships between his painting and theirs. Mangold's individual works, I am suggesting, deserve the prolonged attention he gives to them because they contain within themselves the possibility of such dialogue.

It is, of course, no accident that these three particular painters, whose explicit concerns are so obviously different, can naturally in these ways be associated with one another. Not every painter, now or in the past, opens his work to the possibilities of such dialogue. "Mangold's images," Bill Berkson has written, "come across with the quiet authority of sensible facts. They are memorable and right. . . ." Exactly the same can be said of Matisse's images, and of Piero's. Unless we can thus grasp Mangold's place, as he himself understands it, within the traditions of painting, inevitably his art will be misunderstood. But a proper understanding of the aesthetic qualities of his painting demands, finally, that we turn our attention to the specific qualities of his individual works. Robert Mangold, a classic American abstract painter, has found so apparently simple, so obviously inevitable and entirely direct a way of picture-making, that it is a little shocking to realize that this was his discovery.

THE MARK GOODSON COLLECTION

October 27 – 25 November, 1995

I met Mark Goodson in 1972 when Mort Janklow brought him into the gallery to see a Magritte painting. He wasn't deeply enthusiastic about the work, but he clearly liked it and was considering acquiring it. I suggested that he wait until the right Magritte presented itself. We didn't see each other again for several months during which time a Boston collector whom I had known since the early '60's called to tell me that he wanted to deaccession Magritte's Journal intime, 1951. *I had always considered it a great Magritte—beautifully painted and filled with visual wit. Mark shared my enthusiasm and acquired it. Thus began our relationship of building his collection which gave him enormous pleasure and was catalytic to the development of our friendship that lasted until his death.*

As the collection grew, so did the demands Mark made upon each work he acquired. What was the context within which a work could be positioned in an artistic career? Was it unique and did it stretch the boundaries of his perception? Did it cause Mark to see the world differently? These were the considerations by which the works entered the collection. . . . Mark's collection was integral to his life and a key to the intelligence and complexity of the man. It was our pleasure to exhibit it together one last time.

GEORGE CONDO

Artifices of the Visionary
by Donald Kuspit
Excerpt from Pace catalogue

. . . Condo gives us the myth of the artist and his creations: of Pygmalion having his wish fulfilled—the miracle of art brings the dead statue-machine to life. It is also the myth of postmodernism: Machines can live, independently of their masters, yet we are all machines, eager for a master to program and run us. The puppets—the artist's works—outsmart their master because they are, unexpectedly, more primitive than him. The Psychoanalytic Puppeteer and the Magician are sophisticated, unique human beings compared to their impulsive, unhuman puppets, but the demonic puppets are sophisticated artificial constructions as well as primitively real. The tension between the knowing master and the metaphysical mannequin that he creates, breathes life into, is the emotional core of the allegorical tall tale which Condo's pictures are. It remains unresolved in his pictures, as it should be, because it remains unresolved in the artificial reality that we have created but are clearly not master of.

George Condo: Recent Works

PaceWildenstein

George Condo: Recent Works

PaceWildenstein

George Condo: Recent Works

PaceWildenstein

ANTONI TÀPIES

Porta roja, 1995
soil, paint and iron assembly on wood, 61¼ × 45"

Toward Monumentalism
by Mildred Glimcher
Excerpt from Pace catalogue

During the summer of 1952, while visiting the Massons in Provence, the Calders decided to spend a year in France beginning in July 1953. The Massons found them a house called Mas de Roches in Les Granettes near Aix-en-Provence. The house itself was quite primitive, with no electricity and little running water, and the family spent a good deal of time outdoors. Calder turned the carriage shed into a *gouacherie* and was quite pleased with the large number of gouaches he made.[38] Apparently he had no sculpture studio, so perhaps this propelled him to the blacksmith shop down the road, where he began to make larger outdoor standing mobiles.[39] *Myxomatose* of 1954 is one of the five or six sculptures made in Aix during that year. As was his practice in the studio, Calder worked directly on the metal, drawing and cutting (with help) the forms from the thick metal plates. Whereas an earlier monumental standing mobile, *El Corcovado*, 1951,[40] about 11 feet high, was conceived as an indoor sculpture, these new standing mobiles were made of much heavier steel plate, welded instead of bolted. They were thus conceived from the beginning as outdoor sculptures.[41] These are breakthrough works because Calder was able to transfer his familiar, intuitive studio practice to the production of outdoor pieces. Thus, in the future, he would never hand over the fabrication of monumental pieces, but would remain involved until the completion of the project.

Although Calder had incorporated larger outdoor sculpture into his personal studio practice, the procedures for completing future large-scale commissions would require the more traditional use of a model, both for the proposal and the enlargement of the sculpture. Calder had

ALEXANDER CALDER
THE FIFTIES

actually been making maquettes since the thirties, even then using them as proposals for commissions.[42] This practice continued during the forties and into the fifties, and by mid-decade he was receiving commissions for monumental sculptures. During 1953 he made two maquettes for standing mobiles which were then enlarged: *Model for Ten Restless Disks* and *Model for Rosenhof*. In June 1954, the Rudolf Hoffman Gallery in Hamburg showed both the *Model for Ten Restless Disks* and the enlarged version, which was about 15 feet high, in their Calder exhibition. The same catalogue lists the *Model for Rosenhof* as the "model for the mobile in the Rose garden of *Planten und Blomen* Hamburg 1953." The current whereabouts of this monumental work is unknown, but from one of the existing photographs we can infer that it must have been about 25 feet tall. This was the largest sculpture Calder had made and is the antecedent of *La Spirale* and the numerous monumental standing mobiles of the sixties such as *Southern Cross*, 1963 and *Sandy's Butterfly*, 1964. . . .

Calder's monumental commissions of the fifties seem to have been immune from most of the rancorous debate about the role of abstraction in public sculpture—probably because he created works appropriate to the project, rather than just making a "Calder." Although he never made a war memorial (the monument most open to controversy), three of his projects became symbols of America in an international context: *Hextoped*, 1955, at the American Consulate in Frankfurt; *La Spirale* at UNESCO; and *Whirling Ear* at the Brussels 1958 World's Fair. In 1962 he commented: "They [commissions] give me the opportunity to undertake something of considerable size. . . . I find that everything I do, if it is made for a particular spot, is more successful. . . ."[46] Calder drew on his experience with earlier collaborative efforts to bring these projects to completion. His openness, indeed his willingness, to collaborate with experts,

ALEXANDER CALDER | THE 50'S

November 9 – 29 December, 1995
Los Angeles (Illustrated)
January 19 – 17 February, 1996
57th Street

be they architects, engineers, acoustical engineers as at Aula Magna, or metal workers and welders, meant that he would remain with the project until its completion. Trained as an engineer, he respected the great feats of engineering manifested in bridges or turbines.[47] He enjoyed watching welders do their work, and has said, perhaps with some irony, that he liked playing the role of apprentice during the fabrication of his sculpture.

In 1957, Calder received three commissions for monumental public sculptures. The first, from the Port of New York Authority through Gordon Bunschaft and his firm Skidmore, Owings and Merrill, was for a mobile for the International Arrivals building at Idlewild (now Kennedy) Airport. What would more appropriately express the modernity of flight than a mobile by Calder?. . .

Calder was one of the dozen artists chosen to embellish the new headquarters of UNESCO in Paris.[51] As the fifties drew to a close, the world still hoped for peace through the United Nations, and the ideology of unification though culture and education was the driving force of UNESCO. The works of these artists were to be a material symbol of that hope. In every other public commission of the decade, Calder pushed the visual and philosophical limits of the work, but in *La Spirale*, the piece for UNESCO, he understood its ideological and symbolic significance and was content to stay with the quintessentially familiar. The rising movement suggested by the mobile form was balanced by the steady form of the base, still connected to the earth, creating a work appropriate to its symbolic role. . . .

Edward Durrell Stone and the United States Department of State asked Calder to do a mobile for the United States Pavilion at the Brussels World's Fair in 1958.[54] However, when he examined the plans, Calder was drawn to the pool in front of the pavilion, seeing there another opportunity to develop his fountain ideas. . . .

Still in search of the ultimate expression of his fountain ideal, this time Calder included a sculpture. Titled *Whirling Ear*, it was composed of two parts, an organic "ear" shape, which would sit on a three-dimensional geometric base in the pool. . . .

The "birth" of this new monumentalism had many midwives. An artist's life is never linear, even if the documentation gives that impression. Everything in an artist's environment is inherent in what we perceive as the finished work. . . .

The central issue of the fifties was the global internationalization of politics, the economy, travel, and culture. With the H-bomb and television, isolation was no longer possible. A study of the Chronology in this volume reveals how "in sync" Calder was with the Zeitgeist. He was the first truly international artist, beginning his continuous travel during the thirties. This meant that he and his work could absorb, and be absorbed into, a variety of cultures, in a manner that would be a model for the future. He was prepared, more than others, to take advantage of the opportunities for internationalization that the fifties presented. He never hesitated to expand the limits of a project, with a breadth of vision and "chutzpah" that was born of confidence in himself and his work. The important aspects of that work have been invisible to most of us because they cannot be put on display in a museum. As the size of the stage expanded, opportunities for grand scale expanded as well, and Calder was enthusiastic to meet the challenge. . . .

38. Calder, *Autobiography with Pictures* (New York 1966), p. 214. Later that summer they moved to another house, where Calder concentrated on making gouaches in a third-floor room and felt that he "seemed to develop something new"; ibid., p. 218. These gouaches were exhibited by Christian Zervos in Paris.

39. Ibid.

40. See James Johnson Sweeney, *Alexander Calder* (New York, 1951), p. 71.

41. My thanks to Alexander Rower for pointing this out.

42. My thanks to Alexander Rower for directing me to the Herbert Matter photographs of Calder's February–March 1937 exhibition at the Matisse Gallery, which shows six small maquettes under the large sculpture *Stable/Big Bird/Chick-lett*; see the catalogue of the Calder retrospective at the Louisiana Museum of Modern Art, Humlebaek, 1995, p. 62.

46. Quoted in Katherine Kuh, "Alexander Calder," *The Artist's Voice* (New York, 1962), p. 42.

47. Conversation with Alexander Rower, September 1995.

51. The others were Moore, Miró, Picasso, Tamayo, Matta, Afro, Appel, Noguchi, Arp, Bazaine, and Brassaï.

54. Letters form George W. Staempfli and Edward Durrell Stone, January 31, February 6, and March 1, 1957, at the Archives of The Alexander & Louisa Calder Foundation.

JULIAN SCHNABEL

THE CONVERSION OF ST. PAOLO MALFI/GREENE STREET

February 15 – 23 March, 1996

by Bernice Rose
Excerpt from Pace catalogue

Biographical note:
Paolo Malfi was an itinerant Italian artist. Wandering the world, partially deaf, Paolo supported himself by a variety of jobs, among them apple picker, electrician, gigolo, pizza maker. He was for a time a footsore seeker after enlightenment in the Himalayas. He spent a short time in jail in Asia. In New York he worked as a studio assistant for both Julian Schnabel and Francesco Clemente. Clemente has noted that those close to Paolo "felt he carried a hidden gift. A secret illumination he protected faithfully but was unable to express." Paolo Malfi died in an automobile accident near Rome in the summer of 1995. Schnabel's cycle of paintings, *The Conversion of St. Paolo Malfi*, is a response to his friend's life and death.

The Conversion of St. Paolo Malfi

Like most of Julian Schnabel's work, *The Conversion of St. Paolo Malfi* is conceived as a cycle of paintings. Death by accident provides the pretext for transfiguring an all too familiar event into a sublime occasion for the apotheosis of painting. Schnabel is a true believer: "Art functions as a physical fact to commemorate the existence of being." Representations made of paint are the body in another

form, they are signs for the self. The painter is a phenomenon of nature; his materials are the substances that materialize and convert all spirit to substance and substance to spirit in a magical alchemical process.

In this instance, Schnabel's compulsion to convert a sense of loss into an analogue for his nostalgia for ambitious painting generates a cycle of five related themes, each with a set of multiple variations. . . .

The first two paintings (banners) announce the cycle, the third discloses its formal elements. Schnabel's narrative is indirect; through mundane details and bathos, Paolo's death is likened to the Deluge, a cataclysmic event that figures a larger transfiguration or, in the words of the text, a conversion. To achieve this conversion, Schnabel tears the pictorial elements of the printed detail apart and converts them into abstract material forms by a process known as likeness. The contours, the motion, the marks, and internal patterns of the abstract paint forms echo those of the representational forms, so that, in a sense, the abstract forms remember their origins. . . .

Likeness acted out technically supplies a new connection to this assembly of disparate parts; it even serves

Photo Patrick Demarchelier

as a device to revive discredited genres and makes sense of the violation of aesthetic categories. For instance, in the second set of the cycle, the delicate red form suggesting a drape was drawn by pressing a paint-soaked red rag on the canvas. This imprint and its abstract form recall both the drapery of the women's gowns and the graphic execution of the printed image from which they are derived. As a result of this material transformation, a historical genre in disuse because it has degenerated into sentimentality is reawakened; time is, in a sense, defeated, as the past is reclaimed for the present. In homage to their origins, the newly abstract "figures" begin to assume the role of dramatic personae in an allegorical structure. Another layer of the story is of course the reuse and alteration of similarly discredited images by earlier artists, a tradition that includes the altered found images of Max Ernst's Surrealist creations such as *Rêve d'une jeune fille qui voulut entrer au Carmel*. (For Schnabel, as for Ernst, who also transformed kitsch images to formal signs, kitsch and the discredited represent a challenge and an opportunity.)

Variation 2
This second set, which is composed of seven paintings, illuminates the process of converting the figurative narrative to a fragmented and ungrammatical story of words and forms moving in space. In a complete spatial shift, the genre of landscape comes to the fore as a governing theme that displaces the emblematic character of the initial three works. For the first time we are told that the conversion of Paolo Malfi takes place near Rome in the summer of 1995. The aged yellow ground of the first variation is replaced by a wash of clear Naples yellow contrasted with reds and grand sweeps of translucent resin medium tinted brilliant green. With the new clarity of the colors, the canvas seems less material; it glows with light. . . .

In fact the major part of the cycle was made outdoors in Montauk in the evening and the early morning, and these glowing colors quote the outdoors and sun on the horizon. Nevertheless, the drama of the color scheme and the arbitrary juxtaposition of contradictory modes—the incorporeal and tactile, infinite and near, visual and linguistic—tell us we are looking into an artificial space, one that, while invoking nature, is actually intended to replace it. Grandiloquent gesture—body language—is the natural force at work in the creation of these grand spaces. We begin to liken the process of making these works to performance and perceive the result as a fragmented memorial left in the guise of a stage setting, with the inscription functioning as its soundless text.

Painting as ritual performance
In the fourth canvas, the sensation of the process of painting as ritualistic performance is confirmed. The format shifts for the first time from vertical to horizontal and enlarges drastically, as the veil of translucent Naples yellow parts to reveal a seamless, clean, white canvas ground. The movement of forms is no longer centrifugal; there is a fine balance—a sense of stasis—as the motifs reach out after touching one another to find the edges of the ground as they seek to escape pictorial space. This is landscape as inscape—a landscape of the mind, a synthetic genre in which the space of the mind is projected as the space of painting and acted out by the body. The canvas becomes the realm of spectacle. This fourth painting sets the stage for the three remaining variants in the cycle, which enact a dialogue between pictorial and non-pictorial space. The canvas is no longer conceived as a unified pictorial ground, nor is there a single dominant work. There is rather a series of settings in which motifs are assigned the role of characters. It is the language of fragments. . . .

521

JEAN DUBUFFET | THE RADIANT EARTH

February 22 – 23 March, 1996

by Arne Glimcher
Excerpt from Pace catalogue

Most of Dubuffet's works of the forties have a decidedly urban connotation, whether they are paintings of a jazz band or business lunch,[2] or the portraits of the writers for the *Nouvelle Revue Française* whom he met for lunch at Florence Gould's home on Wednesday afternoons, or the graffiti-inspired works such as *Les Murs*, 1944, or *Danseurs*, 1945. Even the series he called *Paysages grotesques* of 1949 suggests, in the grayness of its coloration, a suburban, if not exactly urban scene. Since Dubuffet believed that the essence of art was "permanent revolution," it is not surprising that, as the fifties opened, he was looking in another direction.

The 1950 painting *Le Géologue*, with its small figure forced to the top, examining the earth with magnifying glass in hand, was an avatar of this new direction. The focus of this exhibition is Dubuffet's investigation of, and journey into, the natural world. In the 1950s, working against abstraction and toward a concrete reality devoid of metaphor, Dubuffet's art moved toward super-realist recreations of fragments of nature. His explorations, moreover, took the form of serial imagery, which has become a hallmark of twentieth-century art. However, unlike most serial imagists, Dubuffet was not seeking to perfect the concept or image, but rather to exhaust all conceivable options. His work of the fifties has several periods but is dominated by cycles concerned with the earth and its fruits. His objective was not the creation of individual masterpieces, although they exist, but the success of the series as a whole. And the series succeed because of the recklessness of his imagination. Always courting perversity, he delighted in the fact that within a series some works were poor, some mediocre, and some were of dazzling excellence.

I recall visiting Dubuffet in 1982, just after he completed the *Psycho-sites* series. In an attempt to select the group of works that would comprise my exhibition, I focused on a set of the most intense, colorful, and complex paintings—the ones that I considered to be the best. Asked to defend my choice, I told Dubuffet that it was based on the presentation of a cohesive group that would allow the public to grasp one aspect of the series, leaving open the possibility of successive shows. As I was speaking, he began to lay out another group of pale, ill-defined, fluid, atmospheric paintings—the antithesis of my choice. "Why didn't you choose any of these paintings, they're so bad?" he asked. "Don't you think it would be interesting for the Americans to see how badly I can paint?" Out of respect and intimidation I took a few. The exhibition, including the "bad" paintings, met with great success. Years later, at the École des Beaux-Arts, I saw an exhibition of the "bad" paintings and they looked radiant, filled with a light that had only become visible to me with time. The forms, still incomplete and pale, now seemed luminous, like metamorphosing embryos floating in amniotic fluid. This truly serial work, and no singular achievement, no matter how radiant, can have the power to express the narrative arc of the series as a whole.

Dubuffet's journey into the natural world began with the *Paysages grotesques* of 1949, a hybrid of figure and "all-over" landscape painting. While landscape painting never lent itself to the iconic imagery of graffiti, by combining graffiti/écriture with the landscape, Dubuffet was able to lose the traditional hierarchy of the figure over landscape. If the *Paysages grotesques* reduced the figures to fossils, the *Terres radieuses*, 1952, and *Sols et terrains*, 1956–60, presented a world where the only human presence was in the markings left in the mud, a concept that evolved toward a microscopic examination of the planet's surface in the *Texturologies*. In these works, devoid of human enterprise, it is possible to perceive a landscape not in the service of man, but rather one whose properties were previously beneath notice and actually underfoot.

In January 1955, Dubuffet moved to Vence in the Midi, where he established a small studio in which he created some of his most controversial work. He has written that this new location contributed to a "new orientation" and "new themes . . . that of small pieces of earth planted with botanical elements/ingredients: clumps of grass, wild plants covering the ground such as *plantains*, *chardons* or *pissenlits* pushing up among the small stones which can be seen at the edges of neglected roads, or barren mountainous pieces of earth as one finds in the environs of Vence."[3] Several series followed one after the other: the second series of *Ailes de papillons* in 1955 (the first had been made during the summer of 1953), the *Personnages monolithes*, 1955, and *Assemblages*, 1956, which often refer to the gardens and patches of earth around Vence.

The *Topographies* and *Texturologies*, begun in September 1957, continued throughout most of 1958. Even today they remain some of the most radical paintings of

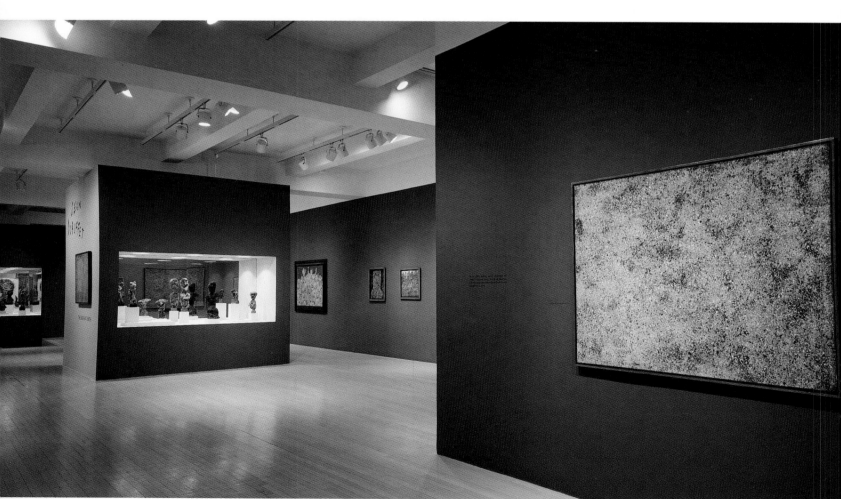

the century. Formally, they can be perceived as staccato responses to the Pollock paintings that had closed the previous decade. But while Pollock established a heroic curvilinear fluidity comparable to symphonic music, Dubuffet created all-over atonal personal scribbles, more evocative of chalk screeching across a blackboard. The scale of Dubuffet's paintings was intimate, Pollock's scale was public. Pollock moved away from visual reality into pure abstraction.

Dubuffet moved away from the abstraction of graffiti to the concrete reality of the *Texturologies*. *Texturologies* became truly all-over paintings, going off the edge, and thus transforming themselves into a fragment of the real world. Pollock's paintings, by regenerating themselves at the edge and moving in and out with a continual tidal pull, isolate themselves from the real world by considering the edges of their supports. Dubuffet's difficult and "ugly" paintings do not immediately seduce the viewer—no color, no painterly texture, no images. They exist outside interpretation, presenting a measure of earth to be accepted and examined like a deed to a specific property. Image and support are congruent. . . .

Each series began with a cognitive plan for the communication of Dubuffet's ideas. However, in the evolution of the process a battle raged between cognition and intuition. The battlefields—the canvases—are of less importance than the process itself, in which intuition overcomes cognition and the most extraordinary fantasies are realized. Among them are the first *Ailes de papillons*, in which Dubuffet incrementally fastened wings to paper supports. Not unlike the work of artists operating outside of society, where an image may evolve out of bottlecaps, landscapes and figures take form, cell by cell. These jigsaw puzzle structures reveal Dubuffet's working method as the proliferation of cells, corresponding to the act of mitosis in the natural world. Functioning without regard for hierarchy, all the individual cells within the image are in the service of the whole. (This process was to become more apparent in the *Paris Circus* paintings of 1961–62 and entirely clear in the *Hourloupe Cycle*, 1962–66.)

With the *Ailes de papillons*, Dubuffet found his images in the material and froze them at the moment of recognition. The *Ailes de papillons* and the *Eléments botaniques*, 1959, are from nature and about nature, and the result is a kind of rudimentary poetry that brings to mind the composite heads of Arcimboldo. But Dubuffet

rejected the linguistically locked associations that Arcimboldo had embraced to create pictures based on metaphoric units—a rose is like a mouth, a mushroom like an ear, a chaff of wheat like eyebrows. In Dubuffet's constructions it is not linguistically satisfactory to say a mouth is like a butterfly wing, an ear is like a butterfly wing, an eyebrow is like a butterfly wing—and yet in the extreme originality and perversity of his art, it is! Both Arcimboldo's "composite images" and Dubuffet's collages are based upon materials that have a totally different existence in the natural world. Arcimboldo spent a great portion of his life curating the art collections and arranging and assembling the legendary *Wunderkammern* (the collections of unusual natural objects) of Maximilian II and Rudolf II in sixteenth-century Prague. In these cabinets, Arcimboldo catalogued nature's rarities and freaks, retrieved from exotic locations. Dubuffet assembled ordinary natural materials from the local environment and turned them into creations as exotic and wondrous as any in nature. None surpasses the *Petites statues de la vie précaire*, 1954–59. . . .

The fifties saw the fulfillment of Dubuffet's concrete reality and the establishment of a new vocabulary for landscape painting. He extended his use of materials to include properties from the natural world and firmly established his process of building images by the proliferation of cells. In the course of the decade, landscapes gave way to sharp-focus fragments of textured mud. Zooming close, Dubuffet revealed the random patterns made by grains of sand, seeds, and fissures in the earth. Eventually, the fruits of the earth—tobacco leaves, banana leaves, and various plant material collages—brought to a close his decade-long obsession with the earth and its radiance. In a final act of cannibalism, he ground up leaves and twigs, mixed them with a binder into material more suited to the production of mud pies than paintings, spread the mixture across the surface of wooden supports, and in this manner created *Mur végétal*, 1959. Like a compost heap, his work had come full circle, turning in upon itself as it recycled the medium.

2. See *Jean Dubuffet: 1943–1963*, exh. cat. (Washington D.C: Hirshhorn Museum and Sculpture Garden, 1993), pls. 10 and 18.
3. Jean Dubuffet, "Memoire," in *Jean Dubuffet: 1942–1960*, exh. cat. (Paris: Musée des Arts Décoratifs, 1960), p. 165.

JIM DINE

Notes on Some Greeks, Some Romans

Three years ago, I went to the Glyptothek in Munich to, yet again, sit in front of, and draw from, the so called "Classical Sculpture". The director, Klaus Vierneisel, charmingly, had always allowed me to come in at night and work undisturbed. This time I was in Munich for only two days and I didn't phone him; I just walked over to the Glyptothek during museum hours. I went directly to the hall of Roman Portrait heads, pulled up my chair and began drawing. There were lots of other visitors and I became embarrassed and shy to work with other people looking over my shoulder. I couldn't concentrate, so I bought a book of portraits at the museum shop and went back to the privacy of my hotel. In my room I made two small portraits very fast using charcoal and some crushed fresh cherries for color. The paper size is A4 and was from a spiral sketch pad. I left the perforations at the top of each page as a kind of conceit that all the drawings would have in common. I was thinking then of maybe making ten drawings. I came back to New York and pinned up the two and made another four or five.

A few months later I was in London and started another "head" there. I couldn't make it happen. The work wasn't coming alive. In my frustration, I slashed it with a knife. I glued the wounds back together and began again. I realized that one of the mediums I use is anger. Anger at not being able to make it work. Angry, because my anger comes forward when I'm defenseless, that is, in the state of making art. When I'm drawing and lose myself, anger sometimes rises up just like joy can, or sadness. Anger rises up not just because the drawing isn't working, but because it's in me always ready to explode. Anyhow, I seemed to have harnessed it with my knife (or lanced it). I sent it back to death and brought it forward to life. That's when I began to make these heads really come alive.

My main purpose in all my work has been to try and take these inanimate inventions and make them live. I stand behind my marks. The marks it takes to depict these Greeks and Romans, with all their warts. All their broken bits. Noses gone. Cuts from falling off pedestals. Erosion by time, war, and gasoline fumes. The page must come alive. To make each mark mean a part of a face, a woman's braid, some guy's sense of power (real or imagined). Each of these faces make up a part of this symphony.

My notes are varied. There are some carefully rendered pieces. Others are drawn from my stomach. Some-

times my eyes see nothing. Then this force screams at me and I can't control the output. Other days I sit and wait.

1. Can I bring to life a head who was an empress?
2. The whore who's missing an ear.
   Where's her beauty?
3. Can I make the stone wounds bleed?
4. Will the marble read as flesh and stone?

I think of all this. Day after day, layer upon layer, there is this vast unconscious well to drill and tap.

It must be clear to you now, reader, that my personal history is intertwined with this subject matter. These Greek and Roman citizens become my history. Each head is the voice of my unconscious. It could be called the subject of the works, along with all the brush strokes, pencil lines, erasures, and smears. These Greeks and Romans become a very large personal vocabulary. I know this can create an enigmatic state for the viewer. Those of you who find the work unavoidable, will eventually understand the secret. Naturally, I remain the keeper of the secret.

–J.D.

Some Greeks, Some Romans, 1992-1996
charcoal, pastel and watercolor with abrasion on two sheets of rough paper attached on verso with paper strip, 11⅝ × 8¼"

Some Greeks, Some Romans, 1992-1996
lithographic crayon, red conte crayon, oil stick and watercolor with incising and abrasion on rough paper, 11⅝ × 8¼"

ROBERT RYMAN

RECENT PAINTINGS/GREENE STREET

May 4 – 21 June, 1996

Photo Bill Jacobson

ROBERT RAUSCHENBERG | ANAGRAMS

September 19 – 19 October, 1996
57th Street (Illustrated)
November 15 – 18 January, 1997
Los Angeles

by Bernice Rose
Excerpt from Pace catalogue

Robert Rauschenberg is an activist; he might almost be said to have taken Ezra Pound's injunction to "go in fear of abstractions" as a moral imperative.[1] Although far from being a "historically propelled technician,"[2] Rauschenberg has, nevertheless, reinvented the terms by which modernism, in a powerful act of the imagination, first made visual representation a fellow traveler in the philosophical quest in which consciousness takes itself as its own object and recasts itself as a part of nature. Rauschenberg can be described as a modernist fundamentalist who clearly perceives that the art of our era is about the role of the visual in the soul's quest for self-knowledge—and, ultimately, enlightenment. In the same way, modern art transformed the role of visual representation by rejecting realism and taking art itself, "its own nature as an artistic medium, as the object for investigation and understanding." Rauschenberg, too, devotes his art to exploring and recording the space and function of imagination, of creativity and of perception. His newest group of works is one of his more extraordinary visual reenactments of that exploration into the world of the sensate: the *Anagrams* are the poetic ciphers of his self's self-discovery as it travels among the objects of the material world and inserts itself into the chaotic, arbitrary world of nature. . . .

The *Anagram* paintings are the newest element in Rauschenberg's expanding universe. One of the most extraordinary episodes in his recent work, they are, like the Dante drawings, visionary—visionary in the sense that Rauschenberg has revealed a world united by art. Once again he uses the particular qualities of medium and paper support as they interact to absorb images of a world fragmented into a seamless whole. Like the *Inferno* drawings, they are made by a transfer process, and light and shadow inhere to both the origin of the image and the technique that produces it. Also as in the *Inferno*, each element in the pictorial structure is assigned multiple tasks, messages, identities. As Rauschenberg washes image over image, "abstract" and representational, foreground and background constantly shift roles, creating spatial ambiguities that escape the expanded Cubist grid structure. . . .

Photography has been the instrument of Rauschenberg's sensibility for some time now, the means by which he designates fragments of the material world as surrogates for himself, the means by which he organizes the "narrative" of his journey through the world. With the camera as impersonal agent of the artist's sensibility, the artist's "eye" gains authority over the world. The camera is the instrument of light and memory; its mechanism instantly and efficiently memorizes a multitude of images, creating databanks of ready-made repeatable, manipulable, mutable images. Each roll of film presents Rauschenberg with his own mass-media images as it records fragments of the world, one after the other, like strings of adjectives that defy conventional grammatical connections, to be cut and reassembled into fields of objects conceived as a form of visual poetry that infinitely extends pictorial form.

The *Anagrams* are both more systematic and ultimately more random than the Dante drawings, although the basic strategy is the same. The narrative is tracked erratically figure by figure, frame by frame, as a far-flung "transposition cipher" (substitution code), through numerous repetitions, reversals, changes of scale, and shifts of focus. Each work in the set is informed by poetry, random musical composition, its movement within the field impelled by the static sounds of the environment, by disorderly impressions registered as if imprinted across a flat-bed press, as a series of layers of incidents and objects, left, as in *Monogram*, as if by some elemental instinctive force. Each change of context effects a transformation of identity that reflects all the others, driving a quest that visually reinforces the work as a shifting memory structure in which public, private, contemporary and historical, real and imaginary contexts are merged. The use of photographic images creates a presentational immediacy and resonance which makes the narrative work in the gap between art and life and gives it urgency and poignancy. There are no improbable polygraphs here, for the shifts of imagery, the doubling and tripling of meanings that give each image new meaning in its new situation also create a gap that leaves room for chaos. The very logic of the system undermines logic. . . .

1. Quoted in Robert Pinsky, *The Situation of Poetry* (Princeton: Princeton University Press, 1976), p. 5; see also note 4.
2. James H. Rubin, *Manet's Silence and the Poetics of Bouquets: Essays in Culture* (Cambridge, Massachusetts: Harvard University Press, 1994), pp. 13–15. Rubin used the phrase in a general context, not in reference to Rauschenberg. The quoted remarks in the first paragraph here are also from Rubin, but my debt to him includes my reliance on his detailed expansion of the concept of subjectivity in modern art, as paraphrased in this paragraph
4. [Riva Castleman, formerly Chief Curator of the Department of Prints and Illustrated Books at The Museum of Modern Art, suggested this reading of the O.]

Fusion, 1996
Color transfer drawing, 60¼ × 144⅝"
Collection Whitney Museum of American Art
Purchase, with funds from Leonard A. Lauder and Thomas H. Lee
© Untitled Press, Inc/Licensed by VAGA, New York

BARBARA HEPWORTH

SCULPTURE/WILDENSTEIN & CO.

October 8 – 30 November, 1996

by Alan G. Wilkinson
Excerpt from Pace catalogue

. . . The life and work of Barbara Hepworth, the first great female sculptor in the history of Western art, have been largely ignored or forgotten since her death in a fire at her home, Trewyn Studio, St. Ives, Cornwall, in 1975. The last important exhibition during her lifetime was organized by the Tate Gallery, London, in 1968. . . . At present, the distinguished art historian Sir Alan Bowness, the artist's son-in-law, is working on the first volume of the *official* biography.

The Wildenstein exhibition marks the first time Hepworth's work has been shown in New York since 1979. How many New Yorkers are aware of the name of the woman who created one of the most successful public sculptures in Manhattan—the 21-foot-high bronze *Single Form* (1962-63), commissioned as a memorial to Secretary-General Dag Hammarskjöld and unveiled in 1964 at the United Nations Headquarters? Perhaps the situation has improved somewhat since I drove past the sculpture in the late 1970s and mentioned to my daughter Anna that I had met the artist on one occasion. The taxi driver quipped knowingly: "She's Turkish . . . it's the latest thing.". . .

From an early age, Hepworth's imagination was intoxicated by the landscape of her native Yorkshire, which was almost mystical in its intensity. She shared with Turner, Constable, Samuel Palmer, and Wordsworth a love of landscape that is often thought to define the quintessential "Englishness" of English art. The most lyrical and poetic of all her writings are descriptions of landscape—the landscape of Yorkshire, of Cornwall, and of Greece. On the one hand, she perceives the separateness of the powerful sculptural forms and shapes; on the other, she herself *becomes* the landscape. . . .

A Note on the Sculpture from the Estate
by Alan Bowness
Excerpt from Pace catalogue

. . . Hepworth was, and always remained, a carver. She loved to shape the wood or stone with the tools in her own hands. She made very few drawings for sculpture, or maquettes (unlike Henry Moore) because she always said that she could envisage the form when she looked at the block of wood or stone. . . . She had a special affinity for the material of her sculpture, responding to the organic nature of wood with its innate quality of tree growth. Each stone also had its color and texture, and its sense of growth, albeit infinitely slow.

She always continued to carve (three quarters of her 579 works are carvings) but just over halfway through her career, in the mid 1950s, she began working in bronze as well. There were several reasons for this. She sensed the fragility and the limitations of wood and stone, and wanted to work on a larger scale. She had also come to feel that her sculpture was often best seen in an outdoor landscape or garden setting, and bronze alone is suitable for this. . . .

Hepworth's bronze sculptures are either versions of carvings, translated into a more permanent material, or what she called "free forms" which can only exist in the medium of bronze. The possibilities of the material fascinated her—she found that she could make forms that were more open and fluid than anything she had done in wood or stone. Cutting and bending a sheet of metal and stringing it was a part of the constructivist element in her work—she had after all been a close friend and associate of Gabo who lived in Hampstead and St. Ives in the 1930s and 1940s. And then she found a way of making the bronze without modeling—first constructing an armature, and then building up and carving down the plaster until she reached the shape and surface she required. . . .

In the final years of her life she was exploring the possibilities of multipart sculpture, often constructed out of discrete parts and not always constricted by one definitive arrangement. The nine part *Family of Man* (1970) is the major example of this new development, presented either as a group or as separate figures. . . .

LUCAS SAMARAS

October 25 – 30 November, 1996

KISS KILL

PERVERTED GEOMETRY

SELF-ABSORPTION

INEDIBLES

"LET THEM EVANESCE, THESE SWIRLING ASSO-CIATIONS WITH ONLY PETITE VARIATIONS AND EFFETE MALLEABILITY, FOR A FEW PERCHED NERVOUSLESS MINUTES WHILE I TAKE A BRAIN BREATH. DON'T TOUCH MY THINKING OR IT WILL BECOME A GREASE-SOAKED TIREDNESS," SAID WAITINGMAN TO NO ONE IN PARTICULAR OTHER THAN HIMSELF, SITTING FIDGETLESS WITH A TYPEWRITER BETWEEN HIS THIGHS WAITING DESPERATELY BUT POLITELY FOR A SPECK OF EMOTIONAL INTELLECTUAL ELECTRIC SHOCK TO FIND ITSELF IMPALED YET PALSIEDLY ACTIVE ON THE SPOTLESS TOILET-CLEAN YIELD-ING TYPEWRITER PAPER. . . . ALTHOUGH HE COULD MANIPULATE AT WILL HIS AWARENESS SELF OVER OR THROUGH ANY PART OF HIS BODY OR ACTIONS, HE DISMALLY REALIZED EARLY THAT HIS THINKING SELF WAS A FREE AGENT WHO COULD COME AND GO UNAN-NOUNCED, AND THE TOPMOST HE COULD DO WAS TO SET TRAPS FOR IT OR PRETEND NOT TO CARE, SHREWDLY KEEPING ON THE ALERT AN EARLY THINKING WARNING SYSTEM. TO HIM-SELF HE WASN'T A PARTICULARLY GLOOMY MAN THOUGH HE FOUND IT REFRESHING DE-FYING COMIC TO TALK OF GRUESOME THINGS. IF YOU WERE TO ASK HIM WHAT HE WAS DO-ING, THAT BEING THE FIRST THING ANYONE ASKED HIM, HE'D TELL YOU HE WAS WATCHING HIS HANDS OR WASHING HIS SOCKS OR THINK-ING OF YOU, OR NOTHING IN PARTICULAR, BUT IF HE ASKED THE SAME QUESTION TO HIM-SELF IT WOULD MORE OFTEN THAN NOT BROIL-BOIL DOWN TO THE FACT THAT HE WAS WAITING FOR DEATH. IT IS NOT POSSIBLE TO KNOW THE SPECIFIC OR GENERAL TIME THAT THIS WAITING BEGAN. IT COULD HAVE BEEN

WHEN AFTER JUGGLING THE WORD DEATH FOR MANY YEARS AS A CHILD ADOLESCENT AND YOUNG ADULT AND LETTING IT DROP BECAUSE OF ITS FEAR POTENTIAL, HE FINALLY GRABBED IT, ANALYZED IT, MONTAGED IT WITH THE DEATH OF SOMEONE HE KNEW AND BEGAN TO REALIZE THE INEVITABILITY OF HAVING TO CONFRONT THIS THING THAT WAS SOMEDAY DOWNING HIM. . . . HE WAS TRYING IN HIS WAY TO DETERRIFY AGING. ALSO HE WAS BEGINNING TO ATTRIBUTE TO DEATH EMBELLISHMENTS THAT HE FORMERLY FOUND IN LOVE. HE HAD PRETTY MUCH DONE EVERYTHING THERE WAS TO DO AND WHAT HE DIDN'T DO HE EXPERIENCED READING OR SEEING. THERE WAS NOTHING ELSE BIG ENOUGH THAT WAS COMING TO HIM OTHER THAN DEATH, AND IF THERE WAS GOING TO BE NO SATISFAC-TION AFTER IT OR BEYOND IT NOW WAS THE TIME TO SQUEEZE SOME OF THE MYSTERY OF ITS PARTS, ITS POSSESSIVENESS. . . .WHEN HE WAS WITH PEOPLE HE SWITCHED INTO THE HIGHGEAR POODLE TITILATION OF TRIVIAL WAITING FOR A CONVOLUTED CONVERSATION, WAITING FOR A NICE VIEW, WAITING FOR UNVOMITABLE FOOD, WAITING FOR A DRINK . . . WAITING FOR DARKNESS, WAITING FOR EXHAUSTION, WAITING FOR SLEEP, WAITING FOR SUBLIMATION, WAITING FOR FRESHNESS, WAITING FOR EXUBERANCE, WAITING TO BE WANTED, WAITING TO TO BE ALONE, WAITING FOR AN AMELIORATION, WAITING FOR THE RIGHT APARTMENT, THE PROCESS OF WAITING HEAVILY ABSORBED MOST OF HIS TIME. HE TURNED ON THE TYPEWRITER AND TYPED THE WORD waiting. . . .

BONNARD ROTHKO
COLOR AND LIGHT

by Bernice Rose
Excerpt from Pace catalogue

Two men, two artists, Pierre Bonnard and Mark Rothko, each with very different stories to tell: Bonnard enclosed himself in place, seeking safety at home in the very geography of his culture; Rothko, an emigrant to a foreign land, carried the "geography" of his culture within him. Each worked from deeply engraved memories both of his own culture and one that came to be shared; each in his own way lost a world. To realize these memories as visual art—painting—both became participants in artistic revolution. They are ultimately united by the idea that color in itself—abstract color—functions as the direct path to emotion, and emotion, flooding the painting with the light of a revelation, opens the way to imagery—to the idea that "whatever is painted lives exclusively through the life of painting."[1] Bonnard's story traces and retraces the path of of the liberation of color; his gift to Rothko—and Rothko's debt to him—is the realization of that liberty. . . .

Bonnard's last exhibition in New York opened in December 1946 and ran through January 1947, the month of his death. It was a small exhibition, with fifteen paintings, shown in a gallery that was well-known at the time, but has since closed, the Bignou Gallery on Madison Avenue. Rothko may well have looked at Bonnard earlier with his friend, the painter Milton Avery, but this

time there seems to have been an immediate reaction: the leap into color. In the paintings he began in that winter of 1946–47, now called Multiforms, Rothko's color patches appear to take up details of Bonnard's paintings and enlarge them, transforming Bonnard's tendency to free the colored paint gesture from object description into a kind of abstraction. For instance, compare the color forms in Rothko's *Untitled* (1948) with the color forms in the ground in front of a characteristic Bonnard, *Large Reclining Nude* (1927). This selection of "abstract" areas from Bonnard was one aspect of what Rothko took away with him from that exhibition. He also took away the sensation of brilliant color as the source of light. In short, he was confronted with a language of light and color that spoke directly to the emotions—and directly through the emotions to the soul. . . .

Rothko also came away with a memory of light that was abstract, since it expanded to fill space beyond the particular representation and even beyond the planes containing the representation. Rothko immediately expanded the scale of the gesture, thus expanding the scale of the individual color areas to accord with what appears to have been his impression of the expansive sensation of Bonnard's color. The irregularity of Rothko's forms also seems to have been a result of looking at Bonnard's more complexly executed color areas and generalizing them. This expansion of scale of color strokes into color areas has the effect of making the color and the corresponding light vibration even more intense than those of Bonnard: they become blatantly the subject. . . .

During this time, Rothko came increasingly to feel that "the familiar identity of things has to be pulverized in order to destroy the finite associations with which our society increasingly enshrouds every aspect of our environment."[26] In the winter of 1947–48, Jackson Pollock made his historic breakthrough, producing his first drip paintings and clearing the way for his contemporaries. Rothko's own catalytic "moment" continued for about two years. This extended period of exploration seems to have been resolved after another encounter with Bonnard during the latter's 1948 retrospective at The Museum of Modern Art. The exhibition at the museum was larger than the Bignou show, with painting after painting creating a strong picture of Bonnard's work. The early Multiforms had taken note of Bonnard's color strategies, the irregular outlines of his forms, and to some extent the brushwork; Rothko had concentrated on Bonnard, plane by color plane, treating each as a whole painting, concentrating on the forms as abstractions. He appears to have overlooked the overall structural scheme of rectangular enclosures. But in the 1948 show, Rothko does appear to have noticed how Bonnard's color forms were "contained" by the planar enclosures structuring the picture, depicted as windows, doorways, and mirrors. The windows and doorways opened onto planes moving back into space, while the mirrors reversed the process, projecting deep space forward onto the plane, even forward of it. Rothko responded to the new stimuli by refining the rendering of his color patches, enlarging and simplifying his composition until what had been the last remnants of referential forms were subsumed into paint and light. His color sense itself seems to have become richer and more refined by his re-encounter with Bonnard. . . .

1. Pierre Schneider, *Matisse* (New York: Rizzoli, 1984), p. 226.
26. Mark Rothko, "The Romantics Were Prompted," *Possibilities 1* (Winter 1947–48), p. 84.

This was the most recent in a series of exhibitions, begun in 1978, devoted to the oeuvre of Mark Rothko in all its multifaceted complexity: "The Seagram Mural Project," (1979); "The Surrealist Years," (1981); "The Classic Paintings," (1983); "The Dark Paintings 1969–1970," (1985); "Multiforms," (1989); and "The Last Paintings," (1994). "Bonnard and Rothko: Color and Light" examined Bonnard's psychological use of color and its influence on Mark Rothko's search for pure color to convey content.

ELIZABETH MURRAY

RECENT PAINTINGS/GREENE STREET

May 1 – 20 June, 1997

An Interview With Elizabeth Murray

by Joan Simon

Excerpt from Pace catalogue

E.M. . . . . I don't know what it is with the shoes. It's a very exciting kind of shape, and they lend themselves to so many variations. I guess there's a kind of narrative—I know I said that once, probably to Kathy Halbreich because the first two shoe paintings were in the show she did.* I wasn't thinking about it very specifically then.

What is it about the shoes? It just has to get worked out—but I think it is very much about the past. There is something about shoes that really is about your history: it's the way you relate to them in terms of time. They are very appealing things for people, for me anyway—I save certain shoes where I've walked certain places. And there's something funny and sad about shoes. Very sad. Like the piles of shoes in some of the Holocaust pictures. The way an old shoe lying around on the street is left. The image has a death connection, an end of something.

J.S. You've spoken before of Cézanne.

E.M. Philip Guston would be the artist I would think about more than Cézanne. When I was doing one of the shoe paintings it hit me like a ton of bricks just how much I owe to Guston. I'd never really thought about it until I started the shoe paintings.

J.S. In what way?

E.M. A way that he flattened the shoe out and used the sole and the heel just as shapes. He found that shape and he really used it in a way that made the eye twist around a little bit more or free it from a situation in a picture. But it's the same thing. I think it's the same interest, which, corny as it may sound, is a formal part of it. How the heel and sole fit together and the sole is the extended heel.

. . . There's always formal stuff in my work. It's the constant. Without the formal considerations, it would be like an automobile without a motor, a body without a soul. That line is just the right line. Why do I want it there? What does it do to the whole thing? But I think that's the visual part of it, the sensate part that makes it work. And it has to work with me first. I will literally change a mark 60 different times, change a color because you're getting it right, but it's an open-ended right.

. . . Cartoons were the first art I saw. I loved them. I had comic books for the pictures more than for the little sto-ries. In was the color, the line, the movement. I had favorite artists: the particular Disney artist that drew Donald Duck, with a lot of detail. Chester Gould's Dick Tracy, Superman. There were also Disney films that opened with a cartoon paintbrush, dripping paint, and then painting the real scene opening up the story. So the images, the shapes, the movement more from the flat, strip comics, the movement frame-to-frame than the films—are all there from the beginning and it's so unconscious to have absorbed so much. In the '70s when my work was called cartoony I resisted it, but it's so much a part of what I am. Also, I realized, looking at that book of Picasso's sketch-books, how interested he was in early French cartoons, and when you look at his stuff, the graphics are all there.

J.S. . . . . You have always described yourself as working alone, and as separate from what's going on around you.

E.M. I think it's totally contradictory things that I have to say about it. I really do like the separation. I don't want the work to be in a sense like any one else's. I used to work hard at that, work harder at that than I do now. I don't think I think about it any more that much. But I always feel like, everything else I see, especially something that provokes me, whether I like it or not, I'm completely influenced by it. That goes for contemporary work but I also love history. I love and try to use all that stuff back there.

I think I use a lot of ideas about clumsiness and awkward shapes coming together and line from Cézanne. I think that's something I really learned from how he painted objects. How to—and this is a very physical thing—how to really paint very lushly and elegantly and then cut the one shape off with a line and go into another color. That's completely just observing how he does that, looking at his paintings so much. It's about how physically he worked on them.

I think I learned a lot from Picasso, and a lot from Pollock. Form Picasso how to make every shape and every image about the paint at the same time. And how to paint a lot of different ways. A good way to keep things interesting is to paint a lot of different ways in a painting, but pick one way that becomes the whole thing and have the little separate ways go off into corners and stuff. And de Kooning has been really, really important. Again, it's how to paint.

How to use a big brush, and a knife, and put the paint on the surface and get it to roll into something. So far everything I've said is paint is image. I've learned a lot from Susan [Rothenberg]—like bringing image up, watching how she uses and builds up the strokes and makes them work for her to build an image. . . .

J.S. I wonder if you knew Lee Bontecou's work or Yayoi Kusama's? I've never seen these artists mentioned in context with your work, and yet, it seems to me, given the timing of your arrival in New York in '67, and the kinds of things you may have been looking at, there are affinities with that they were doing and what you've tried to do. Maybe more than with the cool surfaces of Pop and Minimal work at the time. The sexuality, the construction piecing parts to whole.

E.M. I never saw Kusama's work, believe it or not, until two years ago when Lynn Zelevansky, who was then working as curator at MoMA, talked to me about her when I was doing a show for the Modern.** And I was blown away by it. I couldn't believe she had been working all the time and I had no idea about her. Bontecou. Yes, I don't know why I haven't mentioned her. I saw her work when I first came to New York—no before I moved to New York, at the Albright-Knox when I was teaching in Buffalo [1965–67]. And I think those sculptures are just fierce, they are amazing. Now that's an example of looking at something and it's like you've grafted it onto your body or something. I could never verbalize what an incredible influence. But you can see. The holes, the interior space. I think when I started to put holes in the painting that's where it came out of.

J.S. . . . I'm curious to know what you were looking for when you were rummaging the archives and through the storage [at The Museum of Modern Art], and if what you found turned out to be something different.

E.M. When I started the only idea I had was "women's work at the Modern." To dredge up what they had. At the time WAC [Women's Action Coalition] was going on. I was so excited to be part of this women's group, and so much of what was going on then. When Kirk [Varnedoe] asked me to do a show at the Modern, I thought it was so simple and obvious an idea. But he really liked it. It had never been done before.

J.S. What was the show called?

E.M. "Artist's Choice: Modern Women." I was going to call it Mamas at MoMA. Until I started to do it, I didn't have a grip on what I was digging for. I started to see these women who appeared and disappeared, came and went. There was one woman, Kay Sage, and I remember, there was one little typewritten page in her dossier even though she's better known than many of the others. Her work was very interesting. I included a painting of hers in the show, a gorgeous very spare abstraction, with a bullet-hole in it. Some of the

women were really very strong figures: Baroness Elsa von Freytag Loringhoven; Hannah Höch—I hadn't known her work much. I kept pulling more and more people in from the past, and then more and more in the hanging.

To make a long story short, what I didn't know I'd get out of it when I started—I was just kind of fishing—was how fast people come and go. How fast they are forgotten. The men too. There were hundreds of Tchelitchews; hundreds of works by Ilya Bolotowsky. Most of all, you just see—you're a speck. It's interesting and humbling.

J.S. You once said, "My paintings are all about being on the wall and coming off the wall. The tension between the painting and the wall." Now, it seems the wall is such a given, such a necessary part of the process, that the tension, or the equation is more heavily weighted toward the painting than the wall. And it seems that the pressure on and from within them therefore is even greater.

E.M. What's happened is that I am thinking about what I do in such a different way. I am not sure you should ever listen to what artists say about their work; most of the things sound ridiculous to me, a couple of years later. They don't make any sense any more. And I'm not sure why that is, except that I think the act of painting, and making art brings up so many constant contradictions. You're constantly contradicting yourself within the same painting. It's like, you do something, you take it out. Or you write something, and you go back and all of a sudden because you wrote that the exact opposite thoughts float up. That's what art making starts to do. And then you have to start making a choice. And the painting, or whatever it is, the essay, or novel, is in the end, just a choice. All it stands for is a choice that you made at a significant time in your life. And then you go on to make different choices.

Notes

* "Elizabeth Murray: Painting and Drawings," organized by Kathy Halbreich and Sue Graze for The Dallas Museum of Art and the Albert and Vera List Visual Arts Center, Massachusetts Institute of Technology, 1987.

** "Artist's Choice—Elizabeth Murray, Modern Women," curated by Elizabeth Murray. The Museum of Modern Art, New York, June 20–August 22, 1995.

This interview was conducted January 20, 1997 with follow up conversations in February and March of 1997.

Joan Simon is a Paris-based writer and curator. Author of Susan Rothenberg *and the forthcoming* Ann Hamilton *(both Abrams), Simon is General Editor of* Bruce Nauman *and its catalogue raisonné (Walker Art Center/D.A.P.) and Editor of* Joan Jonas: Documents *(P.A.J./Johns Hopkins) now in preparation. She contributes regularly to* Art in America.

Rain Painting, 1996
oil on canvas on wood, 82 × 72 × 9"

555

ROBERT RAUSCHENBERG

ARCADIAN RETREATS

September 19 – 18 October, 1997

by Bernice Rose
Excerpt from Pace catalogue

Robert Rauschenberg is again on the track of heroes and gods. . . . In this most recent work, *Arcadian Retreats*, Rauschenberg, the hero of his own imagination, is on a parallel quest, again following the "poetic cipher's of his self's self-discovery as it travels among the objects of the material world and inserts itself into the chaotic, arbitrary world of nature."[1] This time Rauschenberg's journey retraces the conquests of the Macedonian hero, Alexander the Great, through the multilayered ruins and contemporary incarnations of the ancient Greek city-states of Asia Minor. . . .

The aesthetic instant in which past and present meet on equal terms is the focal point of Rauschenberg's cosmos, his version of Paradise. Rauschenberg is a visionary of the material world, rescuing all sorts of detritus, the dead and discarded, the disregarded, the broken and ruined; they are the raw stuff of his work—his version of working from nature. His is a landscape of fragments organized according to a self-made law of media variation. Rauschenberg has taken art's material operations as the object of investigation: he is absorbed by the *making* of the making of a work of visual art. . . .

For the *Arcadian Retreats*, Rauschenberg has chosen an ideal form of affective fragment as a model, the ruins of wall paintings, usually described in more familiar terms as "frescoes," after the primary technique in which wall painting was historically executed. . . . But in the now ruined state of most frescoes, the medium incorporates virtues close to Rauschenberg's heart: formal transparency, in its many layers of stories exposed to one another; narrative and authorial opacity, for the original specific meanings of frescoes have often been lost with the passage of time, as has the distinction among hands. To the modern eye, these complex chronicles read either as ravishing formal fragments or pieces of puzzles whose secret messages are to be deciphered. Fresco thus becomes a perfect formal ground for imprinting the constantly shifting field of memory and identity—for the change of substance of material form and ideas; by nature *and* device, wall painting is transparent to time. . . .

As always, Rauschenberg's camera is the initial study means, a machine for copying, for duplicating the world of appearances. Sophisticated developing and printing techniques facilitate the rapid production of numerous replicas—imitations of imitations. The memory of the image inheres to the photographic matrix. And unlike traditional techniques, in which each day's work (a portion of the drawing) had to be transferred to the fresh plaster, continuity is a function of selection, not of time, as Rauschenberg chooses from a profusion of images. . . .

Rauschenberg is a genius at pastiche, and in this case reality presents a ready-made pastiche. As the narrative is tracked erratically figure by figure, panel by panel, through numerous repetitions, reversals, changes of scale, and shifts of focus that duplicate and reduplicate the world of appearances, the elements and layers of reality appropriated by Rauschenberg in his photographic rovings get rearranged to tell the story of "reality"—of images—living through one another more efficiently.

1. Bernice Rose, *Robert Rauschenberg: Anagrams*, exh. cat. (New York: PaceWildenstein, 1996), p. 7.

Estuary, 1996
fresco, 74½ × 75"

On Hold, 1996, fresco, 6'2½" × 9'3"
© Untitled Press, Inc./Licensed by VAGA, New York, NY

KIKI SMITH

RECONSTRUCTING THE MOON
GREENE STREET
September 27 – 25 October, 1997

Reflections on Mondrian/Reinhardt
by Arne Glimcher
Excerpt from Pace catalogue

. . . By the mid-sixties I had moved my gallery from Boston to 9 West 57th Street in New York and began showing the work of two Los Angeles artists, Bob Irwin and Larry Bell, whose immaculate presentations were alien to the 10th Street sensibility of New York's art scene. Both Irwin and Bell loved Ad's work and were influenced by his achievements. It was through their friendship with him that mine began. He came to see their shows, was responsive to their aesthetic, and was unique among the New York artists in his encouragement of my enterprise. Soon after, I was spending at least one afternoon a month in Ad's studio. Often as we talked, he continued to paint: multiple layers of pigment, extended to transparency by turpentine, applied like layers of gossamer laminated miraculously by vanishing brushstrokes. During this precise process, the conversation never faltered. He was a great humorist, and many of his art historical edicts have been misunderstood or quoted out of context. Reinhardt, a cynic who yearned to believe, was not the black monk art historians would have us believe; he was genuinely funny, never losing perspective on the pomposity of the art world and his place in it. Ad asked me to come in during the installation of the 1966–67 Jewish Museum exhibition. His idea was to show a single room of $60 \times 60"$ "Ultimate" or "Timeless" paintings, but Alan Solomon convinced him that a retrospective was necessary to better understand the origins of these perplexing works. Throughout the exhibition *The New Yorker* regularly ran cartoons of characters standing in front of solid black rectangles, making witty comments. Typical of Ad's perverse humor, the last paintings were presented first, inverting the retrospective by relegating all of the early work to the second floor in the hope that people would be so saturated by the black paintings that they would never make it upstairs. His paintings were small in comparison with his contemporaries' and, tongue-in-cheek, he combined four $60 \times 60"$ paintings to create a work of Abstract Expressionistic scale within the exhibition. The intersecting lines of the separate canvases dominated the painting experience, somewhat mitigating the surface phenomenon. When the exhibition came down, the paintings were disassembled and once more became four separate works. . . .

Ad shared his "history of art" with me, and a major figure in that history was Mondrian. Although he was already firmly in my own pantheon of heroes, Ad enlarged my knowledge of Mondrian and transformed my appreciation of him; from a historical presence he became a contemporary force. Years later, Rita Reinhardt was instrumental in helping me to arrange a Mondrian exhibition at The Pace Gallery entitled *Mondrian: The Process Works.*[1] It was an exhibition of Mondrian's drawings and his charcoal studies on canvas, underdrawings for what would have become paintings. The process of translation from color, only imagined in these black-and-white charcoals, into color that was so concrete and specific, was little known at that time. A set of drawings on notebook pages and cigarette packs that were studies for paintings, some black-and-white, with color notations indicated by initials, made it possible to imagine that process. Within the drawings was the 1926 plan for the *Salon de Madame B. . . . à Dresden*, an ideal interior environment Mondrian had described in a text entitled *Home–Street–City*. After reading it, we decided to construct the salon as the centerpiece for the exhibition.[2]

Clearly, Reinhardt responded to Mondrian as one might a mentor, reacting against some aspects of the work, assimilating others, but always inspired by the potential of roads not taken. During the forties, Reinhardt's art evolved as he worked his way through various ideas then current in the art world, including the dominant influences of Picasso and the Surrealists (many of whom, like Mondrian, had fled World War II to shelter in New York). In fact, Reinhardt found his own way by closely examining the tradition of abstract art, working through Stuart Davis' jumpy interlocking forms, as in *Number 30*, 1938, and Paul Klee's mosaic-like compositions of saturated color, exemplified by *Abstract Painting*, 1940. Mondrian was a living force in the New York of the forties. Moving in the same circles, Reinhardt met Mondrian and visited Mondrian's studio. Mondrian made the rounds of the galleries and saw Reinhardt's *Abstract Painting*, 1940; he commented to Harry Holtzman that it could have been larger.[3] In 1944, Mondrian was reported to have admired a collage of Reinhardt's he had seen at the Artist's Gallery. It was "made of deep-dyed papers which suggest window frames in their arrangement; neon lights in their color."[4]

Reinhardt discussed his beliefs in *Art as Art*, and among his personal papers is a draft of an article written for the *New Masses,* "The Fine Artist and The War Effort," in 1942 or 1943 (not published then).

MONDRIAN REINHARDT
INFLUENCE AND AFFINITY

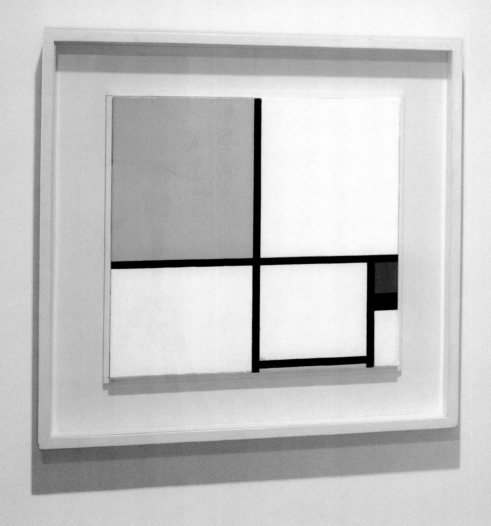

In this article, as Margit Rowell noted, he cited Mondrian's art as "an exemplary solution" to the problem of how abstract art could embody moral, social, and political concerns.[5] Reinhardt himself did not believe the ideology that art could solve the problems of life, and indeed was against art as illustration, however abstract. His reading of Mondrian's work became the key to the realization of his own aspirations for an art as vital as life itself. Reinhardt wrote:

> Consider the recent Mondrian exhibition. These paintings, sensuous and concrete manifestations of a certain kind of thinking and understanding . . . demanded in their limited and concentrated area direct, first-hand experience for its appreciation . . . The intellectual and emotional content was in precisely what the lines, colors and spaces told, and not in anything else (the form and content being one).

> . . . [T]his work claims to have been the most objective approach possible—the recognition of the limitation of the medium and the development of individual sensibility to lines, colors, spaces, in this instance, a preference for the horizontal and vertical lines as the stronger, and for the primary colors as the most dynamic . . . but the concrete result, not the philosophical pretension does the trick. What greater challenge today (in subjective and two dimensions) to disorder and insensitivity; what greater propaganda for integration than this emotionally intense, dramatic division of space?[6]

In the years that followed, Reinhardt created an art of harmony and balance no less emotionally intense than Mondrian's. With access to all of Mondrian's historical work as well as his contemporary New York achievements, by the early 1950s Reinhardt decided that his path was not to be the dynamic asymmetrical "compositional" tensions taken by Mondrian in the 1920s, but rather one of symmetry and balance suggested by Mondrian's 1912–17 work and especially his floating color planes of 1917.

From there Reinhardt had to find his own way to invent the structure of art for himself. Through Mondrian, Reinhardt realized the importance of format: of the thing as thing, of pushing to the limit of where one had decided to go. Mondrian renounced the modular grid; Reinhardt embraced it—as a deductive structure—while renouncing its black lines. Mondrian's color was an element of his dynamic balance, endowing each unit with maximum intensity in a non-hierarchical whole: the equilibrium expressed the underlying laws of art, and art's ultimate absorption into life itself.

Slowly, Reinhardt reduced his palette, to red, blue, and black monochromes composed of rectangles, each element interdependent with the others, and arranged in a non-hierarchical format. Earlier he had painted a "brushstroke" work of shifting planes, *Number 107*, 1950, in white pigment on a white ground. In 1954, after the red and blue monochromes, and prior to the black paintings, Reinhardt again painted a small monochromatic cruciform canvas in white, before renouncing that option forever. Finally, he reached his "ultimate" painting, as he often called it, the last painting that anyone could make: that black painting which seemed to renounce color yet was really about the density of color and, while it renounced illusionism, was all about light and surface. Reinhardt's painting celebrated painting, "art as art," in an art of extreme beauty, of perfect balance, as serene and focused as a mantra. It was about the will to see deeply, extend visual perceptions past the immediate, and integrate time itself as an interdependent element of the painting's experience.

1. Through Rita Reinhardt I met Harry Holtzman, Mondrian's friend and protector in New York, who as the legatee of the Mondrian Estate had inherited these drawings. Rita helped me persuade Holtzman to show these at Pace.

2. Piet Mondrian, *Neo-Plasticisme: De woning–de straat–de stad. (The dwelling–the street–the city)* in *i 10*, first issue (January 1927). A French version appeared in *Vouloir*, no. 25 (early 1927) as, *Le Home–la rue–la cité*, illustrated with Mondrian's design for an interior, *Salon de Madame B. . . . à Dresden*, which was not executed until the Pace exhibition. For the text in English, see Harry Holtzman and Martin S. James, *The New Art–The New Life: The Collected Writings of Piet Mondrian* (Boston: G.K. Hall & Co., 1986), p. 211. In the article Mondrian wrote: "Roughness, rustic appearance (typical of materials in their natural state) must be removed. Therefore: 1. Surfaces will be smooth and bright, which will also relieve the heaviness of the material. This is one of the many cases where Neo-plastic art agrees with hygiene, which demands smooth, easily cleaned surfaces. . . . Home and street must be viewed as the city, as a unity formed by planes composed in neutralizing opposition that destroys all exclusiveness. The same principle must govern the interior . . . {it must be} a construction of planes in color and noncolor unified with the furniture and household objects which will be nothing in themselves but which will function as constructive elements of the whole."
Holtzman lent me some of Mondrian's paint tubes, which he had carefully kept, and I took then to American Cyanamid, which matched the colors, manufacturing just enough of them in *Formica* to construct the room to Mondrian's specifications and his vision.

3. In conversation with Rita Reinhardt, September 1997.

4. Maude Reilly, "Fifty-Seventh Street in Review," *Art Digest*, 18 (February 1944), p. 20. The work referred to is *Study for a Painting*, Collection of the Museum of Modern Art, New York, Gift of the Artist.

5. Margit Rowell, *Ad Reinhardt and Color*, exh. cat. (New York: The Solomon R. Guggenheim Museum, 1980), p. 13.

6. Ad Reinhardt, "The Fine Artist and the War Effort," in Barbara Rose, ed., *Art as Art: The Selected Writings of Ad Reinhardt.* (New York: The Viking Press, 1975; reprint, Berkeley and Los Angeles: University of California Press, 1991), pp. 176–77.

JULIAN SCHNABEL

PORTRAIT PAINTINGS/GREENE STREET

October 31 – 13 December, 1997

Portrait of Vito Maria Schnabel (age 10), 1997
oil and resin on canvas, 108 × 102"

PABLO PICASSO

WORKS FROM THE ESTATE AND SELECTED LOANS/LOS ANGELES

January 22 – 7 March, 1998

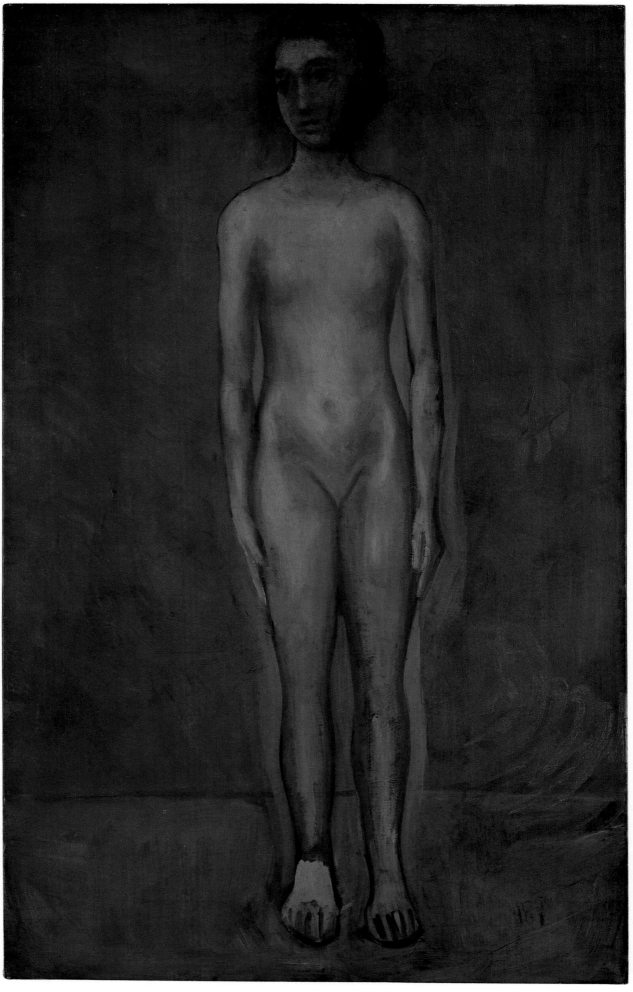

Nu debout, 1902
oil on canvas, 43½ × 27⅝"
© 2001 Estate of Pablo Picasso / Artists Rights Society (ARS),
New York

GEORGE CONDO

COLLAGE PAINTINGS/GREENE STREET
January 30 – 7 March, 1998

Interview with Michael FitzGerald
Excerpt from Pace catalogue
November 9, 1997

M.F. Most of the paintings you have shown in recent years have been focused on single characters. These new works are seemingly opposite. They are very complex compositions, with a wide variety of figures worked into many different materials. Yet, the two groups of work are closely related.

G.C. By taking some of the drawings and the sketches that came as studies for those concrete paintings and reconsidering them, I saw all kinds of new possibilities that led to these collage paintings.

M.F. Viewers can pick out the previous imagery if they look carefully and they follow the way you elaborate. So, in a sense the two groups of work are present in these new pictures. One just has to look for them.

G.C. The two groups of work are present in the picture. They exist separately and are integrated. In a way, it's an alternative to looking at one painting after the next. You see the entire life cycle of the series taking place in each individual canvas. I want the viewer to feel as though the image is going through the same process as the artist himself. And that it's all visible on the canvas.

M.F. One of the things I find particularly interesting about these pictures, besides the layering of imagery within them, is the range of media you used.

G.C. I think the tactility of the materials is an important factor. These paintings are like my sculptures as a painter. I've literally gone and torn the images and put them in place and then taken them off and then repositioned them, painted around them, found they would better serve a different area, and moved them. The process creates a buildup as I shift something and then am left with the residue of whatever it was I took away. And then that becomes the attaching ground for a new image, so the two of them will start combining into one another and certain permutations take place.

Sometimes I'll go with the paint directly onto the canvas and then push the drawing onto the surface. Other times, I'll turn the drawing over and on the reverse side will squeeze the tubes of paints. Quite often I'll work in

five dots on a single sheet. In the newest work, I did some gestural brushstrokes with the paint on the back and stuck that on, so those gestural brushstrokes would come through as an almost invisible color. These things are all that's behind the paper, and that's on the paper. It allows me to work on every dimension—almost like a sculpture, but with paint. . . .

The first thing I do is look back at my own work to see what it is that I've done and to see if where I left off can be enlarged, . . . And from about 1990 until about 1996, I developed a whole new group of concrete images that were ready and just right to go into this language of abstract collage once again.

M.F. If one of the sources for these new paintings is your past work, do they also draw on your contemporary experience?

G.C. These canvases are like the real place where I live. Because I see them in some way as landscapes, sort of psychological landscapes to some degree. The psychological landscapes of not only the characters within the painting but also of the creator who saw them.

M.F. So it's the environment of the studio that is projected into these paintings.

G.C. Living in New York City, I sometimes think, sure, it would be beautiful to be out in the countryside and paint nature. I'd love to go out and sit down in front of a landscape with a lake and paint the reflections and birds and all kinds of wildlife. And start describing each living thing and paint it as I see it. And then I said, well I'm in a landscape already. The landscape I live in is a landscape of ripped drawings, of paint all over the place, of pencil sketches and drawing that have been compiled, images that have been thought about and turned and twisted. And suddenly I realize that I am in the landscape, and this is my landscape, and there's no point in trying to run away. I may as well just make art of it.

JOHN CHAMBERLAIN

CHAMBERLAIN'S FAUVE LANDSCAPE / GREENE STREET
March 11 – 25 April, 1998

John Chamberlain at PaceWildenstein
by Richard Kalina
Originally published in *ART IN AMERICA*
Brant Publications, Inc., July 1998

John Chamberlain presides over what, for an artist, counts as a big industrial operation. A collagist at heart, and a highly productive one at that, he requires plenty of raw material to pick and choose from. In his case that material is automobile metal: bulky, heavy and in need of crushing, wadding, twisting, cutting and spray-painting. . . . This spring's exhibition at PaceWildenstein, titled "Chamberlain's Fauve Landscape," showed a different side of the artist's sensibility. While these new works are still constructed of his signature materials, their compositional format has changed markedly.

The show consists of two huge works (his largest to date) both of which were executed in 1997 in his Sarasota factory-studio. *The Privet* is 12 1/2 feet high, 60 feet long and a little under 2 feet in depth; while *The Hedge*, a row of 16 square units, placed parallel to each other . . . measures 4 by 4 by 50 feet. *The Privet* is composed of long upright rows of crimped, visually interlocking metal ribbons, each a few inches wide, mounted on a low rectangular base of larger crumpled pieces. The ribbons corkscrew upward, then flare out a bit at the top. Not content with mere color variation, Chamberlain loads each ribbon and base element with a mélange of juicily garish tones, patterns and spray treatments. The resulting chromatic cacophony evens itself out, and our eyes travel over the length of the piece, picking out color correspondences and runs, playing vertical rhythms against horizontal ones and reading the subtle interplay of line and volume, transparency and opacity. This is very much the way one looks at paintings, especially big, abstract field paintings.

The title of the show is to the point—the Fauves were painters, and *The Privet* is a very painterly work. It also looks remarkably like a piece of the landscape, a privet hedge, . . . casting a pattern of cool, dappled shade on the floor and wall behind it. . . .

This show marks a particularly interesting turn in the work of a prolific and inventive artist. Lively and upbeat, it seems willing to mount, if not a challenge, then at least a spirited response to the large-scale work of Frank Stella, the Minimalists and even Jackson Pollock. Chamberlain has risked forcing his vision on a format that is unsuitable to it. That he has pulled it off with such visual wit and élan is a testament to his skill, experience and ambition.

ISAMU NOGUCHI | STONES AND WATER
May 1 – 26 June, 1998

Stories of Stone
by Jeremy Strick
Excerpt from Pace catalogue

In 1969, Isamu Noguchi established a studio in the village of Mure, near the city of Takamatsu, on the Japanese island of Shikoku. Until his death in 1988, Noguchi came to Mure twice a year, staying for a period of three months each time. Over the course of a long and prolific career, Noguchi's years at Mure must be counted among the artist's most productive. Working exclusively in stone, Noguchi revisited forms and themes that had preoccupied him for decades, even as he set out in new directions, exploring materials and ideas with a remarkable freedom, assurance, and intensity.

. . . A dilapidated samurai house was found, transported to Mure, and restored to serve as Noguchi's living quarters. A sake storage house, similarly moved and reconstructed, became an exhibition space. A Japanese garden was planted, along with stands of bamboo, and high walls were erected in a traditional Japanese manner.

Noguchi's establishment of a studio in a rural setting was not without significant precedent: among Noguchi's contemporaries, David Smith comes quickly to mind. Like Smith, Noguchi chose a location of considerable natural beauty and relative isolation, a site that discouraged casual visitors and that could suggest transcendent natural and (especially for Noguchi) even cultural values.

But the most important feature of Noguchi's studio at Mure—and also its most significant resemblance to Smith's Bolton Landing—arose from Noguchi's decision to people his new environment with his sculpture. Some of this work he set out on the hill above his home, some in the house itself; many objects were placed in an enclosed yard, while others remained in the studio building. Among the works, some were monumental and clearly site-specific; others were placed only provisionally in the yard as an inspiration for new ideas and new works. During the twenty years he spent at Mure, Noguchi labored intensively to create a private world that both corresponded to his aesthetic ideals and would provide an appropriate setting for the generation of his art.

Yet the two decades during which Noguchi worked at Mure also marked the period of his greatest success as a public artist. Realizing commissions for museums and universities, corporations and cities, he memorably transformed the perception of numerous public spaces. A unique set of talents, experiences, and ambitions contributed to Noguchi's success. Close to a num-

ber of architects and attuned to their sensibilities, he understood his role to be that of a shaper of space as well as a maker of objects. Influenced, perhaps, by the sets he had designed for dance productions, Noguchi viewed space not as a static entity, but rather as a medium through which movement occurs. He was able to address an exceptional range of registers, producing work by turns spectacular or meditative, as the nature of a particular site and commission dictated. Moreover, although Noguchi was committed to preserving traditional techniques, he was also free in his use of new materials and technologies. Above all, he was committed to the idea and purpose of public art, eagerly seeking commissions in order to enrich and even transform the daily life of those who came into contact with his work.

The environmental concerns Noguchi explored in his public art were mirrored in the private world he created for himself at Mure. Indeed, Mure itself can be seen as Noguchi's most complex and significant environmental work. And yet this painstakingly created environment was not intended to function as a finite, fixed monument. Rather, it served as an inspiration for creation and experimentation. It was a setting in which different aspects of the sculptures were revealed as they moved in and out of studio, exhibition space, and yard, leading to new avenues and approaches. So even as the private environment of Mure was inspiring the planning of public parks and gardens, it more directly inspired the unique basalt and granite sculptures that emerged from the Mure studio.

The impetus to establish a studio at Mure came from a public commission. In 1966, the city of Seattle asked Noguchi to produce a monumental sculpture to be erected in a public park. Noguchi proposed an enormous ring of stone, a work he would title *Black Sun*. To carry out this commission, he required the expertise and the equipment of a master stonecarver. Friends spoke to Noguchi of the quarries and workshops near Takamatsu, and proposed that he engage the services of Masatoshi Izumi, a young man of dedication and patience whose family had established a workshop at Mure.

In a sense, Noguchi's studio at Mure can be seen as a public economic development project. The chief of Kagawa prefecture, Governor Kaneko, was involved in the selection of Izumi, and cleared away bureaucratic impediments. Kaneko hoped that Noguchi's activities at Mure would spread the fame of Takamatsu's quarries, and even more enhance the reputation of the region's craftsmen. . . .

ROBERT IRWIN

A SELECTION OF WORKS 1958 TO 1970 / GREENE STREET

May 1 – 24 July, 1998

SOL LEWITT

| **NEW WALL DRAWINGS / GREENE STREET**
September 10 – 10 October, 1998

PHILIP-LORCA DICORCIA

STREETWORK / GREENE STREET

November 18 – 16 January, 1999

Having placed his camera in a location through which people randomly pass, diCorcia documents the effects that inventive and dramatic light have on urban life. The illumination of private moments, removed from urban noise and speed, humanize city dwellers while simultaneously emphasizing their detachment from each other. For example, the two men in the detail to the right, from the work *Calcutta* (below), are highlighted and separated from the crowd by an enigmatic light source.

DiCorcia is a progenitor of the current interest in the cinematization of everyday scenes. A master at capturing a complicated picture using minimal orchestration, diCorcia creates multilayered narratives and visual complexities.

detail

Calcutta, 1998
Ektacolor print mounted to 4-ply board
24¹¹⁄₁₆ × 37⅞"

ELIZABETH MURRAY | RECENT PAINTINGS
February 12 – 13 March, 1999

Turquoise All Along

Elizabeth Murray Interviewed by Bob Holman
January 3, 1999

B.H. When you're in the passion of the work—do you use that word?

E.M. No.

B.H. What word would you use? You never talk about it.

E.M. I never talk about it, right?

B.H. That's why interviews are tough with artists.

E.M. Well, those things should not be discussed, in my opinion. I know when I became suspicious of the word "passion"—it was when I was working at the City of Lights bookstore in San Francisco selling junky romance novels. Customers would come in and ask for novels like *Pride and Passion*. And I thought that was so hilarious, but I would just keep a straight face and lead them to the latest potboilers. And there on the flyleaf would be, "A Tale of Pride and Passion!" The word passion has just never meant the same to me since then.

B.H. So you can hit that moment of passion—I'm kind of joking—could it happen right away in the morning? Does it sound like an opera?

E.M. There are no rules to when you really get it together with your work. The beginnings are always great because anything can happen. I totally enjoy the beginning. And then there is a point where the trouble begins.

B.H. The trouble?

E.M. The trouble is the thing. I mean, I love it, I love the trouble. The trouble is when the painting starts to happen. The trouble is the conflict and the difficulty, the point where I begin to direct the action. Ideas emerge and I have to make decisions, intriguing ideas. You have to paint those decisions, so you can discard them if they don't work. There are definitely bad decisions. It's the process of *making*. I'm sure it would be true if I were a writer or a musician.

I'm most happy with the painting when I can allow the things I left behind to get there to somehow continue to be present. It's hard to describe, but when you look at my paintings I think maybe you can feel it there, the past. By following the impulse to change, I have to paint over its root—and many times I can't get that back, no matter how hard I try, it's gone, music in the air, an underlying aspect that can no longer be seen, but maybe felt.

B.H. With painting, there is the application of paint to the brush, the transferal of paint from the little paper plate to the brush and then to the canvas. That's painting. But then there's squeezing the tubes and walking away from the painting and looking at it, in it, and then going over to where the paint is. When you go to pick up that tube, do you always pick up the tube you're planning to pick up?

E.M. No. Sometimes I look at the array of paints and see other possibilities. I'll think, Oh, instead of carmine, I could use bright red. Sometimes I'll stick with the carmine. Sometimes there's no question—I know what I'm using, I've got it, I just want more of it, as fast as I can get it down.

B.H. Do you ever get annoyed if you run out of a color and have to go get more?

E.M. I'm reluctant to stop painting but I like to go to the paint store. So I stop what I'm doing and go to Pearl. But if I'm open,—say I'm using cobalt turquoise, and I run out, but I have some cerulean blue, and I decide to try it—the painting takes a whole different turn. It turns out the color I wanted was cerulean. You know, maybe there are no bad decisions. Bad decisions make art. No matter how much trouble I have, I know I'm going to get there sooner or later. And then in a couple of weeks I could realize it should have been turquoise all along. It's just too cerulean, you know.

B.H. When you're there standing there, and you're looking—do you see a narrative in the painting?

E.M. I think there are definitely kinds of narratives. But it's not a narrative with a beginning and a middle and an end. The painting gets made all at once, in a way. It's always like a big stew. You add all the ingredients and then you just stir it and stir it and stir it. It's going on all at once in front of you. And I see it like other people see it, although I'm the one who has controlled it and made it. I see it all at once and then, I think, as you look at it, you see the different moments in it. A time traveler experience, maybe, spiraling, all in front of you, but you go deeper into it the longer you look at it. It takes a long time to do it. You can take it all in one quick second, unlike a novel or a movie. Well, a poem is a little different. . . .

Bob Holman is a poet; his latest CD is In With the Out Crowd *(Mouth Almighty/Mercury). He is married to Elizabeth Murray.*

ROBERT MANGOLD

RECENT ZONE PAINTINGS

March 18 – 17 April, 1999

by Nancy Princenthal
Excerpt from Pace catalogue

The biggest of the *Zone* paintings in this exhibition are monumental: 18 feet wide in one case, 27 in another. Majestic as a mountain range[1]—an allusion sustained in their curving upper contours, repeated in irregular arcs from one work to the next—they have all the poise and serenity long associated with Robert Mangold's art. The evolution within this series (which dates to 1996) and the progress of forms within each painting (and study) are logical, clear, unhurried. But the *Zone* paintings also represent a marked disruption. For the first time in thirty years, Mangold introduced areas of paint not coterminous with their supports: that is, he began to drop veils of neutral color (generally gray or pale black, and in a few cases white) over adjoining single-color panels. In doing so, he violated what was for him a last, vestigial rule of Minimalism—that shape and color (or object and image) be congruent. In a long staring contest with a compelling but arbitrary edict, the artist blinked.

And indeed made that blink a principal subject. If all of Mangold's work is in some degree reflexively illustrative of mechanisms of visual perception—if the business of viewing his paintings teaches us about the way we see—the *Zones* are the first to put those illustrations into motion, insisting on the active, time-consuming nature of visual apprehension. The neutral "zones" are executed in thinned acrylic applied with rollers, giving their surfaces a reticulation reminiscent, in some examples, of galvanized metal, in others of a theatrical scrim. These zones interrupt not only fields of unvaried color, but also the procession of penciled ellipses drawn across the fields. An analogy could be made between the *Zone* format and movie film (viewed outside a projector), the zones standing for the intervals between frames—increments of action lost to the camera but recreated in the mind to sustain the illusion of uninterrupted movement. Or, to draw a comparison from reading, the zones could be compared to renderings of the thickness of a page, making vivid a material reality and a perceptual event usually turned out of consciousness. Perhaps most pertinently, the zones suggest the frequent, involuntary, and generally unnoticed blinks that are part of normal vision—perceptual elisions that help support the optical consolidation of a full, animate, continuous world. . . .

This exhibition, with its many studies both on paper and on canvas, offers a welcome opportunity to see Mangold refining his vocabulary, calculating and recalculating the proportions and position of each ellipse, zone, and arch. What becomes clear by comparing the canvases and works on paper is not only the precision with which internal decisions are made, but also the im-

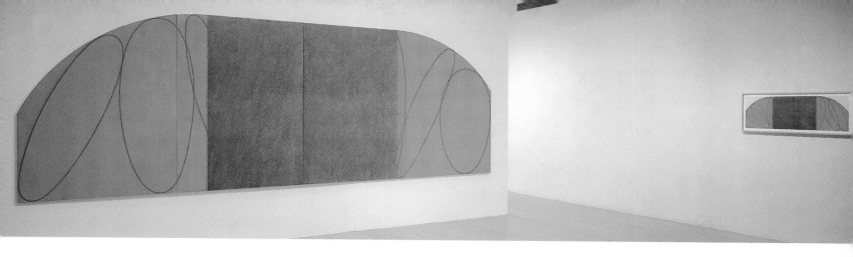

portance attached to determining each painting's overall shape. The distinctive flattened arches evoke the arc of the field of vision as represented, for instance, in 19th-century photographic panoramas, which establishes another implicit link to the experience (if not the literal representation) of landscape. They also suggest the dome of heaven, a connection examined in David Carrier's discussion of the spatial congruence between Piero della Francesca's *Madonna del Parto* and a painting from the *Curved Plane/Figure* series, which preceded the *Zones*.[4]

Mangold's own references include Matisse's several versions of the *Dance*, in particular the one at the Barnes Foundation . . . Mangold also cites Stonehenge, the massive, geometrically hewn stones which have shifted from their original positions to a measure halfway between history and geology. Among other visual relations the artist suggests are those with narrative sequences in the sculptures of the Parthenon pediment, in Giotto's fresco cycle at Padua, in the Sunday comics. And tacitly but inevitably, there is Barnett Newman, whose example has inspired Mangold's work from the beginning, and whose "zips" seem to have returned in the *Zone* paintings as dark, looming ghosts. . . .

What is most striking about the *Zone* paintings, though, is . . . their gravity. To use the language of ancient Greece with which (in the *Attic* series) Mangold began this decade, the *Zones* represent perception as a heroic epic, as a story that is amenable to intimate exercises but can also be writ large. Indeed, there is in the scale, the slow rhythms, and the black-veiled aspect of the *Zones* an invitation to consider their characterization of painting as tragic, as a medium bound to express its own fatal limitations—constraints no more nor less restrictive than those on sight itself. . . .

1. As early as 1965, when Mangold spent a summer away from the city, he found inspiration in the landscape for fundamental aspects of his work. In this early case, the curved bottoms of semicircular paintings were loosely based on drawings made after observing the spaces between hills.

4. David Carrier, "Visual Dialogue and the Acknowledgement of Particularity: Robert Mangold's Curved Plane/Figure Series," *Robert Mangold: Curved Plane/Figure Paintings*, exh. cat. (New York: PaceWildenstein, 1995), pp. 10–11.

Bookworms Harvest, 1998
vegetable dye transfer on polylaminate, 97½ × 61"
© Untitled Press, Inc./Licensed by VAGA, New York, NY

ROBERT RAUSCHENBERG

ANAGRAMS (A PUN) / GREENE STREET

March 19 – 17 April, 1999

ABOUT MY PAINTINGS

WE ALL LIVE FROM DAY TO
TO DAY. (TODAY)
WE MOVE FROM MOMENT TO MOMENT,
MOOD TO MOOD, MAKING DECISIONS
THAT CONTROL OUR ACTS, INSISTING
AND RECOGNIZING THAT FACTS
ARE CHANGING LIKE THE LIGHT
WE ARE SEEING THEM IN AND AS
OUR MOTIVATION TO LOOK.

WE ARE ALL UNIQUE, IT IS A PRECIOUS
THING TO COMPARE OURSELVES TO
NOTHING ELSE. THIS IS MY WORK-
ING ATTITUDE. I DO NOT FEEL
SHAME IN MY JOY NOR REGRET
OR FRIGHT IN HISTORY.

I TRUST IMPULSE, CREATIVE
INTUITION, AND UNMOTIVATED
SPONTANEITY, BUT ABOVE
ALL RESPONSIVE ACTION WITH
AS MANY FILTERS THAT ONE
CAN AVOID.

BOB

ALSO — TO AROUSE SECRETS OR
CELEBRATE THE UNEXPLORED
TRUTH OR LIES.

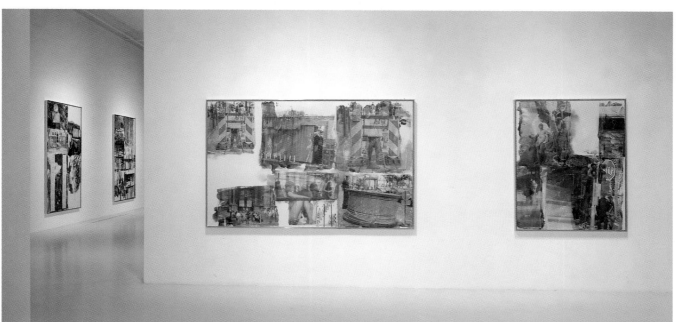

JULIAN SCHNABEL

Portrait of Stella, 1996
oil, plates and Bondo on wood, 80 × 60"

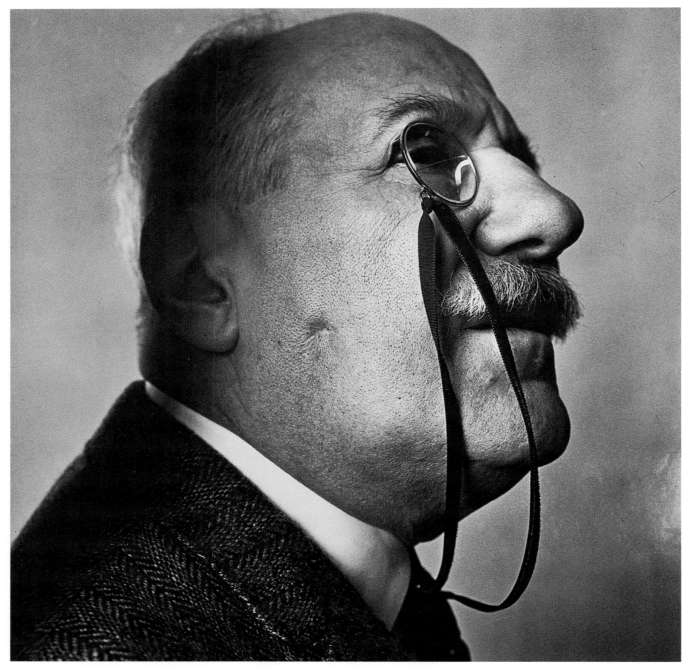

Barnett Newman (B), New York, 1966
platinum palladium print, 17 × 17"
Copyright © 1966 by Irving Penn. Courtesy of Vogue

Mirrors of Marginal Thought

by James L. Enyeart
Excerpt from Pace catalogue

Jim Dine's newest works, large-scale pigment photographs on canvas, are produced by photographic and digital technologies that continue Dine's lifelong devotion to an imaginative mix of materials—in earlier works, lithograph mixed with silkscreen or painting materials mixed with three-dimensional objects. In every case, his use of inventive materials and processes has contributed to a unique way of building and layering his images. Having said this, the question of how the work is made should be put aside because Dine's use of the most current technology is not the primary issue. Dine has made it clear in various publications and interviews that process brings him pleasure, but the real subject of the work is his "primal response" manifested in aesthetic terms. In a recent interview concerning a series of heliogravure photographs (photographs realized as etchings), he said: ". . . there's no difference in the way I choose an image in photography than I do painting. I make the decision, whether I see it after it's been shot or before. What really is important is what I get at the end."[1]

The intricate relationship that Dine has with his materials is essentially one of emotional and psychological impact. Just as certain tools represented in his paintings and drawings have become icons for what he calls "primary subjects," so too have the owl, ravens and Pinocchio puppet become icons in his current pigment canvases. All such objects are primary references to his own psyche, his emotional ties to experiences and events. Referring to them as "objects of my affection,"[2] Dine selects them because they represent memorable experiences from his life, whether in childhood or the present. The raven that appears with a little boy (Dine himself) in *North Crescent* was discovered at a taxidermist's shop in Germany a few years ago, but its importance as a visual tool has earlier resonance. As a child of three or four, he visited a zoo with his family and came across a talking raven named Jimmy. This experience, so powerful for a young child, has remained with him, cropping up in his dreams and memories and consequently in his work.

Dine cultivates his emotions and feelings as aesthetic conduits that can connect him in a transformative way to life's experiences. Whatever intensities he feels or recalls are turned into an artistic reality, mirroring the fact that physical reality itself is also made up of enigma, dreams, and memories. Since Dine works hard to stay in touch with his feelings, he was more than prepared for the adult encounter with stuffed ravens. Not every object, of course, has a direct correlation to Dine's personal history. Some, like the heart and bathrobe, are appropriated from a variety of sources and used by Dine as extensions of his artistic personality. "I have appropriated [the heart] so much," he remarked, "that it has become mine—something to hang landscape on or whatever emotionally I wanted to say or formally I wanted to say with paint." The same motive, however, explains his appropriation of the Pinocchio doll in *Me Dangling:* . . . the puppet harks back to a formative childhood issue about "bringing a talking stick to life, which represents a wonderful idea for art." The figure of Pinocchio in the current work is both emotionally charged by virtue of its Pop references and at the same time an object of veritable aesthetic play within the syntax of photographic imaging technology. . . .

Dine does not portray himself as a photographer; he calls himself a painter because that is how he started as an artist. In the realm of printmaking he has been quite open about how much he enjoys collaboration with technicians of exceptional talent "who have a lot to say technically and, therefore, help me to speak clearly." The same holds true for his interest in photography. It is not that he has any desire to become a photographer, but rather that he is excited about the timeliness of being able to use the medium in a new and innovative way: "photography, to me, is a pure, reproductive medium. It mirrors . . . it mirrors the marginal thought . . . very quickly, so that you could have many, many thoughts in a roll of film . . . it's like the way I dream."[4] . . .

1. Jim Dine, interview by Jean-Luc Monterosso, in *Jim Dine: Photographies récentes*, exh. cat. (Paris: Maison Européenne de la Photographie, 1998), p. 8.

2. All quotations from Jim Dine, unless otherwise attributed, are from a videotaped interview with Dine by the author on May 1, 1999 at the Museum of Fine Arts, Santa Fe, New Mexico.

4. Quoted in Monterosso, *Jim Dine*, p. 8.

Following pages: The Veronica, 1999
digital pigment print on canvas, 68¾ × 96½", overall

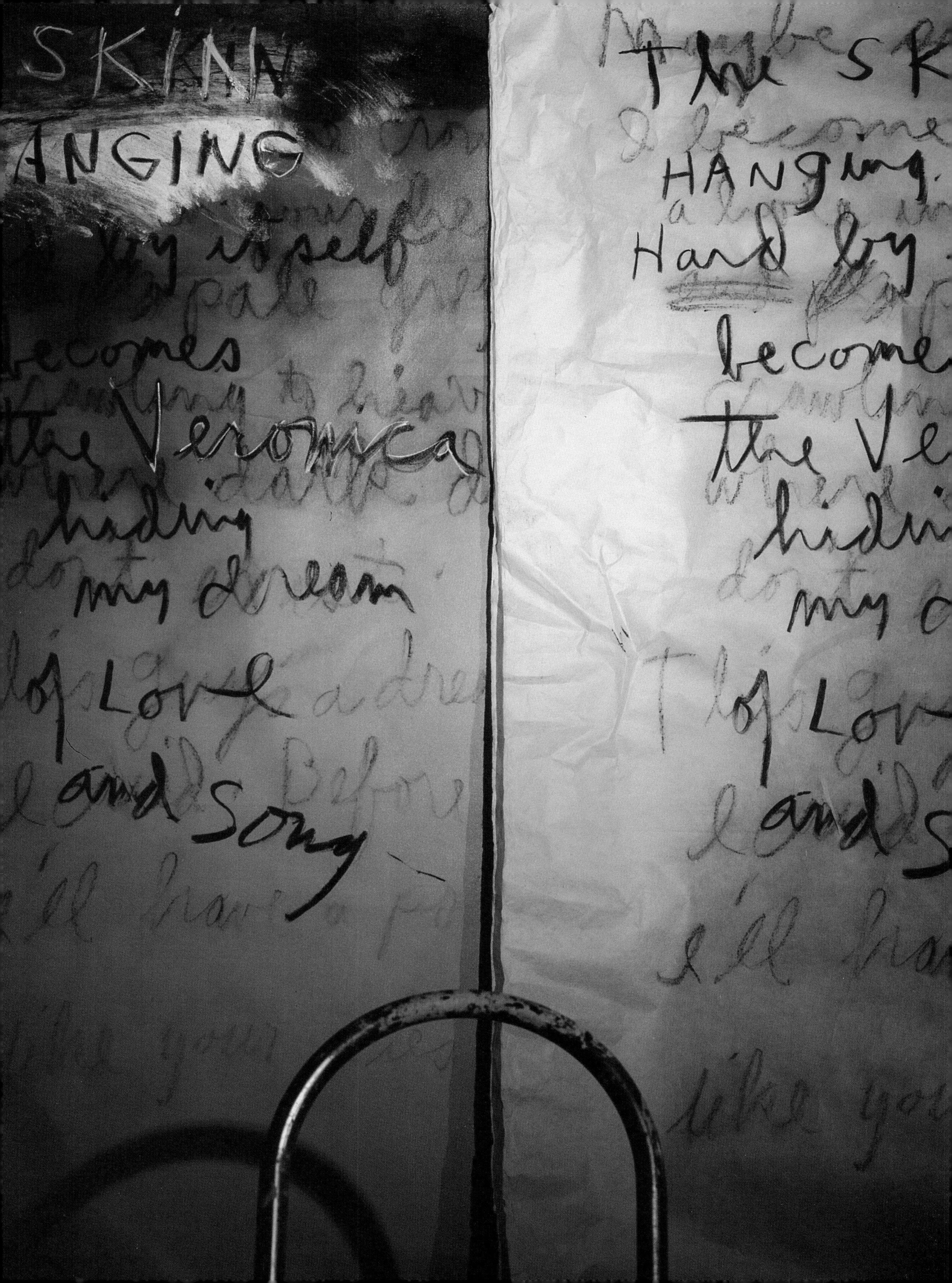

SKINN
ANGING

my itself
becomes
the Veronica
hiding
my dream
of Love a dre
and Song

The sk
HANGING.
Hard by
become
the Ve
hidi
my o
of Lov
and s

IF I Travel
far afield,
~~FIT~~ my god
cant Yield
the ALCoHoL
that burns
my envy of
a life!
Heart's door

SAUL STEINBERG | DRAWING INTO BEING
October 1 – 30, 1999

Saul Remembered
by Arne Glimcher
Excerpt from Pace catalogue

1980. The Picasso Retrospective at MoMA.
We are at the Museum of Modern Art standing in front of Picasso's *Still Life with a Hat*, 1909. I turn to Saul and say "The hat is supposed to be Cézanne's." Saul responds with, "Imagine!", cocks his head, steps forward for a closer look, straightens up, steps back and says "What would really be useful is to know Cézanne's hat size."

Obsessed with detail, minutiae and obscure information, Saul examines, concludes, and non-judgmentally presents his view of the world through a spy glass. Like Klee, Steinberg allows us a glimpse of a private universe, a world of his own making, where the ordinary transforms by scrutiny into the extraordinary. Like Picabia, an artist with whom he identified (especially the early work), his universe runs like a pointless machine caught up in the manufacture of the absurd. At the controls of this machine, Steinberg is creating himself.

A Restaurant on 57th St. where we frequently met.
Saul says "Imagine, the gorilla lost its cat . . . imagine the sadness." He chuckles nervously. He is referring to Koko the signing gorilla. He is fascinated with her, not because she signs but because she has a pet, a cat. That morning the newspaper reported that Koko's cat was killed by a car; she is sad and keeps signing for the cat. Saul is touched by the loss and moved by the gorilla's grief. Saul himself has a pet cat, an alter-ego who appears in several of his works, observing the scene. In *Persian Table*, 1981, the cat is curled up on a kilim. All angles and no curves, the cat appears to be woven into the rug, becoming the rug, Saul's rug.

Saul's Apartment on East 75th St: a place for serious discussions.
Loss hovers over Saul's life and its fog infiltrates the work. In the Gogol drawings and objects, a man is in search of his lost nose. In the documents, he is in search of his foggy identity, and in the maps, whole cities and countries are lost in the myopic perception of a New Yorker's view of America. When we discuss this, Saul says "Today you get from here, where you board the plane, to there, where you get off. There's nothing in between, not like it used to be. The discovery of Bozeman, Montana is lost."

Being with Saul was seeing a layered world whose reality was heightened by the gift of his perception. We were friends for 25 years and had several exhibitions to-gether. Annually we would plan shows and Saul would postpone them, annually. Each exhibition that actually took place was a minor miracle, as he worried about the critical reception of his work. He feared the classification of cartoonist. For him, the idiom was a springboard, a kind of shorthand whose style was captivating, a seduction that instantly brought the viewer into his arena of ideas both intellectual and pictorial.

The representational aspect of his art separated him from his friends, the cognitive content of his work and the sharpness of his observation endeared him to them. He belonged to a generation of artists whose abstract work depended on a scale that never suited the presentation of his ideas. The scale of Saul's work is portable—a refugee's scale, something to fold up and take away. In a constant state of notation rather than conclusion, it never settles down. Yet he was close to all the Abstract Expressionists (especially de Kooning) and was married to Hedda Sterne, one of the "Irascibles", the only woman in the group.[1] Saul and the Abstract Expressionists had more in common than it appeared. Their torment and ecstasy was expressed in gymnastic action, or dynamic fields of color, in search of the "sublime." Steinberg's torment was masked by carefully drafted humor and by his celebration of New York streets jammed with yellow cabs where he found the sublime. He dramatized human behavior with its attendant inventions, achievements, festivals, and changing social mores. He was always contemporary—contemporaneous to the moment dated now only by his death.

Saul once showed me a drawing of a group of women parading down a street in Los Angeles, where each one is dressed in a costume from a different era. Each one is safeguarding the period within which she blossomed and to which she forever belongs. Unlike Saul, each one is dated, but together they are a timeline woven into the fabric of contemporary memory, reaching back and looking forward and like Saul Steinberg, trying to make sense of the carnival we call the 20th century.

---

1. *The Irascibles*, photograph by Nina Leen, *LIFE Magazine*, January 15, 1951. William Baziotes, James Brooks, Richard Pousette-Dart, Jimmy Ernst, Adolph Gottlieb, Willem de Kooning, Robert Motherwell, Barnett Newman, Jackson Pollock, Ad Reinhardt, Mark Rothko, Theodoros Stamos, Hedda Sterne, Clyfford Still, Bradley Walker Tomlin.

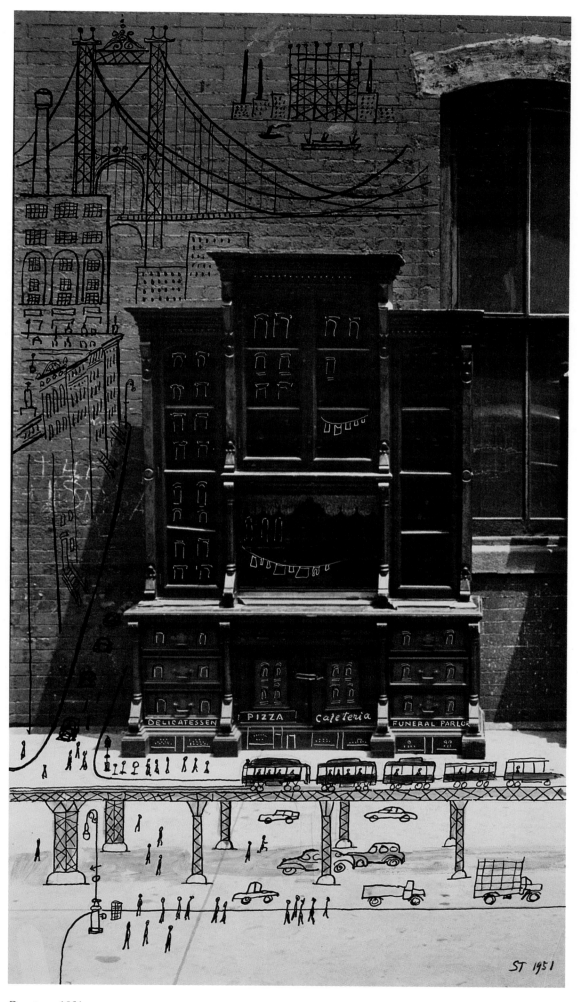

Downtown, 1951
ink on black and white photograph, 15 × 9"

Untitled (after Millet's The Angelus), c. 1968
oil, ink and rubber stamp on canvas, 22⅝ × 16¼"

NAUM GABO | PIONEER OF ABSTRACT SCULPTURE
November 4 – 8 January, 2000

Constructed Head No. 2, 1916
galvanized steel on wood base, 17⅝ × 17 × 17⅛"
Photo © Nina & Graham Williams
The Works of Naum Gabo © Nina Williams

GEORGE CONDO

JAZZ PAINTINGS / GREENE STREET

December 3 – 29 January, 2000

THELONIOUS MONK

Thelonious Monk, 1999
oil, acrylic and collage on canvas, 60 × 60"

ARP, CALDER AND NOGUCHI

EARTHLY FORMS: THE BIOMORPHIC SCULPTURES

February 18 – 20 March, 2000

The Epiphany of Abstraction

by Marc Glimcher

Excerpt from Pace catalogue

There is a spirit in art that strives to expose the essential and elementary characteristics of nature. This search, though as old as consciousness, reached new heights in the early years of Abstract Art. Since that time, abstraction in visual art has been exhaustively considered by historians and critics. Although the human mind willingly accepts such perceptual leaps in the form of music, bringing abstraction into the visible world has required the intellectual and philosophical preparation of all human history. . . . To the artist working at the dawn of abstraction, it must have seemed like the first glimpse of microbes made apparent by a primitive microscope or of Jupiter's moons made visible through the first telescope; thrilling in its implication, but disturbingly improbable at the same time.

To the twenty-first century eye, abstraction is more like an autopsy than an adventure. It has been dissected to expose the evolutionary process, which led to its development. As a result, our contemporary view of abstraction is thoroughly dry and analytical. The force of will and originality of purpose that was demonstrated by the artists is nearly impossible for us to feel today.

The first three decades of the twentieth century saw several strong currents flow through abstraction. Of these the Suprematists and Dadaists saw abstraction as more than culture or style, they saw it as a way to elevate art to the highest level of philosophical, intellectual and spiritual exploration. The Suprematists and their elaborate doctrines led to the right angles of Malevitch, Kandinsky and Mondrian. . . . Geometry became a gate to a Platonic Ideal of the non-physical essence of art. It allowed artists to evade representation of the physical world entirely, in an effort to explore the pure Art. In contrast, the Dadaists, led by Arp and others, sought to expose through their work, the essence of nature. Dada was not a satiric commentary on art and culture (a common misreading of the movement based on a common misreading of Duchamp). Rather, the movement was concerned with how chance and the "order" it created reflected life and the Universe most clearly. This central precept provided the backdrop for the development of the forms recognized in this exhibition, commonly known as biomorphic or organic forms. These forms, like the idea of "chance," relate to natural processes. They allow artists to explore the natural world without representing it directly. The result was an expression of nature's laws and character, rather than its imagery.

This strain of abstraction will be examined through the lens of Arp, Calder and Noguchi in an effort to understand how the passage through the early part of their own art histories led to biomorphic abstraction.

ARP

Dada is a moral revolution. Dada is for nonsense. Which does not mean bunk. Dada is as senseless as nature and life. Dada is for nature and against art . . .[1]

While the ashes of WWI bore witness against a civilization that claimed to have mastery and dominion over nature, artists in Paris . . . as well as others in Zurich . . . Cologne . . . and Berlin, formed a web of revolution known as Dada . . . Dada would become art history's tool for illustrating the incompatibility of Art's search for invisible Truth and Modern Society's imposition of Order. . . .

To Jean Arp, these ideas and the coming together of like minds to explore them, were the prime movers of his life as an artist. . . .

The forms Arp began to work with first in wall reliefs and later in plaster and stone, followed exactly the Dadaist prescription to abandon reason and order. These shapes did not follow any systematic or art historical guidelines. Arp furthered their Dadaist nature by using these Earthy Forms, as he dubbed them, as willing subjects in his obscience to the Laws of Chance. These forms, with no particular symmetry or hierarchy, were assembled by Arp into groups. . . .

CALDER

. . . Calder's work in abstraction led to the invention of the mobile, which was rapidly folded into the collective unconscious as a "form" like painting and sculpture. For Calder however, this invention, which flowed from the kineticism of the wire pieces and the circus, was the nat-

Alexander Calder, *Untitled*, 1939
plastic, wood, bone, string, wire and paint
24 × 20½ × ¾"
© 2001 Estate of Alexander
Calder/Artists Rights
Society (ARS), New York

ural extension of abstraction. Like other members of *Abstraction-Création*, including Arp, Calder saw the essence of the natural world embodied more in its processes than in its images. For these artists, more dynamic rules of composition, which engaged gravity, motion and chance, had replaced the golden section. . . .

NOGUCHI

. . . Noguchi returned to New York [from China and Japan in 1930] to begin another cycle of portraiture, but not before he had finished at least one work that would presage his role in the future of organic abstraction. Almost immediately upon his return, Noguchi made a sculpture of a figure which hung from the ceiling. Titled by Buckminster Fuller, *Miss Expanding Universe*, the piece is one of the first to show how Noguchi would use biomorphic forms to evoke the universal elements of his subjects. . . .

Arp, Calder and Noguchi believed in the reality of what they were uncovering and that its existence predated their own.

This deep belief in their work exemplifies the optimism that lies at the heart of the modern era. For centuries, original thinkers have striven to reveal, mostly through institutions, the elementary aspects of the Universe. In the early part of the twentieth century, they began to believe that such an understanding was within the grasp of the individual. Concurrently, in the scientific community, theoretical physicists, cyberneticists and geneticists felt an elementary understanding of the Universe lay within reach. Today, the search for technology (in the sciences) and fashion (in the arts) often preempts the search for understanding. (As a result, the disparity between the arts and the sciences has grown). . . .

1. Jan Hans Arp, *Notes from a Diary*, 1932.

611

Self-Portrait, 1997
oil on canvas, 102 × 84"

CHUCK CLOSE

RECENT PAINTINGS / GREENE STREET
March 12 – 6 May, 2000

Mark, Image, Medium, Interference
by Richard Shiff
Excerpt from Pace catalogue

Meticulous Invention

Chuck Close's art strikes most viewers as superhuman in execution yet perfectly straightforward in concept: whether engaged in painting, drawing, or printmaking, he "copies" photographs of people's faces, aiming for informational accuracy, albeit by means that may seem odd, indirect, and even grotesque. In his earlier work, he often enlarged the source image so greatly that the slightest pores and blemishes became major pictorial events; in his recent work, he has been using whimsical abstract forms as independent constructive elements without losing the general effect of verism. It can't be easy, the casual observer thinks, but perhaps you just commit yourself to the task, concentrate, and put in the time. After all, it simply amounts to transferring a picture from one flat surface to another. Some kind of drafting machine—or better, a programmed computer and printer—might serve the same ends, getting the job done that much faster.

This commonsense view of Close's enterprise persists despite the artist's precise and characteristically soul-searching statements, which leave a very different impression of his intentions and methods. On what basis does he claim that his painting ends up looking "more like" the person it represents? Additional questions of this nature arise from recent art criticism which touches on a number of historical and social issues that lend both artistic and extra-artistic significance to Close's practice. There is much that may be relevant to an analysis of his work in its proper late twentieth-century context: the break that his artistic generation of the 1960s made with a romantic-modernist tradition of gestural expressiveness (a change in how the self is conceived and projected as an image); why that generation investigated the look of ordinary photographic and commercially processed imagery (the issue of commodity culture); why these artists were concerned with the material basis of perceptual and psychological effects (an interest Close has shared with Minimalist sculptors and performance artists); why they have sought an indeterminate realm between organicism and mechanicity (perhaps to reassess human mentality in an age of electronic information). Many more issues potentially linked to an understanding of Close could surely be identified.

Granted, considerations of this sort would demand a lot from the casual consumer of Close's art, which simply attracts and fascinates the eye, no questions asked. But it's possible that professional viewers, those educated in the ways of modern art and criticism, also have a tendency to avoid the more complicated paths into Close's practice. Despite all the available information, it seems that there remains something deeply challenging about his creativity, something counterintuitive for typical viewers. The hard thing to admit is that Close's work forces every one of us to become a "typical" viewer; confronted with it, we revert to a naive attitude. A background in art, in science, in aesthetics—none of this seems to make much difference. Just this year, a cognitive psychologist used Close's art to investigate the degree to which the perceived size of elements of a representation can affect recognition of the larger image those elements constitute. The scientist was studying a phenomenon of great interest to Close himself—in the artist's words, the shift from a local "distribution of marks on a flat surface" to a comprehensive "illusion" of volume and depth. The scientist accepted Close's rigorous probe of visual experience as a worthy foundation for his own empirical study. His highly appreciative account nevertheless describes Close's procedure in a way that can only mislead, as it refers to the painter's process of "meticulously copying one square [grid unit] at a time from photo to canvas."[2]

The problem is not with "one square at a time," but with the words "meticulous" and "copy," which seem to come so naturally to the scientist; they emphasize the systematic element in Close's work, a mechanical-reproduction directness. I suspect that this type of description of his practice (which probably comes naturally to all of us) is a defense against what isn't so natural—the sense of the uncanny that each of Close's completed pictures generates. If we can understand the placement of the little "copied" detail, we think we ought to be able to grasp the rationality of the whole. I doubt that we do, however, for the specific nature of Close's details appears largely unrelated to their ultimate representational function.

These details, these individual marks, assume arbitrary form, while paradoxically proving essential to rendering the general image fixed in advance by the photographic source. If anything at all is "copied," it must be some immaterial feature of the image (perhaps certain conceptualized, informational elements of it), not the actual material components of a photographic image produced by lenses and light-sensitive chemicals. As for photography itself, Close has always been conscious of the arbi-trariness of its mark, a feature that normally goes unnoticed because it lurks just below the threshold of visual resolution: "The surface of a photographic image is so consistent [that is, continuous, coherent] and yet the dots of which it consists have nothing to do with the images they project."[3] To notice the form of the photographic mark is to stand too close to the image, an error in perceptual judgment. . . .

Like most other artists, either representational or

abstract, Close is much more the imitator than the copyist. His project amounts to a willful transformation of his photographic source image, never its literal reproduction, even though the perceptual effects of the two images—the mechanically generated source and its manual translation, both of them two-dimensional—can appear remarkably similar; and this, to be sure, is part of the artistry. To a great extent, the similarity requires special conditions because, as Close readily confesses, his work is designed to reveal "both the device that makes the illusion and the illusion itself.". . .

2. Denis G. Pelli, "Close Encounters–An Artist Shows That Size Affects Shape," *Science*, 285 (August 6, 1999), p. 844.
3. Close, in Cindy Nemser, "An Interview with Chuck Close," *Artforum*, 8 (January 1970), p. 54. Close's reference to "dots" evokes both the grain of photographic emulsion and the halftone dots of photoprinting. The (in)visibility of the grain and the dots varies considerably according to the type of process used and the representational intentions of the producer of the image.

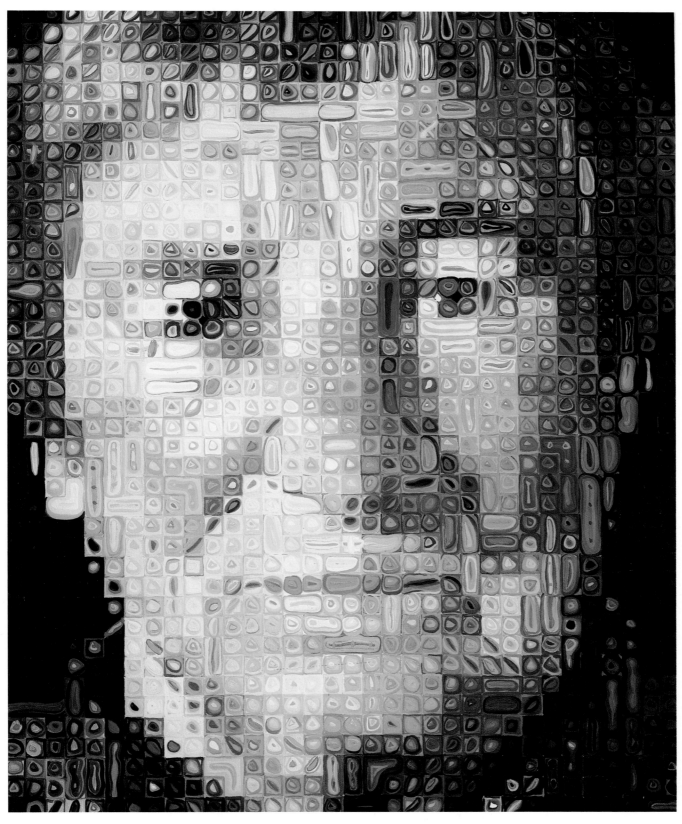

Agnes, 1998
oil on canvas, 102 × 84"

GEORG BASELITZ

| **RECENT PAINTINGS**
March 24 – 22 April, 2000

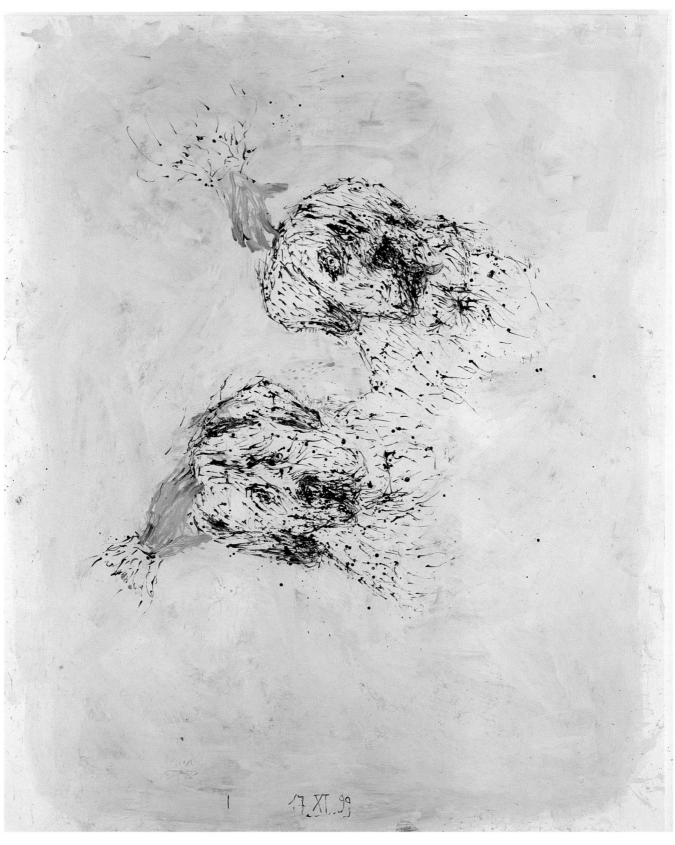

Porträhund, November 17, 1999
oil on canvas, 98½ × 72¾"

618

JOHN CHAMBERLAIN

RECENT SCULPTURE / GREENE STREET
May 12 – 14 July, 2000

Left: Installation of *Atmosphere and Environment V*
Below: Louise Nevelson, *Atmosphere and Environment V,* 1967
black epoxy on magnesium and aluminum base
102 × 96 × 48"
Photos Charles Uht

By the late 1950s, Louise Nevelson's reputation was already firmly fixed in American art as the progenitor of the installations she called atmospheric environments. Unlike her contemporaries Calder and Smith, whose sculpture evolved in scale and material to withstand the elements, Nevelson used found wood objects, which did not transfer to the outdoors, although her work too was heroic in scale. To extend her sensibility of environment to exterior spaces, she experimented with aluminum forms, some found and some manufactured, and then created a series of screenlike sculptures designed to incorporate the landscape.

In 1967 Pace presented Louise Nevelson's first exhibition of aluminum sculpture. Nelson Rockefeller, one of a small group of patrons who enthusiastically supported contemporary art, saw most of the exhibitions at our original location at 9 West 57th Street. When the Museum of Modern Art acquired the largest work in the Nevelson exhibition, both Alfred Barr and Dorothy Miller encouraged Rockefeller to see the exhibition. I remember staying late at the gallery to accommodate his schedule. By the time he visited the show all the sculptures had been sold. Eager to own one of the works, he commissioned Nevelson to create a variant on the series.

Nelson decided to place the work on the crest of a hill at Pocantico Hills, the Rockefeller family estate that overlooks the Hudson River landscape. But the selected site was next to the great house, and it was difficult for construction vehicles to reach without damaging the landscape. It was decided to construct the work of magnesium instead of aluminum, which sufficiently reduced the weight so that it could be transported to the site by helicopter. Nevelson agreed to the use of magnesium so long as it could be painted black!

Nevelson's 1971 exhibition took place at a time when industry was beginning to assume the mantel of the Medicis, by commissioning sculptures for urban and rural corporate headquarters. The Chase Manhattan Bank and Pepsico were, and still are, exemplary in creating significant collections of contemporary art and in enthusiastically commissioning works of major significance.

The seventies also saw the government patronage of contemporary artists. Under the auspices of the GSA (General Services Administration) a "one percent clause" took effect, whereby one percent of the construction cost of a federal building was earmarked for the commissioning of art for the public space outside the building. Dubuffet, Nevelson, Calder, Tony Smith, Claes Oldenburg, Joel Shapiro, Richard Serra, and John Chamberlain all benefited from the program, as did the country benefit from the artists' achievements.

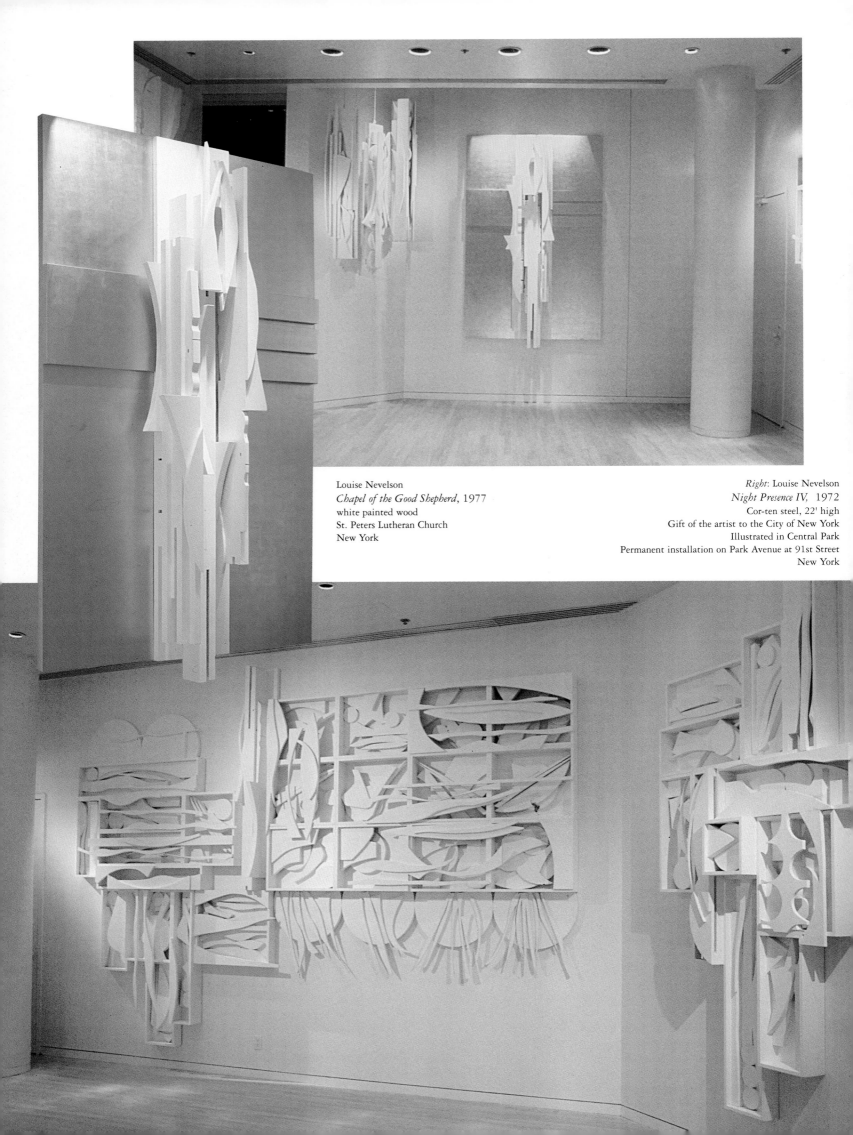

Louise Nevelson
Chapel of the Good Shepherd, 1977
white painted wood
St. Peters Lutheran Church
New York

Right: Louise Nevelson
Night Presence IV, 1972
Cor-ten steel, 22' high
Gift of the artist to the City of New York
Illustrated in Central Park
Permanent installation on Park Avenue at 91st Street
New York

Louise Nevelson
Nightwave Moon, 1984
black painted wood
12' × 35' × 20"
Kentucky Center for the Arts
Louisville, Kentucky
Photos Balthazar Korab

Louise Nevelson
Transparent Horizon, 1975
black painted Cor-ten steel, 20' high
Massachusetts Institute of Technology
Cambridge, Massachusetts

Below: Louise Nevelson
Atmosphere and Environment XIII, 1972
Cor-ten steel, 14' × 14' 7½" × 5'
Scottsdale, Arizona

Above: Louise Nevelson
Dawn Shadows, 1982
black painted steel, ca. 30' high
Madison Plaza
Chicago, Illinois

Above: Louise Nevelson
Celebration II, 1976
black painted Cor-ten steel
28 × 10½ × 13½'
Pepsico Corporation
Purchase, New York

Left: Louise Nevelson
Trilogy, 1978–79
black painted Cor-ten steel
three sculptures, tallest 44' high
Bendix Corporation
Smithfield, Michigan

Joel Shapiro, *Conjunction,* 1999
bronze, ca. 40' high
United States Embassy, Ottawa
Ontario, Canada
Photos Pierre St-Jacques

Right: Joel Shapiro, *Untitled,* 1994
bronze, unique
21 × 18 × 14'
Sony Corporation
New York

Joel Shapiro
Three Figures/Fifteen Elements, 1994–1996
cast bronze
Above: 8 × 21 × 9', 15 × 12.5 × 7.5'
Below: 8 × 21 × 9'
Kansas City International Airport
Kansas City, Missouri

Lucas Samaras
Chair Transformation #20, 1996
patinated bronze
14' × 84" × 27"
National Gallery of Art
Washington, D.C.

Jean Dubuffet
Monument à la bête debout, 1969–1982
polyester resin and fiberglass over stainless steel framework
painted with polyurethane, 29½' high
Interfirst Plaza
Chicago, Illinois
© 2001 Artists Rights Society (ARS), New York/ADAGP, Paris

Jean Dubuffet
Group of Four Trees, 1972
epoxy paint on polyurethane over
metal structure, 38 × 40 × 34'
Chase Manhattan Plaza
New York
Photo Tom Crane
© 2001
Artists Rights Society (ARS), New
York/ADAGP, Paris

Above: Claes Oldenburg
Houseball, in Berlin Site—with Bear, 1997
charcoal and pastel on paper
37¾ × 49¾"

Left: Claes Oldenburg
Houseball, 1996
mixed media, 32' diameter
Jerusalem, Israel

Jim Dine
Looking Toward the Avenue, 1989
patinated bronze, three sculptures
14, 18, and 23' high
Avenue of the Americas
New York

Back row, from left: Peter Boris, Richard Solomon, Peter MacGill,
Susan Dunne, Marc Glimcher, Douglas Baxter, Guy Wildenstein
Front row: Bernice Rose, Arne Glimcher

Alumni
Back row, from left: Jay Grimm, Peter Blum, Renato Danese
Front row: Christopher D'Amelio, Anthony Grant, Matthew Marks
Not pictured: Jeffrey Hoffeld and Marc Selwyn

Anniversary Publication Staff
Back row, from left: Suzi Steiger
Front row: Kevin Parise, Mildred Glimcher, Amy Greenspon

Senior Staff
Back row, from left: Jeff Burch, Jerry Reilly, Howard Fuhr, Andrea Bundonis, David Goerk, Linda Ashcraft, Catherine Davis, Signe Howard
Front row: Chris Harnden, Cay Rose, Bill Wood, Alina Pellicer, Ward Ackerman
Photo at right: Judy Harney

Diverse Support Staff
Back row, from left: Bernadette Dirr, Tomoko Konami, Ellen Wilson, Motohiko Tokuta, Angie Fredrickson, April Howard, Tucker Capparell
Front row: Sonny Fitzsimonds, Caroline Comack

Dealer Support Staff
Back row, from left: Elizabeth Sullivan, Kevin Hart, Elyse Buxbaum, Alexandra Whitney, Maria de Madariaga
Front row: Patricia Hughes, Kate Gillespie

Registrar and Preparator Staff
Back row, from left: Alan Weiner, Bill Scanga, Seamus McIlvenny, Susanna Patrick,
Lissa McClure, Kate McSweeney, Jay Rice, Bruce Gluck
Front row: Wayne Letitia, Kerry McFate, Kristin Casey
Not pictured: Frank Lentini

Accounting
Back row, from left: Carmen Diaz, Renee Sadinsky, Jerry Reilly, Tim Gutch
Front row: Sonia Roldan, Sloane Simpson

Pace Prints
Back row, from left: Therese Albers, Stephanie Sloane,
Kristina Sumption, Barbara Delano
Front row: Kristin Heming, Richard Solomon

Pace Master Prints and Pace Primitive
From left: Chantal Salomon-Lee, Paola Quintero,
Alexandra Schwartz, Carlo Bella, Lisa Bradley

Pace/MacGill
Back row, from left: Joshua Chuang, Lauren Panzo,
Pak So, Matthew Sullivan, Alexis Smith
Front row: Julie Braniecki, Michelle Ellwood, Frank Salinas,
Peter MacGill, Kimberly Jones, Alissa Schoenfeld

Pace Editions, Inc. and Pace Editions, Ink.
Back row, from left: Donald Traver, Julia D'Amario,
Kathy Kuehn, Richard Solomon, Ruth Lingen, Mae Shore,
Bill Hall, Denis Timm, Jeff Hauger
Front row: Jean-Yves Noblet, Mara Leimanis, Jessica Miller,
Laura Meyers, Andre Ribuoli

COMPREHENSIVE CHRONOLOGY
OF EXHIBITIONS

BOSTON

Selected Exhibitions

1960–61

April 25	The Pace Gallery opened at 125 Newbury Street, Boston, with paintings by Albert Alcalay, David Berger, Jason Berger, Lawrence Kupferman, and Robert S. Neuman, and sculpture by Mirko.
May 23–June 20	*Master Graphics*
October 24–November 14	ALBERT ALCALAY: *Paintings and Works on Paper* Catalogue.
December	*Three British Artists: Alan Davie, Eduardo Paolozzi, William Scott*
January 23–February 11	GEORGE GROSZ/JULES PASCIN: *Paintings, Drawings, Prints*
March 6–25	MIRKO: *Recent Small Bronzes*
March 27–April 15	JASON BERGER: *Recent Paintings*
April 17–May 6	LAWRENCE KUPFERMAN: *Recent Paintings*
May 8–27	WALTER FELDMAN: *Recent Paintings*
May 29–June 24	LOUISE NEVELSON: *Sculpture* Exhibition of painted wood sculptures, organized in association with the Martha Jackson Gallery, New York.

1961–62

October 10–October 24	*Four Sculptors: Arp, César, Mallary, Mirko*
November 12–December 2	J.J. THARRATS: *Recent Paintings*
December 5–31	*Posters by Toulouse-Lautrec*
January 3–23	*New Directions*
February 12–March 3	HUGH TOWNLEY: *Sculpture*
March 12–31	VICTOR VASARELY: *Paintings* Catalogue with introduction by Sam Hunter.
April 9–28	ROBERT S. NEUMAN: *Paintings*
May 6–27	ALBERT ALCALAY: *Paintings* Catalogue.

1962–63

October 10–31	*European Masters* Jean Arp, Constantin Brancusi, Alberto Giacometti, Henry Moore, Pablo Picasso, Auguste Rodin
November 11–24	JOSEF ALBERS: *Paintings*
November 26–December 8	ROBERT S. NEUMAN: *Prints*
December 10–January 2	*Stock Up for the Holidays: An Anthology of Pop Art* Jim Dine, Robert Indiana, Marisol, Claes Oldenburg, James Rosenquist, George Segal, Andy Warhol, Tom Wesselmann
January 28–February 16	JAN COX: *Paintings*
April 1–20	ERNEST TROVA: *Falling Man Paintings* Catalogue with introduction by Ivan Karp.
May 13–June 6	ELEANOR MIKUS: *Paintings*

1963–64

October 23–November 11	RICHARD STANKIEWICZ: *Recent Sculpture*
March 24–April 11	LOUISE NEVELSON: *Sculpture*
May 11–June 6	CLAES OLDENBURG: *Recent Work*

1964–65

November 16–December 7	JOHN CHAMBERLAIN: *Sculpture*
February 13–March 13	JEAN ARP: *Sculpture*
March 20–April 17	*Formal Art (Op Art)*
April 20–May 15	HUGH TOWNLEY: *Sculpture*
December 9–January	*Collage-Assemblage Exhibition* Jean Arp, César, Joseph Cornell, Louise Nevelson, Lucas Samaras, Kurt Schwitters, Michael Todd, Tom Wesselmann, and others

NEW YORK

The dates of exhibitions are those that appear in the printed catalogues and announcements. Exhibitions were occasionally extended and actual dates may vary.

1963–64

October 28	The Pace Gallery opened at 9 West 57th Street.
October 28–c. December 1	ERNEST TROVA: *Falling Man Paintings* Inaugural exhibition.
November 27–December 21	BARRIE C. MCDOWELL: *Sculpture*
January	*American and European Paintings*
January 28–February 15	ALAN FENTON: *Recent Paintings*
February 18–March 7	ELEANOR MIKUS: *Recent Tablets*
March 11–28	MICHAEL TODD: *Sculpture*
March 31–April 18	VICTOR VASARELY: *Paintings, Sculpture, Prints*
April 28–May 16	HUGH TOWNLEY: *Wood Sculptures*
Summer	*Group Exhibition of Gallery Artists* Aldcroftt, Billy Apple, Sven Lukin, Novak, Marjorie Strider, Michael Todd, Ernest Trova

1964–65

October 13–November 7	SVEN LUKIN: *New Paintings*
November 17–December 12	LOUISE NEVELSON: *Recent Work* First solo exhibition at Pace/New York. Catalogue with introduction by William C. Seitz.
December 15–January 7	*Masterworks: Modern Sculpture*
January 7–25	*First International Girlie Show* Ben Johnson, Al Hansen, Roy Lichtenstein, Marjorie Strider, Tom Wesselmann
February 2–February 27	ERNEST TROVA: *Falling Man Sculptures*
April 6–May 1	ELEANOR MIKUS: *Tablets*
May 4–29	*Beyond Realism* Richard Artschwager, Chryssa, Robert Morris, Claes Oldenburg, Michelangelo Pistoletto, James Rosenquist, Lucas Samaras, Marjorie Strider, Paul Thek, Michael Todd, Ernest Trova Catalogue with introduction by Michael Kirby.
May 11–September 30	*American Artists: Summer Painting Exhibition*

1965–66

October 9–November 3	VICTOR VASARELY: *Paintings* Catalogue.
October 31–November 29	LARRY BELL: *Recent Work* First solo exhibition at Pace.
December 4–January 2	MARJORIE STRIDER: *Recent Works* First solo exhibition at Pace of works that bridged the gap between painting and sculpture.
January 8–February 2	EDUARDO PAOLOZZI: *Sculpture, Drawings, Prints* First solo exhibition at Pace, arranged in cooperation with the Robert Frazer Gallery.

	Catalogue with dedication poem by Louise Nevelson.
February 5–March 2	**SVEN LUKIN:** *Recent Works*
March 12–April 6	**CHRYSSA:** *Sculpture*
	First solo exhibition at Pace. Catalogue.
April 2–May 4	**PAUL THEK:** *Recent Work*
	First solo exhibition at Pace of sculptural objects that shocked and disturbed some viewers.
May 7–June 11	**LOUISE NEVELSON:** *Four Enameled Aluminum Sculptures*

1966–67

October 8–November 5	**LUCAS SAMARAS:** *Selected Works 1960–1966* First solo exhibition at Pace of 44 works, including *Mirrored Room #2*, which was built in the gallery and later sold to the Albright-Knox Art Gallery, Buffalo. Catalogue with essay by Lawrence Alloway.
November 12–December 10	**ROBERT IRWIN:** *Dot Paintings* First solo exhibition at Pace.
December 15–January 10	*American Artists: Winter Group Exhibition*
January 14–February 11	**ERNEST TROVA:** *Selected Works 1953–1966* Catalogue with essay by Lawrence Alloway.
February 18–March 15	**CRAIG KAUFFMAN:** *Recent Work* First solo exhibition at Pace, consisting of vacuum-molded wall reliefs.
March 18–April 15	**NICHOLAS KRUSHENICK:** *Paintings* First solo exhibition at Pace.
April 22–May 20	**LARRY BELL:** *Boxes*

1967–68

October 17–November 7	**ROBERT WHITMAN:** *Dark* Three works in which laser beams— one wavy, one straight, one wide—each circumscribed its own space constructed within the gallery. Upon meeting its end, each commenced erasing itself and then retracing itself, the two cycles repeating themselves continually. The exhibition was eventually closed by the Board of Health due to concern about ocular damage to gallery visitors.
November 18–December 16	**EDUARDO PAOLOZZI:** *New Sculpture*
December 16–January 10	*Prints by Krushenick, Nevelson and Trova*
January 13–February 14	**LOUISE NEVELSON:** *Transparent Sculptures*
February 17–March 13	**CHRYSSA:** *Selected Works 1955–1967* Catalogue with essay by Diane Waldman.
March 15–April 11	**ROBERT IRWIN:** *Aluminum Discs*
April 13–May 18	**JEAN DUBUFFET:** *Painted Sculptures* First solo exhibition at Pace of recent work. Catalogue with statement by the artist.

This was the final exhibition at the 9 West 57th Street location. During the summer, reconstruction of the third floor at 32 East 57th Street was under-taken by I.M. Pei and Associates.

1968–69

October 12–November 12	**LUCAS SAMARAS:** *Boxes/Transformations* The first exhibition at the gallery's new location. The exhibition included the first publication by Pace Editions; Samaras'

Book, which was published in conjunction with the Whitney Museum of American Art.

November 16–December 11	**SVEN LUKIN:** *Shaped Paintings*
January 4–February 4	**ERNEST TROVA:** *New Sculptures*
February 18–March 15	**CRAIG KAUFFMAN:** *Wall Sculptures*
March 22–April 22	**LOUISE NEVELSON:** *Recent Wood Sculpture*
April 26–May 21	**NICHOLAS KRUSHENICK:** *Paintings* Catalogue.

1969–70

October 4–29	**ROBERT IRWIN:** *Acrylic Discs*
November 8–January 1	**JEAN DUBUFFET:** *Simulacres* The black and white epoxy assemblages were virtually three-dimensional drawn simulacra of figures, tables, and landscapes. Catalogue with letter, discussing the work, from Dubuffet to Arne Glimcher.
February 14–March 11	**LARRY BELL:** *New Work*
March 21–April 8	**CRAIG KAUFFMAN:** *Recent Work*
April 11–May 6	**PIET MONDRIAN:** *The Process Works* Exhibition traveled to several museums. Catalogue with excerpts from Mondrian's writings and essay by Harry Holtzman.
Summer	*Group Exhibition of Gallery Artists* Larry Bell, Jean Dubuffet, Robert Irwin, Craig Kauffman, Sven Lukin, Louise Nevelson

1970–71

October 3–31	**LUCAS SAMARAS:** *Chair Transformations* Catalogue with statement by the artist.
November 7–25	*A Decade of California Color* Peter Alexander, Chuck Arnoldi, Larry Bell, Billy Al Bengston, Fred Eversley, Patrick Hogan, Robert Irwin, Craig Kauffman, John McCracken, Ed Moses, Kenneth Price, Ed Ruscha, Dewain Valentine Catalogue with chronology of each artist.
January 9–February 3	**ERNEST TROVA:** *New Sculpture* Catalogue with foreword by Arne Glimcher.
February 13–March 10	**JACK YOUNGERMAN:** *Recent Paintings and Sculpture* Catalogue.
March 13–April 7	**JEAN DUBUFFET:** *Works on Paper*
April 10–May 5	**LARRY BELL:** *Recent Work*
May 8–June 19	**LOUISE NEVELSON:** *Seventh Decade Garden* Three-dimensional outdoor metal sculpture.
Summer–Autumn	Following construction, the second floor of 32 East 57th Street became an additional gallery space, shared by The Pace Gallery and the newly established Pace Editions, which also inaugurated a Master Print Gallery. A spiral staircase allowed access between the two floors.

1971–72

September 25–October 14	**LUCAS SAMARAS:** *Part I: Autopolaroids* The intimate Polaroid photographs that Samaras took of himself between December 1969 and May 1971 became the most influential and revealing of self-portraits, published in a limited edition album by Pace Editions in association with the Whitney Museum of American Art.
October 16–November 2	**LUCAS SAMARAS:** *Part II: Stiff Boxes* 15 Cor-ten steel sculptures

November 6–December 31	*Beyeler at Pace* Modern masterworks from the Beyeler Gallery, Basel, shown on both floors. Jean Arp, Francis Bacon, Pierre Bonnard, Alexander Calder, André Derain, Jean Dubuffet, Alberto Giacometti, Paul Klee, Fernand Léger, Henri Matisse, Joan Miró, Piet Mondrian, Claude Monet, Louise Nevelson, Pablo Picasso, Mark Rothko, Mark Tobey Catalogue.
January 8–February 2	LARRY BELL: *Terminal Series of Boxes* Catalogue.
January 8–February 2	NICHOLAS KRUSHENICK: *New Paintings and Collages*
February 5–March 15	FERNAND LÉGER: *The Late Works*
March 25–April 30	JEAN DUBUFFET: *Praticables* Studies for pieces that were part of *Coucou Bazar (Le bal de l'hourloupe)*, the performance work Dubuffet presented at the Guggenheim Museum during his 1973 retrospective. At selected times the exhibition also included dancers wearing costumes used in *Coucou Bazar*.
May 6–June 7	ALFRED JENSEN: *Paintings* First solo exhibition at Pace.
Summer	*Group Exhibition of Gallery Artists* Jean Dubuffet, Alexander Calder, Alfred Jensen, Donald Judd, Fernand Léger, Louise Nevelson, Isamu Noguchi, Lucas Samaras, Ernest Trova, Victor Vasarely

1972–73

September 20	*Art for McGovern* Exhibition organized by Pace and the Janis Gallery with works donated by the artists, to be sold for the benefit of the presidential campaign of Senator George McGovern.
September 23–October 21	JACK YOUNGERMAN: *New Work*
October 28–November 28	LOUISE NEVELSON: *Columns, Dream-Houses and Collages*
December 2–January 3	LUCAS SAMARAS: *New Chicken Wire Boxes*
January 7–February 10	*Group Exhibition of Gallery Artists* Jean Dubuffet, Fernand Léger, Louise Nevelson, Isamu Noguchi, Eduardo Paolozzi, Ernest Trova
January 6–February 7	LARRY BELL: *New Work*
February 10–March 7	GEORGES NOËL: *Paintings* First solo exhibition at Pace.
March 10–April 4	CRAIG KAUFFMAN: *New Work*
March 10–April 4	WASSILY KANDINSKY: *Watercolors and Drawings 1911–1943* Exhibition organized with the cooperation of Mme. Nina Kandinsky. Catalogue.
April 7–May 2	ERNEST TROVA: *The Profile Cantos* Catalogue with text by Udo Kultermann.
May 5–June 7	JEAN DUBUFFET: *Studies for a Spectacle* Sculptural works that were studies for the costumes for *Coucou Bazar (Le bal de l'hourloupe)* presented concurrently at the Guggenheim Museum. Catalogue.
Summer	*Group Exhibition* Josef Albers, Jean Arp, Milton Avery, Jean Dubuffet, Ellsworth Kelly, Joan Miró, Louise Nevelson, Georges Noël, Lucas Samaras, Ernest Trova

1973–74

| September 22–October 20 | *Archipenko at Pace*
Retrospective of 61 works, organized with the assistance of Frances Grey and the Estate of Alexander Archipenko. Catalogue. |

October 27–November 24	ALFRED JENSEN: *Recent Paintings* Catalogue with foreword by the artist.
December 1–28	ROBERT IRWIN: *"Hard Wall"*
January 10–February 7	GUY DILL: *Recent Sculpture*
February 9–March 12	*American Painters of the Fifties* Josef Albers, Milton Avery, William Baziotes, Willem de Kooning, Sam Francis, Ashile Gorky, Adolph Gottlieb, Philip Guston, Hans Hofmann, Franz Kline, Alexander Liberman, Conrad Marca-Relli, Robert Motherwell, Clyfford Still, Jack Tworkov
March 23–April 27	LUCAS SAMARAS: *Photo-Transformations* Catalogue with foreword by Arne Glimcher.
May 4–June 8	LOUISE NEVELSON: *Sky Gates and Collages* Catalogue with foreword by the artist.
Summer	*Group Exhibition* Milton Avery, William Baziotes, Jean Dubuffet, Robert Irwin, Alfred Jensen, Fernand Léger, Louise Nevelson, Georges Noël, Lucas Samaras, Kurt Schwitters, Ernest Trova

1974–75

September 21–October 19	*African Accumulative Sculpture* Collaboration with Pace Primitive. Catalogue with foreword by Bryce Holcombe and essay by Arnold Rubin.
November 2–30	DAVID VON SCHLEGELL: *New Sculpture* First solo exhibition at Pace. Catalogue with statement by the artist.
December 7–January 4	*Works on Paper* Stuart Davis, Willem de Kooning, Robert Delaunay, Jean Dubuffet, Hans Hofmann, Wassily Kandinsky, Fernand Léger, René Magritte, Henri Matisse, Joan Miró, Piet Mondrian, Henry Moore, Pablo Picasso, Mark Rothko, Kurt Schwitters, Mark Tobey
December 7–January 4	ROBERT IRWIN: *"Soft Wall"*
January 11–February 22	*Five Americans* Alexander Calder, Joseph Cornell, Louise Nevelson, Isamu Noguchi, David Smith
March 1–April 1	AGNES MARTIN: *New Paintings* First solo exhibition at Pace and first show of new work in New York in 13 years.
April 5–May 6	ERNEST TROVA: *Profile Canto and Gox Series*
May 10–June 27	ISAMU NOGUCHI: *Steel Sculptures* First solo exhibition at Pace. Catalogue with introduction by Bryan Robertson.
Summer	*Group Exhibition* Alexander Archipenko, Larry Bell, Guy Dill, Jean Dubuffet, Alfred Jensen, Louise Nevelson, Georges Noël, Isamu Noguchi, Lucas Samaras, Ernest Trova, Jack Youngerman

1975–76

September 20–October 18	JEAN DUBUFFET: *Recent Paintings: Paysages Castillans, Sites Tricolores* Catalogue with slides of the works.
October 25–November 27	LUCAS SAMARAS: *Samaras and Some Others* Catalogue.
December 6–January 3	JACK YOUNGERMAN: *New Sculpture*
December 6–January 3	GEORGES NOËL: *Recent Paintings*
January 10–February 7	ALFRED JENSEN: *Selected Works 1961–1974*

January 10–February 7	**GUY DILL:** *Recent Sculpture*
February 14–March 13	**LOUISE NEVELSON:** *Dawn's Presence–Two; Moon Garden+Two* Catalogue.
March 27–April 24	**JULIO GONZÁLEZ:** *100th Anniversary Exhibition* Exhibition presented with the cooperation of Roberta González and Miriam Prévost Douatte. Catalogue with reprint of "González: First Master of the Torch" by David Smith, which originally appeared in *Art News*, February 1956.
April 24–May 29	*African Spirit Images and Identities* Exhibition presented in collaboration with Pace Primitive. Catalogue with foreword by Bryce Holcombe and essay by Leon Siroto.
May 1–June 5	**AGNES MARTIN:** *Recent Paintings*
Summer	*Group Exhibition of Gallery Artists* Alfred Jensen, Lee Krasner, Louise Nevelson, Georges Noël, Isamu Noguchi, Lucas Samaras, Ernest Trova, Jack Youngerman
Autumn	Dedication of *Bicentennial Dawn*, by Louise Nevelson, commissioned by the General Services Administration's Fine Arts Program for the entrance vestibule of the newly erected James A. Byrne U.S. Courthouse, Philadelphia.

1976–77

October 2–30	**AD REINHARDT:** *Paintings* First solo exhibition at Pace.
November 5–December 1	**ERNEST TROVA:** *Recent Sculpture* Catalogue.
December 4–January 8	**LUCAS SAMARAS:** *Phantasmata* Polaroid SX-70 photographs. Catalogue with poem by the artist.
January 15–February 12	**JIM DINE:** *Paintings, Drawings, Etchings* First solo exhibition at Pace. Catalogue.
February 19–March 19	**LEE KRASNER:** *Eleven Ways to Use the Words To See* First solo exhibition at Pace. Catalogue.
March 26–April 23	**JEAN DUBUFFET:** *Théâtres de mémoire* Catalogue with essay by Arne Glimcher.
April 30–June 4	**CHUCK CLOSE:** *Recent Work* First solo exhibition at Pace. Catalogue.
Summer	*Group Exhibition of Gallery Artists*

1977–78

September 17–October 15	**DAVID VON SCHLEGELL:** *New Sculpture*
September 17–October 15	**AGNES MARTIN:** *New Paintings*
October 22–November 19	*Masterpieces of Japanese Screen Painting* Catalogue.
November 26–January 7	**LOUISE NEVELSON:** *Recent Wood Sculpture* Included her monumental three-dimensional room entitled *Mrs. N's Palace*. Catalogue.
January 14–February 11	**GEORGES NOËL:** *Recent Paintings*
February 18–March 18	**LUCAS SAMARAS:** *Reconstructions* Catalogue with interview with the artist by Barbara Rose.
March 25–April 22	**AGNES MARTIN:** *Watercolors*
March 25–April 22	*Group Exhibition of Gallery Artists*
April 29–June 9	**JIM DINE:** *New Paintings* Catalogue.
Summer	*Group Exhibition of Gallery Artists*

1978–79

September 23–October 21	**BRICE MARDEN:** *The Annunciation Paintings* First solo exhibition at Pace. Catalogue with statements by the artist and essay by Jean-Claude Lebensztejn.
October 23–December 2	**MARK ROTHKO:** *1958–59 Murals* The "Seagram Murals." Catalogue with interview by Arne Glimcher with Dan Rice (Rothko's studio assistant at the time).
December 16–January 20	**GRIDS:** *Format and Image in 20th-Century Art* Josef Albers, Carl Andre, Jennifer Bartlett, Max Bill, Chuck Close, Joseph Cornell, Agnes Denes, Fritz Glarner, Adolph Gottlieb, Eva Hesse, Patrick Ireland, Robert Irwin, Alfred Jensen, Jasper Johns, Ellsworth Kelly, Paul Klee, Lee Krasner, Sol LeWitt, Roy Lichtenstein, Brice Marden, Agnes Martin, Piet Mondrian, Eadweard Muybridge, Louise Nevelson, Georges Noël, Kenneth Noland, Larry Poons, Ad Reinhardt, Edda Renouf, Bridget Riley, Lucas Samaras, Frank Stella, Andy Warhol, Frank Lloyd Wright, Joe Zucker Catalogue with essay by Rosalind E. Krauss.
February 3–March 10	**LEE KRASNER:** *Paintings 1959–1962* Catalogue with a conversation between the artist and Richard Howard.
March 17–April 21	**JEAN DUBUFFET:** *Théâtres de mémoire: Scènes champêtres* Exhibition in collaboration with the Richard Gray Gallery. Catalogue.
April 27–June 9	**TONY SMITH:** *Ten Elements and Throwback* Catalogue with essay by Sam Hunter.
Summer	*Group Exhibition of Gallery Artists*

1979–80

September 21–October 13	**AGNES MARTIN:** *Paintings*
September 21–October 13	*Five Action Painters of the 50's* Willem de Kooning, Franz Kline, Lee Krasner, Robert Motherwell, Jackson Pollock Catalogue with a reprint of Harold Rosenberg's "Action Painting," originally published in *Art News*, December 1952.
October 26–November 24	**CHUCK CLOSE:** *Recent Work* Catalogue with essay by Kim Levin.
October 27–November 24	*Group Exhibition of Gallery Artists*
November 29–January 5	**LUCAS SAMARAS:** *Reconstructions* Catalogue with essay by Kim Levin.
January 11–February 9	**JIM DINE:** *Paintings* Catalogue with essay by James R. Mellow.
February 16–March 15	**ISAMU NOGUCHI:** *75th Birthday Exhibition* Catalogue with essay by Sam Hunter.
March 28–April 19	**ERNEST TROVA:** *The Poet Series/Table Figures* Catalogue with essay by Udo Kultermann.
March 28–April 26	*Eight Painters of the 60's: Selections from the Tremaine Collection* Jim Dine, Jasper Johns, Roy Lichtenstein, Claes Oldenburg, Robert Rauschenberg, James Rosenquist, Andy Warhol, Tom Wesselmann
May 2–June 27	**LOUISE NEVELSON:** *Maquettes in Steel and Related Works* Concurrent exhibition at Wildenstein & Co. of wood sculptures and collages. Catalogue with text by David L. Shirey and audio cassette of an interview with the artist by Barbaralee Diamonstein.
Summer	*Group Exhibition of Gallery Artists*

1980–81

September 19–October 25	*Yoruba Beadwork: Art of Nigeria* Exhibition presented in collaboration with Pace Primitive. Catalogue.
September 26–October 25	BRICE MARDEN: *New Paintings and Drawings*
October 31- November 29	JEAN DUBUFFET: *Brefs exercices d'école journalière* Catalogue with essay by Peter Schjeldahl.
November 14–December 13	AGNES MARTIN: *1980 Paintings*
December 5–January 10	LUCAS SAMARAS: *Sittings 8 x 10* 8 × 10" and 20 × 24" Polaroid portraits. Catalogue with essay by Carter Ratcliff.
December 17–January 24	*Group Exhibition of Gallery Artists*
January 30–March 14	PABLO PICASSO: *The Avignon Paintings* Catalogue with essay by James R. Mellow.
March 20–April 18	LEE KRASNER: *Solstice* 22 new mixed-media works. Catalogue with interview with the artist by Barbara Novak.
April 3–May 2	DAVID VON SCHLEGELL: *Recent Wood Sculpture*
April 14	Death of Alfred Jensen.
April 24–May 30	MARK ROTHKO: *The Surrealist Years* Catalogue with essay by Robert Rosenblum.
Summer	*Group Exhibition of Gallery Artists*

1981–82

September 25–October 31	AGNES MARTIN: *Paintings*
October 2–31	JULIO GONZÁLEZ: *Sculpture and Drawings* Catalogue with essay by Rosalind E. Krauss.
November 6–December 5	JIM DINE: *New Paintings and Drawings* Catalogue.
December 11–January 9	HANS NAMUTH: *Artists 1950–1981* 58 portraits of artists. Catalogue with introduction by Calvin Tomkins.
December 11–January 9	AD REINHARDT: *Paintings and Watercolors 1945–1951*
January 15–February 13	*Group Exhibition of Gallery Artists*
January 15–February 13	*From Chicago: Seven Chicago Artists* Roger Brown, Philip Hanson, Jim Nutt, Ed Paschke, Suellen Rocca, H.C. Westerman, Karl Wirsum Catalogue with essay by Russell Bowman.
February 19–March 20	LUCAS SAMARAS: *Pastels and Bronzes* Catalogue with text by Donald Kuspit.
April 2–May 8	SAUL STEINBERG: *Still Life and Architecture* First solo exhibition at Pace. Catalogue with essay by Italo Calvino.
May 14–June 12	ROBERT IRWIN: *A Summary of Exhibitions at Pace*
Summer	*Group Exhibition of Gallery Artists*

1982–83

September 16–October 23	PABLO PICASSO: *The Sculpture of Picasso* 43 sculptures (3 lent by The Museum of Modern Art), 22 unique ceramic and terracotta pieces, 21 drawings related to the sculptures. Catalogue with essay by Robert Rosenblum.
October 29–November 27	BRICE MARDEN: *Marbles, Paintings and Drawings* Catalogue with essay by William Zimmer.
November 5–27	ERNEST TROVA: *Bronze Poets* Catalogue.

December 3–January 8	AGNES MARTIN: *New Paintings*
December 3–January 8	JEAN DUBUFFET: *Partitions, Psycho-sites* Catalogue with puzzle, and text by Carter Ratcliff.
January 14–February 19	LOUISE NEVELSON: *Cascades, Perpendiculars, Silence, Music* Catalogue.
February 25–March 26	DAVID VON SCHLEGELL: *New Sculpture*
February 25–March 26	CHUCK CLOSE: *Recent Work* Catalogue with essay by John Perreault.
April 1–30	MARK ROTHKO: *Paintings 1948–1969* Catalogue with essay by Irving Sandler.
May 6–June 4	ISAMU NOGUCHI: *New Sculpture* Catalogue with essay by Dore Ashton.
Summer	*Group Exhibition of Gallery Artists*

1983–84

September 23–October 22	TONY SMITH: *Paintings and Sculpture* Catalogue with essay by Robert Hobbs.
October 28–November 26	BARRY FLANAGAN: *Sculpture* First solo exhibition at Pace. Catalogue with essay by Michael Compton.
December 2–January 7	ALFRED JENSEN: *The Late Works* Catalogue.
January 13–February 11	*Group Exhibition of Gallery Artists*
January 13–February 11	LUCAS SAMARAS: *Chairs, Heads, Panoramas* Simultaneous exhibitions at Pace/MacGill Gallery and Wildenstein & Co. Catalogue with interview with the artist by Douglas Blau.
January 20–February 11	AGNES MARTIN: *Paintings*
February 17–March 31	JIM DINE: *Sculpture and Drawings* Catalogue.
March 7–April 21	*Group Exhibition of Gallery Artists* Alexander Calder, Chuck Close, Robert Irwin, Brice Marden, Agnes Martin, Louise Nevelson, Ad Reinhardt, Mark Rothko, Tony Smith, Jim Dine, Barry Flanagan, Alfred Jensen, Lucas Samaras, Saul Steinberg, Frank Stella
April 27–June 9	JOAN MIRÓ: *The Sculpture of Miró* Catalogue with text by Peter Schjeldahl.
Summer	*Group Exhibition of Gallery Artists*

1984–85

	Commencing with this season, Pace Editions occupied the third floor of 32 East 57th Street and The Pace Gallery rebuilt the second floor as its primary exhibition space.
September 28–October 27	BRICE MARDEN: *Recent Work* Catalogue.
November 2–December 1	JULIAN SCHNABEL: *Paintings* First solo exhibition at Pace. Catalogue with essay by Gert Schiff.
December 7–January 12	JEAN DUBUFFET: *Mires* Catalogue with essay by Daniel Abadie.
January 18–February 16	AGNES MARTIN: *New Paintings*
February 23–March 23	*Nevelson at 85*
March 29–April 27	MARK ROTHKO: *The Dark Paintings 1969–1970* Catalogue with essay by Brian O'Doherty.
May 1–June 15	ALEXANDER CALDER: *Calder's Calders* First solo exhibition at Pace. Selected works from the artist's collection, about 40 mobiles and stabiles and 6 household items. Catalogue with reprint of an excerpt

May 12	of Jean Lipman's text from *Calder's Universe*, exhibition catalogue of the artist's 1976 retrospective at the Whitney Museum of American Art.
May 12	Death of Jean Dubuffet.
Summer	*Group Exhibition of Gallery Artists*

1985–86

September 13–October 12	**ROBERT IRWIN** Site-conditioned projects and two new installations.
October 18–November 16	**LUCAS SAMARAS:** *Paintings: The Art World* Catalogue.
November 21–January 11	**RICHARD AVEDON:** *In The American West: 1979–1984* The New York venue of the exhibition, in conjunction with Pace/MacGill Gallery; toured seven major American museums from 1985 to 1987.
January 17–February 15	**JIM DINE:** *Paintings, Drawings, Sculpture* Catalogue with excerpts from a talk by Dine at the 92nd Street YMHA on November 12, 1985.
February 21–March 22	**CHUCK CLOSE:** *Recent Work* Catalogue with interview with the artist by Arne Glimcher.
March 28–April 26	**ISAMU NOGUCHI:** *Seven Stones* Catalogue with manifesto by the artist.
May 2–August 1	**PABLO PICASSO:** *Je suis le cahier: The Sketchbooks of Picasso* One of the gallery's most significant efforts; exhibiting (some for the first time) 45 of Picasso's 175 sketchbooks. The items were loaned by the heirs, the Musée Picasso, Paris, and various other museums. The exhibition was curated by Marc Glimcher and Matthew Marks and traveled to many museums internationally. Catalogue published by Atlantic Monthly Press with texts by E.A. Carmean, Robert Rosenblum, Theodore Reff, Rosalind E. Krauss, Sam Hunter, Gert Schiff, Claude Picasso, and Françoise Gilot.

1986–87

September 19–October 25	**LOUISE NEVELSON:** *Mirrors-Shadows*
September 19–October 25	**AGNES MARTIN:** *New Paintings*
October 31–November 29	**JULIAN SCHNABEL:** *Recent Paintings* Kabuki scrim paintings. Catalogue with essay by Wilfried Dickhoff.
December 5–January 31	**JOSEPH CORNELL:** *Works from the Artist's Collection* First solo exhibition at Pace with works from the artist's estate. Catalogue with text by Brian O'Doherty (from his book *American Masters: The Voice and the Myth*).
February 6–March 7	**LUCAS SAMARAS:** *Chairs and Drawings* Catalogue with text by Gary Indiana.
March 20–April 18	**ALFRED JENSEN:** *Major Paintings*
March 20–April 18	**ALEXANDER CALDER:** *Bronzes*
April 24–June 13	**JEAN DUBUFFET:** *Towards an Alternative Reality* A major retrospective at Pace and Wildenstein & Co., which included works from European and American private collections that had rarely been shown, with loans from The Museum of Modern Art in New York, Centre Pompidou in Paris, and other museums around the

June 19–July 24	world. Catalogue published by Pace Publications and Abbeville Press, with an introduction by Mildred Glimcher and a selection of the artist's writings translated into English (some for the first time).
June 19–July 24	**CHUCK CLOSE:** *Drawings: 1974–1986* Catalogue.
Summer	*Group Exhibition of Gallery Artists*

1987–88

September 25–October 24	**RICHARD SERRA:** *Wall Props and Drawings* Exhibition and catalogue in association with the Castelli Gallery.
October 31–November 28	**SAUL STEINBERG:** *Recent Work* Catalogue with essay by Adam Gopnik.
December 4–January 2	**ROTHKO AND MIRÓ:** *Magnetic Fields and Murals*
January 8–30	**CY TWOMBLY:** *Works on Paper* Catalogue.
February 5–March 5	**JIM DINE:** *New Paintings* Catalogue with essay by Carter Ratcliff.
March 11–April 2	**GEORGE CONDO:** *Paintings and Drawings* First solo exhibition at Pace. Catalogue with introduction by Henry Geldzahler.
April 8–May 7	**BARNETT NEWMAN:** *Paintings* Exhibition organized with the cooperation of Annalee Newman, with loans from The Metropolitan Museum of Art and The Museum of Modern Art. Catalogue with essay by Yve-Alain Bois.
April 17	Death of Louise Nevelson.
May 13–June 11	**ISAMU NOGUCHI:** *Bronze and Iron Sculpture* Catalogue with essay by Dore Ashton.
June 27–September 16	*Group Sculpture Exhibition* Alexander Calder, John Chamberlain, Jean Dubuffet, Louise Nevelson, Isamu Noguchi, Lucas Samaras, Richard Serra, David Smith, Tony Smith

1988–89

September 23–October 22	**CHUCK CLOSE:** *New Paintings* Catalogue with introduction by Klaus Kertess.
October 28–November 26	**LUCAS SAMARAS:** *Boxes and Mirrored Cell* Catalogue with essay by Germano Celant.
December 2–January 7	**MALCOLM MORLEY:** *New Work* First solo exhibition at Pace. Catalogue with interview with the artist by Arne Glimcher.
December 30	Death of Isamu Noguchi.
January 20–February 11	**AGNES MARTIN:** *New Paintings*
February 24–March 25	**JOHN CHAMBERLAIN:** *New Sculpture* First solo exhibition at Pace/New York. Catalogue with essay by Donald Judd.
March 31–April 29	*Louise Nevelson Remembered* Memorial exhibition. Catalogue with photographs, quotes by Nevelson and others, and memorial letters written by many of her friends.
May 5–June 17	**ALEXANDER CALDER:** *Stabiles* Catalogue.
June 23–September 1	*Sculpture by Painters* George Condo, Willem de Kooning, Jim Dine, Jean Dubuffet, Jasper Johns, Ellsworth Kelly, Roy Lichtenstein, Joan Miró, Malcolm Morley, Barnett Newman, Pablo Picasso, Julian Schnabel, Cy Twombly, Andy Warhol

1989–90

September 15–October 14	**RICHARD SERRA:** *Recent Work* Catalogue with statement by the artist.
October 20–November 25	**JOSEPH CORNELL:** *Dovecotes, Hotels and Other White Spaces* Catalogue with essay by Brian O'Doherty.
December 1–January 6	**JULIAN SCHNABEL:** *Fox Farm Paintings* Catalogue with essay by Thomas McEvilley.
January 12–February 10	**MARK ROTHKO:** *Multiforms* Catalogue with essay by Mark Stevens.
February 16–March 17	**JIM DINE:** *Drawings* Catalogue.
April 6–May 10	**ROBERT RYMAN:** *New Paintings* First solo exhibition at Pace. Catalogue with essay by Yve-Alain Bois.
May 11–June 30	**RENÉ MAGRITTE:** *Paintings, Drawings, Sculpture* (and photography at Pace/MacGill Gallery) Catalogue with statement by the artist.
July 16–August 31	*Large-Scale Works by Gallery Artists*

As the stable of artists grew and the
need for larger exhibition space arose, a
new space at 142 Greene Street was
opened in SoHo, New York.

1990
Greene Street

May 1–June 29	**JULIAN SCHNABEL:** *Sculpture 1987–1990* Inaugural exhibition. Catalogue.

1990–91
57th Street

September 14–October 13	**BARRY FLANAGAN:** *Sculpture* Catalogue.
October 19–November 24	**GEORG BASELITZ:** *The Women of Dresden* First solo exhibition at Pace. Exhibition and catalogue, with text by Thomas McEvilley, in conjunction with Greene Street.
November 30–January 5	**DE KOONING/DUBUFFET:** *The Women* 25 works by de Kooning and 22 by Dubuffet, paintings and works on paper, including loans from major museums in the United States and Europe. Catalogue with essay by Mildred Glimcher.
January 25–March 2	**MALCOLM MORLEY:** *Recent Paintings and Sculpture*
March 8–April 13	**JOHN CHAMBERLAIN:** *New Sculpture* Catalogue with excerpts from a conversa- tion between the artist and Julie Sylvester.
April 19–May 24	**GEORGE CONDO:** *Recent Paintings* Catalogue with essay by Wilfried Dickhoff.
Summer	*Group Exhibition of Gallery Artists*

Greene Street

September 12–October 13	*Painting Alone* Juan Uslé, Callum Innes, Stefan Mattes, Patricio Cabrera, Jonathan Lasker, Georg Herold, Ian Davenport Curated by Rainer Crone and David Moos. Catalogue with essay by Rainer Crone and David Moos.
October 19–December 1	**GEORG BASELITZ:** *45* Exhibition and catalogue in conjunction with 57th Street.

December 7–January 12	**AGNES MARTIN:** *Recent Paintings*
January 19–March 2	**ALFRED JENSEN:** *Paintings* Catalogue with facsimile of a working manuscript by the artist.
March 9–May 7	*Sculpture* Alexander Calder, John Chamberlain, Donald Judd, Louise Nevelson, Isamu Noguchi, Claes Oldenburg, Richard Serra
May 11–September 14	*Changing Group Exhibition* *of Gallery Artists*

1991–92
57th Street

September 13–October 20	**DONALD JUDD:** *New Sculpture* First solo exhibition at Pace. Catalogue with essay by Yve-Alain Bois.
October 25–November 30	**LUCAS SAMARAS:** *Slices of Abstraction, Slivers of Passion* *and/or Mere Decor* Catalogue with "auto-interview" by the artist.
December 6–January 4	**AGNES MARTIN:** *Recent Paintings*
January 10–February 8	*Group Exhibition* Willem de Kooning, Franz Kline, Louise Nevelson, Barnett Newman, Jackson Pollock, Ad Reinhardt, Mark Rothko, David Smith, Clyfford Still
February 14–March 14	**ROBERT MANGOLD:** *The Attic Series* First solo exhibition at Pace. Catalogue with essay by Klaus Kertess.
March 20–April 18	**GEORG BASELITZ:** *Recent Paintings*
April 24–May 30	**JULIAN SCHNABEL:** *Olatz* Catalogue with essay by Gabriella De Ferrari, in conjunction with Greene Street shows.
Summer	*Group Exhibition of Gallery Artists*

Greene Street

September 21–October 26	**JIM DINE:** *New Paintings and Sculpture* Catalogue with interview with the artist by Martin Friedman.
November 2–December 7	**CHUCK CLOSE:** *Recent Paintings* Catalogue with essay by Peter Schjeldahl.
December 12–January 8	*Group Exhibition of Gallery Artists*
February 15–March 14	**DAN FLAVIN:** *Colored Fluorescent Light 1964 and 1992* First solo exhibition at Pace.
March 21–April 18	**RICHARD SERRA:** *Deadweights 1991–1992* Recent drawings. Catalogue with statement by the artist.
April 24–May 23	**JULIAN SCHNABEL:** *The End of Summer*
May 26–June 26	**JULIAN SCHNABEL:** *Hurricane Bob* Exhibition and catalogue in conjunction with 57th Street.
Summer	*Group Exhibition of Gallery Artists*

1992–93
57th Street

September 18–October 17	**CLAES OLDENBURG:** *New Work* First solo exhibition at Pace/New York. Catalogue with interview with the artist by Arne Glimcher.
October 23–November 28	**LOUISE NEVELSON:** *Black, White and Gold* Catalogue.
December 4–January 2	**ROBERT RYMAN:** *Versions* Exhibition and catalogue, with introduction by Christel Sauer and interview with the artist by Urs Raussmüller, in conjunction with the Hallen für neue Kunst in Schaffhausen, Switzerland.

January 15–February 6	*Sculpture and Color* Alexander Calder, John Chamberlain, Jim Dine, Dan Flavin, Donald Judd, Ellsworth Kelly, Roy Lichtenstein, Joan Miró, Joel Shapiro
February 19–March 20	**ANTONI TÀPIES:** *Recent Works* First solo exhibition at Pace. Catalogue with essay by Robert S. Lubar.
March 26–April 24	*Drawing into Film: Directors' Drawings* Robert Benton, Tim Burton, Sergei Eisenstein, Rainer Werner Fassbinder, Federico Fellini, Terry Gilliam, Alfred Hitchcock, John Huston, Akira Kurosawa, David Lynch, Martin Scorsese, Orson Welles, Fred Zinnemann Documented the role of process in film-making from annotated idea to completed scene. Catalogue with essay by Annette Michelson.
April 30–June 18	**JOEL SHAPIRO:** *Sculpture and Drawings* First solo exhibition at Pace. Exhibition and catalogue, with text by Peter Schjeldahl, in conjunction with Greene Street.
Summer	*Group Exhibition of Gallery Artists*

Greene Street

September 19–October 17	**ROBERT IRWIN:** *1°2°3°4°* Site-conditioned installation.
October 24–November 28	**JOHN CHAMBERLAIN:** *Recent Work* Large-scale wall reliefs and free-standing sculptures. Catalogue with interview with the artist by Henry Geldzahler.
December 5–January 9	**SAUL STEINBERG:** *The Discovery of America* Catalogue published with Alfred A. Knopf, Inc. with essay by Arthur C. Danto.
January 16–February 13	*Coenties Slip* Robert Indiana, Ellsworth Kelly, Agnes Martin, James Rosenquist, Jack Youngerman Crucible of young artists as a "band of outsiders." Catalogue with essay by Mildred Glimcher.
February 20–March 20	**LUCAS SAMARAS:** *Pastels* Catalogue with essay by Mildred Glimcher.
March 27–April 24	**DONALD JUDD:** *Large-Scale Works*
April 30–June 18	**JOEL SHAPIRO:** *Recent Work* Exhibition and catalogue in conjunction with 57th Street.
July 5–September 10	*Wall/Floor* Carl Andre, Donald Judd, Ellsworth Kelly, Claes Oldenburg, Richard Serra, Joel Shapiro

1993–94
57th Street

September 17–October 16	**DE KOONING/DUBUFFET:** *The Late Works* Second meeting of these giants at Pace. Catalogue with essay by Peter Schjeldahl.
October 22–November 27	**JIM DINE:** *Ape and Cat* Catalogue.
December 3–January 8	**GEORG BASELITZ:** *Paintings and Sculpture* Catalogue with essay by Donald Kuspit.
December 3–January 15	**HENRY MOORE:** *A Sculptor's Drawings* Catalogue with essay by Bernice Rose.
January 14–February 12	*Sculptor's Maquettes* Alexander Calder, Jim Dine, Jean Dubuffet, Henry Moore, Louise Nevelson, Claes Oldenburg/Coosje van Bruggen, Richard Serra, Joel Shapiro
February 4–March 12	**JOSEPH CORNELL:** *Collages*
March 18–April 23	**ROBERT MANGOLD:** *Recent Paintings and Drawings* Exhibition and catalogue, with essay by John Yau, in conjunction with Greene Street.

February 18–March 19	**MARK ROTHKO:** *The Last Paintings* 12 small paintings from 1969. Previously ignored, these works project an image of peace not usually associated with Rothko's terminal year. Catalogue with essay by Brian O'Doherty.
March 25–April 23	**JULIAN SCHNABEL:** *Boni Lux* Catalogue.
April 29–June 11	*Saul Steinberg on ART*
April 29–June 30	**BARRY FLANAGAN:** *Recent Sculpture* Catalogue.
June 24–September 9	*Summer Academy I* (drawings) Claes Oldenburg, Roy Lichtenstein, Tom Otterness, Ed Ruscha
July 8–August 9	*White Works* Jean Arp, Alexander Calder, John Chamberlain, Joseph Cornell, Dan Flavin, Ellsworth Kelly, Sol LeWitt, Piero Manzoni, Agnes Martin, Claes Oldenburg, Lucas Samaras, Joel Shapiro, Cy Twombly

Greene Street

September 18–October 16	**LOUISE NEVELSON:** *Large Outdoor Metal Sculptures* Catalogue.
October 22–November 27	**CHUCK CLOSE:** *Recent Works* Catalogue with essay by Arthur C. Danto.
December 3–January 15	**DAN FLAVIN:** *Tall Cornered Fluorescent Light* Catalogue.
December 3–January 22	**ROBERT RYMAN:** *New Paintings*
January 29–March 12	**SOL LEWITT:** *Wall Drawings* Catalogue (with Addison Gallery of American Art).
March 18–April 23	**ROBERT MANGOLD:** *Recent Paintings and Drawings* Exhibition and catalogue in conjunction with 57th Street.
April 30–June 11	**GEORGE CONDO:** *Paintings* Catalogue.
June 14–September 9	**JULIAN SCHNABEL:** *Jane Birkin Paintings*

1994–95
57th Street

September 16–October 15	**DONALD JUDD:** *Sculpture* Catalogue with essay by William C. Agee.
September 16–October 15	**JIM DINE:** *Flowers and Plants* Drawings.
October 21–November 26	**BARNETT NEWMAN:** *The Sublime Is Now:* *The Early Work of Barnett Newman* Exhibition organized with Annalee Newman, in conjunction with the Walker Art Center and St. Louis Art Museum; included works borrowed from museum and private collections. Catalogue with essay by Jeremy Strick.
October 21–November 26	**KIKI SMITH:** *Drawings* First solo exhibition at Pace.
December 2–January 7	**CLAES OLDENBURG/COOSJE VAN BRUGGEN:** *Large-Scale Projects* Brochure announcement and major publication by Monacelli Press.
December 2–January 7	*Drawings of the 60's* Georg Baselitz, Joseph Beuys, John Chamberlain, Jim Dine, François Dufrêne, Raymond Hains, Eva Hesse, David Hockney, Jasper Johns, Edward Kienholz, Roy Lichtenstein, Agnes Martin, Claes Oldenburg, Blinky Palmero, Sigmar Polke, Robert Rauschenberg, Robert Ryman, Lucas Samaras, Jean Tinguely, Cy Twombly
January 13–February 11	**ALFRED JENSEN:** *Where the Gods Reside:* *Paintings 1963–1968* Brochure with statement by the artist.

January 27–March 18	*Drawings*
	Georg Baselitz, Chuck Close, Max Ernst, Jim Dine, Arshile Gorky, Ellsworth Kelly, Piero Manzoni, Henri Matisse, Bruce Nauman, Barnett Newman, Claes Oldenburg, Pablo Picasso, Henry Moore, Auguste Rodin, Mark Rothko, Julian Schnabel, Richard Serra
February 12	Death of Donald Judd.
February 17–March 18	**AGNES MARTIN:** *Recent Paintings*
March 24–April 22	**JOEL SHAPIRO:**
	Painted Wood Sculpture and Drawings
	Catalogue with a conversation between the artist and Ellen Phelan.
April 28–June 2	**PABLO PICASSO:**
	Picasso and Drawing
	Works from the estate augmented by loans from private collections and major museums, including The Metropolitan Museum of Art and The Museum of Modern Art. Catalogue with essay by Bernice Rose.
June 26–September 23	*Summer Academy 2* (drawings)
	Georg Baselitz, Chuck Close, Sherrie Levine, Sol LeWitt, Allan McCollum, Malcolm Morley, Claes Oldenburg, Ellen Phelan, Lucas Samaras, Kiki Smith
Summer	*Group Exhibition of Gallery Artists*

Greene Street

September 17–October 15	**JOHN CHAMBERLAIN:**
	Recent Sculpture
	Catalogue with essay by Brian O'Doherty.
October 22–November 26	**LUCAS SAMARAS:**
	Cubes Pragmata + Trapezoids
	Catalogue with essay by Jan Avgikos.
December 3–January 21	**ISAMU NOGUCHI:**
	Beginnings and Ends
	Catalogue with unpublished statements by the artist.
January 27–April 4	**ANTONI TÀPIES:** *Recent Work*
March 11–May 15	**ROBERT WHITMAN:** *Backtrack*
	An environment in a constant state of flux where liquid dripped, leaked, fell and spouted in five of the six installations. The exhibition included light, objects, and video projections that addressed the themes of regeneration and the passage of time.
Summer	*Group Exhibition of Gallery Artists*

Los Angeles

May–August	**HENRY MOORE:**
	Monumental Sculptures
	10 sculptures installed in a four-block radius near City Hall and one in City Hall, Beverly Hills.

1995–96
57th Street

September 15–October 21	**GEORGE CONDO:**
	Paintings and Drawings
	Catalogue with essay by Donald Kuspit.
September 15–October 21	**JULIO GONZÁLEZ:**
	Drawing for Sculpture
	Catalogue with essay by Bernice Rose.
October 27–November 25	*The Mark Goodson Collection*
	Jean Arp, Milton Avery, Francis Bacon, Max Beckmann, Joseph Cornell, Jean Dubuffet, Lyonel Feininger, Alberto Giacometti, Wassily Kandinsky, Henri Laurens, Fernand Léger, René Magritte, Joan Miró, Louise Nevelson, Isamu Noguchi, Pablo Picasso
	Catalogue with introduction by Arne Glimcher.
November 3–December 2	**BRICE MARDEN:**
	Drawings: 1964–1994
	Catalogue.

November 30–January 13	**ANTONI TÀPIES:** *New Paintings*
	Catalogue with a conversation between the artist and Manuel J. Borja-Villel.
December 8–January 13	**ROBERT RYMAN:** *Core Drawings*
January 19–February 17	**ALEXANDER CALDER:** *The 50's*
	Exhibition and catalogue, with essay by Mildred Glimcher, in conjunction with Los Angeles (see below).
February 2–17	*Master Drawings*
	Constantin Brancusi, Jean Dubuffet, Max Ernst, Arshile Gorky, Fernand Léger, Henry Moore, Pablo Picasso
February 22–March 23	**JEAN DUBUFFET:**
	The Radiant Earth
	50 paintings and sculptures that focused on the artist's investigation of the natural world. Catalogue with essay by Arne Glimcher.
February 22–March 23	**GEORG BASELITZ:** *Drawings*
March 28–April 27	**AGNES MARTIN:**
	New Drawings and Watercolors
May 3–June 8	**ELIZABETH MURRAY:** *Drawings*
	First solo exhibition at Pace.
March 28–April 27	**JIM DINE:** *Some Greeks, Some Romans*
	150 mixed-media works on paper depicting classical heads that Dine made in London, Munich, and New York from 1992 to 1996. Catalogue with statement by the artist.
May 3–June 8	**JOHN CHAMBERLAIN:**
	Recent Sculpture
Summer	*Summer Academy 3* (drawings)
	Jim Dine, Raymond Hains, Edward Kienholz, Brice Marden, Agnes Martin, Bruce Nauman, Claes Oldenburg, Lucas Samaras, Richard Serra, Andy Warhol
	Group Exhibition of Gallery Artists

Greene Street

September 16–October 21	**KIKI SMITH:** *New Work*
	Catalogue.
October 28–November 25	**ROBERT MANGOLD:**
	Curved Plane/Figure Paintings
	Catalogue with essay by David Carrier.
December 2–January 13	**CHUCK CLOSE:** *Recent Paintings*
	Exhibition and catalogue, with essay by John Yau, in conjunction with Los Angeles (see below).
January 20–February 10	*Group Exhibition of Gallery Artists*
February 15–March 23	**JULIAN SCHNABEL:**
	The Conversion of St. Paolo Malfi
	Catalogue with essay by Bernice Rose.
March 30–April 27	**DAN FLAVIN:** *Recent Work*
May 4–June 21	**ROBERT RYMAN:** *Recent Paintings*
Summer	*Group Exhibition of Gallery Artists*

Los Angeles

September 29	PaceWildenstein Los Angeles opened at 9540 Wilshire Boulevard in Beverly Hills.
September 29–October 28	**CHUCK CLOSE:** *Recent Paintings*
	Exhibition and catalogue in conjunction with Greene Street, December 1995.
September 29–October 28	**GEORG BASELITZ:** *Drawings*
November 9–December 29	**ALEXANDER CALDER:** *The 50's*
	Exhibition and catalogue in conjunction with 57th Street.
November 9–December 9	**SOL LEWITT:** *Gouaches*
January 12–February 3	**AGNES MARTIN:** *New Paintings*
January 12–February 3	**GEORGE CONDO:**
	Drawings 1976–1996
February 9–March 9	**ALFRED JENSEN:** *A Survey*
March 15–April 20	**JOEL SHAPIRO:**
	Sculpture and Drawings
	Catalogue with essay by Michael Brenson.
April 25–June 1	**DONALD JUDD:**
	Stacks and Progressions
	Catalogue.
Summer	*Group Exhibition of Gallery Artists*

1996–97
57th Street

October 8–November 30
BARBARA HEPWORTH:
Sculptures from the Estate
Exhibition at Wildenstein and Co., New York.
Catalogue with foreword by Sir Alan
Bowness and essay by Alan G. Wilkinson.

September 19–October 19
ROBERT RAUSCHENBERG:
Anagrams
Exhibition and catalogue, with essay
by Bernice Rose, in conjunction with
Los Angeles.

October 25–November 23
LUCAS SAMARAS:
*Kiss Kill, Perverted Geometry,
Inedibles, Self-Absorption*
Highlights of 40 years, including *Photo-
Transformations* at Greene Street. Catalogue,
with excerpt from "Waitingman," 1967, by
the artist, in conjunction with Greene Street.

November 26–January 4
JIM DINE: *Recent Work*
Exhibition and catalogue, with statement
by the artist, in conjunction with Los Angeles.

January 16–February 15
AGNES MARTIN: *Recent Paintings*

February 19–March 22
BONNARD/ROTHKO:
Color and Light
13 Rothko paintings, 21 Bonnard
paintings. Explored Rothko's debt to
Bonnard's use of color. Catalogue with
essay by Bernice Rose.

March 28–April 26
LOUISE NEVELSON:
Sculpture 1957–1987
Catalogue with a collection of quotes from
the artist.

May 2–June 20
ALFRED JENSEN AND TONY SMITH:
Personal Geometry
Double catalogue.

Summer
Group Exhibition of Gallery Artists

Greene Street

September 27–November 2
JOEL SHAPIRO: *Recent Sculpture*

November 8–December 14
LUCAS SAMARAS:
Photo-Transformations 1973–1976
Catalogue in conjunction with 57th Street.

December 20–January 4
Group Exhibition of Gallery Artists

January 11–February 8
ROBERT WHITMAN: *Great Lakes*
An installation conceived in 1995–96 with
three mixed-media pieces using found
objects, a scrim, and video projectors.

February 14–March 15
GEORG BASELITZ: *Recent Paintings*
Catalogue with essay by Richard Shiff.

March 21–April 26
ROBERT MANGOLD: *Zone Paintings*
Exhibition and catalogue, with essay by
Alexander van Grevenstein, in conjunction
with Los Angeles.

May 1–June 20
ELIZABETH MURRAY:
Recent Paintings
Catalogue with interview with the artist by
Joan Simon.

Summer
Group Exhibition of Gallery Artists

Los Angeles

August 8–September 28
Group Exhibition of Gallery Artists

August 8–September 28
KIKI SMITH: *Field Operation*

October 4–November 9
JIM DINE: *Recent Work*
Exhibition and catalogue in conjunction
with 57th Street.

November 15–January 18
ROBERT RAUSCHENBERG: *Anagrams*
Exhibition and catalogue in conjunction
with 57th Street.

November 15–January 18
LUCAS SAMARAS: *Pastels*

January 24–March 1
ELIZABETH MURRAY:
Recent Paintings

January 24–March 1
DONALD JUDD: *Furniture*

March 7–April 19
JULIAN SCHNABEL:
Selected Paintings

April 25–June 7
ROBERT MANGOLD:
*Paintings 1990–1997/Drawings for
Zone Paintings*
Exhibition and catalogue in conjunction
with Greene Street.

June 20–July 26
GEORGE CONDO:
Collage Abstractions

July 10–September 6
LUCIO FONTANA: *Works on Paper*

Summer
Group Exhibition of Gallery Artists

1997–98
57th Street

September 19–October 18
ROBERT RAUSCHENBERG:
Arcadian Retreats
Frescoes made in 1996; exhibition
coincided with retrospective at the
Guggenheim Museum. Catalogue with
essay by Bernice Rose.

October 24–December 13
MONDRIAN/REINHARDT:
Influence and Affinity
Catalogue with "reflections" by
Arne Glimcher.

December 19–January 15
Winter Group Exhibition
Carl Andre, Georg Baselitz, John
Chamberlain, Giorgio De Chirico, Willem
de Kooning, Jim Dine, Jean Dubuffet,
Alberto Giacometti, Joan Miró, Elizabeth
Murray, Claes Oldenburg, Mark Rothko,
Robert Ryman, Lucas Samaras, Julian
Schnabel, Joel Shapiro, Antoni Tàpies

February 3–March 14
DONALD JUDD:
Early Fabricated Work
Catalogue with essay by Rosalind E. Krauss.

March 27–April 25
AGNES MARTIN: *New Paintings*

May 1–June 26
ISAMU NOGUCHI: *Stones and Water*
Basalt and granite sculptures and fountains.
Catalogue with essay by Jeremy Strick.

Summer
Group Exhibition of Gallery Artists

Greene Street

September 6–20
Emerging Artists
Ward Ackerman, Yugi Agematsu, Sunny
Beirs, Jeff Burch, Manuel Cancel, Tucker
Capparell, Cayse Cheatham, Michael
Coughton, Jory Felice, Bruce Gluck, David
Goerk, Derrick Hilbertz, Joey Kötting,
Jose Marin, Jon McCafferty, Amy Olson,
Edward Pantalon, Tami Philion, Cay Rose,
Bill Scanga, Robert Selwyn, Motohiko
Tokuta, Alan Wiener, William Wood

September 25–October 25
KIKI SMITH:
Reconstructing the Moon
Mixed-media installations and sculptures,
works on paper and a video. Catalogue.

October 31–December 13
JULIAN SCHNABEL:
Portrait Paintings
Exhibition and catalogue in conjunction
with Los Angeles.

December 19–January 24
Group Exhibition of Gallery Artists

January 30–March 7
GEORGE CONDO: *Collage Paintings*
Catalogue with interview with the artist
by Michael FitzGerald.

March 11–April 25
JOHN CHAMBERLAIN:
Chamberlain's Fauve Landscape
Two monumental sculptures: *The Privet*
and *The Hedge*. Catalogue.

May 1–June 19
ROBERT IRWIN:
A Selection of Works 1958 to 1970
Catalogue.

Summer
Group Exhibition of Gallery Artists

Los Angeles

September 26–November 8
PHILIP-LORCA DICORCIA:
Hollywood Pictures 1990–1992

November 14–January 10
JOHN CHAMBERLAIN:
Sculpture and Photographs

November 14–January 10	**LOUISE NEVELSON:** *Collages*
January 22–March 7	**PABLO PICASSO:** *Works from the Estate and Selected Loans*
March 12–April 4	*Group Exhibition of Gallery Artists*
February 14–28	*Portraits from the Collection of Mr. Chow*
April 10–May 23	**JULIAN SCHNABEL:** *Portrait Paintings* Exhibition and catalogue in conjunction with Greene Street.
July 2–August 29	**SOL LEWITT:** *Flat and Glossy Colors*

1998–99
57th Street

September 11–October 10	**GEORG BASELITZ:** *New Paintings* Catalogue with essay by Pamela Kort.
October 16–November 14	**JOEL SHAPIRO:** *New Wood and Bronze Sculpture* Exhibition and catalogue, with essay by Klaus Kertess, in conjunction with Greene Street.
November 18–January 2	**LUCAS SAMARAS:** *Gold* Gold jewelry, x-ray film portraits, and an installation of strings of glass beads. Catalogue with essay by Barbara Rose.
January 15–February 6	**ROBERT RYMAN:** *Paintings* Catalogue.
February 12–March 13	**ELIZABETH MURRAY:** *Recent Paintings* Catalogue with interview with the artist by Bob Holman.
March 18–April 17	**ROBERT MANGOLD:** *Recent Zone Paintings* Catalogue with essay by Nancy Princenthal.
April 22–July 5	**JULIAN SCHNABEL:** *Plate Paintings 1978–1997* Portraits. Exhibition and catalogue in conjunction with Greene Street.
May 12	Death of Saul Steinberg.

Greene Street

September 10–October 10	**SOL LEWITT:** *New Wall Drawings*
October 16–November 14	**JOEL SHAPIRO:** *New Wood and Bronze Sculpture* Exhibition and catalogue in conjunction with 57th Street.
November 18–January 16	**PHILIP-LORCA DICORCIA:** *Street Work* Photographs taken in Japan, Mexico, Germany, India, and New York.
January 21–March 13	*Group Exhibition of Gallery Artists*
March 19–April 17	**ROBERT RAUSCHENBERG:** *Anagrams (A Pun)* New paintings utilizing photography and special printing techniques. Catalogue with statement by the artist.
April 22–July 5	**JULIAN SCHNABEL:** *Plate Paintings 1978–1997* Large-format paintings. Exhibition and catalogue in conjunction with 57th Street.
Summer	*Group Exhibition of Gallery Artists*

Los Angeles

September 3–October 3	*Sculpture*
October 9–31	**AGNES MARTIN:** *New Paintings*
October 8–31	**ROBERT IRWIN:** *Early Paintings*
November 6–December 23	**ANTONI TÀPIES:** *Recent Paintings*
November 6–December 23	**ISAMU NOGUCHI:** *Small Stones*
January 13–March 20	**GEORG BASELITZ:** *New Paintings*
January 13–March 20	**JOEL SHAPIRO:** *Recent Sculpture*
March 26–May 1	**DONALD JUDD:** *Wall Works*
March 26–May 1	**ALFRED JENSEN:** *Crossing the Equator*
May 6–July 3	**JOHN MCLAUGHLIN:** *Paintings*

1999–2000
57th Street

September 1–25	**IRVING PENN:** *New and Unseen* Catalogue with foreword by Peter MacGill and several written homages by various curators and friends.
October 1–30	**SAUL STEINBERG:** *Drawing into Being* Memorial exhibition. Catalogue with foreword by Arne Glimcher and essay by Bernice Rose.
November 4–December 11 (exhibition extended to January 8)	**NAUM GABO:** *Pioneer of Abstract Sculpture* First American exhibition of Gabo's work since 1953. Catalogue with introduction by Graham Williams.
January 14–February 12	**ANTONI TÀPIES:** *Recent Work* Catalogue with essay by Dan Cameron.
February 18–March 20	*Earthly Forms: The Biomorphic Sculpture of Arp, Calder and Noguchi* Catalogue with essay by Marc Glimcher.
March 24–April 22	**GEORG BASELITZ:** *Recent Paintings* Catalogue.
April 27–June 3	**AGNES MARTIN:** *Recent Paintings* Catalogue.
Summer	*Group Exhibition of Gallery Artists*

Greene Street

September 24–October 23	**JIM DINE:** *Color Photographs* Digital prints on canvas of Dine's familiar subjects. Catalogue with essay by James L. Enyeart.
October 29–November 27	**KIKI SMITH:** *Of Her Nature* Sculpture, drawings, and prints.
December 3–January 29	**GEORGE CONDO:** *Jazz Paintings* Catalogue with introduction by the artist and essays by Olivier Berggruen and Paul D. Miller a.k.a. DJ Spooky.
February 5–March 11	*Group Exhibition of Gallery Artists*
March 17–April 29	**CHUCK CLOSE:** *New Work* Catalogue with essay by Richard Shiff.
May 12–June 10	**JOHN CHAMBERLAIN:** *Recent Sculpture* Catalogue with selected quotations from critical literature.
Summer	*Group Exhibition of Gallery Artists*

This concludes the record of exhibitions at Pace Gallery/PaceWildenstein for the first 40 years. PaceWildenstein continues vigorously both at 57th Street and at its new location at 534–548 West 25th Street.

Pace Editions: Selected Publications

1968

Lucas Samaras, *Book*, 1968
Three-dimensional multiple in the form of an 18-page book, each leaf ³⁄₁₆" thick; overall dimensions, 10 × 10 × 2". Produced using five processes: serigraphy, lithography, embossing, thermography, and die-cutting. Signed and numbered edition of 100.

Ernest Trova, *Manscapes*, 1968
Portfolio of 10 original silkscreens measuring 28 × 28" in a signed and numbered edition of 175.

1969

Nicholas Krushenick, *Amberbahn*, 1969
Silkscreen print measuring 34 × 30" in a signed and numbered edition of 100.

Sven Lukin, *Portfolio #1*, 1969
Portfolio of 8 silkscreen prints. 4 measuring 29 × 33" and 4 measuring 33 × 29", in a signed and numbered edition of 175.

1970

List Art Poster Program
Acquisition of 40 posters created by HKL Ltd. for Lincoln Center and other non-profit institutions to publicize and commemorate activities and events.

George Segal, *Sleeping Girl*, 1970
Cast-plaster fragment multiple sculpture measuring 19 × 13 × 11" in a signed and numbered edition of 125. Published in collaboration with Galerie der Speigel, Cologne, Germany.

Jack Youngerman, *Changes*, 1970
Portfolio of 8 silkscreen prints measuring 43 × 33", in a signed and numbered edition of 175.

1971

Ernest Trova, *F.M. Shadow Figure*, 1971
Nickel-plated bronze shadow figure mounted in a Plexiglas box measuring 7 × 11 × 7⅜", in a signed and numbered edition of 150.

Jean Dubuffet, *Le Tétrascopique*, 1971
Four-sided multiple measuring 36 × 20 × 20" composed of 4 shaped acrylic panels mounted on a metal base to form a three-dimensional rectangular sculpture. Each panel measures 36 × 20 × 1" and is silkscreened in 4 colors on the front and 2 colors on the back. Each multiple in a signed and numbered edition of 45.

Lucas Samaras, *Autopolaroids*, 1971
104-page book containing reproductions of self-photographed Polaroid portraits in an edition of 2,000 plus 100 deluxe copies, each containing a signed and numbered Polaroid. Published in collaboration with the Whitney Museum of American Art.

1972

Louise Nevelson, *Night Tree*, 1972
Lead intaglio collage print consisting of an assemblage of wood-grained lead foil relief elements bonded to paper measuring 30⅛ × 25" in a signed and numbered edition of 150.

Gloria F. Ross, *Tapestry Collection*
First exhibition of tapestries commissioned and published by Gloria F. Ross from maquettes created by Helen Frankenthaler, Adolph Gottlieb, Robert Goodnough, Robert Motherwell, Louise Nevelson, Kenneth Noland, Frank Stella, Ernest Trova, and Jack Youngerman.

1973

Alfred Jensen, *Untitled (Print #1)*, 1973
Portfolio of 4 silkscreen prints measuring 35 × 35" in a signed and numbered edition of 150.

1974

Louise Nevelson, *Dark Ellipse,* 1974
Black three-dimensional sculpture of polyester resin measuring 17 × 6 × 6". Each multiple is signed in a numbered edition of 125.

1975

Jean Dubuffet, *Solitude Illuminée*, 1975
Three-color silkscreen measuring 38 × 28" in a signed and numbered edition of 50.

Louise Nevelson, *Dawnscape*, 1975
White cast-paper relief print of 100 percent cotton fiber pulp, measuring 27 × 31" in a signed and numbered edition of 75.

1976

Jim Dine, *A Robe with 13 Kinds of Oil Paint*, 1976
Soft-ground etching measuring 42 × 30" in a signed and numbered edition of 10.

Jean Dubuffet, *Fables*, 1976
Portfolio of 6 silkscreen prints measuring 34 × 27" in a signed and numbered edition of 50.

Chuck Hinman, *Untitled*, 1976
Portfolio of 4 silkscreen and embossed prints measuring 38 × 41" in a signed and numbered edition of 100.

Georges Noël, *Untitled*, 1976
Suite of 2 silkscreen prints on sandpaper, each measuring 27 × 27" in a signed and numbered edition of 100.

1977

Gene Davis, *Royal Canoe* and *Davy's Locker*, 1977
Suite of 2 silkscreen prints, each measuring 37 × 42" in a signed and numbered edition of 100.

Jim Dine, *The Brown Coat*, 1977
Color etching with aquatint and soft-ground etching measuring 42 × 30" in a signed and numbered edition of 50.

Jean Dubuffet, *Le Fugitif*, 1977
Multiple consisting of a four-color silkscreened abstract background on a metal sheet with a die-cut magnetized four-color silkscreened figure attached that can be moved to different positions on the background. Each multiple measures 27⅝ × 19⅜" overall in a signed and numbered edition of 50.

Bridget Riley, *Untitled*, 1977
Portfolio of 3 five-color silkscreened prints measuring 38 × 19⅝" in a signed and numbered edition of 100.

1978

Stephan Antonakos, *Pink Incomplete Square* and *Pink Incomplete Square on Blue*, 1978
2 die-cut etchings, each measuring 38 × 25" in a signed and numbered edition of 30.

Agnes Denes, *Probability Pyramid*, 1978
Color lithograph measuring 29 × 41" in a signed and numbered editions of 40.

Jim Dine, *Temple of Flora*, 1977–78
Portfolio of 9 hand-colored etchings, each measuring 39 × 27" in a signed and numbered edition of 30.

Jean Dubuffet, *Faits Mémorables*, 1978
Portfolio of 3 silkscreened images with over 80 printings of multiple elements within the final image. Each measures 29 × 38", in a signed and numbered edition of 70.

1979

Jean Dubuffet, *Site de Mémoire I, II, III*, 1979
3 black-and-white silkscreen prints on canvas, mounted to stretchers. They vary in scale as follows: I: 99 × 67⅝"; II: 84 × 58"; III: 57 × 83". Each in a signed and numbered edition of 10.

Louise Nevelson, *Celebrations*, 1979
Suite of 6 multicolored aquatint etchings on Arches cover measuring 44 × 31" in a signed and numbered edition of 50.

1980

Jim Dine, *Yellow Robe*, 1980
Three-color lithograph measuring 50 × 35" in a signed and numbered edition of 40.

Louise Nevelson, *Full Moon*, 1980
Polyester resin multiple mounted on a black wood frame measuring 18 × 18 × 2" in a signed and numbered edition of 125.

Don Nice, *American Still Life*, 1980
Suite of 3 color lithographs each measuring 30 × 22" in a signed and numbered edition of 50.

Joe Zucker, *Toucans*, 1980
Series of 25 handmade paper monoprints. Each print silkscreened with the same black-and-white Toucan image on which the artist applied a variety of colored pulps to create unique color variations of the image. Each measures 36 × 36" and is signed.

1981

Chuck Close, *Phil/Fingerprint*, 1981
Black-and-white lithograph, created by the artist with his thumbprint, measuring 50 × 38" in a signed and numbered edition of 36.

Jim Dine, *A Heart on the Rue de Grenelle*, 1981
Hand-painted etching with soft-ground etching and aquatint measuring 41⅞ × 29⅝" in a signed and numbered edition of 36. Printed and published by Aldo Crommelynck.

Jean Dubuffet, *Parcours*, 1981
Black-and-white silkscreen printed on silk in the form of a scroll measuring 20 × 240", in a signed and numbered edition of 80. Each scroll is attached at each end with a dowel and is enclosed in a wood box with a two-color screened top.

1982

Chuck Close, *Phil/Manipulated*, 1982
Hand-made paper pulp print on a gray background, with twenty-four-color pulp variations from white to black, measuring 38 × 28" in a signed and numbered edition of 25.

Jim Dine, *Fourteen Color Woodcut Bathrobe,* 1982
Fourteen-color woodcut produced from only two blocks, measuring 77 × 42" in a signed and numbered edition of 75.

Michael Mazur, *Amaryllis/Calla Lilly I*, 1982
Hand-inked single-plate etching measuring 44 × 31" in a signed and numbered edition of 20. Published in collaboration with the Harkus-Krakow Gallery, Boston.

Louise Nevelson, *Sky Gate*, 1982
Cast-paper relief print on gray handmade paper measuring 33 × 20" in a signed and numbered edition of 90.

1983

Jim Dine, *The Heart and the Wall*, 1983
Large four-part soft-ground etching with aquatint. Each of the 4 sheets of paper measures 42 × 33⅜", creating a print that measures 84 × 67" in a signed and numbered edition of 28. Printed by Graphicstudio, Tampa, Florida.

Tom Holland, *Santa Del Series*, 1983
Series of 12 three-dimensional cast-paper, hand-painted constructions, each print measuring 24 × 36", signed and framed in a Plexiglas box.

1984

Chuck Close, *Georgia*, 1984
Handmade paper print in 24 gradations of color from black to white, measuring 56 × 44" in a signed and numbered edition of 35.

Jim Dine, *Nine Views of Winter*, 1984
Series of 9 prints of the artist's *Venus* image, created with variations of a jigsawed woodblock that was transformed into 3 sections. Sections of the simple woodblock were used for each print, together with another block or stainless steel plate. Colors of a variety of materials were applied in various printing

sequences and, in one print, a screen printing was also employed. Each print measures 52 × 37" and is signed and numbered in an edition of 24.

1985

Jim Dine, *Rise Up Solitude*, 1985
Drypoint with hand-painting, the artist's *Venus* and *Tree* images, measuring 52 × 58", in a signed and numbered edition of 35.

Julian Schnabel, *Mother*, 1985
Etching printed over a nine-color photo-lithographed map measuring 71 × 47" in a signed and numbered edition of 35.

1986

James Brown, *Untitled*, 1986
Portfolio of 7 prints, the first printed in Pace Prints' facilities at 115 East 23rd Street. Each a combination of etching and drypoint with watercolor and each a unique variant measuring 30 × 22" in a signed and numbered edition of 15.

Chuck Close, *Leslie/Fingerprint*, 1986
Black-and-white carbon transfer print created from an image of Close's thumbprints of wife, Leslie, measuring 54 × 41" in a signed and numbered edition of 45.

Jim Dine, *The Side View*, 1986
Black-and-white print, combining etching, soft-ground etching, and drypoint, depicting a profile view of a skeletal skull, measuring 45 × 43" in a signed and numbered edition of 20.

Robert Stackhouse, *Niagara Dance*, 1986
Color lithograph measuring 37⅛ × 45" in a signed and numbered edition of 45.

The Next Development
In 1987, Pace Editions established printing facilities, the Spring Street Workshop (SSW), at its new 72 Spring Street location. The workshop had the capacity to produce intaglio and relief prints and a paper mill to produce handmade paper.

1987

Richard Bosman, *Sunset*, 1987
An eleven-color linocut measuring 33 × 25" in a signed and numbered edition of 40. Printed at SSW.

Jim Dine, *Youth and the Maiden*, 1987
Large triptych woodcut with etching and hand painting, with an overall measurement of 78⅛ × 140⅝". Each woodcut in a signed and numbered edition of 16.

April Gornik, *Light After the Flood*, 1987
Soft-ground etching measuring 28 × 42" in a signed and numbered edition of 23. Printed at SSW.

Alan Shields, *Soft and Fluffy Gear Series*, 1987
Series of 9 assembled, punched, and glued handmade paper prints in varying sizes in signed and numbered editions of 15. Printed at SSW.

In 1988, Pace Editions formed Aldo Crommelynck/ New York (AC), a joint venture with the French master printer Aldo Crommelynck, who established an etching atelier at 72 Spring Street to create prints exclusively for distribution by Pace Editions.

1988

Donald Baechler, *Tree*, 1988
Stenciled handmade paper print measuring 34 × 34" in a signed and numbered edition of 22. Printed at SSW.

Richard Bosman, *Adrift I*, 1988
Soft-ground and spitbite etching measuring 24 × 29" in a signed and numbered edition of 50. Printed by AC.

Chuck Close, *Self-Portrait*, 1988
Spitbite aquatint measuring 20 × 15⅝" in a signed and numbered edition of 50. Printed by AC.

Michael David, *Lingen*, 1988
Linocut with pochoir and soft-ground etching on handmade paper measuring 20 × 24" in a signed and numbered edition of 12. Printed at SSW.

Jim Dine, *Glyptotek*, 1988
Book of 40 etchings with aquatint from his drawings of classical sculptures in Munich's Glyptotek, the museum of ancient art. Each plate in the book measures 27 × 21" and the book is signed and numbered in an edition of 90.

Gary Stephan, *Untitled*, 1988
Suite of 3 monochrome etchings of varying sizes with chine collé in editions of 15. Printed at SSW.

1989

James Brown, *The Five Sorrowful Mysteries*, 1989
Portfolio of 5 etchings measuring 31 × 26" in a signed and numbered edition of 35. Printed at SSW.

Francesco Clemente, *Untitled*, 1989
Portfolio of 6 etchings with aquatint measuring 21⅞ × 15⅝" in a signed and numbered edition of 35. Printed by AC.

George Condo, *Untitled*, 1989
Portfolio of 7 etchings measuring 18 × 14⅞" in a signed and numbered edition of 55. Printed by AC.

Glenn Goldberg, *Duster Plus*, 1989
Portfolio of 3 relief prints measuring 25⅞ × 19⅝" in a signed and numbered edition of 35. Printed at SSW.

Peter Halley, *A Tour of the Monuments of Passaic, New Jersey*, 1989
Portfolio of 5 line engravings measuring 16 × 20" in a signed and numbered edition of 50. Printed at SSW.

Robert Stackhouse, *Sources and Structures*, 1988–89
Portfolio of 6 color spitbite etchings measuring 31 × 21" in a signed and numbered edition of 50. Printed at SSW.

Meyer Vaisman, *Summer Suite*, 1989
Portfolio of 6 screenprints measuring 49 × 34" in a signed and numbered edition of 75.

Pace Prints   *The Latest Development*
The name of the contemporary print gallery was changed from Pace Editions to Pace Prints.

1990

John Alexander, *Untitled*, 1990
Portfolio of 4 etchings with aquatint and hand-coloring measuring 25 × 29" in a signed and numbered edition of 35. Printed at SSW.

Joe Andoe, *Untitled*, 1990
Portfolio of 5 etchings with aquatint measuring 20 × 21" in a signed and numbered edition of 50. Printed at SSW.

Chuck Close, *Lucas/Book*, 1990
Accordian-fold letterpress book illustrating 7 color reduction black linocuts. Printed at SSW.

Michael David, *The Archer's Plum*, 1990
Portfolio of 4 multicolor relief prints measuring 16 × 26" in a signed and numbered edition of 45. Printed at SSW.

Jim Dine, *Fo Dog in Hell*, 1990
Etching with hand-coloring measuring 48 × 31⅞" in a signed and numbered edition of 30.

Mary Heilmann, *Untitled*, 1990
Portfolio of 4 etchings on handmade paper measuring 16 × 12" in a signed and numbered edition of 30. Printed at SSW.

Julian Schnabel, *Untitled*, 1990
Suite of 3 prints that appropriate photographs by Jean Kallina, combining photolithography, woodcut, etching, and screenprinting. These oversized prints vary in size and are signed and numbered in an edition of 35.

Joel Shapiro, *Untitled*, 1990
Portfolio of 4 color aquatints measuring 37⅜ × 27" in a signed and numbered edition of 60. Printed by AC.

Joe Zucker, *Cochise*, 1990
Portfolio of 3 spitbite etchings measuring 16 × 30" in a signed and numbered edition of 30. Printed at SSW.

1991

Jennifer Bartlett, *Galls of Water I*, 1991
Color aquatint measuring 16 × 20⅛" in a signed and numbered edition of 40. Printed by AC.

Chuck Close, *Alex*, 1991
A 95-color, 47 block printed in the Ukiyo-e technique on paper measuring 28 × 23" in a signed and numbered edition of 75.

John Chamberlain, *Melon Collie Gondola Series*, 1991
Series of 3 color etchings measuring 14 × 28" in a signed and numbered edition of 18. Printed at SSW.

Alfred Leslie, *Montauk*, 1991
Portfolio of 3 aquatint etchings measuring 16 × 17" in a signed and numbered edition of 50. Printed at SSW.

Robert Stackhouse, *Blue Diviners*, 1991
A 23-color, 17 block printed in the Ukiyo-e technique on paper measuring 26 × 18" in a signed and numbered edition of 75.

1992

Chuck Close, *Self-Portrait*, 1992
Etching measuring 19 × 15" in a signed and numbered edition of 70. Printed at SSW.

Jim Dine, *Summer*, 1992
Five-color woodcut triptych on 3 sheets of paper, each measuring 45 × 36", each in a signed and numbered edition of 33. Printed at SSW.

Alfred Leslie, *Melena*, 1992
Etching with soft-ground etching, aquatint, and hand-coloring measuring 49 × 39⅛" in a signed and numbered edition of 20. Printed at SSW.

Claes Oldenburg, *Proposed Colossal Monument for Mill Rock, East River, New York City: Slice of Strawberry Shortcake*, 1992
Color etching measuring 23 × 29" in a signed and numbered edition of 60. Printed by AC.

Joel Shapiro, *Untitled*, 1992
2 color etchings measuring 32 × 24" in a signed and numbered edition of 60. Printed by AC.

Terry Winters, *Field Notes*, 1992
Portfolio of 25 etchings measuring 13 × 10" in a signed and numbered edition of 75. Printed by AC.

1993

John Chamberlain, *After Dogberry*, 1993
Silkscreen and relief print measuring 82 × 29" in a signed and numbered edition of 33.

Chuck Close, *Alex/Reduction Print*, 1993
Three-color silkscreen print, from screens created from mylar positives printed from each state of a 7-state reduction linocut, measuring 79⅜ × 60⅜" in a signed and numbered edition of 35.

Jim Dine, *The Colorful Wall*, 1993
Woodcut with hand-painting measuring 55 × 42" in a signed and numbered edition of 18. Printed at SSW.

Günther Förg, *Untitled*, 1993
3 color etchings with aquatints in varying sizes, each in a signed and numbered edition of 55. Printed by AC.

Robert Mangold, *Plane/Figure Series, Folded*, 1993
Portfolio of 4 etchings with soft-ground etching and aquatint on paper with a fold, measuring 22 × 30" in a signed and numbered edition of 60. Printed at SSW.

Santiago Moix, *The Nocturnal World*, 1993
Portfolio of 5 color woodcuts measuring 19 × 17" in a signed and numbered edition of 20. Printed at SSW.

Claes Oldenburg, *Proposal for a Colossal Monument in Downtown New York City: Sharpened Pencil Stub with Broken-Off Tip of the Woolworth Building*, 1993
Color etching measuring 32 × 22" in a signed and numbered edition of 60. Printed by AC.

Donald Sultan, *Black Flowers and Vase*, 1993
Etching with aquatint measuring 31 × 29" in a signed and numbered edition of 50. Printed by AC.

1994

Jim Dine, *Raven on White Paper*, 1994
Intaglio print created with a cardboard plate, measuring 53 × 42" in a signed and numbered edition of 15. Printed at SSW.

April Gornik, *Diving Water*, 1994
Color etching with soft-ground etching and aquatint measuring 32 × 31" in a signed and numbered edition of 30. Printed at SSW.

Red Grooms, *Main Concourse, Grand Central Terminal*, 1994
A 65-color etching with aquatint and soft-ground etching measuring 31 × 33" in a signed and numbered edition of 75. Printed by AC.

Peter Halley, *Exploding Cell*, 1994
Portfolio of 9 silkscreen prints measuring 37 × 48" in a signed and numbered edition of 32.

Mary Heilmann, *Charm*, 1994
Color aquatint measuring 40 × 28" in a signed and numbered edition of 40. Printed at SSW.

Santiago Moix, *Gypsy*, 1994
Portfolio of 13 drypoints, measuring 14 × 15" in a signed and numbered edition of 20. Printed at SSW.

Joel Shapiro, *Untitled*, 1994
Etching measuring 38⅝ × 32" in a signed and numbered edition of 30. Printed by AC.

1995

Jim Dine, *Winter Dream (for V)*, 1995
Portfolio of 12 woodcuts measuring 67 × 51" in a signed and numbered edition of 12.

Jim Dine, *Very Picante*, 1995
Color intaglio print created with a cardboard plate, measuring 57⅝ × 42⅛" in a signed and numbered edition of 40. Printed at SSW.

Robert Mangold, *Curved Plane/Figure II and III*, 1995
2 color woodcuts, each measuring 20 × 15" in a signed and numbered edition of 60. Printed at SSW.

Saul Steinberg, *Las Vegas*, 1995
Color etching and aquatint measuring 17⅝ × 14" in a signed and numbered edition of 50. Printed by AC.

Terry Winters, *Vorticity Field*, 1995
Color aquatint measuring 29 × 36" in a signed and numbered edition of 50. Printed by AC.

1996

Polly Apfelbaum, *Eclipse,* 1996
Series of monotypes combining relief printing and collage in varying sizes. Printed at SSW.

Ed Baynard, *Poppies*, 1996
3 color linocuts, each measuring 30 × 24" in a signed and numbered edition of 28. Printed at SSW.

Jim Dine, *A Beautiful Heart*, 1996
Multicolor etching with aquatint and soft-ground etching measuring 31 × 25⅝" in a signed and numbered edition of 60. Printed by AC.

Sol LeWitt, *Straight Lines in All Directions*, 1996
Series of 30 unique 5-color silkscreen monotypes, each measuring 56 × 56" and signed by the artist.

Claes Oldenburg, *Pizza Palette*, 1996
Lithograph measuring 29 × 38" in a signed and numbered edition of 100.

Ed Ruscha, *Sunliners*, 1996
Portfolio of 7 etchings and aquatints measuring 17 × 13" in a signed and numbered edition of 50. Printed by AC.

Donald Sultan, *Flowers in a Flower Vase*, 1996
Color aquatint measuring 31 × 29" in a signed and numbered edition of 50. Printed by AC.

Terry Winters, *Potential Surface of Density*, 1996
Etching and aquatint measuring 18⅛ × 21⅛" in a signed and numbered edition of 30. Printed by AC.

1997

Jennifer Bartlett, *Bridge, Boat, Dog*, 1997
Multicolor etching and aquatint printed as a triptych on 3 sheets of paper, measuring 27⅝ × 27" in a signed and numbered edition of 50. Printed by AC.

Chuck Close, *Self Portrait I* and *II*, 1997
2 reduction linocuts measuring 24 × 18" in signed and numbered editions of 70. Printed at SSW.

April Gornik, *Moon Bay*, 1997
Soft-ground etching measuring 26 × 33" in a signed and numbered edition of 50. Printed at SSW.

Red Grooms, *To the Lighthouse*, 1997
Color etching and aquatint measuring 22 × 30" in a signed and numbered edition of 50. Printed by AC.

Alfred Leslie, *Bellevue Hospital, circa 1945; Elevator Operator, Empire State Building, circa 1940; New York City, circa 1934; Leaving Oklahoma on Route 66, circa 1935; Entering New Mexico on Route 66, circa 1935,* all 1997
Series of 5 black-and-white silkscreen prints from photographs, each measuring 30 × 35" in signed and numbered editions of 50.

Robert Mangold, *Brown/Black Zone Print,* 1997
Color woodcut measuring 21 × 29" in a signed and numbered edition of 50. Printed at SSW.

Kiki Smith, *Jersey Crows*, 1997
Portfolio of 3 Iris prints measuring 17 × 41" in a signed and numbered edition of 40.

Kiki Smith, *Jesus*, 1997
Letterpress print measuring 26 × 18" in a signed and numbered edition of 30. Printed at SSW.

Kiki Smith, *Untitled*, 1997
Series of 8 Iris prints in varying sizes, signed and numbered in editions of 20.

In 1998, Pace Editions moved its offices, curatorial, warehousing, and production facilities from 72 Spring Street to 44 West 18th Street. The Spring Street Workshop was renamed Pace Editions Ink (PEI). Crommelynck returned to his permanent residence in Paris.

1998

John Chamberlain, *Seawater #27, #45, #63*, 1998
Series of 3 silkscreen prints of varying sizes in signed and numbered editions of 63.

Chuck Close, *John*, 1998
26-color silkscreen print measuring 64 × 54" in a signed and numbered edition of 63.

Jim Dine, *Pinocchio*, 1998
Iris print with intaglio printing and hand-coloring measuring 47 × 31" in a signed and numbered edition of 20. The intaglio was printed at PEI.

Robert Mangold, *Four Figures*, 1998
Portfolio of 4 intaglio prints measuring 30 × 22" in a signed and numbered edition of 50. Printed at PEI.

April Gornik, *Light and Trees*, 1998
Etching measuring 35 × 25" in a signed and numbered edition of 35. Printed at PEI.

Mary Heilmann, *Mint Boy* and *Mint Print*, 1998
2-color etchings measuring 38 × 29" in a signed and numbered edition of 40. Printed at PEI.

Agnes Martin, *Untitled*, 1998
Portfolio of 4 offset lithographs measuring 12 × 12" in a signed and numbered edition of 75.

Ed Ruscha, *Clown Speedo* and *Tumbling Snowman Speedo*, 1998
2 aquatints measuring 36 × 26" in a signed and numbered edition of 35. The prints were created in collaboration with AC and printed at PEI.

Kiki Smith, *Tidal*, 1998
Folded print/object to be displayed in an accordian style with an overhanging element; created using a combination of photogravure, photolithography, and silkscreen. The work measures 19 × 126" in a signed and numbered edition of 39. Published by the LeRoy Neiman Center for Print Studies at Columbia University and distributed by Pace Prints.

Kiki Smith, *Dandelions*, 1998
Portfolio of 6 mezzotints measuring 9 × 8⅝" in a signed and numbered edition of 24. Printed at PEI.

Pat Steir, *Summer Dawn Group*, 1998
Portfolio of 3 silkscreen prints with aquatint measuring 24 × 23" in a signed and numbered edition of 30. The aquatint was printed at PEI.

1999

Donald Baechler, *Abstract Compositions with Birds*, 1999
Portfolio of 3 woodblock and linoblock prints on handmade paper measuring 34 × 24" in a signed and numbered edition of 53. The paper was made at the Dieu Donné Paper Mill and printed at PEI.

Jennifer Bartlett, *Boat*, 1999
Suite of 2 multicolor etchings measuring 28 × 35" in a signed and numbered edition of 25. The plates were created in collaboration with AC and printed at PEI.

Karin Davie, *Smother I, II, III*, 1999
Multicolored soft-ground etchings with aquatint measuring 18 × 23" in a signed and numbered edition of 20. Printed at PEI.

Jim Dine, *Red Pants II*, 1999
Hand-made paper print with etching and hand-coloring measuring 55 × 34" in a signed and numbered edition of 20. The paper was made at the Dieu Donné Paper Mill and printed at PEI.

David Hockney, *Still Life*, 1999
Series of 10 color and black-and-white etchings of varying sizes in a signed and numbered edition of 35.

David Hockney, *Portraits*, 1999
Series of 4 etchings measuring 44 × 30" in a signed and numbered edition of 35.

David Hockney, *Dog Wall*, 1999
Suite of 15 etchings of varying sizes in a signed and numbered edition of 35.

Pat Steir, *Blue Moon Waterfall*, 1999
Hand-colored photogravure printed with chine collé on paper measuring 28 × 25" in a signed and numbered edition of 30. Printed at PEI.

Donald Sultan, *Smoke Rings*, 1999
Portfolio of 4 Iris prints measuring 27 × 20⅞" in a signed and numbered edition of 20.

Donald Sultan, *Smoke Rings*, 1999
Set of 2 aquatints measuring 43 × 22" in signed and numbered editions of 26. Printed at PEI.

William Wegman, *Untitled*, 1999
Portfolio of 6 soft-ground etchings and aquatints with a laser-copied chine collé image on paper measuring 14 × 16" in a signed and numbered edition of 20. Printed at PEI.

2000

Joe Andoe, *Mare and Foal*, 2000
Iris print measuring 37⅝ × 29" in a signed and numbered edition of 30.

Richmond Burton, *Solex* and *Barok*, 2000
2 etchings with relief printing and pochoir measuring 28 × 39" in a signed and numbered edition of 35. Printed at PEI.

Chuck Close, *Self-Portrait*, 2000
111-color silkscreen print measuring 65 × 54⅛" in a signed and numbered edition of 80.

Chuck Close, *Scribble/Etching*, 2000
Twelve-color soft-ground etching measuring 18 × 15" in a signed and numbered edition of 60. Printed at PEI.

George Condo, *Invocations of Miles*, 2000
Multicolored silkscreen measuring 30⅜ × 45" in a signed and numbered edition of 50.

Jim Dine, *The Dog*, 2000
Intaglio and relief print measuring 31 × 46" in a signed and numbered edition of 18. Printed at PEI.

Robert Indiana, *Love and 2000*, 2000
2 color aquatints measuring 35 × 35" in a signed and numbered edition of 50.

Jonathan Lasker, *Untitled*, 2000
Etching and linocut on handmade paper with a collage element, measuring 22 × 30" in a signed and numbered edition of 30. The paper was made at the Dieu Donné Paper Mill and printed at PEI.

Pat Steir, *August Waterfall* and *Starry Night*, 2000
2 photogravure prints with aquatint measuring 28⅞ × 24" in a signed and numbered edition of 30. Printed at PEI.

Pace Primitive: Selected Exhibitions

September 21–October 19, 1974	*African Accumulative Sculpture*
March 1–29, 1975	*Gopes, Agibas & Spatulas*
April 24–May 29, 1976	*African Spirit Images and Identities*
November 20–December 31, 1976	*African Art from a French Collection*
April 2–May 14, 1977	*Recent African Acquisitions*
January 14–February 11, 1978	*African, Pre-Columbian, American Indian, Oceanic: The Ulfert Wilke Collection*
September 23–October 21, 1978	*African Art: New Acquisitions*
May 5–June 16, 1979	*African Art: New Acquisitions*
March 14–April 14, 1980	*African Art: Important Acquisitions*
June 9–July 25, 1980	*African Art: Masks and Figures*
September 18–October 25, 1980	*Yoruba Beadwork: Art of Nigeria*
April 25–May 23, 1981	*Thirteen African Masks*
October 9–November 22, 1981	*African Art: Recent Acquisitions*
February 20–March 20, 1982	*Yoruba Sculpture of West Africa*
May 1–June 11, 1982	*African Art: New Acquisitions*
November 1–December 30, 1982	*Art of the Yoruba*
January 15–February 27, 1983	*African Art: Important Acquisitions*
September 23–October 26, 1983	*African Art: Important Acquisitions*
October 28–December 10, 1983	*African Art: Images of Power and Mystery*
May 4–June 9, 1984	*African Art: Figures and Masks*
November 9–December 17, 1984	*African Art: Important Acquisitions*
September 27–November 2, 1984	*African Art: Important Acquisitions*
April 8–May 9, 1986	*African Art*
October 24–December 6, 1986	*African Art: Recent Acquisitions*
October 16–November 21, 1987	*African Art: Recent Acquisitions*
April 1–May 1, 1988	*Rural Indian Ritual: Wall Hangings from the Provinces of Gujarat and Kutch*
May 5–June 10, 1989	*African Art: Recent Acquisitions*
November 14–December 16, 1989	*African Art: Recent Acquisitions*
October 26–December 8, 1990	*Masks of the Himalayas*
May 10–June 28, 1991	*African Art & Artifacts*
October 4–November 30, 1991	*A Sacred Presence: Masks of Africa and the Himalayas*
May 17–July 12, 1992	*African Masterpieces from Private Collections*
May 14–June 13, 1993	*The Art of African Beadwork*
May 31, 1994	*New Acquisitions: African Art, Oceanic Art*
February 24–April 1, 1995	*The Linear Image in African Art*
October 26–December 2, 1995	*The Art of Yoruba: Sculpture and Beadwork*
October 1–November 30, 1996	*Important African Sculpture*
October 17–November 12, 1997	*Masterpieces of African Art*
October 7–November 18, 1998	*African Art: New Acquisitions*
February 5–March 13, 1999	*Art of the Himalayas*
October 1–30, 1999	*New Acquisitions of African Art*
March 3–April 1, 2000	*African Art*

Pace Master Prints: Selected Exhibitions

May 6–June 4, 1983	*American Prints*
February 17–March 17, 1984	*19th and 20th Century American Prints*
November 1985	*British Modernist Prints: 1900–1940*
January 11–February 2, 1985	*American Prints*
January 17–February 15, 1986	*American Prints*
October 17–November 29, 1986	*European Master Prints: 1935–1965*
February 27–March 21, 1987	*David Smith: The Prints*
May 12–June 13, 1987	*Old Master Prints: Sixteenth to Eighteenth Century*
January 1988	*Important Italian Old Master Drawings*
November 11–December 17, 1988	*Piranesi: Views of Rome*
February 17–March 11, 1989	*Five Centuries of Master Prints*
May 5–May 27, 1989	*Francisco Goya: La Tauromaquia, Los Caprichos*
November 1989	*Views of Venice: 1492–1880*
February 22–26, 1990	*Masterpieces from Five Centuries: Prints and Drawings*
October 5–November 24, 1990	*Prints from the Twenties and Thirties: Bellows, Chagall, Hopper, Kandinsky, Matisse, Miró, Morandi, Picasso*
October 25–November 30, 1991	*The Portrait Tradition: Master Printmakers*
November 8–December 7, 1991	*Miró: Early Prints 1935–1955*
June 5–July 31, 1992	*Pace in Bloom: Botanical Prints from the 17th to 19th Centuries*
October 16–December 19, 1992	*Henri Matisse: Etchings, Lithographs, Linocuts & Aquatints*
February 12–March 6, 1993	*Albrecht Dürer: Woodcuts and Engravings*
March 24–April 21, 1993	*19th and 20th Century French Prints*
September 17–October 8, 1993	*Views of Rome: Giovanni Battista Piranesi & Giovanni Battista Nolli*
October 22–December 4, 1993	*The Surrealist Spirit*
January 28–February 26, 1994	*Nudes: Chagall, Dürer, Giacometti, Matisse, Picasso, Rembrandt*
May 6–June 11, 1994	*New Acquisitions: Dürer, Rembrandt, Canaletto, Steinlen, Matisse, Leger, Miró*
November 1994	*Piranesi: Views of Paestum*
October 20–November 25, 1995	*Cassatt, Cézanne, Dubuffet, Matisse, Miró Picasso, Vuillard*
July 5–August 5, 1996	*Henri Matisse: La Capeline de Paille d'Italie*
October 11–November 2, 1996	*New Acquisitions: Braque, Cézanne, Giacometti, Matisse, Miró, Picasso, Toulouse-Lautrec*
January 17–February 15, 1997	*Twentieth Century French Prints*
May 9–June 13, 1997	*Prints of Fantasy: Goya, Piranesi, Tiepolo*
October 17–November 12, 1997	*New Acquisitions: Braque, Cassatt, Dubuffet, Matisse, Miró, Picasso, Renoir, Vuillard*
October 29–November 27, 1999	*Henri Matisse: Lithographs 1913–1929*

Pace/MacGill Gallery: Selected Exhibitions

November 5–December 17, 1983	*André Kertesz: Distortions*
January 13–February 11, 1984	*Lucas Samaras: Panoramas*
March 23–April 21, 1984	*Joel-Peter Witkin: Photographs and Drawings*
October 18–November 24, 1984	*Paul Strand: Exhibition Prints from 291*
October 1–November 16, 1985	*Charles Sheeler: Vintage Photographs*
November 29–January 5, 1985	*O. Winston Link*
November 29–January 5, 1985	*Harold Edgerton*
November 21–January 4, 1986	*Richard Avedon: In the American West*
January 9–February 15, 1986	*Chuck Close: Maquettes*
February 20–March 22, 1986	*Fredrick Sommer: Photographs and Drawings*
March 27–April 26, 1986	*Herbert List: Vintage Photographs*
May 2–August 1, 1986	*Photographs of and by Pablo Picasso*
May 2–August 1, 1986	*Bill Brandt: Vintage Photographs*
January 22–March 7, 1987	*William Eggelston: Photographs from* The Guide
January 22–March 7, 1987	*Crime Photographs*
October 15–November 28, 1987	*Large-Scale Self-Portraits*
October 15–November 28, 1987	*Harry Callahan: Vintage Photographs*
December 3–January 16, 1988	*Ralph Eugene Meatyard: Vintage Photographs*
January 21–March 5, 1988	*Robert Rauschenberg: A Survey*
May 5–June 17, 1988	*Nan Goldin: Recent Works*
September 23–October 22, 1988	*Ed Rauscha: Parking Lots*
December 1–January 14, 1989	*Irving Penn: Cranium Architecture*
January 19–March 4, 1989	*Alexander Rodchenko: A Retrospective*
April 27–June 10, 1989	*Emmet Gowin: Petra*
December 1–January 6, 1990	*Dennis Oppenheim: Conceptual work from the 1960s*
February 22–March 24, 1990	*René Magritte: Vintage Photographs*
March 30–April 28, 1990	*Irving Penn: Other Ways of Being; Ethnographic Photographs, 1948–1990*
January 24–February 23, 1991	*Martin Kippenberger: Recent Large-Scale Work*
January 16–February 22, 1992	*William Wegman: Early Black and White Photographs*
February 27–March 28, 1992	*William Christenberry: Photographs and Sculpture*
April 2–May 2, 1992	*Gary Winogrand: One Unrelated Photographer, Vintage Prints 1956–1963*
September 10–October 24, 1992	*Harry Callahan: City Pictures, 1950*
October 29–November 28, 1992	*Frederick Sommer: Horizonless Landscapes*
September 9–October 23, 1993	*Alfred Stieglitz: Vintage Photographs from the Collection of Georgia O'Keefe*
December 2–January 15, 1994	*Francesca Woodman: A Survey*
October 27–December 3, 1994	*Robert Frank: 27 Photographs*
March 30–April 29, 1995	*Doug and Mike Starn: New Editions*
September 7–October 14, 1995	*Dieter Appelt: Self-Portraits*
September 7–October 14, 1995	*Edward Weston: Vintage Photographs*
January 11–February 24, 1996	*Kiki Smith: Photographs*
February 9–March 9, 1996	*Cindy Sherman: Recent Work* (Pace/MacGill Gallery, Los Angeles)
February 29–April 6, 1996	*Harry Callahan: Theme and Variation*
April 26–June 1, 1996	*Diane Arbus: Photographs* (Pace/MacGill Gallery, Los Angeles)
September 12–October 19, 1996	*Philip-Lorca diCorcia: Street Pictures*
February 27–April 5, 1997	*Jim Dine: Berlin . . . etc.*
April 10–May 10, 1997	*John Szarkowski: Mr. Bristol's Barn*
October 30–November 29, 1997	*Michal Rovner: Photographic Works*
October 30–November 29, 1997	*Lazlo Maholy-Nagy: Early Experiments 1922–1932*
December 4–January 17, 1998	*Diana Michener: Solitaire*
September 10–October 24, 1998	*Harry Callahan: Themes Revisited*
September 10–October 24, 1998	*Robert Rauschenberg: Postcard Pictures, 1952*
October 29–November 28, 1998	*Jim Dine: Kali in New York*
December 3–Janury 16, 1999	*Fazal Sheikh: The Victor Weeps*
January 21–March 6, 1999	*Guy Bourdin: Early Work 1950s*
January 21–March 6, 1999	*Cropping and Picture Making: Kertesz, Man Ray, Weston and Winogrand*
March 11–April 24, 1999	*Robert Frank*
April 29–June 12, 1999	*Dieter Appelt*
April 29–June 12, 1999	*John Szarkowski*
September 1–September 25, 1999	*Irving Penn: New and Unseen* (PaceWildenstein)
September 9–October 16, 1999	*Irving Penn: Process* (Pace/MacGill Gallery)
September 24–October 23, 1999	*Jim Dine: Recent Photographs* (PaceWildenstein, Greene Street)
October 28–November 27, 1999	*Frederick Sommer: 1945*
October 28–November 27, 1999	*Man Ray: Important Vintage Photographs*
December 2–January 15, 2000	*Hiro*
January 20–March 4, 2000	*Duane Michals*
March 9–April 22, 2000	*Chuck Close: Daguerreotypes*
April 27–June 17, 2000	*The Scientist and Aesthetics: Selections by Torsten Wiesel*
April 27–June 17, 2000	*Charles Jones: Vintage Photographs*

ACKNOWLEDGEMENTS

In producing a history of The Pace Gallery/PaceWildenstein, we sought to create a living record of a gallery in process, documenting exhibitions through photographs and catalogue excerpts. We are proud of the texts we've been honored to publish, just as we are of the artists whose work it's been our privilege to show.

The completion of this project was truly a collaborative effort. Leonardo Mondadori's enthusiasm for this monumental work was catalytic to its completion. We are grateful for the encouragement of all the artists and writers who permitted the reproduction their work. The selfless participation of the entire staff of PaceWildenstein brought this to completion and the gallery itself would not exist without their support.

We gratefully recognize the dedication and stamina of Amy Greenspon, Kevin Parise and Suzi Steiger, as well as Marc Glimcher, Lucas Samaras, Giuseppe Lamastra, Giorgio Gardel, Isabella Borromeo, Barbara Rose, Bernice Rose, Douglas Baxter, Susan Dunne, and Peter Boris. Special thanks to Sheila Schwartz and Janet Hicks and the staff at Artists' Rights Society, for their advice and support. It is our hope that this volume documents the valuable historical contribution made by the artists, and in some small way describes the climate of the art world during this period.

Milly Glimcher

Staff Photographers: Ferdinand Boesch, Al Mozell, William Suttle, Bill Jacobson, Ellen Wilson and Gordon Christmas.

Daniel Abadie William C. Agee Lawrence Alloway Dore Ashton Jan Avgikos Olivier Berggruen Douglas Blau Yve-Alain Bois Manuel J. Borja-Villel Russell Bowman Alan Bowness Michael Brenson Italo Calvino Dan Cameron E.A. Carmean David Carrier Germano Celant Michael Compton Arthur C. Danto Gabriela De Ferrari Barbaralee Diamonstein Wilfried Dickhoff Jean Dubuffet James L.Enyeart Michael FitzGerald Henry Geldzahler Françoise Gilot Arne Glimcher Marc Glimcher Mildred Glimcher Adam Gopnik Robert Hobbs Bryce Holcombe Bob Holman Harry Holtzman Richard Howard Sam Hunter Gary Indiana Donald Judd Ivan Karp Klaus Kertess Michael Kirby Pamela Kort Rosalind E. Krauss Udo Kultermann Donald Kuspit Jean-Claude Lebensztejn Kim Levin Jean Lipman Robert S. Lubar Peter MacGill Thomas McEvilley James R. Mellow Annette Michelson Paul D. Miller Barbara Novak Brian O'Doherty John Perreault Ellen Phelan Claude Picasso Nancy Princenthal Urs Raussmüller Carter Ratcliff Theodore Reff Bryan Robertson Barbara Rose Bernice Rose Robert Rosenblum Arnold Rubin Irving Sandler Christel Sauer Lucas Samaras Gert Schiff Peter Schjeldahl William C. Seitz Richard Shiff David L. Shirey Joan Simon Leon Siroto Mark Stevens Jeremy Strick Julie Sylvester Calvin Tomkins Alan G. Wilkinson Diane Waldman Graham Williams John Yau William Zimmer Daniel Abadie William C. Agee Lawrence Alloway Dore Ashton Jan Avgikos Olivier Berggruen Douglas Blau Yve-Alain Bois Manuel J. Borja-Villel Russell Bowman Alan Bowness Michael Brenson Italo Calvino Dan Cameron E.A. Carmean David Carrier Germano Celant Michael Compton Arthur C. Danto Gabriela De Ferrari Barbaralee Diamonstein Wilfried Dickhoff Jean Dubuffet James L.Enyeart Michael FitzGerald Henry Geldzahler Françoise Gilot Arne Glimcher Marc Glimcher Mildred Glimcher Adam Gopnik Robert Hobbs Bryce Holcombe Bob Holman Harry Holtzman Richard Howard Sam Hunter Gary Indiana Donald Judd Ivan Karp Klaus Kertess Michael Kirby Pamela Kort Rosalind E. Krauss Udo Kultermann Donald Kuspit Jean-Claude Lebensztejn Kim Levin Jean Lipman Robert S. Lubar Peter MacGill Thomas McEvilley James R. Mellow Annette Michelson Paul D. Miller Barbara Novak Brian O'Doherty John Perreault Ellen Phelan Claude Picasso Nancy Princenthal Urs Raussmüller Carter Ratcliff Theodore Reff Bryan Robertson Barbara Rose Bernice Rose Robert Rosenblum Arnold Rubin Irving Sandler Christel Sauer Lucas Samaras Gert Schiff Peter Schjeldahl William C. Seitz Richard Shiff David L. Shirey Joan Simon Leon Siroto Mark Stevens Jeremy Strick Julie Sylvester Calvin Tomkins Alan G. Wilkinson Diane Waldman Graham Williams John Yau William Zimmer Daniel Abadie William C. Agee Lawrence Alloway Dore Ashton Jan Avgikos Olivier Berggruen Douglas Blau Yve-Alain Bois Manuel J. Borja-Villel Russell Bowman Alan Bowness Michael Brenson Italo Calvino Dan Cameron E.A. Carmean David Carrier Germano Celant Michael Compton Arthur C. Danto Gabriela De Ferrari Barbaralee Diamonstein Wilfried Dickhoff Jean Dubuffet James L.Enyeart Michael FitzGerald Henry Geldzahler Françoise Gilot Arne Glimcher Marc Glimcher Mildred Glimcher Adam Gopnik Robert Hobbs Bryce Holcombe Bob Holman Harry Holtzman Richard Howard Sam Hunter Gary Indiana Donald Judd Ivan Karp Klaus Kertess Michael Kirby Pamela Kort Rosalind E. Krauss Udo Kultermann Donald Kuspit Jean-Claude Lebensztejn Kim Levin Jean Lipman Robert S. Lubar Peter MacGill Thomas McEvilley James R. Mellow Annette Michelson Paul D. Miller Barbara Novak Brian O'Doherty John Perreault Ellen Phelan Claude Picasso Nancy Princenthal Urs Raussmüller Carter Ratcliff Theodore Reff Bryan Robertson Barbara Rose Bernice Rose Robert Rosenblum Arnold Rubin Irving Sandler Christel Sauer Lucas Samaras Gert Schiff Peter Schjeldahl William C. Seitz Richard Shiff David L. Shirey Joan Simon Leon Siroto Mark Stevens Jeremy Strick Julie Sylvester Calvin Tomkins Alan G. Wilkinson Diane Waldman Graham Williams John Yau William Zimmer Daniel Abadie William C. Agee Lawrence Alloway Dore Ashton Jan Avgikos Olivier Berggruen Douglas Blau Yve-Alain Bois Manuel J. Borja-Villel Russell Bowman Alan Bowness Michael Brenson Italo Calvino Dan Cameron E.A. Carmean David Carrier Germano Celant Michael Compton Arthur C. Danto Gabriela De Ferrari Barbaralee Diamonstein Wilfried Dickhoff Jean Dubuffet James L.Enyeart Michael FitzGerald Henry Geldzahler Françoise Gilot Arne Glimcher Marc Glimcher Mildred Glimcher Adam Gopnik Robert Hobbs Bryce Holcombe Bob Holman Harry Holtzman Richard Howard Sam Hunter Gary Indiana Donald Judd Ivan Karp Klaus Kertess Michael Kirby Pamela Kort Rosalind E. Krauss Udo Kultermann Donald Kuspit Jean-Claude Lebensztejn Kim Levin Jean Lipman Robert S. Lubar Peter MacGill Thomas McEvilley James R. Mellow Annette Michelson Paul D. Miller Barbara Novak Brian O'Doherty John Perreault Daniel Abadie William C. Agee Lawrence Alloway Dore Ashton Jan Avgikos Olivier Berggruen Douglas Blau Yve-Alain Bois Manuel J. Borja-Villel Russell Bowman Alan Bowness Michael Brenson Italo Calvino Dan Cameron E.A. Carmean David Carrier Germano Celant Michael Compton Arthur C. Danto Gabriela De Ferrari Barbaralee Diamonstein Wilfried Dickhoff Jean Dubuffet James L.Enyeart Michael FitzGerald Henry Geldzahler Françoise Gilot Arne Glimcher Marc Glimcher Mildred Glimcher Adam Gopnik Robert Hobbs Bryce Holcombe Bob Holman Harry Holtzman Richard Howard Sam Hunter Gary Indiana Donald Judd Ivan Karp Klaus Kertess Michael Kirby Pamela Kort Rosalind E. Krauss Udo Kultermann Donald Kuspit Jean-Claude Lebensztejn Kim Levin Jean Lipman Robert S. Lubar Peter MacGill Thomas McEvilley James R. Mellow Annette Michelson Paul D. Miller Barbara Novak Brian O'Doherty John Perreault Ellen Phelan Claude Picasso Nancy Princenthal Urs Raussmüller Carter Ratcliff Theodore Reff Bryan Robertson Barbara Rose Bernice Rose Robert Rosenblum Arnold Rubin Irving Sandler Christel Sauer Lucas Samaras Gert Schiff Peter Schjeldahl William C. Seitz Richard Shiff David L. Shirey Joan Simon Leon Siroto Mark Stevens Jeremy Strick Julie Sylvester Calvin Tomkins Alan G. Wilkinson Diane Waldman Graham Williams John Yau